Get the eBook FREE!

(PDF, ePub, Kindle, and liveBook all included)

We believe that once you buy a book from us, you should be able to read it in any format we have available. To get electronic versions of this book at no additional cost to you, purchase and then register this book at the Manning website.

Go to https://www.manning.com/freebook and follow the instructions to complete your pBook registration.

That's it!
Thanks from Manning!

Python How-To

63 TECHNIQUES TO IMPROVE YOUR PYTHON CODE

YONG CUI

MANNING

SHELTER ISLAND

For online information and ordering of this and other Manning books, please visit
www.manning.com. The publisher offers discounts on this book when ordered in quantity.
For more information, please contact

> Special Sales Department
> Manning Publications Co.
> 20 Baldwin Road
> PO Box 761
> Shelter Island, NY 11964
> Email: orders@manning.com

 Manning Publications Co.
20 Baldwin Road
PO Box 761
Shelter Island, NY 11964

Development editor:	Marina Michaels
Technical development editor:	René van den Berg
Review editor:	Aleksandar Dragosavljević
Production editor:	Keri Hales
Copy editor:	Keir Simpson
Proofreader:	Melody Dolab
Technical proofreaders:	Ignacio Beltran Torres and Walter Alexander Mata Lopez
Typesetter:	Gordan Salinovic
Cover designer:	Marija Tudor

ISBN 9781617299742
Printed and bound by CPI Group (UK) Ltd, Croydon, CR0 4YY

To my wife, Tingting Gu,
who sat next to me on numerous late nights
while I was writing this book.

contents

        *Appendices A–E can be found in the digital and online versions
        of this book.*

We're probably the luckiest generation in human history. We're no longer in the Neolithic Age or the Industrial Age; we've entered the Information Age. Advanced information technologies, particularly computers and networks, have transformed human life. We can take a flight from our hometown to another place thousands of miles away in less than half a day. We can make a doctor's appointment using a smartphone and attend the appointment through a video call, if we prefer. We can order almost anything from online stores and get it delivered within days or even hours.

These transformations have been accompanied by the accumulation of tremendous amounts of data over the past couple of decades. The work of processing and analyzing this data has contributed to the emergence of a new interdisciplinary subject: data science. As a behavioral scientist, I spend a significant amount of time dealing with data, so you might say that I'm applying data science to behavioral research. It takes more than paper and pencil to process data of this magnitude, however. Instead, I've been writing code to clean data and run statistical models with a wonderful programming language: Python.

As a self-taught coder, I know it's not easy to grasp Python or any other programming language—not because it takes a long time to learn all the techniques (and know which ones to use when), but because too many learning resources are available, such as online courses, tutorial videos, blog articles, and certainly books. How do you choose the ones that are most suitable for you?

I had the same question when I started learning Python. Over the years, I've tried a variety of resources, and I've found that the best learning resources are books, because books have well-structured content that makes it possible to take a deep dive into the language. During the learning process, you can set your own pace. Whenever you need to, you can slow down to digest hard topics. In addition, you can refer to the books on your bookshelf quickly should any questions arise.

Most of the Python books on the market are written for beginners (providing detailed coverage of the language's basic features) or advanced users (covering specialized techniques that are less generalizable). Without doubt, a few of those books are great. From the learning-curve perspective, however, I felt that a book was missing: one for Python learners at the late-beginner and early-intermediate levels. These stages are critical, as learners are forming the right coding habits and figuring out the proper Pythonic techniques for a given context. From the content perspective, I thought the missing book should address general programming problems that most readers could relate to their work, no matter what they do with Python: web development or data science. In other words, more readers could benefit from such a book because it would provide general domain-independent knowledge.

I wrote this book to fill the gap between beginner and advanced books. I hope you'll feel that you've learned a few things after reading it.

acknowledgments

I'd like to thank my mentors, Dr. Paul Cinciripini and Dr. Jason Robinson at the University of Texas MD Anderson Cancer Center, for supporting me as I pursued the use of Python as the language for our analytic work. That effort eventually led to this book.

I also want to thank the Manning team: Publisher Marjan Bace for leading the excellent editorial and production teams; Associate Publisher Michael Stephens for inviting me to write this book; Senior Development Editor Marina Michaels for coordinating and editing; René van den Berg for technical editing; Walter Alexander and Ignacio Torres for providing code review; Aleksandar Dragosavljević for organizing peer reviews; as well as the production staff for their hard work in formatting this book.

Finally, thank you to the reviewers, who provided valuable feedback: Alexei Znamensky, Alexey Vyskubov, Ariel Andres, Brent Boylan, Chris Kolosiwsky, Christopher Kardell, Christopher Villanueva, Claudiu Schiller, Clifford Thurber, Dirk Gomez, Ganesh Swaminathan, Georgios Doumas, Gerald Mack, Gregory Grimes, Igor Dudchenko, Iyabo Sindiku, James Matlock, Jeffrey M. Smith, Josh McAdams, Keerthi Shetty, Larry Cai, Louis Aloia, Marcus Geselle, Mary Anne Thygesen, Mike Baran, Ninoslav Cerkez, Oliver Korten, Piergiorgio Faraglia, Radhakrishna M.V., Rajinder Yadav, Raymond Cheung, Robert Wenner, Shankar Swamy, Sriram Macharla, Giri S. Swaminathan, Steven Herrera, and Vitosh K. Doynov. Their suggestions helped make this a better book.

about this book

In this book, I focus on teaching the essential techniques of Python from a specialty-independent perspective. Although a variety of Python packages are available for different specialties, such as data science and web development, these packages are built on the core features of Python. No matter what domain-specific Python packages you use for your job, you must have a good understanding of essential techniques, such as choosing the proper data models and writing well-structured functions and classes. These techniques make it possible for you to use your domain-specific packages comfortably.

Who should read this book

If you've been self-teaching and using Python for some time, but feel that your Python knowledge is unstructured, I consider you to be a late-beginner or early-intermediate user. This book is right for you because you need to reinforce and synthesize your Python knowledge in a structured way. In this book, I identify several topics in each chapter to address common problems that you may encounter in your work. My coverage of these topics teaches you more than how to address a specific problem; it also frames the content in a larger context, showing why and how the topic matters when you're working on a project. This way, you're not learning individual techniques to complete separate tasks; you're completing a project and learning these techniques in the process.

How this book is organized: A road map

This book consists of six parts, as shown in the following figure. In the first part (chapters 2–5), you study the built-in data models, such as strings, lists, and dictionaries. These data models are the building blocks of any project. In the second part (chapters

6 and 7), you learn about best practices for defining functions. Functions are integral to any project because they're responsible for manipulating data to create the desired output. In the third part (chapters 8 and 9), you learn techniques for defining custom classes. Instead of using built-in classes, we define custom classes to better model the data in our project. In the fourth part (chapters 10 and 11), you learn the fundamentals of using objects and manipulating files on your computers. In the fifth part (chapters 12 and 13), you learn a variety of techniques to safeguard your programs, including logging, exception handling, and testing. In the sixth part (chapter 14), you

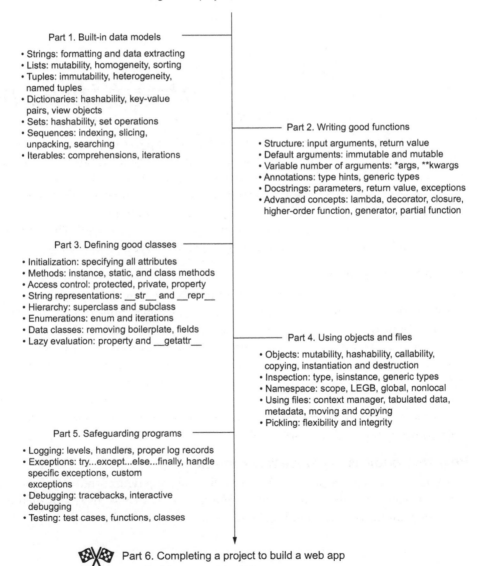

Working on the project as the shared context

Part 1. Built-in data models

• Strings: formatting and data extracting
• Lists: mutability, homogeneity, sorting
• Tuples: immutability, heterogeneity, named tuples
• Dictionaries: hashability, key-value pairs, view objects
• Sets: hashability, set operations
• Sequences: indexing, slicing, unpacking, searching
• Iterables: comprehensions, iterations

Part 2. Writing good functions

• Structure: input arguments, return value
• Default arguments: immutable and mutable
• Variable number of arguments: *args, **kwargs
• Annotations: type hints, generic types
• Docstrings: parameters, return value, exceptions
• Advanced concepts: lambda, decorator, closure, higher-order function, generator, partial function

Part 3. Defining good classes

• Initialization: specifying all attributes
• Methods: instance, static, and class methods
• Access control: protected, private, property
• String representations: __str__ and __repr__
• Hierarchy: superclass and subclass
• Enumerations: enum and iterations
• Data classes: removing boilerplate, fields
• Lazy evaluation: property and __getattr__

Part 4. Using objects and files

• Objects: mutability, hashability, callability, copying, instantiation and destruction
• Inspection: type, isinstance, generic types
• Namespace: scope, LEGB, global, nonlocal
• Using files: context manager, tabulated data, metadata, moving and copying
• Pickling: flexibility and integrity

Part 5. Safeguarding programs

• Logging: levels, handlers, proper log records
• Exceptions: try...except...else...finally, handle specific exceptions, custom exceptions
• Debugging: tracebacks, interactive debugging
• Testing: test cases, functions, classes

Part 6. Completing a project to build a web app

synthesize all the knowledge you've gained to produce a web app—a project that serves as the teaching frame in all the other chapters.

To follow along with the teaching, I recommend that you use a computer while you're studying this book, which will allow you to get familiar with Python syntax and techniques faster. I've uploaded all the code in GitHub, and you can find my public repository at https://github.com/ycui1/python_how_to. In this book, however, whenever I show you some code, I provide the necessary explanations and output, so it's fine if you don't have a computer around while you're reading this book.

If you do intend to use a computer, your computer's operating system doesn't matter. Windows, macOS, and Linux are all fine because Python is a cross-platform programming language. (See appendix A online for Python installation instructions.) Because I focus on the essential techniques, which have stabilized in recent Python releases, it's not too important whether your computer runs Python 3.8 or earlier, but to get the most out of the book, I recommend that you install Python 3.10 or later.

About the appendices

The online version of this book has five appendices. Appendix A, Learning Python with REPL in IDLE, shows how to write Python code interactively. Appendix B, Managing Python packages with pip, shows how to manage Python packages. Appendix C, Using Jupyter Notebook: A web-based interactive Python editor, shows how to work with Jupyter Notebook. Appendix D, Integrating version control into your project, shows the importance of version control in your codebase. Appendix E, Preparing your package for public distribution, shows how to publish your package.

About the code

This book contains many examples of source code, both in numbered listings and inline with normal text. In both cases, source code is formatted in a `fixed-width font like this` to separate it from ordinary text. Sometimes, code is also **in bold** to highlight changes from previous steps in the chapter, such as when a new feature adds to an existing line of code.

In many cases, the original source code has been reformatted; I've added line breaks and reworked indentation to accommodate the available page space in the book. In rare cases, listings include line-continuation markers (➥). Additionally, comments in the source code have been removed from the listings when the code is described in the text. Code annotations accompany many of the listings, highlighting important concepts.

You can get executable snippets of code from the liveBook (online) version of this book at https://livebook.manning.com/book/python-how-to. The complete code for the examples in the book is available for download from the Manning website at https://www.manning.com/books/python-how-to and from GitHub at https://github.com/ycui1/python_how_to.

liveBook discussion forum

Purchase of *Python How-To* includes free access to liveBook, Manning's online reading platform. Using liveBook's exclusive discussion features, you can attach comments to the book globally or to specific sections or paragraphs. It's a snap to make notes for yourself, ask and answer technical questions, and receive help from the author and other users. To access the forum, go to https://livebook.manning.com/book/python-how-to/discussion. You can learn more about Manning's forums and the rules of conduct at https://livebook.manning.com/discussion.

Manning's commitment to our readers is to provide a venue where meaningful dialogue between individual readers and between readers and the author can take place. It is not a commitment to any specific amount of participation on the part of the author, whose contribution to the forum remains voluntary (and unpaid). We suggest that you try asking the author some challenging questions, lest their interest stray! The forum and the archives of previous discussions will be accessible on the publisher's website as long as the book is in print.

Other online resources

You can find official documentation, including tutorials and references, at https://docs.python.org/3. The author, Dr. Yong Cui, regularly writes blogs on Python and related data science topics at Medium (https://medium.com/@yongcui01).

about the author

DR. YONG CUI is a scientist who has been working in the biomedicine field for more than 15 years. His research focuses on developing mobile health apps for behavioral interventions using Swift and Kotlin. As his favorite language, Python is his go-to language for data analysis, machine learning, and research-tool development. In his spare time, he likes to write blog posts on a variety of technical topics, including mobile development, Python programming, and artificial intelligence.

about the cover illustration

The figure on the cover of *Python How-To* is titled "Paysanne des environs de Soleure," or "Peasant woman around Solothurn," taken from a collection by Jacques Grasset de Saint-Sauveur, published in 1788. Each illustration is finely drawn and hand-colored.

In those days, it was easy to identify where people lived and what their trade or station in life was by their dress alone. Manning celebrates the inventiveness and initiative of the computer business with book covers based on the rich diversity of regional culture centuries ago, brought back to life by pictures from collections such as this one.

Developing a pragmatic learning strategy

1

This chapter covers

- What being pragmatic means
- What Python can do
- When you should consider alternative languages
- What you can expect to learn from this book

Python is an amazing programming language. Its open source, general-purpose, platform-independent nature has given it an enormous developer community, along with an incredible ecosystem that includes tens of thousands of freely available libraries for web development, machine learning (ML), data science, and many other domains. I hope that we share this belief: knowing how to code in Python is great, but knowing how to write truly efficient, secure, and maintainable applications gives you a tremendous advantage. This book will help you go from a Python beginner to confident programmer.

In the Python ecosystem, we use domain-specific Python tools, such as web frameworks and ML libraries, to complete various tasks in our jobs. The effective employment of these tools is nontrivial, as it requires considerable familiarity with essential Python skills, such as processing texts, dealing with structured data, creating control flows, and handling files. Python programmers can write different solutions to address the same tasks. Among these solutions, one is generally better than the others because it may be more concise, more readable, or more efficient, which we collectively term as *Pythonic:* an idiomatic coding style that all Python programmers strive to acquire. This book is about how to write Pythonic code to address programming tasks.

Python is so well developed and has so many features to learn that it would be impossible or unwise to try to learn everything about it from this book. Instead, I'll take a pragmatic approach to defining what I'll teach in this book: the essential skills that you'll most likely use in your projects. Equally important, I'll frequently mention how to use these skills with the consideration of readability and maintainability so that you can form good coding habits, which I'll bet that you and your teammates will greatly appreciate.

> **NOTE** You'll see callouts like this one throughout the book. Many of them are devoted to tips regarding readability and maintainability. Don't miss them!

1.1   Aiming at becoming a pragmatic programmer

We code for purposes, such as building websites, training ML models, or analyzing data. Whatever our purposes are, we want to be pragmatic; we write code to solve real problems. Thus, before we learn to code from the beginning or advance our coding skills in the middle of our career, we should be clear about our intentions. But even if you're unsure of what you desire to achieve with Python at this stage, the good news is that core Python features are universal knowledge. After you grasp the core features, you can apply them to any domain-specific Python tools.

Aiming to become a pragmatic programmer means that you should focus on the techniques that are most useful. Mastering these skills is just the first milestone in your journey, however; the long-term game in coding is writing readable code that not only works, but also fosters maintainability.

1.1.1   Focusing on writing readable Python code

As a developer, I'm obsessed with readability. Writing code is like speaking a real-world language. When we speak a language, don't we want others to understand us? If your answer is yes, you probably agree with me that we want others to understand our code too. Whether our code's readers possess the necessary technical expertise to understand our code is out of our control. What we can control is how we write the code—how readable we make it. Consider some simple questions:

- *Are your variables named properly to indicate what they are?* No one can appreciate your code if it's full of variables named var0, temp_var, or x, for example.
- *Do your functions have proper signatures to indicate what they do?* People are lost if they see functions named do_data(data) or run_step1().

- *Do you organize your code consistently across files?* People expect different files of the same type to use similar layouts. Do you place `import` statements at the top of your files, for example?
- *Is your project folder structured with specific files stored in the desired folders?* When your project's scope grows, you should create separate folders for related files.

These example questions pertain to readability. We don't just ask them from time to time; instead, we ask these kinds of readability questions throughout our projects. The reason is simple: *good* practice makes perfect. Trained as a neuroscientist, I know exactly how the brain works when it comes to behavioral learning. By practicing readability through these self-checking questions, we're training our brain's neural circuits. In the long term, your brain will be trained to know what behaviors constitute good practice in coding, and you'll write readable and maintainable code without even thinking about it.

1.1.2 Considering maintainability even before you write any code

In rare cases, we write code for one-time use. When we write a script, we almost always succeed in convincing ourselves that we'll never use the script again; thus, we don't care about creating good variable names, laying out the code properly, or refactoring functions and data models, not to mention making sure that we leave no comments (or outdated ones). But how many times did it turn out that we had to use the same script the next week or even the following day? This has probably happened to most of us.

The previous paragraph describes a mini-scale maintainability problem. In this case, it affects only your own productivity in a short span of time. If you work in a team environment, however, problems introduced by individual contributors add up to large-scale maintainability problems. The team members fail to follow the same naming rules for variables, functions, and files. Countless incidents of commented-out code remain. Outdated comments are everywhere.

To address maintainability problems in a later stage of your own projects, you should build a good mindset when you're learning to code. Following are some questions that you might consider to help you develop a good "maintainability" mindset for the long run:

- *Is your code free of outdated comments and commented-out code?* If the answer is no, update or delete them! These situations are even worse than those without any comments because they may provide conflicting information.
- *Is there considerable duplication in the code?* If the answer is yes, refactoring is probably warranted. A rule of thumb in coding is *DRY* (Don't Repeat Yourself). By removing duplicates, you'll deal with a single shared portion, which is less prone to bugs than changes in repeated parts.
- *Do you use version-control tools such as Git?* If the answer is no, look at the extensions or plugins of your integrated development environment (IDE). For Python, common IDEs include PyCharm and Visual Studio Code. Many IDEs have integrated version-control tools that make it much easier to manage versions.

Being a pragmatic Python programmer requires this type of maintainability training. After all, almost all Python tools are open source and evolving rapidly. Thus, maintainability should be the cornerstone of any viable project. Throughout the book, where applicable, we'll touch base on how to implement maintainability practices in our daily Python coding. Please remember that readability is the key to sustained maintainability. When you focus on writing readable code, your codebase's maintainability improves consequentially.

1.2 What Python can do well or as well as other languages

Python owes its growing popularity to the characteristics of the language itself. Although none of these characteristics is unique to Python, when they were organically combined, Python was set to grow into a widely adopted language. The following list summarizes Python's key characteristics:

- *Cross-platform*—Python runs on common platforms, such as Windows, Linux, and MacOS. Thus, Python code is transferrable. Any code that you write on your own platform can run on other computers without any restrictions imposed by the differences between platforms.
- *Expressive and readable*—Python's syntax is simpler than that of many other languages. The expressive, readable coding style is widely adopted by Python programmers. You'll find that well-written Python code is enjoyable to read, just like well-written prose.
- *Fast for prototyping*—Given its simple syntax, Python code is generally more concise than code written in other languages. Thus, it requires less work to produce a functional prototype in Python than in other languages.
- *Standalone*—When you install Python on your computer, it becomes ready to use right after "unboxing." The basic Python installation package consists of all essential libraries that you need to perform any routine coding work.
- *Open source, free, and extensible*—Although Python works standalone, you can write and use your own packages. If others have published any packages you need, you can install them with a one-line command without worrying about license or subscription fees.

These key characteristics have attracted many programmers, forming a tremendous developer community. The open source nature of Python allows interested users to contribute to this language and its ecosystem in general. Table 1.1 summarizes some notable domains and their respective Python tools. This table isn't an exhaustive list, and you're encouraged to explore Python tools in the specialty domain of your own interest.

Table 1.1   Overview of domain-specific Python tools

Domain	Tool	Highlights
Web development	Flask	A micro web framework; good for building lightweight web apps; flexible extensibility for third-party functionalities

Table 1.1 Overview of domain-specific Python tools

Domain	Tool	Highlights
Web development	Django	A complete web framework; good for building database-driven web apps; highly scalable as an enterprise solution
	FastAPI	A web framework for building application programming interfaces (APIs); data validation and data conversion; automatic generation of API web interfaces
	Streamlit	A web framework for easy building of data-related apps; popular among data scientists and ML engineers
Data science	NumPy	Specialized for processing large, multidimensional arrays; high computational efficiency; integral to many other libraries
	pandas	A versatile package for processing spreadsheet-like two-dimensional data; comprehensive data manipulations
	statsmodels	A popular package for statistics, such as linear regression, correlation, Bayesian modeling, and survival analysis
	Matplotlib	An object-oriented paradigm for drawing histograms, scatter plots, pie charts, and other common figures with a variety of customizable settings
	Seaborn	An easy-to-use visualization library for drawing attractive graphics; high-level APIs based on Matplotlib
Machine learning	Scikit-learn	A wide range of preprocessing tools for building ML models; implementation of common ML algorithms
	TensorFlow	A framework with both high- and low-level APIs; Tensor board visualization tool; good for building complex neural networks
	Keras	High-level APIs for building neural networks; easy to use; good for building low-performance models
	PyTorch	A framework for building neural networks; more intuitive code styles than TensorFlow; good for building complex neural networks
	FastAI	High-level APIs for building neural networks on top of PyTorch; easy to use

Frameworks, libraries, packages, and modules

When we discuss tools, we use several closely related terms, including *frameworks*, *libraries*, *packages*, and *modules*. Different languages may use some of these terms and have slightly different meanings. Here, I discuss the meanings of these terms that most Python programmers accept.

Frameworks have the largest scope. Frameworks provide a complete set of functionalities that are designed to perform a dedicated job at a high level, such as web development.

> *(continued)*
>
> *Libraries* are building blocks of frameworks, consisting of packages. Libraries provide functionalities without users having to worry about the underlying packages.
>
> *Packages* provide specific functionalities. More specifically, packages bundle modules, and each module consists of a set of closely related data structures and functions in a single file, such as a .py file.

1.3   What Python can't do or can't do well

Everything has limits, and so does Python. There are many things that Python can't do, or at least can't do well compared with alternative tools. Although some people are trying to push Python in such a way that we can use it for other purposes, at this stage, we should know its limits in two important areas:

- *Mobile applications*—In this mobile age, we all have smartphones and use apps in almost every aspect of life, such as banking, online shopping, health, communications, and certainly gaming. Unfortunately, there have been no great Python frameworks for developing smartphone apps despite attempts such as Kivy and BeeWare. If you work in mobile development, you should consider mature alternatives such as Swift for iOS apps and Kotlin for Android apps. As a pragmatic programmer, you choose a language that leads to a product with the best user experience.
- *Low-level development*—When it comes to developing software that interacts directly with hardware, Python isn't the best choice. Due to the interpreted nature of Python, the overall execution speed isn't fast enough for developing low-level software, such as device drivers, which require instant responsiveness. If you're interested in developing software at a low level, you should consider alternative languages that are better at interfacing with the hardware. C and C++ are good options for developing device drivers, for example.

1.4   What you'll learn in this book

We've talked a little bit about what it means to be a pragmatic programmer. Now let's talk about how you're going to get there. As you write programs, you'll inevitably run into new programming challenges. In this book, we've identified the programming techniques you'll need to take for the tasks you're most likely to encounter.

1.4.1   Focusing on domain-independent knowledge

All things are connected in some way directly or indirectly, and so is Python knowledge. To put this discussion in a context, consider figure 1.1. We can conceptualize Python features and its applications as three related entities.

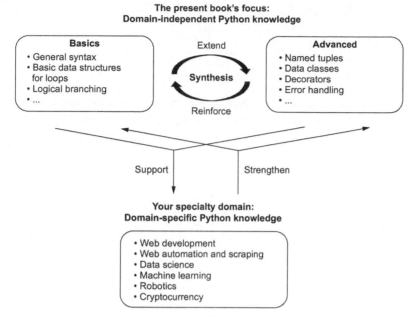

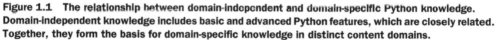

Figure 1.1 The relationship between domain-independent and domain-specific Python knowledge. Domain-independent knowledge includes basic and advanced Python features, which are closely related. Together, they form the basis for domain-specific knowledge in distinct content domains.

The goal of learning Python for most of us is to apply Python to address problems in the domain where we work, which requires *domain-specific Python knowledge,* such as web development and data science. As a prerequisite for fulfilling your job, your knowledge base should encompass essential Python features—more specifically, *domain-independent Python knowledge.* Even when your job role switches or evolves, you can apply the essential Python knowledge to your new position.

In this book, you'll focus on gaining domain-independent Python knowledge. To facilitate the learning process, we can operationally define domain-independent Python knowledge as two building components: the basic and the advanced.

For the basics, we should know common data structures and their manipulations. We also need to know how to evaluate conditions to construct the if...else... statement. When we perform repeated work, we can take advantage of for and while loops. To reuse blocks of code, we can refactor them into functions and classes. Mastering these basics is sufficient for writing useful Python code to perform your job tasks. If you know most of the basics, you're ready to learn the advanced skills.

The advanced skills enable you to write better code that's more efficient and that takes advantage of versatile Python features. Let's see a simple example to feel the versatility of Python. When we use a for loop to iterate a list object, we often need to show the position of each item beside the item itself, such as

```
prime_numbers = [2, 3, 5]

# desired output:
Prime Number #1: 2
Prime Number #2: 3
Prime Number #3: 5
```

If we use only the basic features, we may come up with the following solution. In the solution, we create a `range` object that allows retrieval of the 0-based index to produce the position information. For the output, we use string concatenation:

```
for num_i in range(len(prime_numbers)):
    num_pos = num_i + 1
    num = prime_numbers[num_i]
    print("Prime Number #" + str(num_pos) + ": " + str(num))
```

However, after you read this book, you'll become a more experienced Python user and should be able to produce the following solution that is cleaner and more Pythonic:

```
for num_pos, num in enumerate(prime_numbers, start=1):
    print(f"Prime Number #{num_pos}: {num}")
```

The above solution involves three techniques: tuple unpacking to obtain `num_pos` and `num` (section 4.4), creating the `enumerate` object (section 5.3), and formatting the output using f-strings (section 2.1). I'm not going to expand the discussion of these techniques here since they'll be covered in their respective sections. Nevertheless, this example is simply showing you what this book is all about—*how to use a variety of techniques to produce Pythonic solutions.*

Besides these techniques, you'll learn and apply advanced function concepts, such as decorators and closures, for example. When you define classes, you'll know how to make them work together to minimize the code and reduce the potential for bugs. When your program is done, you'll know how to log and test your code to make it production-ready.

This book is all about synthesizing domain-independent Python knowledge. You'll not only learn pragmatic advanced features, but also basic Python features and fundamental computer programming concepts where applicable. The key term here is *synthesizing*, as discussed in section 1.4.2.

1.4.2 *Solving problems through synthesis*

A common dilemma that beginners run into is that they seem to know a variety of techniques, but don't know how and when to use them to solve problems. For each technique we discuss in this book, we'll show you how it works independently, and we'll also show you how it fits with other techniques. We hope that you'll start to see how all the different pieces can be composed into an infinite number of new programs.

As a fundamental note on learning and synthesizing various techniques, you should expect that learning to code isn't a linear path. After all, Python's technical features are closely interrelated. Although you'll focus on learning intermediate and advanced Python techniques, they can't be isolated completely from basic topics. Instead, you'll notice that I'll frequently make remarks on basic techniques or intentionally reiterate techniques that I've already covered.

1.4.3 *Learning skills in context*

As we mentioned earlier, this book focuses on learning skills that are built on domain-independent Python knowledge. Being domain-independent means that you can apply the skills covered in this book to any domain where you'd like to use Python. It's almost impossible to learn anything without an example, however. We'll show most techniques in this book by using an ongoing project to provide a consistent context within which to discuss specific skills. If you're familiar with a particular skill, you can skip to the section's Discussion part, in which I'll discuss some key aspects of the covered skills.

As a heads-up, the generic project is a task-management web app. In the application, you can manage tasks, including adding, editing, and removing tasks—everything that will be implemented with pure Python, such as data models, functions, classes, and anything else you can think of that an application may have. Moving forward, the important thing to note is that the goal is not to get a perfect, shiny application from this book. Instead, you want to learn all the essential Python techniques in the process of creating this web app so you can apply your domain-independent knowledge to projects in your own jobs.

Summary

- It's critical for you to build a pragmatic learning strategy. By focusing on learning the domain-independent features of Python, you'll get yourself ready for any Python-related job role.
- Python is a general-purpose, open source programming language that fosters a tremendous community of developers who make and share Python packages.
- Python is competitive in many domains, including web development, data science, and ML. Each domain has specific Python frameworks and packages that you can use.
- Python has its limitations. If you consider developing mobile apps or low-level device drivers, you should use Swift, Kotlin, Java, C, C++, Rust, or any other applicable language.
- I make a distinction between *domain-independent* Python knowledge and *domain-dependent* Python knowledge. This book focuses on teaching domain-independent Python knowledge.

- Learning to code is not a linear path. Although you'll learn advanced features in this book, I'll frequently mention basic ones. Also, you'll encounter some difficult topics, which will create an upward spiral learning path.
- The essential recipe for learning Python or any programming language is synthesizing individual technical skills to form a comprehensive skill set. Through the synthesis process, you'll learn the language in a pragmatic way, knowing what works for the problem that you're addressing.

Part 1

Using built-in data models

We build applications to address problems in our daily lives. People build online shopping websites so we can order clothes and books online. They build human resources software so companies can manage employees. And they build text-processing software so we can edit documents. From the application-development perspective, no matter what problems our application addresses, we must extract and process information about the problems. In programming, to model various kinds of information in our applications, such as product descriptions and employees, we must use proper data structures. These data structures provide a standardized way to represent real-life entities in our applications, making it possible to enable specific rules, organizations, and implementations to address our business needs. In this part, we focus mainly on using built-in data models, including strings, lists, tuples, dictionaries, and sets. Moreover, you learn techniques that are shared by various types of data structures, such as sequence-like data and iterables.

Processing and formatting strings

2

This chapter covers

- Using f-strings to interpolate expressions and apply formatting
- Converting strings to other applicable data types
- Joining and splitting strings
- Using regular expressions for advanced string processing

Textual information is the most important form of data in almost every application. Textual data as well as numeric data can be saved as text files, and reading them requires us to process strings. On a shopping website, for example, we use text to provide production descriptions. Machine learning is trending, and you may have heard about one machine learning specialty: natural language processing, which extracts information from texts. Because of the universal use of strings, text processing is an inevitable step in preparing data in these scenarios. Using our task management app as the context, we need to convert a task's attributes to textual data so that we can present them at the frontend of our web app. When we obtain data entry at the frontend of our app, we must convert these strings to a proper type, such as an integer, for further processing. In numerous real-life cases like these, we need to process and format strings properly. In this chapter, we tackle some common text processing problems.

2.1 How do I use f-strings for string interpolation and formatting?

In Python, you can format text strings in a variety of ways. One emerging approach is to use an f-string, which allows you to embed expressions inside a string literal. Although you can use other string formatting approaches, an f-string offers a more readable solution; thus, you should use f-strings as the preferred approach when you prepare strings as output.

> **TRIVIA** F-strings were introduced in Python 3.6. Both f and F (which mean *formatted*) can be the prefix for the f-string. A *string literal* is a series of characters enclosed within single or double quotation marks.

When you use strings as an output, you often need to deal with nonstring data, such as integers and floats. Suppose that our task management application has the requirement of creating a string output from existing variables:

```
# existing variables
name = "Homework"
urgency = 5

# desired output:
Name: Homework; Urgency Level: 5
```

In this section, you'll learn how to use f-strings to interpolate nonstring data and present strings in the desired format. As you'll discover, f-strings are a more readable solution for formatting strings from existing strings and other types of variables.

2.1.1 Formatting strings before f-strings

The `str` class handles textual data through its instances, which we refer to as *string variables*. Besides string variables, textual information often involves data types such as integers and floats. Theoretically, we can convert nonstring data to strings and concatenate them to create the desired textual output, as shown in the next listing.

> **Listing 2.1 Creating string output using string concatenation**

```
task = "Name: " + name + "; Urgency Level: " + str(urgency)

print(task)
# output: Name: Homework; Urgency Level: 5
```

There are two potential problems with the code creating the `task` variable. First, it looks cumbersome and doesn't read smoothly, as we're dealing with multiple strings, each of which is enclosed in quotation marks. Second, we must convert urgency from int to str before it can be joined with other strings, further complicating the string concatenation operation.

Old string formatting techniques

Before the f-string was introduced, two other solutions were available. The first solution is the classic C-style involving the % sign, and the other uses the format method. You'll find these solutions in the following code snippet:

```
task1 = "Name: %s; Urgency Level: %d" % (name, urgency)
```
The % sign separates the string literal and the tuple object.
```
task2 = "Name: {}; Urgency Level: {}".format(name, urgency)
```

The C-style approach uses % within the string literal to denote that one variable will be formatted, following which are the % sign and the tuple of the corresponding variables. The format method approach has a similar usage. Instead of using % signs in the literal, it uses curly braces as the marker for string interpolation, and the corresponding variables are listed in the format method.

Notably, both approaches are still supported in Python, but they have become obsolete, and you rarely need to use them. Thus, I don't expand on them here. It's important to know that what they do can be done with f-strings—a more readable string interpolation and formatting approach, as we'll explore in section 2.1.2.

CONCEPT In general, methods are functions that are defined within a class. Here, format is a function defined in the str class, and we call these methods on str instance objects.

2.1.2 Using f-strings to interpolate variables

Formatting strings often involves combining string literals and variables of different types, such as integers and strings. When we integrate variables into an f-string, we can interpolate these variables to convert them to the desired strings automatically. In this section, you'll see a variety of interpolations involving common data types using f-strings. Let's see first how we use f-strings to create the output shown in listing 2.1:

```
task_f = f"Name: {name}; Urgency Level: {urgency}"

assert task == task_f == "Name: Homework; Urgency Level: 5"
```

In this example, we create the task_f variable by using the f-string approach. The most significant thing is that we use curly braces to enclose variables for interpolation. As f-strings integrate string interpolation, they're also referred to as *interpolated string literals*.

CONCEPT The term *string interpolation* isn't Python-specific, as most common modern languages (such as JavaScript, Swift, and C#) have this feature. In general, it's a more concise and readable syntax for creating formatted strings than string concatenations and alternative string formatting approaches.

The assertion statement

assert is a Python keyword used to create an assertion statement, which evaluates the supplied condition. When the condition is True, the program continues its execution. When the condition is False, execution stops, and the program raises an AssertionError.

As a convention in this book, I use the assertion statement to show the equivalence of the involved variables in a comparison. As a special case, when the evaluated variable is Boolean, it's technically preferred to use assert true_var and assert not false_var. To explicitly show the variable's Boolean value, however, I opt to use assert true_var == True and assert false_var == False.

We've seen that an f-string interpolates string and integer variables. How about other types, such as list and tuple? These types are supported by f-string, as shown in this code snippet:

```
tasks = ["homework", "laundry"]                                    Interpolates
assert f"Tasks: {tasks}" == "Tasks: ['homework', 'laundry']"  ◁───┘ a list object

                                                         Interpolates a tuple object
task_hwk = ("Homework", "Complete physics work")
assert f"Task: {task_hwk}" == "Task: ('Homework', 'Complete physics work')"  ◁───┘

                                                                      Interpolates
task = {"name": "Laundry", "urgency": 3}                              a dict object
assert f"Task: {task}" == "Task: {'name': 'Laundry', 'urgency': 3}"  ◁───┘
```

PEEK   F-strings also support custom class instances. When we're learning about creating our own custom classes in chapter 8, we'll revisit how string interpolation works with the custom instances (section 8.4).

2.1.3 *Using f-strings to interpolate expressions*

We've seen how f-string interpolates variables. As a more general usage, f-strings can also interpolate expressions, which eliminates the need to create intermediate variables. You may access an item in a dict object to create string output, for example, or use the result of calling a function. In these common scenarios, you can plug these expressions into f-strings, as shown in the following code snippet:

```
tasks = ["homework", "laundry", "grocery shopping"]              Accesses an
assert f"First Task: {tasks[0]}" == 'First Task: homework'  ◁───┘ item in the list

                                                                Calls a function
task_name = "grocery shopping"
assert f"Task Name: {task_name.title()}" == 'Task Name: Grocery Shopping'  ◁───┘

number = 5
assert f"Square: {number*number}" == 'Square: 25'  ◁───── Direct calculation
```

These expressions are enclosed within curly braces, allowing f-strings to evaluate them directly to produce the desired string output: {tasks[0]} -> "homework"; {task_name .title()} -> "Grocery Shopping"; {number*number} -> 25.

As a key programming concept, we often encounter the term *expression*. Some beginners may confuse this term with a related concept *statement*. An expression usually is one line of code (it can expand to multiple lines, such as a triple-quoted string) that evaluates to a value or an object, such as a string or a custom class instance. Applying this definition, we can easily figure out that variables are a kind of expression.

By contrast, statements don't create any value or object, and a statement's purpose is to complete an action. We use assert, for example, to create an assertion statement, which ensures that something is valid before proceeding. We aren't trying to produce a True or False Boolean value; we're checking or asserting a condition. Figure 2.1 illustrates the differences between expressions and statements.

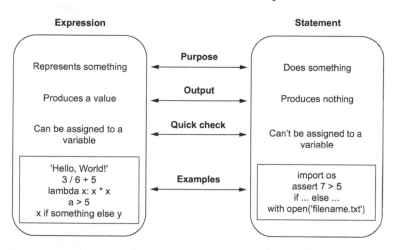

Figure 2.1   Differences between expressions and statements. Expressions represent something and are evaluated to a value or an object, whereas statements execute specific actions and can't be evaluated to a value.

Although f-strings interpolate expressions natively, we should use this skill with caution because any complicated expressions in an f-string compromise the readability of your code. The following example represents a misuse of an f-string that uses a complex expression:

```
summary_text = f"Your Average Score: {sum([95, 98, 97, 96, 97, 93]) /
➥ len([95, 98, 97, 96, 97, 93])}."
```

A rule of thumb for checking your code's readability is to determine how much time a reader needs to digest your code. In the preceding code, it may take tens of seconds for a reader to know what you want to achieve. As a direct contrast, consider the following refactored version:

```
scores = [95, 98, 97, 96, 97, 93]

total_score = sum(scores)
subject_count = len(scores)
average_score = total_score / subject_count

summary_text = f"Your Average Score: {average_score}."
```

This version has several things to note. First, we use a list object to store the scores to remove the duplication of the data. Second, we use separate steps, with each step representing a simpler calculation. Third, the key thing for improved readability is that each step uses a sensible name to indicate the calculation result. Without any comment, your code is comfortable to read; everything is clear by itself.

> **READABILITY**   Create necessary intermediate variables with sensible names to clearly indicate each step of your operations. For these simple operations, you don't even need to write any comment because the sensible names indicate the purpose of each operation.

2.1.4   *Applying specifiers to format f-strings*

The proper formatting of textual data, such as alignment, is key to conveying the desired information. As they are designed to handle string formatting, f-strings allow us to set a *format specifier* (beginning with a colon) to apply additional formatting configurations to the expression in the curly braces (figure 2.2). In this section, you'll learn how to apply the specifiers to format f-strings.

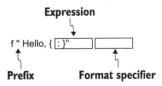

Figure 2.2   **Components of an f-string. The expression is the first part and is required. The expression is evaluated first, and a corresponding string is created. The second part, which is the format specifier, is optional.**

As an optional component, the format specifier defines how the interpolated string of the expression should be formatted. An f-string can accept different kinds of format specifiers. Let's explore some of the most useful ones next, starting with text alignment.

ALIGNING STRINGS TO CREATE A VISUAL STRUCTURE

One way to improve communication efficiency is to use a structured organization, which is also true for presenting textual data. As shown in figure 2.3, scenario B provides clearer information than scenario A due to its more organized structure, with the columns aligned.

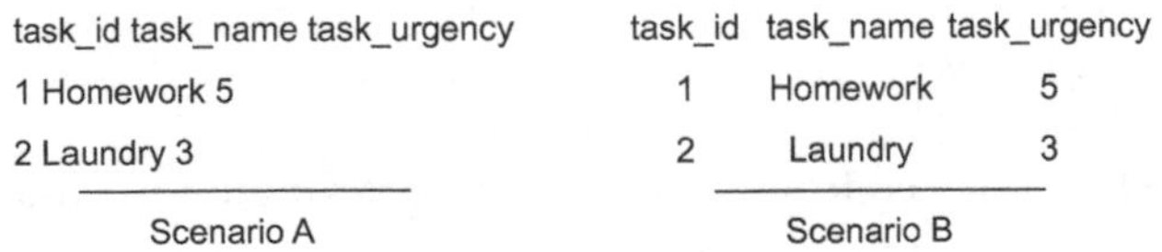

task_id task_name task_urgency		task_id	task_name	task_urgency
1 Homework 5		1	Homework	5
2 Laundry 3		2	Laundry	3
Scenario A			Scenario B	

Figure 2.3   **Improved clarity when the texts are presented in an organized structure (scenario B) compared with the default left alignment (scenario A)**

Text alignment in f-strings involves three characters: <, >, and ^, which align the text left, right, and center, respectively. If you're confused about which is which, remember to focus on the arrow's tip; if it's on the left side, for example, the text is left-aligned.

To specify text alignment as the format specifier, we use the syntax f"{expr:x<n}", in which expr means the interpolated expression, x means the padding character (when omitted, it defaults to spaces) for alignment, < means left alignment, and n is an integer that the string expands in width. Applying this syntax, the code in the next listing shows how to create two properly aligned records with improved clarity.

Listing 2.2   Applying format specifiers in f-strings

```
task_ids = [1, 2, 3]
task_names = ['Do homework', 'Laundry', 'Pay bills']
task_urgencies = [5, 3, 4]                              Applies format specifiers
                                                          to the expressions
for i in range(3):
    print(f'{task_ids[i]:^12}{task_names[i]:^12}{task_urgencies[i]:^12}')  ◁

# Output the following lines:
     1       Do homework       5
     2         Laundry         3
     3        Pay bills        4
```

One thing that should catch your attention is that you apply the same format specifier for all the expressions, which represents repetition. When you see repetitions in your code, you're likely violating the DRY (Don't Repeat Yourself) principle, which is a signal for refactoring.

The DRY principle and refactoring

We can apply many principles to our coding. One famous one is the DRY principle. When your program includes repeated code, it's likely that you can refactor it to remove such repetitions. Some IDEs, such as PyCharm, include features that automatically detect duplications, and you should take advantage of those features to better your program.

When I say *refactor*, I mean taking steps to update existing code to improve its design, structure, and thus maintainability. Refactoring isn't intended to add features to your program; instead, it's meant to restructure existing code without inducing any changes in its external behavior. Whenever applicable, you'll see examples of refactoring throughout the book.

In listing 2.2, if we have a new text alignment requirement, we must update the code in three locations, which is inconvenient and error-prone. Thus, the objective of refactoring is to have a mechanism to use a variable for the format specifier. Listing 2.3 shows a possible solution that extracts the repetitive part: the format specifier. Taking the refactoring a step further, we define a function to accept the format specifier as a parameter, allowing us to try different format specifiers. To improve readability, we create separate variables for the task's information.

Listing 2.3   Refactored function to take any format specifier

```
def create_formatted_records(fmt):
    for i in range(3):
        task_id = task_ids[i]
        name = task_names[i]
        urgency = task_urgencies[i]
        print(f'{task_id:{fmt}}{name:{fmt}}{urgency:{fmt}}')
```

One important thing to note in listing 2.3 is that the format specifier fmt is enclosed within curly braces, embedded within the outside curly braces. Python knows how to replace {fmt} with the proper format specifier. Let's try this function with different format specifiers:

```
>>> create_formatted_records('^15')
       1            Do homework         5
       2             Laundry            3
       3             Pay bills          4
>>> create_formatted_records('^18')
       1              Do homework          5
       2               Laundry             3
       3               Pay bills           4
```

As you can see, the refactored code allows us to set any format specifier, and this flexibility highlights the benefit of refactoring. When we use format specifiers for text alignment, text forms distinct columns, creating visual boundaries to separate different pieces of information.

> **MAINTAINABILITY**   We constantly spot opportunities to refactor our code, usually at a "local" level. The local optimization may seem to be insignificant, but these small improvements add up and determine the entire project's overall maintainability.

We have been using spaces as padding for the alignment; we can use other characters as padding too. Our choice of characters depends on whether they make the information stand out. Table 2.1 shows some examples of using different paddings and alignments.

Table 2.1   F-string format specifiers for text alignment

F-string	Output	Description
f"{task:*>10}"[a]	"**homework"	Right alignment, * as padding
f"{task:*<10}"	"homework**"	Left alignment, * as padding

Table 2.1   F-string format specifiers for text alignment

F-string	Output	Description
`f"{task:*^10}"`	`"*homework*"`	Center alignment, * as padding
`f"{task:^10}"`	`" homework "`	Center alignment, space as padding

[a]We define the task as a string variable: `task = "homework"`.

FORMATTING NUMBERS

Numbers are integral sources of information that we often include in textual material. There are multiple forms of numeric values, such as large integers, floating-point numbers, and percentages. In this section, you'll learn how f-strings can represent numeric values with proper formatting specifiers to improve their readability.

There is an infinite number of prime numbers. By doing a quick Google search, we can find that the smallest prime number greater than 1 billion is 1000000007. To show this large integer, it's a good idea to use separators between digits, and a common approach is to use commas every three digits. To apply separators to integers in an f-string, the format specifier is `xd`, where `x` is the separator and `d` is the specific format specifier for integers:

```
large_prime_number = 1000000007

print(f"Use commas: {large_prime_number:,d}")
# output: Use commas: 1,000,000,007
```

Floating-point numbers, or decimal numbers in general, can be found in almost any scientific or engineering report. As you probably expect, f-strings have format specifiers that allow us to format decimals in a readable manner. Consider the following examples:

```
decimal_number = 1.23456

print(f"Two digits: {decimal_number:.2f}")
# output: Two digits: 1.23

print(f"Four digits: {decimal_number:.4f}")
# output: Four digits: 1.2346
```

As with `d` for integers, we use `f` as a format specifier for decimal values. Although the `f` format specifier can be used alone, it's more often used to specify how many digits we want to keep after the decimal symbol: `.2` to keep two digits, `.4` to keep four digits, and so on.

In a similar fashion to using `f` for decimals, we can use `e` as the format specifier for scientific notations. Consider the following examples of this feature:

```
sci_number = 0.00000000412733

print(f"Sci notation: {sci_number:e}")
```

```
# output: Sci notation: 4.1227330e-09

print(f"Sci notation: {sci_number:.2e}")
# output: Sci notation: 4.13e-09
```

Another common form of numeric values is percentages, and the format specifier for percentages is the percent sign (%). As we do with the e and f specifiers, we can use the % specifier alone or in conjunction with the precision specification, such as .2 for two-digit precision:

```
pct_number = 0.179323

print(f"Percentage: {pct_number:%}")
# output: Percentage: 17.932300%

print(f"Percentage two digits: {pct_number:.2%}")
# output: Percentage two digits: 17.93%
```

In addition to these format specifiers, f-strings support other specifiers. Table 2.2 shows common specifiers that you can apply to f-strings when you deal with numbers.

Table 2.2 **Common format specifiers for formatting numbers with f-strings**

Numeric type	F-string	Output	Description
int	f"{number:b}"	"1111"	Binary format, using base 2
	f"{number:c}"	"\x0f"	Unicode representation of the integer
	f"{number:d}"	"15"	Decimal format, using base 10
	f"{number:o}"	"17"	Octal format, using base 8
	f"{number:x}"	"f"	Hexadecimal format, using base 16
float	f"{point:.2e}"	"1.23e+00"	Scientific notation
	f"{point:.2f}"	"1.23"	Fixed-point notation with two-digit precision
	f"{point:.2g}"	"1.23"	General format, automatically applying e or f
	f"{point:.2%}"	"123.45%"	Percentage with two-digit precision[a]

[a]We define the number as an integer variable (number = 15) and the point as a float variable (point = 1.2345). Please note that the .2 portion in the format specifiers for floats is optional. When you use .3, you'll have three-digit precision.

2.1.5 *Discussion*

Although directly interpolating expressions by f-strings makes code cleaner, avoid using complicated expressions in f-strings, which may confuse your readers. Instead, create intermediate variables with sensible names when the expressions are complicated.

Python still supports the conventional C-style and format-based approaches, but there is no real need for you to learn them (you may see them in legacy code, though). Whenever you need to create string output, use f-strings. Don't forget about aligning your text and formatting numeric values to improve the text output's clarity.

2.1.6   Challenge

James works in a wholesale company's IT department and is preparing a template of price tags. Suppose that the product's data is saved as a dict object: {"name": "Vacuum", "price": 130.675}. How can James write an f-string if the desired output is Vacuum: {130.68}? Note that the price requires two-digit precision and that the output includes curly braces, which are coincidentally the characters for string interpolation in f-strings.

> **HINT**   Curly braces are special characters in f-strings. When a string literal includes special characters, you need to escape them in such a way that they're no longer evaluated as special characters. To escape curly braces, you use an extra curly brace: {{ means {, and }} means }.

2.2   *How do I convert strings to retrieve the represented data?*

Although strings are textual data on their surface, the actual data represented by strings can be integers, dictionaries, and other data types. The built-in input function, for example, is the most basic way to collect users' input in a Python console:

```
>>> age = input("Please enter your age: ")
Please enter your age: 35
>>> type(age)        <─────┐
<class 'str'>              │  Checks the variable's type
```

As shown in the preceding code snippet, the user's input is taken as a string. Suppose that we wanted to check whether the user's age is over 18. We think we can run the following code:

```
>>> age > 18
# ERROR: TypeError: '>' not supported between instances of 'str' and 'int'
```

Unfortunately, the comparison didn't work because age is a string, and you can't compare a string with an integer. This example highlights the necessity of converting a string to an integer. More broadly, many other scenarios require that we convert strings to lists, dictionaries, and other applicable data types. Such conversion is essential for subsequent data processing. In this section, you'll learn how to check the data types represented by the strings and the proper ways to convert strings to the desired data types.

2.2.1   *Checking whether strings represent alphanumeric values*

In Python, strings can be anything you can type with your keyboard. One common need is to check whether strings include only alphanumeric characters. In this section, you'll learn a variety of ways to check the nature of a string's characters.

Suppose that the task management app requires users to set a username, which must be alphanumeric. We can implement this functionality by using the isalnum method, which examines whether a string contains only a-z, A-Z, and 0-9. Some examples follow:

```
bad_username0 = "123!@#"
assert bad_username0.isalnum() == False

bad_username1 = "abc..."
assert bad_username1.isalnum() == False

good_username = "1a2b3c"
assert good_username.isalnum() == True
```

Suppose that when a user creates a task, we require the name to contain letters only. For this feature, we can use the isalpha method, which returns True or False. As you've probably noticed, all these is- methods return Boolean values:

```
assert "Homework".isalpha() == True

assert "Homework123".isalpha() == False
```

In a similar fashion, you can use the isnumeric method to check whether all characters in the string are numeric characters:

```
assert "123".isnumeric() == True

assert "a123".isnumeric() == False
```

Here, I want to discuss a couple of gotchas about checking whether a string represents a numeric value when we use the isnumeric method:

- *Strings that represent floats won't pass the* isnumeric *check.* It would be reasonable to expect that strings with valid numeric values would return True on this method call. Unfortunately, that's not the case:

  ```
  assert "3.5".isnumeric() == False
  ```

- *Strings that represent negative integers won't pass the* isnumeric *check.* It probably goes against many people's intuition, too, as in this example:

  ```
  assert "-2".isnumeric() == False
  ```

- *Empty strings are evaluated as* False *with* isnumeric. Evaluating empty strings as non-numeric is probably a desired behavior. We should understand this behavior when we deal with conversions from strings to numbers.

To avoid these gotchas, remember that a string produces a True value by means of the isnumeric method only if all the characters in a nonempty string are numeric characters. Please note that numeric characters don't include the decimal symbol or the negative sign. For this reason, the isnumeric method evaluates floats and negative numbers as False.

Differences between isnumeric, isdigit, and isdecimal

Related to the isnumeric method, the methods isdigit and isdecimal are often used to check whether strings contain only digits or decimal characters. These names seem to mean the same thing, and they produce the same Boolean values in most cases, such as "123". But some nuances make them produce different values for some strings, especially when numeric strings are not Arabic numerals.

By definition, these three methods have the following relationships in terms of their strictness of checking numerics: isdecimal < isdigit < isnumeric. When you're confused about these methods, your best bet is to use isnumeric, which is the most inclusive.

Besides the discussed is- methods for checking the numeric nature of strings, as a refresher, Python strings have other is- methods that perform other checking tasks, such as islower and isupper. Although I don't cover these other is- methods in this book, you should be familiar with them.

> **TRIVIA** Among these is- methods, isidentifier is interesting because it tests whether a string is a valid identifier to name a variable, a function, or an object in general.

2.2.2 Casting strings to numbers

In the preceding section, you learned to examine whether a string represents a positive integer. But there seems to be no easy way to tell whether a string represents a numeric value, particularly when it's a floating-point or negative number. Converting strings to numbers is important because we can't do any numeric calculations with strings, such as comparing age with 18. Thus, in many cases, we must derive the represented numeric values of strings for subsequent processing. In this section, you'll learn to convert strings to numbers—a process termed *casting*.

> **CONCEPT** In programming, the process of converting a data type to another data type, such as converting a string to an integer, is known as *casting*.

The two common data types for numeric values are float and int. The syntax for creating these instances from strings is float("string") and int("string"). Python evaluates the string objects to cast them to a proper float or int object—if possible.

If you expect a float with a string, you can send it to the built-in `float` constructor. In the following examples, all the casted numbers are of the `float` type, even if the string represents an integer:

```
>>> float("3.25")
3.25
>>> float("-2")
-2.0
```

A float is created even though the string appears to be an integer.

> **CONCEPT**   A *constructor* refers to a special kind of function that creates an instance object of a class. For more on this topic, see chapter 8. Here, we use `float` and `int` constructors to create objects of the `float` and `int` types, respectively.

If you expect an integer with a string, you can use the built-in `int` constructor:

```
>>> int("-5")
-5
>>> int("123")
123
```

Note that when these strings have desired numeric values, these casting operations succeed. When they don't, however, these castings result in errors, which cause your entire program to halt, as shown in the following code snippet:

```
>>> float("3.5a")
# ERROR: ValueError: could not convert string to float: '3.5a'

>>> int("one")
# ERROR: ValueError: invalid literal for int() with base 10: 'one'
```

To prevent your program from being terminated due to this error, it is important to use the try…except… statement to handle the exception. Although I'm not expanding the discussion here, the next listing shows such usage. I'll discuss this feature in chapter 12 (section 12.3).

Listing 2.4   Casting numbers from strings

```
def cast_number(number_str):
    try:
        casted_number = float(number_str)
    except ValueError:
        print(f"Couldn't cast {repr(number_str)} to a number")
    else:
        print(f"Casting {repr(number_str)} to {casted_number}")

# Use the above function in a console
>>> cast_number("1.5")
Casting '1.5' to 1.5
>>> cast_number("2.3a")
Couldn't cast '2.3a' to a number
```

Uses the repr function to have the string in a quoted format

2.2.3 *Evaluating strings to derive their represented data*

Besides numeric values, our application often has textual data that represents other data types, such as lists and tuples. For example, in a web application, data are commonly entered as text, such as "[1, 2, 3]" which resumes a `list` object. Because of the data type as `str`, you can't apply any `list` methods to this textual data—that is, you can only call `list` methods on `list` objects. In this case, data conversion is required. In this section, you explore how to derive the underlying data, other than numbers, from strings.

In the previous section, you learned to use `float` and `int` constructors to cast strings to derive numeric values. The approach of using the constructor with a string object won't always work, however. Consider the three common data types—`list`, `tuple`, and `dict`—which are represented by strings in the following code snippet:

```
numbers_list_str = "[1, 2]"
numbers_tuple_str = "(1, 2)"
numbers_dict_str = "{1:'one', 2: 'two'}"
```

When we attempt to send the strings directly to their respective constructors, unexpected outcomes happen:

```
>>> list(numbers_list_str)
['[', '1', ',', ' ', '2', ']']
>>> tuple(numbers_tuple_str)
('(', '1', ',', ' ', '2', ')')
```

Lists and tuples can instantiate from strings.

```
>>> dict(numbers_dict_str)
# ERROR: ValueError: dictionary update sequence element #0 has length 1; 2 is
➥ required
```

Although the `list` and `tuple` constructors do create a `list` and a `tuple` object by treating strings as iterables, the created objects wouldn't be the data that you would expect to extract from these strings. Specifically, strings are iterables that consist of characters. When you include a string in a `list` constructor, its characters become items of the created `list` object. The same operation happens to a `tuple` constructor.

> **CONCEPT** *Iterables* are objects that can render items one by one. Strings, lists, and tuples are common examples of iterables. For further discussion of iterables, see chapter 5.

To solve this unpredicted behavior, use the built-in `eval` function, which takes a string as though you typed it in the console and returns the evaluated result:

```
assert eval(numbers_list_str) == [1, 2]

assert eval(numbers_tuple_str) == (1, 2)

assert eval(numbers_dict_str) == {1: 'one', 2: 'two'}
```

By evaluating these strings, we can retrieve the data that these strings represent. This transformation is useful because we often use texts as the data interchange format. The benefit of using `eval` is that the evaluation result of the supplied text is guaranteed to be what you expect from running the same text as code in a console.

Using `eval` and `exec` with caution

You may want to restrict the use of `eval` to trusted data sources because `eval` will evaluate the string as though the code is part of the program. The following snippet shows such a problem. The evaluation of the improper code results in a `Syntax-Error`, which could crash your program:

```
>>> eval("[1, 2")
...(omitted lines)
SyntaxError: unexpected EOF while parsing
```

Another built-in `exec` function is similar to `eval`. The `exec` function can run a string as though that string is part of the program. The most notable difference between `exec` and `eval` is that `eval` evaluates and returns an expression, whereas `exec` can accept expressions and statements such as `if...else...` but doesn't return anything. Although both functions can provide dynamicity to your application, when used improperly, they can jeopardize your application or even your computer. You could send the string `"os.system('rm -rf *')"`, for example, to the `exec` function, which would remove all folders and files from your computer.

Thus, you should be cautious when your application needs to process strings as code dynamically by using `eval` and `exec`. As an alternative to `eval`, you can look into the `ast` module in the standard library, which has the `literal_eval` function to evaluate the strings safely.

If your application is concerned with the validity of the data source, I recommend that you parse the strings yourself. If you need to get a `list` object of integers from a string, for example, you can remove the square brackets and split the strings to recreate the applicable `list` object. A trivial example follows for your reference. Please note that the code snippet involves a few techniques, such as string splitting and list comprehension, that I cover later (sections 2.3 and 5.2):

```
list_str = "[1, 2, 3, 4]"
stripped_str = list_str.strip("[]")
number_list = [int(x) for x in stripped_str.split(",")]

print(number_list)
# output: [1, 2, 3, 4]
```

> **MAINTAINABILITY** Using `eval` without verifying the integrity of the string object can cause bugs or even catastrophic outcomes. Be cautious whenever you need to use this method.

2.2.4 Discussion

When we use the `float` or `int` constructor to derive the actual numeric values that strings represent, consider using `try...except...` because successful casting is never guaranteed, and when casting fails, it crashes the program if the exception isn't handled. When you use `eval` to obtain the underlying data, you should be cautious, as it can introduce danger to a program if you use untrusted sources. Thus, when data security is a concern, you should consider parsing the data yourself or using a more secure tool, such as the `ast` module. If you work on your own data, such as a script for processing data, you can just use `eval` to obtain the underlying data.

2.2.5 Challenge

At the beginning of this section, you learned that you can use the `input` function to collect a user's input. Mary is an elementary school teacher who wants to write a simple toy program for her students. Suppose that she wants to ask the students about today's temperature in Celsius degrees, using a Python console. How can she write the program so that it meets the following requirements? x represents the value that the user enters:

- When the temperature is < 10 degrees, output `You entered x degrees. It's cold!`
- When the temperature is between 10 and 25 degrees, output `You entered x degrees. It's cool!`
- When the temperature is > 25 degrees, output `You entered x degrees. It's hot!`
- The x value should have one decimal precision. If the user enters `15.75`, for example, it should be displayed as `15.8`.

HINT   The entered string input needs to be casted to a float number before it can be compared with other numbers. To create a string output, use f-strings. Don't forget about format specifiers!

2.3 How do I join and split strings?

Strings are not always in the format that you want them to be. In some cases, individual strings represent discrete pieces of related information, and we need to join them to form a single string. Suppose that a user enters multiple strings, with each representing a fruit that they like. We may join the strings to create a single string to display the user's likes, as shown here:

```
# initial input
fruit0 = "apple"
fruit1 = "banana"
fruit2 = "orange"

# desired output
liked_fruits = "apple, banana, orange"
```

At other times, we need to split strings to create multiple strings. Suppose that a user enters all the countries that they've been to as a single string. We want to have a list of these countries, as shown here:

```
# initial input
visited_countries = "United States, China, France, Canada"

# desired output
countries = ["United States", "China", "France", "Canada"]
```

These two scenarios are plausible examples of basic string processing jobs that you might encounter in a real-life project. In this section, we explore key functionalities for joining and splitting strings, using realistic examples.

2.3.1   *Joining strings with whitespaces*

When you join multiple strings, you can use the explicit concatenation operator: the + symbol, which you saw in listing 2.1. When you have multiple string literals, you can join them if they're separated by whitespaces, such as spaces, tabs, and newline characters. In this section, you'll see how strings separated by whitespaces can be joined.

Suppose that we have multiple configurations to set a display style for our application. We separate each configuration as a string literal, and these individual configuration settings are joined automatically:

```
style_settings = "font-size=large, " "font=Arial, " "color=black, "
➥ "align=center"

print(style_settings)
# output: font-size=large, font=Arial, color=black, align=center
```

Automatic concatenation can only occur among string literals, however, and you can't use this technique with string variables or a mixture of string literals and variables. F-strings also support automatic concatenation. This feature is useful when you construct a long f-string by breaking distinct string literals into separate lines of code for clarity:

```
settings = {"font_size": "large", "font": "Arial", "color":
➥ "black", "align": "center"}

styles = f"font-size={settings['font_size']}, " \
         f"font={settings['font']}, " \
         f"color={settings['color']}, " \        Uses the backslash as the
         f"align={settings['align']}"            line continuation character
```

READABILITY   When a string is long, consider breaking it into multiple lines, with each line representing a meaningful substring. These substrings can be joined automatically when they're separated by whitespaces.

2.3.2   Joining strings with any delimiters

Joining strings separated by spaces can be a little confusing because the boundaries (spaces) between string literals don't make it easy for us to eyeball the individual strings. Moreover, it can occur only between string literals, which is an additional restriction. As a general scenario, joining strings with any delimiters is ideal. In this section, you'll learn to join strings with any applicable delimiter.

Still, consider the style setting example. We can use the `join` method to concatenate these separate strings:

```python
style_settings = ["font-size=large", "font=Arial", "color=black",
    "align=center"]
merged_style = ", ".join(style_settings)

print(merged_style)
# output: font-size=large, font=Arial, color=black, align=center
```

The `join` method takes a `list` of strings as its argument. The items of the `list` are joined sequentially with the delimiter string that we use to call the method. Although we use a `list` object here, more broadly speaking, it can be any iterable, such as `tuple` or `set`.

> **`str.join` or `list.join`**
>
> Frankly, the method call `"separator".join(the_list)` puzzled me a bit when I started to use Python, because in daily life, I was used to saying that I wanted to join these items with a specific separator. With that logic, you might expect the `list` object to appear before the specifier. In fact, in another common language, JavaScript, the `Array` (like `list` in Python) has the `join` method, which creates a delimited string from its items. Applying this logic, you would expect Python `list` objects to have the `join` method.
>
> Unfortunately, that is not the case. Instead, Python's strings have the `join` method. Thus, there appears to be a mismatch between the expectation and the actual implementation. Later, I found out that the best way to remember the correct method call signature is to think of this feature this way: I want to use the specific separator to join each of the items in the `list` object.
>
> When you learn more about Python, you'll find out that Python's design of having `join` as a string method is brilliant. Not only items in a list can be joined by a separator; we can also use `join` with tuples, sets, dictionaries, map objects, and any other iterables. If Python were to have `join` as a list method, to have the same feature for other iterables, Python would have to implement `join` for each type of the iterables, which violates DRY!

Compared with the direct concatenation, `join` is more readable, as contributing strings are separate items; thus, it's easy for us to know what is to be joined. More importantly, `join` has an extra advantage: we can manipulate the items dynamically in the `list` object.

Suppose that we want to have a string to list the tasks that we want to complete for the week in our task management application. To begin, we have the following tasks. We can join these strings to generate a string as a note to display on our desktop:

```
tasks = ["Homework", "Grocery", "Laundry", "Museum Trip", "Buy Furniture"]
note = ", ".join(tasks)

print("Remaining Tasks:", note)
# output: Remaining Tasks: Homework, Grocery, Laundry, Museum Trip, Buy
➥ Furniture
```

After some hard work, a few tasks are done, so we're removing these tasks:

```
tasks.remove("Buy Furniture")
tasks.remove("Homework")
```

After removing these tasks, we can still use the `join` method to create the needed string:

```
print("Remaining Tasks: ", ", ".join(tasks))
# output: Remaining Tasks:  Grocery, Laundry, Museum Trip
```

This example shows a use case with a list of strings that is subject to dynamic changes. When we have additional tasks, we can add the tasks to the `list` object and regenerate the desired string with the `join` method to create an updated string.

2.3.3 *Splitting strings to create a list of strings*

We often use text files to save and transfer data. We can save tabulated data to a text file, for example, with each line representing a record. When we read the text file, each row is a single string containing multiple substrings, and each substring represents a value for the record. To process the data, we need to extract these values with split strings to obtain separate substrings. This section covers topics related to string splitting.

Suppose that we have a text file named `"task_data.txt"` that stores some tasks. Each row represents a task's information, including task ID number, name, and urgency level, as shown in the following code snippet. Because you're going to learn how to read data from a file in chapter 11, assume that you've read the text data and saved it as a multiline string, using triple quotes:

```
task_data = """1001,Homework,5
1002,Laundry,3
1003,Grocery,4"""
```

> **TRIVIA** You can use single or double quotes to create a triple-quoted string that expands multiple lines. F-strings also support triple quotes for a multiline f-string.

To process this string, we can use the `split` method, which can locate the specified delimiters and separate the string accordingly. The next listing shows a possible solution.

Listing 2.5   Processing text data by splitting strings

```
processed_tasks = []
for data_line in task_data.split("\n"):
    processed_task = data_line.split(",")    ⟵——— Splits each line's text
    processed_tasks.append(processed_task)

print(processed_tasks)
# output the following line:
[['1001', 'Homework', '5'], ['1002', 'Laundry', '3'], ['1003', 'Grocery', '4']]
```

One limitation of the `split` method is that it allows us to specify only one separator, which can be a problem when strings are separated with different separators. Suppose that we have a text file that mixes the use of commas and underscores as separators. For simplicity, only one separator exists between words. For demonstration purposes, consider a single line of data: `messy_data = "process,messy_data_mixed,separators"`.

The problem is likely to occur in real life when we deal with uncleaned raw data. When we encounter this problem, we must think about a programmatic way to solve the problem because chances are that the text file has tons of records. Apparently, using the `split` method on these records won't work, as we can set only one kind of separator. Thus, we must consider alternative solutions:

1   Use separators sequentially:
   a   We split the strings by using commas to create a list.
   b   We examine whether the item in the list contains any underscores. If no, the
       item is ready. If yes, we perform a second split using underscores:

```
separated_words0 = []
for word in messy_data.split(","):       │ When no match is found,
    if word.find("_") < 0:         ⟵——— │ the result will be –1.
        separated_words0.append(word)
    else:                                                     │ The extend method
        separated_words0.extend(word.split("_"))   ⟵——— │ appends all items of
                                                          │ the split strings.
```

2   Consolidate the separators.
       Because we know that there are only two possible separators, we can convert
       one separator to the other, which allows us to call the `split` method just
       once to complete the needed operation:

```
                                                 │ Uses the replace method
consolidated = messy_data.replace(",", "_")   ⟵—│ to replace a substring
separated_words1 = consolidated.split("_")
```

These two solutions are straightforward. If you know the basic operations with strings and lists, they are perfect solutions if performance isn't a concern, because they require multiple passes to examine the separators, particularly when you must deal with multiple separators. In that case, the operations are more expensive in terms of computation.

Is there any more performant solution? The answer is yes. Regular expressions are designed to handle this more complicated pattern matching and searching, as I discuss in sections 2.4 and 2.5.

> **CONCEPT** *Regular expressions*, often shortened to *regex* or *regexp*, are sequences of characters that define specific search patterns.

2.3.4 *Discussion*

Choosing string concatenation, f-string, or `join` should be evaluated on a case-by-case basis. The key is making your code readable. When you have a small number of strings to join, you can use concatenation operators to join them. When you have more strings, you should consider using f-strings first to bring related strings together. The `join` method is particularly useful for joining individual strings when these strings are saved in an iterable.

Besides `split`, strings have another method: `rsplit`, which has a similar functionality to `split`. The only difference is that you set a maximal number of items to the `maxsplit` parameter to be created from the split. Section 2.3.5 explores `split` and `rsplit` further.

2.3.5 *Challenge*

The `split` and `rsplit` methods have the following calling signature. Both methods take an argument to specify the separator and another to specify the maximal number of created items. Can you write a few strings to split to make them behave the same way and differently?

```
str.split(separator, maxsplit)
str.rsplit(separator, maxsplit)
```

> **HINT**   Both methods typically behave the same way. When the number of maximal splits is smaller than the number of split items, you'll see a difference.

2.4 *What are the essentials of regular expressions?*

Python's `str` class has useful methods, such as `find` and `rfind`, for searching substrings. Many scenarios go beyond what these basic methods can address, however, particularly when it comes to complex pattern matching. In these cases, we should consider using regular expressions. In the previous section, I mentioned that you can use regular expressions to split a string containing multiple kinds of separators—a use case that isn't easy to address with pure `str`-based methods. Here's a peek at the solution using regular expressions:

```
import re

regex = re.compile(r"[,_]")        ◁———  Compiles the desired
separated_words2 = regex.split(messy_data)      regular expression
```

From the performance perspective, we traverse the string only one time to complete the split. When there are more separators, regular expressions perform much better than the other two solutions (section 2.3.3), which require multiple traverses of the string. Because of its flexibility and performance, the regular-expressions approach is the irreplaceable technique for conducting advanced string processing. In this section, I use string searching as the teaching topic to explain the mechanisms of regular expressions.

> **TRIVIA** Regular expressions are considered to be independent entities, and all common programming languages support regular expressions despite some variations in terms of the syntax. Regular expressions are similar, however, and you can think of different programming languages as having their own dialects for them.

2.4.1 Using regular expressions in Python

To learn regular expressions, you'll start with getting the big picture: the pertinent module and its core syntax. This section provides a 10,000-foot overview of regular expressions in Python.

Python's standard library includes the `re` module, which provides features related to regular expressions. There are two ways to use this module. The first approach pertains to the object-oriented programming (OOP) aspect of Python. Applying the OOP paradigm to regular expressions (figure 2.4), we carry out our operations with a focus on `Pattern` objects. In this approach, we first create a `Pattern` object by compiling the desired string pattern. Next, we use this `Pattern` object to search the occurrences that match the pattern.

> **CONCEPT** *OOP* stands for *object-oriented programming,* which is a programming design model with a central focus on data and objects rather than functions and procedures.

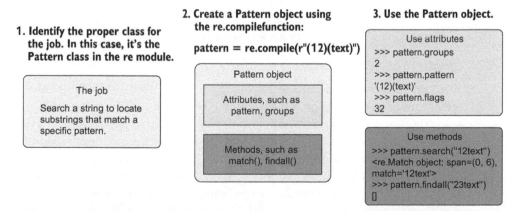

Figure 2.4 Applying the general OOP in pattern matching. In a general OOP approach, we first determine the proper class for the task. In this case, we use the `Pattern` class in the `re` module. The second step is creating the instance object. In the OOP paradigm, an object consists of attributes, which are accessible via dot notations, and methods, which are callable via parentheses. The third step is using the created `Pattern` object, such as by accessing its attributes or calling the methods.

The following code snippet shows how to apply the OOP paradigm to use regular expressions for pattern searching:

```
import re
```

Accesses   regex = re.compile("do")   ◁——— **Creates a pattern**
attributes ↳ regex.pattern
              regex.search("do homework")
              regex.findall("don't do that") | **Uses methods**

The other style adopts a functional approach. Instead of creating a `Pattern` object, we call the functions directly in the module. In the function call, we specify the pattern as well as the string against which the pattern is tested:

```
import re

re.search("pattern", "the string to be searched")
re.findall("pattern", "the string to be searched")
```

Behind the scenes, when we call `re.search`, Python creates the `Pattern` object for us and calls the `search` method on the pattern. Thus, using the module to call these functions is a convenient way to use regular expressions. You should be aware of a difference, however: when you use the `compile` function to create a `Pattern` object, the compiled pattern is cached in such a way that it's more efficient to use the pattern multiple times because there is no need to compile the pattern the second time.

> **CONCEPT**   *Cache* or *caching* is a mechanism used in programming (and computing in general) to store pertinent data so that the data can serve any future requests faster.

By contrast, the functional approach creates the pattern on the fly, so it doesn't have the benefit of improved efficiency of the cached pattern. Thus, if you use the pattern once, you don't need to worry about the difference between these two approaches.

2.4.2   *Creating the pattern with a raw string*

The key manifestation of the power of regular expressions is the conciseness of a pattern to match a wide range of possibilities. To create a pattern, we often need to use raw strings, such as a string literal with the prefix r, as in r"pattern". In this section, you'll see why it's necessary to use raw strings to build a regular-expression pattern.

In regular expressions, we use \d to match any digit and \w to denote a Unicode word character. These are examples of special characters in regular expressions, and we use backslashes as the prefixes to indicate that these characters have special meanings beyond what they appear to be. Notably, Python strings also use backslashes to denote special characters, such as \t for tab, \n for newline, and \\ for backslash.

When these coincidences are combined, we end up using weird-looking patterns. Suppose that we want to search for \task in strings. Notably, \t is a literal here; it really means a backslash and a letter t, but not the tab character. We must use \\task so Python can search for \task. Making things even more complicated, when we create such a pattern, both backslashes must be escaped, which leads to four backslashes (\\\\task) to search \task in strings. Sounds confusing? Examine the following code:

```
task_pattern = re.compile("\\\\task")
texts = ["\task", "\\task", "\\\task", "\\\\task"]
for text in texts:
    print(f"Match {text!r}: {task_pattern.match(text)}")

# output the following lines:
Match '\task': None
Match '\\task': <re.Match object; span=(0, 5), match='\\task'>
Match '\\\task': None
Match '\\\\task': None
```

As match searches a string at the beginning, our pattern can match only "\\task". This behavior is expected; the two consecutive backslashes are interpreted as a literal backslash, which makes the string effectively "\task", matching the pattern that we want to search.

Apparently, using so many backslashes is confusing. To address this problem, we should use raw-string notation in such a way that Python doesn't process any backslashes. As in f-string notation, we use r instead of f as the prefix to convert a regular string literal to a raw string. Applying raw strings to the pattern, we get the following solution:

```
task_pattern_r = re.compile(r"\\task")
texts = ["\task", "\\task", "\\\task", "\\\\task"]
for text in texts:
    print(f"Match {text!r}: {task_pattern_r.match(text)}")

# output the following lines:
Match '\task': None
Match '\\task': <re.Match object; span=(0, 5), match='\\task'>
Match '\\\task': None
Match '\\\\task': None
```

As you can tell, the raw string defines a cleaner pattern than the regular string literal, with which we had to use four consecutive backslashes. As you can imagine, when you build a more complex pattern, you need more backslashes to denote special characters. Without raw strings, your patterns will look like puzzles. Thus, it's always a good practice to use raw strings to create regular-expression patterns.

READABILITY   Using raw strings to build a pattern eliminates the need to escape the special character backslash, making it easier for users to read.

2.4.3   *Understanding the essentials of a search pattern*

The syntax of regular expressions confuses most programmers. As mentioned at the beginning of section 2.4, regular expressions constitute a separate language with its own unique syntax. The good news is that Python adopts regular expressions' syntax in general. In this section, I go over the essential components of a pattern.

BOUNDARY ANCHORS

When you work with strings, you may want to know whether a string begins or ends with a particular pattern. These use cases are concerned with the boundaries of the strings, and we refer to them as boundary anchors, including the beginning and the end of a string, as illustrated in the following code:

```
^hi          starts with hi
task$        ends with task
^hi task$    starts and ends with "hi task", and thus exact matching
```

The ^ symbol signifies that the pattern is concerned about the start of the string, whereas the $ symbol signifies that the pattern is concerned about the end of the string. The following code snippet shows some examples of these anchors:

```
re.search(r"^hi", "hi Python")
# output: <re.Match object; span=(0, 2), match='hi'>

re.search(r"task$", "do the task")
# output: <re.Match object; span=(7, 11), match='task'>

re.search(r"^hi task$", "hi task")
# output: <re.Match object; span=(0, 7), match='hi task'>

re.search(r"^hi task$", "hi Python task")
# output: None (omitted output in an interactive console)
```

You may know that there are `startswith` and `endswith` methods in the `str` class, which work in simple cases. But when you have a more complex need, such as searching a string that starts with one or more instances of h followed by i, it's impossible to use `startswith` because you must account for hi, hhi, hhhi, and more. In such a scenario, regular expressions become very handy.

> **MAINTAINABILITY**   Although regular expressions are powerful, it's always a good idea to see whether a simpler solution would work, such as `startswith` or `endswith`. These solutions are more straightforward and less error-prone.

QUANTIFIERS

In the previous section, I brought up the question of searching for a variable number of characters, which requires creating a pattern that accounts for the quantity. Regular expressions address this problem by supporting the quantifiers category. This category includes several special characters:

```
hi?        h followed by zero or one i
hi*        h followed by zero or more i
hi+        h followed by one or more i
hi{3}      h followed by iii
hi{1,3}    h followed by i, ii, or iii
hi{2,}     h followed by 2 or more i
```

As you can see, there are four general quantifiers: ? for 0 or 1, * for 0 or more, + for 1 or more, and {} for a range. One important thing to note: searching a string with the patterns using ?, *, and + is greedy, which means that the pattern matches the longest sequence whenever possible. To modify this default behavior, we can append the suffix ? to these quantifiers:

```
test_string = "h hi hii hiii hiiii"
test_patterns = [r"hi?", r"hi*", r"hi+", r"hi{3}", r"hi{2,3}", r"hi{2,}",
                  r"hi??", r"hi*?", r"hi+?", r"hi{2,}?"]

for pattern in test_patterns:
print(f"{pattern: <9}-->  {re.findall(pattern, test_string)}")

# output the following lines:
hi?        --->  ['h', 'hi', 'hi', 'hi', 'hi']
hi*        --->  ['h', 'hi', 'hii', 'hiii', 'hiiii']
hi+        -- >  ['hi', 'hii', 'hiii', 'hiiii']
hi{3}      --->  ['hiii', 'hiii']
hi{2,3}    --->  ['hii', 'hiii', 'hiii']
hi{2,}     --->  ['hii', 'hiii', 'hiiii']
hi??       --->  ['h', 'h', 'h', 'h', 'h']
hi*?       --->  ['h', 'h', 'h', 'h', 'h']
hi+?       --->  ['hi', 'hi', 'hi', 'hi']
hi{2,}?    --->  ['hii', 'hii', 'hii']
```

These search results should be consistent with what you can expect. Among these results, the last several patterns involve the use of the ? suffix, which makes the pattern match the shortest possible sequence that satisfies the pattern instead of the longest one.

CHARACTER CLASSES AND SETS

The flexibility of regular expressions arises from the simplicity of using a few characters to denote multiple possibilities of characters. When I introduced raw strings in section 2.4.2, I mentioned that you can use \d to denote any digit. You can specify many other character sets with regular expressions. Here, I focus on the most common ones:

```
\d     any decimal digit
\D     any character that is not a decimal digit
\s     any whitespace, including space, \t, \n, \r, \f, \v
\S     any character that isn't a whitespace
\w     any word character, means alphanumeric plus underscores
\W     any character that is not a word character
.      any character except a newline
[]     a set of defined characters
```

You should note a few things about using [] to define a character set:

- *You can include individual characters.* [abcxyz] will match any of these six characters, and [0z] will match "0" and "z".
- *You can include a range of characters.* [a-z] will match any character between "a" and "z", and [A-Z] will match any character between "A" and "Z".
- *You can even combine different ranges of characters.* [a-dw-z] will match any character between "a" and "d" and "w" and "z".

The best way to remember what each character set does is to study specific examples, as shown in the following code snippet:

```
test_text = "#1$2m_ M\t"
patterns = ["\d", "\D", "\s", "\S", "\w", "\W", ".", "[lmn]"]
for pattern in patterns:
    print(f"{pattern: <9}--->  {re.findall(pattern, test_text)}")

# output the following lines:
\d         --->  ['1', '2']
\D         --->  ['#', '$', 'm', '_', ' ', 'M', '\t']
\s         --->  [' ', '\t']
\S         --->  ['#', '1', '$', '2', 'm', '_', 'M']
\w         --->  ['1', '2', 'm', '_', 'M']
\W         --->  ['#', '$', ' ', '\t']
.          --->  ['#', '1', '$', '2', 'm', '_', ' ', 'M', '\t']
[lmn]      --->  ['m']
```

The identified matches form several pairs of complements. \d locates all digits, for example, and \D locates all the nondigits. Recognizing that these character classes make the opposite matches helps you remember them. The key to mastering regular expressions is practice!

LOGICAL OPERATORS

Like other programming languages, regular expressions have logical operations in terms of defining the patterns. These operations are the most common ones:

```
a|b        a or b
(abc)      abc as a group
[^a]       any character other than a
```

Use a pair of parentheses to denote an exact group of characters that must be present, and use the caret sign to create a character set by negating a specific one. If you want to find any character that is not s, for example, you can use [^s]. Here are some examples for your reference:

```
re.findall(r"a|b", "a c d d b ab")
# output: ['a', 'b', 'a', 'b']

re.findall(r"a|b", "c d d b")
# output: ['b']
```

```
re.findall(r"(abc)", "ab bc abc ac")
# output: ['abc']

re.findall(r"(abc)", "ab bc ac")
# output: []

re.findall(r"[^a]", "abcde")
# output: ['b', 'c', 'd', 'e']
```

2.4.4   *Dissecting the matches*

When you've learned to build a proper pattern, one obvious task is finding all the matches, as you did with the `findall` method (section 2.4.3). The `findall` method may be the most useful when the involved texts are short and we can easily figure out where the matches are. In actual projects, we'll likely deal with a large chunk of text, so showing us what the matches are doesn't help. Instead, we want to know where and what the matches are. This task is what `Match` objects are all about. This section shows how to process the matches.

CREATING MATCH OBJECTS

The `match` and `search` methods are often used for pattern searching. The major difference between `match` and `search` is where they look for matches. The `match` method is interested in whether a match exists at the beginning of the string; the `search` method scans the string until it finds a match (if one exists). Despite this difference, both methods return a `Match` object when the pattern finds a match. For the sake of learning `Match` objects, focus on an example that calls the `search` method:

```
match = re.search(r"(\w\d)+", "xyza2b1c3dd")

print(match)
# output: <re.Match object; span=(3, 9), match='a2b1c3'>
```

The key information about a `Match` object is its matched string and the span. We can retrieve them with their respective methods: `group`, `span`, `start`, and `end`, as shown in the next listing.

Listing 2.6   Methods of a `Match` object

```
print("matched:", match.group())
# output: matched: a2b1c3

print("span:", match.span())
# output: span: (3, 9)

print(f"start: {match.start()} & end: {match.end()}")
# output: start: 3 & end: 9
```

When we use regular expressions, we perform specific operations only if a match is identified. To make our life easy, a Match object always evaluates to True when used in a conditional statement. Here's a general-use style:

```
match = re.match("pattern", "string to match")
if match:
    print("do something with the matched")
else:
    print("found no matches")
```

> **READABILITY** When you use if...else... with regular expressions, you can include a Match object directly in the if clause as a Match object evaluates to True.

WORKING WITH MULTIPLE GROUPS

One thing that may puzzle you is why these pieces of information are retrieved by calling methods instead of attributes: match.span() vs. match.span. If you're wondering why, congratulations; you're developing a good sense of the OOP principle. I agree with you that from the OOP perspective, your intuition that the data should be attributes is correct. But you implement the feature by using method invocations because pattern searching can result in multiple groups. If you pay close attention to listing 2.6, you'll notice that you use the group method to retrieve the matched string. Are you wondering when a match can have multiple groups? Find out through an example:

```
match = re.match(r"(\w+), (\w+)", "Homework, urgent; today")
print(match)
# output: <re.Match object; span=(0, 16), match='Homework, urgent'>

match.groups()
# output: ('Homework', 'urgent')

match.group(0)
# output: 'Homework, urgent'

match.group(1)
# output: 'Homework'

match.group(2)
# output: 'urgent'
```

This pattern involves two groups (enclosed within parentheses), each of which searches for one or more word characters separated by a comma and a space. As mentioned previously, the matching is greedy because the longest possible sequence is 'Homework, urgent'. The identified match creates separate groups that correspond to the pattern's groups.

By default, group 0 is the entire match. The subsequent groups are matched based on the pattern's groups. Because of the multiple groups that a pattern can match, it's better to use methods to retrieve each group's information instead of an attribute, which can't accept arguments. The same grouping also applies to span:

```
match.span(0)
# output: (0, 16)

match.span(1)
# output: (0, 8)

match.span(2)
# output: (10, 16)
```

2.4.5   *Knowing the common methods*

To use regular expressions effectively in our projects, we must know what functionalities are available for us to use. Table 2.3 summarizes the key methods; each method is accompanied by an example for illustration purposes.

Table 2.3   Common regular expression methods

Method	Code example	Match/return value
search: Returns a Match if a match is found anywhere in the string.	re.search(r"\d+", "ab12xy")	'12'
	re.search(r"\d+", "abxy")	None
match: Returns a Match only if a match is found at the string's beginning.	re.match(r"\d+", "ab12xy")	None
	re.match(r"\d+", "12abxy")	'12'
findall: Returns a list of strings that match the pattern. When the pattern has multiple groups, the item is a tuple.	re.findall(r"h[ie]\w", "hi hey hello")	['hey', 'hel']
	re.findall(r"(h|H)(i|e)", "Hey hello")	[('H', 'e'), ('h', 'e')]
finditer: Returns an iterator[b] that yields the Match objects.	re.finditer(r"(h|H)(i|e)", "hi Hey hello")	An iterator
split: Splits the string by the pattern.	re.split(r"\d+", 'a1b2c3d4e')	['a', 'b', 'c', 'd', 'e']
sub: Creates a string by replacing the matched with the replacement.	re.sub(r"\D", "-", '123,456_789')	'123-456-789'

[b]An *iterator* is an object that can be iterated, such as in a for loop. I cover iterators in chapter 5.

For the methods in table 2.3, I want to highlight the key points regarding their usages:

- Both search and match identify a single Match object. The biggest difference is that match is anchored to the beginning of the string, whereas search scans the string, and a match in the middle is also valid.

- When you try to locate all matches, the `findall` method returns all the matches without providing any information about where they are. Thus, more commonly, you want to use `finditer`. That method returns an iterator that yields each `Match` object, which has more descriptive information about the match (such as location).
- The `split` method splits the string by all the matched patterns. Optionally, you can specify the maximum number of splits that you want.
- The `sub` method's name means *substitute*, and you use this method to replace any identified pattern with the specified replacement. In an advanced use case, you can specify a function instead of a string literal, which takes a `Match` object as its argument to produce the desired replacement.

2.4.6 *Discussion*

The key steps in using regular expressions are (1) creating a pattern, (2) finding matches, and (3) processing matches. These steps should be built on a clear understanding of the exact needs of your text processing job. Think of the pattern at a higher level. Do you need boundary anchors, quantifiers, or character sets? Then drill down to the syntax for these categories. Be prepared for your pattern not to work as you expect. You must test your pattern by evaluating the matches with a subset of your text. There are almost always some edge cases that will surprise you. Ensure that the pattern accounts for rare cases before you deploy anything to production.

2.4.7 *Challenge*

Jerry is a graduate student. One of his projects requires him to extract data from text. Suppose that the text data is `"abc_,abc__,abc,,__abc_,_abc"`, where abc stands for the needed data values. That is, the data values are separated by one or more separators. How can he use regular expressions to extract the data values?

> **HINT** When you need to create a pattern that involves a variable number of characters, think about using pattern quantifiers.

2.5 *How do I use regular expressions to process texts?*

Regular expressions are not the easiest topic to grasp because we're creating a general pattern that can match a variety of possibilities. In most cases, the pattern looks rather abstract and thus is confusing to many beginners. Therefore, don't feel frustrated if the concept is not making sense to you now; it takes time to master regular expressions. When you grasp them, you'll find them powerful for processing textual data.

Using our task management app as an example, suppose that we have the text shown in the following listing to begin with. The text, which is the data recovered from a database crash, contains multiple valid records of the tasks, but unfortunately, random text appears throughout the data.

Listing 2.7 Text data to be processed

```
text_data = """101, Homework; Complete physics and math
some random nonsense
102, Laundry; Wash all the clothes today
54, random; record
103, Museum; All about Egypt
1234, random; record
Another random record"""     ←——— Triple quotes for multiline strings
```

Our job is to extract all the valid records from the text data, leaving out invalid records. Suppose that there are several thousand lines of text, making it unrealistic to go through the data manually. We need to use a general pattern-searching approach to conquer this job, which is exactly what regular expressions are designed to do. In this section, I go over the key steps in solving this problem.

2.5.1 Creating a working pattern to find the matches

The string shown in listing 2.7 highlights a common task when we deal with texts: cleaning up the data. Often, the needed data is mixed with unneeded data. Thus, we want to implement a programmatic solution, taking advantage of regular expressions, to keep only the needed data. In this section, you'll learn the first step: creating the pattern.

After making a careful inspection of the raw data, you notice that the valid records have three contributing groups: the task ID number in the form of three digits, the title of the task, and the description of the task. The first two groups are separated by a comma, and the last two groups are separated by a semicolon. Based on these pieces of information, you might build the following pattern, with each of the components analyzed in detail:

```
r"(\d{3}), (\w+); (.+)"
```

```
(\d{3}):    a group of 3 digits
, :         string literals, a comma and a space
(\w+):      a group of one or more word characters
; :         string literals, a semicolon and a space
(.+):       a group of one or more characters
```

Applying this pattern to the text data, you can have a quick look at the outcome. At this stage, don't worry about processing the matches, because you want to make sure that the pattern works as expected. You can run the following code after you test and modify the pattern multiple times before you reach the desired pattern:

```
regex = re.compile(r"(\d{3}), (\w+); (.+)")
for line in text_data.split("\n"):
    match = regex.match(line)
    if match:
        print(f"{'Matched:':<12}{match.group()}")
    else:
        print(f"{'No Match:':<12}{line}")
```

Splits the data rows to extract each row

Uses the match method to search for the pattern at the beginning of the string

Uses the group method to show the matched string

```
# output the following lines:
Matched:     101, Homework; Complete physics and math
No Match:    some random nonsense
Matched:     102, Laundry; Wash all the clothes today
No Match:    54, random; record
Matched:     103, Museum; All about Egypt
No Match:    1234, random; record
No Match:    Another random record
```

As mentioned in section 2.4.4, an important feature of the Match object is that it evaluates to True, allowing us to work on the Match object only if it is created by the match method. From the printout, you see that you obtain valid records from the matched objects. By contrast, in those unmatched cases, those records are indeed invalid.

2.5.2 *Extracting the needed data from the matches*

Because the pattern works as expected, it's time to extract the data and prepare it for further processing. To be specific, you want to save each record (ID, title, and description) as a tuple object, and the tuple objects form a list object.

Notably, when you built your pattern, you included three separate groups that accounted for each of the task's data fields. These groups allow you to access these individual matches for each group. The next listing shows how groups work.

Listing 2.8   Extracting data from individual groups

```
regex = re.compile(r"(\d{3}), (\w+); (.+)")
tasks = []
for line in text_data.split("\n"):              Creates a
    match = regex.match(line)                   tuple from
    if match:                                   multiple
        task = (match.group(1), match.group(2), match.group(3))  ◁── groups
        tasks.append(task)

print(tasks)
# output the following line
[('101', 'Homework', 'Complete physics and math'),
➥ ('102', 'Laundry', 'Wash all the clothes today'),
➥ ('103', 'Museum', 'All about Egypt')]
```

As shown in listing 2.8, we use the group method and access the identified three groups in a sequential manner: group 1 for the ID, group 2 for the title, and group 3 for the description. As a related note, when we omit the number parameter in the group method, we'll retrieve the entire match across the groups (see section 2.4.4).

In our example, we have three groups in the pattern. When our records get more complicated, we may have to deal with more groups. Using the integers to track these groups sequentially can be error-prone; it's not difficult to miscount by one, which can lead to unexpected behaviors.

Isn't a better solution available? That question leads to the discussion in section 2.5.3.

2.5.3 Using named groups for text processing

In general, texts provide more semantic information than numbers do. If the integers that refer to the groups can be confusing, do we have the option of using texts for group referencing? Fortunately, Python supports this feature, which is called *named groups*. In essence, this feature allows you to give a name to the group in such a way that you can use the name to refer to the group for later processing.

To name a group, you use the syntax (?P<group_name>pattern), in which you name the pattern group as group_name. The name should be a valid Python identifier because you must be able to retrieve it by calling the name. Now you can use the named groups technique to update the code in listing 2.8, as the next listing shows.

Listing 2.9 Using named groups to extract data

```
regex = re.compile(r"(?P<task_id>\d{3}), (?P<task_title>\w+);
    (?P<task_desc>.+)")
tasks = []
for line in text_data.split("\n"):
    match = regex.match(line)
    if match:
        task = (match.group('task_id'), match.group('task_title'),
        ⇒ match.group('task_desc'))
        tasks.append(task)
```

In the code snippet, we named the three groups task_id, task_title, and task_desc, which clearly indicate the data for each group. Later, instead of passing an integer to the group method, we can pass the group name directly. Compared with the implementation in listing 2.8, using named groups in listing 2.9 improves code readability; more important, it decreases the likelihood of referencing a wrong group, particularly if a pattern contains many more groups.

> **MAINTAINABILITY** Always use sensible identifiers to name variables or any objects. This approach not only improves readability, but also leads to fewer possible mistakes because you know what data you're dealing with by looking at the names.

Although we use the group method to retrieve the individual items from the identified groups, named groups give us another option for retrieving the identified data: the groupdict method. For the first identified match, we might have the following data:

```
>>> match.groupdict()
{'task_id': '101', 'task_title': 'Homework', 'task_desc':
⇒ 'Complete physics and math'}
```

If you prefer using this dict object for data processing, it's also a good choice in terms of code readability.

2.5.4 *Discussion*

The first step in using regular expressions is knowing what business needs we want to achieve and creating a pattern accordingly. You shouldn't feel obsessed with making the pattern correct on the first try. You must test your pattern with the text, and it'll take multiple rounds of back-and-forth effort to find the correct pattern (figure 2.5).

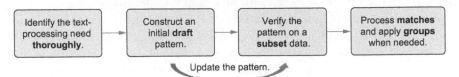

Figure 2.5   The general process of using regular expressions in processing texts

When you work with more groups identified through a pattern, I recommend that you use named groups, as by naming these groups, you're clearly telling the readers what data a group holds. Later, it'll be easier to refer to the groups because of their sensible names.

2.5.5 *Challenge*

When we processed the text data to extract the records, we split the text into separate rows. Assuming that each row indeed has one valid record or no record, could you find a pattern that processes all the text without splitting the data into multiple rows?

HINT   Each row ends with a newline character (\n). Integrate that character into your pattern.

Summary

- An f-string is a concise way to interpolate variables and expressions.
- Applying a proper text alignment to an f-string makes the information clear by creating visual boundaries for distinct pieces of data.
- F-strings are also good at formatting numbers, such as scientific notations and precisions for decimals.
- Python strings have `isalnum`, `isnumeric`, and many other `is-` methods. You can use them to determine the nature of a string.
- All Python data, such as integers and lists, can have the appearance of a string (such as when data is transferred over the internet and all of it consists of strings). We convert these strings to their native data types by evaluating them, so we can use the data type–specific methods.
- When we need to join a few strings, it's fine to use the concatenation symbols. When we deal with multiple strings, however, it's better to use the `join` method.
- The `split` method splits strings, which is a useful data processing tool as well as the basis for processing tabulated text files. Although built-in modules are

available, such as `csv`, knowing these fundamentals is key to writing a script for your own job.

- The key to using regular expressions is building a pattern that addresses your needs. When we build a pattern, we need to start our thinking at a higher level. Relevant questions can include these: Do I need multiple groups? How about boundary anchors, character sets, or quantifiers?

- Named groups make it easier to refer to specific information when you use regular expressions to process complicated text data.

Using built-in
data containers

This chapter covers

- Choosing lists over tuples and vice versa
- Sorting lists that consist of complex data types
- Using named tuples as a data container model
- Accessing a dictionary's data
- Understanding hashability and its implications for dictionaries and sets
- Applying set operations to manipulate nonset data

As a general-purpose programming language, Python provides a range of built-in data types for different purposes, including collection types. These collection types of data serve as containers to hold integers, strings, instances of custom classes, and all other kinds of objects. In every project, we deal with multiple objects at the same time, and these scenarios often require data containers to handle these objects. Every modern language has data containers as its core data models, highlighting the importance of data containers as building blocks for any programming project. As you'll see in chapter 14 when we build our task management app, we'll use data containers for a variety of jobs, such as using a `list` to hold custom instances of the `Task` class (chapter 8). In this chapter, we'll discuss the most common built-in data containers, including lists, tuples, dictionaries, and sets. Please note that this chapter isn't intended to provide an exhaustive review of all the functionalities related to these data models. Instead, we'll focus on essential topics that matter most in our projects.

CONCEPT   *Data containers*, such as lists and tuples, are objects that contain other objects. By contrast, strings and integers are not data containers, as they don't contain other objects.

3.1   How do I choose between lists and tuples?

We often discuss lists and tuples together because of their similarity as data containers. Both can hold objects in an ordered fashion, and the objects are accessible through indexing. In many cases, we use them interchangeably. But some other cases may require us to pick one over the other. Suppose that you need a data container to store transaction records in a bank account. Should you use `list` or `tuple`? As another example, if you need to show a transaction's information, such as its amount and date, should you use `list` or `tuple`?

There are numerous scenarios like these in which both options seem to be plausible, but we end up choosing one over the other. In this section, we'll discuss the key distinguishing factors that guide our selection between lists and tuples.

3.1.1   Using tuples for immutability and using lists for mutability

One major difference between lists and tuples is *mutability*. Lists are mutable in such a way that we can modify the data of a `list` object: we can append new items to the end of a `list`, insert items into the middle, change the items, and remove items. To support this mutability, Python provides a series of methods in the `list` class, such as `append`, `extend`, and `remove`, and you should be familiar with them. Figure 3.1 shows these methods.

Operations		Items in the list
numbers = [1, 2, 3]	Creating a list	[1, 2, 3]
numbers.insert (0, 0)	Inserting an item at specified index	[0, 1, 2, 3]
numbers.append (4)	Appending an item to the end	[0, 1, 2, 3, 4]
numbers.extend ([5, 6, 7])	Extending the list with multiple items	[0, 1, 2, 3, 4, 5, 6, 7]
numbers.remove (5)	Removing an item by specifying the value	[0, 1, 2, 3, 4, 6, 7]
del numbers [3]	Removing an item at specified index	[0, 1, 2, 4, 6, 7]

Figure 3.1   Basic operations with lists as mutable objects

TRIVIA　Lists' remove method deletes only the first matching item. When you're removing an item that isn't in the list, you encounter a ValueError.

By contrast with lists, tuples are immutable; we can't modify the data of a tuple object. To support this immutability feature and prevent any unnecessary confusion, Python has no methods to modify tuple objects. Changing a tuple's items is syntactically possible, but such action results in exceptions: calling a nonexistent method leads to an AttributeError, and reassigning a tuple's item leads to a TypeError, as the next listing shows.

Listing 3.1　**Immutability of tuple objects**

```
integers_tuple = (1, 2, 3)                    Attempts to use a nonexistent
integers_tuple.append(4)          ◀───────    method on the tuple object
# ERROR: AttributeError: 'tuple' object has no attribute 'append'

integers_tuple[0] = 'zero'     ◀───────  Attempts to assign a new value to a tuple's item
# ERROR: TypeError: 'tuple' object does not support item assignment
```

Because of the mutability difference, you should use lists instead of tuples when you expect to update the data. For the task management app, we use lists to store the tasks because we add new tasks or remove old tasks. When you don't change the stored data, you should use tuples, given their immutability. For the task app, we can use tuples to store a task's metadata, such as creation time and user, because they are fixed. Although we can use lists where tuples are used, we prefer using tuples over lists in these cases for several reasons:

- *It prevents any unexpected changes to the data.* Attempting to change the tuples' data would result in either an AttributeError or a TypeError (listing 3.1).
- *It makes clear our intention that the pertinent data should stay unchanged.* We use (creation_time, user) to store a task's information instead of [creation_time, user] to signify that these two values are fixed.
- *Tuples are more memory-efficient than lists.* When a list and a tuple hold the same data, the list has a larger size than the tuple. The greater memory cost of lists results from extra overheads to support mutability. Thus, in situations that require many instances, we prefer using tuples because of their memory efficiency.

TRIVIA　You can check an object's memory usage by calling __sizeof__.

3.1.2　*Using tuples for heterogeneity and using lists for homogeneity*

We can store any data types in lists and tuples. When the items are of different types, or when the items hold the same type but with distinct information, we say that they're *heterogeneous* from the semantic perspective. Consider a real-life object—say, a box. The information related to the box can include the size, material, and color. This information is heterogeneous, as it represents different aspects of the box's characteristics.

When the items are of the same type—or, more strictly, when the data refers to the same kind of information—we say that they're *homogeneous*. When you move your home, for example, you may use multiple boxes. These boxes are homogeneous because they represent the same kind of objects.

Lists and tuples can hold both heterogeneous and homogeneous data. Does that fact mean that we give lists and tuples no preference? Certainly, the major determinant is the mutability requirement for the data, as discussed in section 3.1.1. But when mutability is a lesser concern, you should use data's homogeneity to guide your choice.

Let's consider a more concrete example in the task application. In section 3.1.1, I mentioned that from the data-mutability perspective, it's preferable to use a tuple (creation _time, user) to refer to a task's metadata, as it consists of distinct pieces of information: when the task was created versus who created the task. You may hear people say that tuples are structural because each item carries independent information that contributes to the tuple object. As a result, tuples are the preferred data structure to hold semantically heterogeneous data.

By contrast, the data stored in lists is semantically homogeneous. In the task application, the tasks belong to the same semantic category; thus, we should use lists to store tasks. By default, we can store the tasks based on the creation time in ascending order. Therefore, as shown in figure 3.2, a list is viewed as a linear data structure that holds homogeneous items.

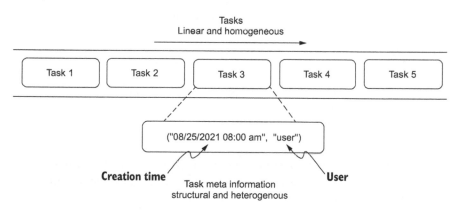

Figure 3.2   Homogeneity of list items and heterogeneity of tuple items. Lists are often used to hold data of the same kind, termed *homogeneous data*. In the figure, we use a list to store multiple tasks. By contrast, tuples are often used to hold data with different meanings, termed *heterogeneous data*. As shown in the figure, we use a tuple to store the metadata of a task, which is fixed, distinct information.

3.1.3   Discussion

From the readability perspective, using tuples to hold data gives readers a clear signal that the data isn't changing. From the maintainability perspective, we prefer using tuples to avoid any accidental changes in the pertinent data if it's expected to stay the same.

I should note that tuples' immutability doesn't prevent you from changing their items' data. If a tuple contains lists, such as numbers = ([1, 2], [1, 2]), it's valid to change the inner lists, such as adding an item to the first list (numbers[0] .append(3)). This operation is valid because although we change the content of the inner object, the reference to the object stays the same. As you'll see in chapter 10, we'll make a distinction between objects and their references.

3.1.4 Challenge

Zoe works in a software company in the geography field. She's building a location-based application, and we know that a place has a name, description, and coordinates (latitude and longitude). For the series of places that a user has visited, does she use list or tuple to store them? For each place, she needs a data model to host its coordinates. Should she choose list or tuple to store the latitude and longitude?

> **HINT** Consider whether the stored data is mutable and/or homogeneous to help you make the decision.

3.2   How do I sort lists of complicated data using custom functions?

Lists are sequence data (see chapter 4) whose order is determined by the insertion order. Because of the supported mutability, we often rearrange a list into orders other than the initial insertion order. Suppose that our project has a list object that holds tasks for a given day, as shown in the following listing.

Listing 3.2   A list object consisting of multiple dict objects

```
tasks = [
    {'title': 'Laundry', 'desc': 'Wash clothes', 'urgency': 3},
    {'title': 'Homework', 'desc': 'Physics + Math', 'urgency': 5},
    {'title': 'Museum', 'desc': 'Egyptian things', 'urgency': 2}
]
```

Suppose that we display the tasks in the order of their creation time or their urgency levels. As you'll find out, if we sort this list of dictionaries, we'll encounter a TypeError because Python doesn't know how to compare dictionaries:

```
tasks.sort()
# ERROR: TypeError: '<' not supported between instances of 'dict' and 'dict'
```

In this section, you'll learn how to sort lists, particularly those consisting of complicated data (such as dict objects as opposed to integers and strings) with custom requirements.

3.2.1 Sorting lists using the default order

Because sorting lists is a common task, Python has a built-in method designed for sorting: the sort method. The next listing shows some simple examples of using sort.

Listing 3.3 Sorting lists using the `sort` method

```
numbers = [12, 4, 1, 3, 7, 5, 9, 8]
numbers.sort()                        ⟵——— Sorts the numbers in place
print(numbers)
# output: [1, 3, 4, 5, 7, 8, 9, 12]

names = ['Danny', 'Aaron', 'Zack', 'Jennifer', 'Mike', 'David']
names.sort(reverse=True)                                     ⟵———
print(names)
# output: ['Zack', 'Mike', 'Jennifer', 'David', 'Danny', 'Aaron']

mixed = [3, 1, 2, 'John',  ['c', 'd'], ['a', 'b']]
mixed.sort()
# ERROR: TypeError: '<' not supported between instances of 'str' and 'int'
```

Sorts the strings in place but requests that the order be reversed

Note that the sorting operation is conducted in place, meaning that sorting changes the order of the original `list` instead of creating a new `list`. Related to this in-place feature, `sort` returns `None`. Thus, in the interactive Python console, you don't see any output after running `numbers.sort()` because `None` is automatically omitted for the output in the console. Another thing to note is that the default sorting order is ascending. If you specify the `reverse` parameter as `True`, you'll get the list in descending order.

> **CONCEPT**   When we say that something happens to an object in place, it means that the process modifies the object itself. The `sort` method modifies the `list` object in place.

It seems that Python can't sort a `list` containing different data types. In listing 3.3, we encountered a `TypeError` when the `list` had integers, strings, and lists because by default, Python doesn't know how to compare objects of different types. Is there any way to instruct Python to compare these objects? Section 3.2.2 discusses the answer.

3.2.2 Using a built-in function as the sorting key

Besides `reverse`, the `sort` method has a `key` parameter. As indicated by its name, this parameter provides a key to the sorting problem. Specifically, you should set `key` with a function, which produces a value from each item in the list. These derived values are used for comparison, and the derived order determines the order of the list's items.

> **TRIVIA**   Not only the `sort` method has the `key` parameter. Some other functions, such as `max` and `min`, have the `key` parameter too. What you learn here can be applied to these functions.

As mentioned at the end of section 3.2.1, Python doesn't know how to compare between integers, strings, and lists. Notably, Python *does* know how to compare strings. Thus, a strategy for sorting data of different types is to convert it to strings by setting the key parameter:

```
mixed = [3, 1, 2, 'John',  ['c', 'd'], ['a', 'b']]
mixed.sort(key=str)

print(mixed)
# output: [1, 2, 3, 'John', ['a', 'b'], ['c', 'd']]
```

In the code, we use the str function (strictly, a class constructor; see section 10.5) as the key argument, which converts each item to a string. Python sorts these strings as proxies, ['3', '1', '2', 'John', "['c', 'd']", "['a', 'b']"], producing ['1', '2', '3', 'John', "['a', 'b']", "['c', 'd']"]. Notably, each converted string is associated with its original object, and Python renders the sorted list with the raw items.

3.2.3   *Using custom functions for more complicated sorting needs*

Section 3.2.2 discussed how to use key to sort a list of objects of various types, but the example is too trivial to be useful in a real-life project. In listing 3.2, our task management app has a list object consisting of dict objects. In this section, you'll see how to sort this kind of list object.

Although we can set str to key to make these dict objects comparable, the sorted list isn't what we want; the objects are not ordered by their urgency levels. To address this need, we can create a custom function and set it to the key parameter, as the next listing shows.

> Listing 3.4   **Sorting tasks by setting a key**

```
def using_urgency_level(task):
    return task['urgency']

tasks.sort(key=using_urgency_level, reverse=True)
print(tasks)

# output the following lines (re-arranged for readability):
[{'title': 'Homework', 'desc': 'Physics + Math', 'urgency': 5},
{'title': 'Laundry', 'desc': 'Wash clothes', 'urgency': 3},
{'title': 'Museum', 'desc': 'Egyptian things', 'urgency': 2}]
```

Each item of the list is sent to the function using_urgency_level. It's important to note that this key function must take exactly one parameter, which corresponds to each item of the list object. This function extracts the tasks' urgency levels according to which the sorting is conducted. Figure 3.3 shows the sorting process intuitively.

> **PEEK**   We can set key with a lambda function, an anonymous function created by using the lambda keyword. To obtain the same sorting result by using a lambda function, we could use tasks.sort(key=lambda x: x['urgency'], reverse=True). We'll discuss lambda functions in section 7.1.

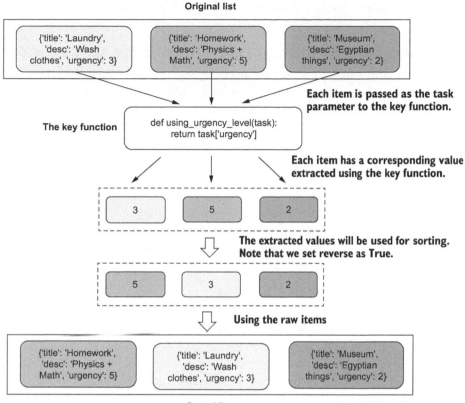

Figure 3.3 The sorting process using a key function. A key function converts each item of the list to a corresponding value. The generated values will be used as intermediate items to sort the list. After the sorting, the original items are rendered in the order created by the intermediate items.

3.2.4 Discussion

The sort method works only with lists because it's an instance method of lists. When we sort other container data types, such as tuples, sets, and dictionaries, we can use sorted, which can take any iterable and return a sorted list. You can specify a custom sorting function for sorted, too. Remember that the function to be set to the key argument should take exactly one parameter. When the function for the key argument performs a small operation, we should consider using a lambda function (see section 7.1).

3.2.5 Challenge

In this chapter, you learned to sort tasks by using their urgency levels, as shown in listing 3.4. Can you come up with a solution to order the tasks by their descriptions' lengths? The longer the description is, the higher the task's rank.

HINT   Custom sorting requires setting the key parameter in the `sort` function. The built-in function `len` can check the length of a string.

3.3   How do I build a lightweight data model using named tuples?

The core of any project is data. If you're building a social network app, the users and their connections are the data. If you're building an e-commerce website, the merchandise and client information are the data. If you're building a machine learning model, the features and targets are the data. For our task management app, we need to have a mechanism to process and handle task-related data.

If you come from an object-oriented programming (OOP) background, your intuitive response is probably to create custom classes to manage data. But it's a nontrivial task to write a class. (You'll learn best practices for creating a class in chapter 8.) With the increasing complexity of our applications, we may have multiple classes to handle different aspects of the data flow. For simpler data models, named tuples can be a perfect solution, especially when our primary concern is to have a lightweight data model that is easy to use and holds data with little memory overhead.

3.3.1   Understanding alternative data models

Before we build a data model using named tuples, it's essential for us to know our options. In this section, we're going to explore at least four other ways to manage the data: lists, tuples, dictionaries, and custom classes.

To create a context, let's say that each task in our application has the following pieces of information that we need to manage: title, description, and urgency level. The next listing shows what the data models look like using `list`, `tuple`, and `dict`.

Listing 3.5   Using built-in data models for data management

```
task_list = ['Laundry', 'Wash clothes', 3]      ⟵—— Uses a list

task_tuple = ('Laundry', 'Wash clothes', 3)     ⟵—— Uses a tuple

task_dict = {'title': 'Laundry', 'desc': 'Wash clothes', 'urgency': 3}  ⟵—┐
                                                          Uses a dictionary┘
```

As shown in listing 3.5, these pieces of information are stored as individual items in `list` and `tuple` and as key-value pairs in `dict`. Besides using the built-in classes, we can create a custom class to store the data. You can find a skeleton of a custom class in the following code snippet (and no worries if you're unfamiliar with defining custom classes; it'll be covered in chapter 8):

```
class Task:
    def __init__(self, title, desc, urgency):
        self.title = title
        self.desc = desc
        self.urgency = urgency

task_class = Task('Laundry', 'Wash clothes', 3)
```

Although each approach is plausible in some scenarios, various drawbacks make them less ideal for our business need: a lightweight model to hold data.

Lists are mutable, making them vulnerable to intentional and accidental changes. Section 3.1 also discussed that we usually use lists to hold homogenous data. Using a list to hold heterogeneous data isn't a good idea. Although tuples are immutable, and we don't worry about data changes, to retrieve an attribute such as title, we must use either the unpacking technique (section 4.4) or indexing (section 4.2). Neither technique is straightforward.

Lists and tuples don't have meta information about what data they're holding. A coworker who's unfamiliar with the application won't have any clues about the data model when they review your code. Compared with lists and tuples, dictionaries provide meta information, as the keys inform what the data is. To retrieve these attributes, however, we must use the corresponding keys (such as `task_dict['title']`). If we misspell the keys or miss a quote, we'll encounter a `KeyError` or `SyntaxError`.

Lists, tuples, and dictionaries are generic types, and they have no ideas about the specifics of the data model. Thus, modern integrated development environments (IDEs) such as PyCharm and Visual Studio Code provide no useful autocompletion hints for these data structures, decreasing your coding efficiency. We can overcome this drawback by creating a custom class. When a `Task` instance is created, after we key in the instance and a dot, the available attributes (such as `title` and `desc`) are prompted automatically by your IDEs, facilitating coding speed.

> **CONCEPT**   An IDE provides comprehensive functionalities, such as autocompletion hints and real-time code analysis, to facilitate software development.

The solution of implementing a custom class can have a few complications, however:

- Creating a custom class requires a considerable amount of boilerplate, and for a simple data model such as a data holder, it is overkill to implement an entire custom class.
- The memory cost is not negligible, particularly if you must deal with tons of instances.

Each instance of a custom class consumes more memory than an instance of named tuples, as discussed in section 3.3.2. When our project evolves, we want our data model to do more things; we'll move the lightweight data model to a fully equipped custom class (chapter 8).

3.3.2   *Creating named tuples to hold data*

As indicated by the name, a named tuple is a kind of tuple. Named tuples are special because the items they hold have names associated with them. Unlike regular tuples, whose items are accessible by indices, named tuples support *dot notation*, accessing items just like accessing attributes of a custom class instance. We can observe these features in an example:

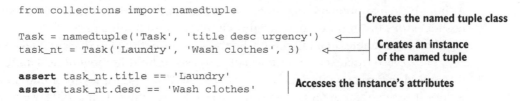

```
from collections import namedtuple
```
Creates the named tuple class

```
Task = namedtuple('Task', 'title desc urgency')
task_nt = Task('Laundry', 'Wash clothes', 3)
```
Creates an instance
of the named tuple

```
assert task_nt.title == 'Laundry'
assert task_nt.desc == 'Wash clothes'
```
Accesses the instance's attributes

Note a few significant things about the named tuple technique:

- *The instance of the named tuple has the advantage of accessing its attributes with dot notation.* It's not only faster to code because of the autocompletion hints, but is also more readable, with a clean access pattern.
- *The* namedtuple *is a factory function in the* collections *module.* Because it's a factory function, calling it returns a new class or a new instance object. In this case, we got the Task class.

READABILITY   Follow the convention of naming classes in Python by using the uppercase camel form: ClassName. When you have multiple words, every word's first letter should be uppercase, as in TaskUser.

- In the namedtuple function, we specified the class name and its attributes for the class. Notably, the data model's attributes can be set as either a single string (with spaces or commas as separators) or a list object (figure 3.4):

```
Task = namedtuple('Task', 'title, desc, urgency')
```

```
Task = namedtuple('Task', ['title', 'desc', 'urgency'])
```

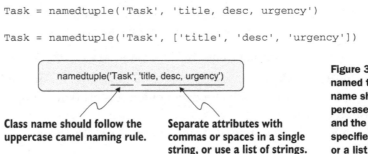

Class name should follow the uppercase camel naming rule.

Separate attributes with commas or spaces in a single string, or use a list of strings.

Figure 3.4   Creating a named tuple. The class name should follow the uppercase camel naming rule, and the attributes should be specified by a single string or a list of strings.

READABILITY   Specify the attributes by using a single string with spaces or commas in the namedtuple function. The code is easier to type and read.

Now that you know about the named tuple, you can use the Task class to process the data used in our application. For simplicity, suppose that our data source is a string object that we receive from a particular application programming interface (API):

```
task_data = '''Laundry,Wash clothes,3
Homework,Physics + Math,5
Museum,Epyptian things,2'''
```

CONCEPT An API defines a set of ways to build and integrate different components, including software and hardware. A common kind of API refers to various defined functions that your application can call to retrieve data from another source.

To convert the text data to `Task` instance objects, here's a possible solution:

```
for task_text in task_data.split('\n'):
    title, desc, urgency = task_text.split(',')
    task_nt = Task(title, desc, int(urgency))
    print(f"--> {task_nt}")

# output the following lines
--> Task(title='Laundry', desc='Wash clothes', urgency=3)
--> Task(title='Homework', desc='Physics + Math', urgency=5)
--> Task(title='Museum', desc='Epyptian things', urgency=2)
```

Splits the text data into multiple rows

Splits the text data with commas

This solution uses a few techniques that you've learned so far, including string splitting and f-strings, and shows exactly how small things add up to make something work. To take this a step further, we can take advantage of the named tuple class method `_make`, which maps an iterable (the list created by `split` is an iterable; we'll discuss iterables in detail in chapter 5) to the named tuple. Here's an updated solution:

```
for task_text in task_data.split('\n'):
    task_nt = Task._make(task_text.split(','))
```

PEEK You'll learn about class methods in section 8.2.

Unlike custom classes, whose instances have per-instance `dict` representations through `__dict__`, named tuples don't have the underlying `dict` representations, which makes named tuples a lightweight data model with negligible memory costs. Named tuples can save significant amounts of memory when you need to create thousands of instances.

Curious readers are encouraged to explore Python's official website (https://docs.python.org/3/library/collections.html) to find out about other features of named tuples, such as creating a new named tuple from an existing one by replacing field values and inspecting the fields' default values.

3.3.3 Discussion

Compared with built-in types (such as lists, tuples, and dictionaries) and custom classes, named tuples are a more proper, lightweight data model if your business concern is a model to hold data with mostly read-only access requirements. The popular data science Python library pandas, for example, allows you to access each row of its `DataFrame` data model as a named tuple.

TRIVIA Most data scientists use pandas in their daily data processing jobs. The library's key data structure `DataFrame` represents data in the form of spreadsheets.

Because named tuples represent a new type, you should use a descriptive name with the first letter uppercase, as in other custom classes. In the meantime, make the named tuple class obvious. It is a good idea to place the code for creating a named tuple class at the top of a module. After all, the code is only one line, and you don't want it buried.

> **MAINTAINABILITY**   Place the code of creating a named tuple class in a noticeable location, such as at the top of a module. The code is one line, but it's significant: it creates a new class.

3.3.4   Challenge

For the task management app, suppose that we need to update a named tuple `Task(title='Laundry', desc='Wash clothes', urgency=3)` by setting the urgency level to 4. Can you change the level directly? If not, how can you change it?

> **HINT**   A named tuple is a tuple object, so it's immutable, and changing its stored data directly is not allowed.

3.4   How do I access dictionary keys, values, and items?

The most-used built-in data types include `int`, `float`, `bool`, `str`, `list`, `tuple`, `set`, and `dict`. The first four types are primitive types because they're the building blocks of other data types. The other four types are data containers (figure 3.5). What makes `dict` different from `list`, `tuple`, and `set` is the fact that it contains key-value pairs instead of individual objects. Through storing the key-value pairs, dictionaries can hold two categories of information.

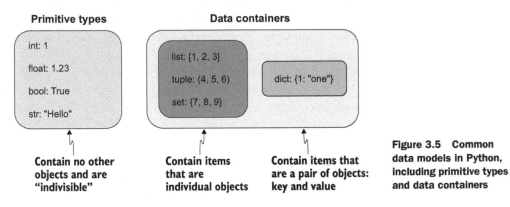

Figure 3.5   Common data models in Python, including primitive types and data containers

Suppose that we have the following dictionary to store the urgencies of some tasks in the task application. This `dict` object holds two sets of information, which are the titles as the keys and the urgency levels as the values:

```
urgencies = {"Laundry": 3, "Homework": 5, "Museum": 2}
```

When we include dictionaries in our project, we often need to access their stored data: the keys, the values, and the key-value pairs. In this section, we're going to explore different ways to access this data. Because we use dictionaries frequently in our projects, knowing how to access a `dict`'s data is essential for using this powerful data type.

3.4.1   *Using dynamic view objects (keys, values, and items) directly*

Besides providing access to individual key-value pairs in a dictionary, such as `urgencies ["Laundry"]`, Python provides three basic methods for retrieving a dictionary's stored data across all the pairs: keys, values, and items to access the keys, values, and the key-value pairs, respectively. Let's observe their basic uses:

```
urgencies = {"Laundry": 3, "Homework": 5, "Museum": 2}
urgen_keys = urgencies.keys()
urgen_values = urgencies.values()
urgen_items = urgencies.items()
print(urgen_keys, urgen_values, urgen_items, sep="\n")

# output the following lines:
dict_keys(['Laundry', 'Homework', 'Museum'])
dict_values([3, 5, 2])
dict_items([('Laundry', 3), ('Homework', 5), ('Museum', 2)])
```

One assumption that many people make is that the objects created from these methods (keys, values, and items) are list objects. They're not, however. They're `dict_keys`, `dict_values`, and `dict_items`, respectively. What's most special about these data types is the fact that they're all *dynamic view objects*. If you're familiar with database terms, you should have heard of *views*, which refer to the virtual results computed or collated dynamically from data in the database.

> **TRIVIA**   *Views* are the results of stored queries in a database. When the pertinent data is updated, the views are updated too.

Like views in a database, dictionary view objects are dynamic, updated automatically with the change of the `dict` object. That is, whenever you modify the key-value pairs stored in a `dict` object, these view objects get updated. Observe this effect:

```
urgencies["Grocery Shopping"] = 4

print(urgen_keys)
# output: dict_keys(['Laundry', 'Homework', 'Museum', 'Grocery'])

print(urgen_values)
# output: dict_values([3, 5, 2, 4])

print(urgen_items)
# output: dict_items([('Laundry', 3), ('Homework', 5), ('Museum', 2),
➥    ('Grocery, 4)])
```

This dynamic provides great convenience when we access a dictionary's data because the data is in perfect sync with the `dict` object. By contrast, the following example, which doesn't take advantage of the `view` object, is antipattern:

```
urgencies = {"Laundry": 3, "Homework": 5, "Museum": 2}

urgen_keys_list = list(urgencies.keys())
print(urgen_keys_list)
# output: ['Laundry', 'Homework', 'Museum']

urgencies["Grocery"] = 4
print(urgen_keys_list)
# output: ['Laundry', 'Homework', 'Museum']
```

We create a `list` for the keys. After we update the dictionary, the `list` stays the same and doesn't sync with the `dict` object. Thus, you may encounter unexpected errors, such as trying to access a deleted item, when you use a `list` to track the keys of a dictionary instead of using the `dict_keys` view object.

> **MAINTAINABILITY** Always use view objects to access a `dict`'s data because these view objects are dynamic; they will update when the dictionary's data is updated.

3.4.2 *Being cautious with the KeyError exception*

In section 3.4.1, we discussed three ways to access all the keys and/or values in a dictionary. Most of the time, however, we need to access a single value by using *subscript notation*, which encloses the key in a pair of square brackets:

```
assert urgencies["Laundry"] == 3

assert urgencies["Homework"] == 5
```

> **CONCEPT** Subscript notation is a common way to access data in a collection data type. For `dict` objects, using subscript notation means using keys enclosed in square brackets to access the corresponding values.

The major advantage of this method is its straightforwardness. If you have used dictionaries in other languages, you should be familiar with this approach. Thus, it is natural for you to use this feature when you access items of a dictionary. But unexpected errors can happen if you're not careful with the key. The following code snippet shows such a problem:

```
urgencies["Homeworks"]
# ERROR: KeyError: 'Homeworks'
```

When you're accessing a key that doesn't exist in the dictionary, you encounter the `KeyError` exception. When an exception is raised, unless it's handled with the `try...except...` statement (section 12.3), your program crashes. We certainly don't want our program to crash, so we should avoid this error by using alternative approaches.

3.4.3 Avoiding KeyError with a hygiene check first: The non-Pythonic way

Because we know that `KeyError` exceptions occur only when the keys aren't in the dictionary object, we can check the key's existence before retrieving the value, as in this example:

```
if "Homework" in urgencies:        ◁——— Checks whether the
    urgency = urgencies["Homework"]      key is in the dictionary
else:
    urgency = "N/A"
```

This solution helps us avoid the `KeyError` exception, but in the meantime, it's cumbersome and non-Pythonic, because Pythonic code should be concise. Now, we're accessing only one item. Can you imagine accessing multiple items? We would have to repeat this block of code, leading to distractive duplication in the codebase. Code duplication should remind you of the DRY (Don't Repeat Yourself) principle; we should refactor our code to remove unnecessary repetitions. Consider this code:

```
def retrieve_urgency(task_title):
    if task_title in urgencies:
        urgency = urgencies[task_title]
    else:
        urgency = "N/A"
    return urgency
```

With the refactored code, we can retrieve a task's urgency level without worrying about the `KeyError` exception anymore:

```
retrieve_urgency("Homework")
# output: 5

retrieve_urgency("Homeworks")
# output: 'N/A'
```

The `retrieve_urgency` function is handy for retrieving a task's urgency level, but it is hardcoded, including the `dict` object (urgencies) and specific semantics (urgency). If we access another `dict`'s data, we must define a similar function to avoid a `KeyError`.

The more dictionary objects we have, the more functions we'll have to create. Are you seeing a higher level of repetition here? Our Python pioneers have already considered this problem and have created a built-in function: the `get` method, discussed in section 3.4.4.

3.4.4 Using the get method to access a dictionary item

Because it is a `dict` method, we can call the `get` method on any `dict` object by specifying the key and a default value when the key doesn't exist. When the default argument is omitted, Python uses `None` as the default value. The following code snippet shows some examples:

```
urgencies.get("Homework")
# output: 5

urgencies.get("Homeworks", "N/A")
# output: 'N/A'

urgencies.get("Homeworks")
# output: None (None is automatically hidden in an interactive console)
```

The `get` method has the advantage of not raising `KeyError` when the key isn't in the dictionary. More importantly, it allows you to set a proper default value as the fallback value. You can use `get` whenever you retrieve values from dictionaries, but I prefer subscript notation, which I find to be more readable.

There are scenarios in which `get` is preferable to subscript notation, however. One such scenario is when you need to deal with the variable number of keyword arguments (`**kwargs`) in a function definition. We'll cover using `**kwargs` in section 6.4. For the time being, you only need to know that `kwargs` is a `dict` object used in a function and that these parameters are usually optional. Suppose that you're building a Python package for the Python community, and this package has the following function:

```
def calculate_something(arg0, arg1, **kwargs):
    kwarg0 = kwargs.get("kwarg0", 0)
    kwarg1 = kwargs.get("kwarg1", "normal")
    kwarg2 = kwargs.get("kwarg2", [])
    kwarg3 = kwargs.get("kwarg3", "text")
    # ... and so on

# possible invocations:
calculate_something(arg0, arg1)
calculate_something(arg0, arg1, kwarg0=5)
calculate_something(arg0, arg1, kwarg0=5, kwarg3="text")
```

In this example, `calculate_something` accepts multiple keyword arguments besides two positional arguments. For conciseness, you may not want to list all optional keyword arguments when their default values are almost always used; thus, you can wrap them to a `dict` kwargs in the function header. In the function body, you'll notice that we use `get` multiple times, which allows us to set default values when the keys are missing from calling the function, and we include these proper default values in the `get` method.

3.4.5   *Watching for the setdefault method's side effect*

When people talk about alternatives to the `get` method, some may mention the `setdefault` method. This method is like the `get` method in that it also takes two parameters: the key and a default value as the fallback. Observe some uses of `setdefault`:

```
urgencies = {"Laundry": 3, "Homework": 5, "Museum": 2}
urgencies.setdefault("Homework")
# output: 5

urgencies.setdefault("Homeworks", 0)
# output: 0

urgencies.setdefault("Grocery")
# output: None (None is automatically hidden in an interactive console)
```

This code snippet shows the similarity between setdefault and get. But what makes setdefault differ from get is that when you call setdefault, an extra operation (dict[key] = default_value) occurs when the key isn't in the dictionary:

```
print(urgencies)
# output: {'Laundry': 3, 'Homework': 5, 'Museum': 2, 'Homeworks': 0,
         'Grocery': None}
```

We previously called setdefault with the keys "Homework", "Homeworks", and "Grocery". Because the latter two keys were not in the dict initially, the following operations occurred under the hood:

```
urgencies["Homeworks"] = 0
urgencies["Grocery"] = None
```

Because of this side effect, I don't recommend using the setdefault method. The name is confusing—typically, we don't expect things to be returned by calling a method that involves setting a value—and an implicit operation that many people may not know (setting the specified default value or None if the key doesn't exist) is involved.

> **MAINTAINABILITY**   Avoid using the setdefault method, as it can set the missing key's value in an unexpected way. Use a more explicit approach, such as the get method.

3.4.6   Discussion

Dictionary view objects are a brilliant design that dynamically tracks a dictionary's keys, values, and key-value pairs. As iterables, they can be used in a for loop (section 5.3) if you want to iterate the data of a dict object.

Don't feel obligated to use get whenever you access a key's value. If you're used to subscript notation, feel free to use it. Sometimes, it's a good idea to use subscript notation in your own codebase, as you want any problems to surface during development, and raising errors is an essential mechanism for identifying any problems. If you misspell a key, using the get method may hide the KeyError exception by providing the fallback value.

3.4.7   Challenge

The built-in id function checks an object's memory address. Running id("Hello") returns the address of the "Hello" object. Can you use the id function to track the changes of a dictionary view object, such as dict_keys? You expect the view object's data to change with the update of the dict object. You should expect the view object's memory address to stay.

> **HINT** An object has the same memory address throughout its lifecycle. Even though the data of the object can change, the memory address should stay.

3.5   When do I use dictionaries and sets instead of lists and tuples?

We have extensively discussed two data containers: tuples and lists. Python has no restriction regarding the data types that can be saved in them, and such flexibility makes them attractive data models in any project. Section 3.4 mentions that dict is useful because it stores key-value pairs, but how about sets? In addition, you may know that not all data types can be stored in dictionaries and sets, as the next listing shows.

Listing 3.6   Failed creation of dict and set objects

```
failed_dict = {[0, 2]: "even"}
# ERROR: TypeError: unhashable type: 'list'

failed_set = {{"a": 0}}
# ERROR: TypeError: unhashable type: 'dict'
```

When objects are unhashable, they can't serve as dict keys or set items. At first glance, this fact appears to be a deficit that harms the usefulness of these two data structures. But there are good reasons for this design. In this section, we'll explore how the hashable restriction benefits data retrieval with these two data structures and when we should use it. We'll also study the hashable-versus-unhashable concept.

3.5.1   Taking advantage of the constant lookup efficiency

Dictionaries store key-value pairs, and this storage pattern allows us to retrieve data by accessing the keys. Moreover, dictionaries have a significant advantage: superior lookup efficiency for retrieving specific items. Because sets have the same underlying storage mechanism (a hash table; see section 3.5.2) as dictionaries, they have the same characteristics—efficient item lookup. In this section, we'll see when to prefer dictionaries or sets over lists and tuples.

Suppose that our application requires a considerable number of item retrievals or lookups. From a theoretic perspective, we could use a list or a set to store the data. We can run a simple experiment to compare the speed of retrieving a random item from each object with the help of timeit and random modules, as shown in the next listing.

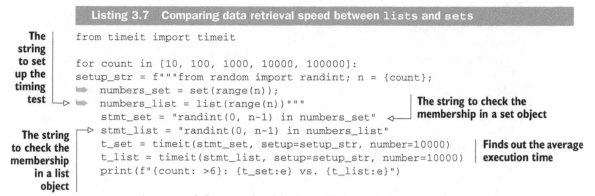

Listing 3.7 Comparing data retrieval speed between `lists` and `sets`

The string to set up the timing test

The string to check the membership in a list object

```
from timeit import timeit

for count in [10, 100, 1000, 10000, 100000]:
    setup_str = f"""from random import randint; n = {count};
        numbers_set = set(range(n));
        numbers_list = list(range(n))"""
    stmt_set = "randint(0, n-1) in numbers_set"
    stmt_list = "randint(0, n-1) in numbers_list"
    t_set = timeit(stmt_set, setup=setup_str, number=10000)
    t_list = timeit(stmt_list, setup=setup_str, number=10000)
    print(f"{count: >6}: {t_set:e} vs. {t_list:e}")
```

The string to check the membership in a set object

Finds out the average execution time

TRIVIA As part of the standard Python library, the `timeit` module allows us to examine our operations' performance, and the `random` module provides functionalities for creating random numbers. The availability of these built-in tools is another manifestation of how comprehensive Python is in terms of routine tools for our work.

In listing 3.7, we use a `for` loop to go over multiple conditions in which the `list` and `set` objects have varied numbers of items. After running the code, you'll see the following output:

```
    10: 1.108225e-02 vs. 9.955332e-03
   100: 9.514037e-03 vs. 1.533820e-02
  1000: 1.051638e-02 vs. 7.346468e-02
 10000: 1.034654e-02 vs. 6.189157e-01
100000: 1.086105e-02 vs. 6.290399e+00
```

Expect to see different results due to different computers.

READABILITY We used f-strings to format the string output. Specifically, we applied the text alignment format specifier to create a visual structure for better readability.

With the increase in the number of the items in the `set`, the lookup time stays at the same magnitude, which represents constant time, known as the O(1) time complexity. That is, no matter how large the `set` grows, item lookup takes about the same time. By contrast, the magnitude of lookup time increases linearly as a function of the `list`'s size. Unlike sets, which use hash tables to index objects with hash values (section 3.5.2), lists require traverses to examine whether an item is contained, and the time for such traversing depends directly on the number of the `list`'s items. This contrast in time complexity highlights the benefit of using sets instead of lists when your business need is item lookup.

This example uses a `set` object as the test subject for item-lookup efficiency to observe how we achieve O(1) time complexity. The same efficiency holds for `dict` objects, as the underlying storage mechanism is the same: using a hash table. Each key in a `dict` object and each item in a `set` object has a corresponding hash value. But what does *hash* mean? Section 3.5.2 discusses that topic.

Time complexity of algorithms

In computer science, algorithms can be conceptualized as defined instructions for solving a problem, such as sorting a list or fetching an item from a sequence. Not all algorithms have the same problem-solving speed. To quantify performance, we use time complexity to describe the amount of time required to run an algorithm. To denote the time complexity, we use so-called Big O notation, in which we use a pair of parentheses to include a function of the number of involved items, typically denoted as n. O(n), for example, means that the time needed for the algorithm is linearly dependent on the number of items involved; O(n^2) means that the time needed is quadratically related to the items' count; and O(1) means that the time is constant and doesn't depend on the number of items involved. The following figure provides a brief overview of the time complexities.

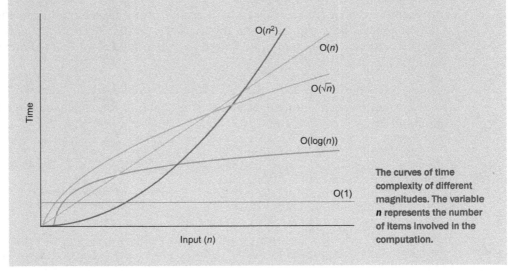

The curves of time complexity of different magnitudes. The variable *n* represents the number of items involved in the computation.

3.5.2   *Understanding hashable and hashing*

When you create dictionaries or sets, you don't want to experience the `TypeError` exception (listing 3.6). This exception is raised because we're trying to use unhashable objects as dictionary keys or set items. As you can imagine, the opposite of *unhashable* is *hashable*, and it appears that only hashable objects can be used with dictionaries and sets. But what does hashable mean? In this section, you're going to learn about both hashable and unhashable objects.

> **CONCEPT**   When your Python program encounters an error, we say that it raises an exception. Other programming languages may use *throw* to signify an error or exception.

Hashable isn't an isolated concept. You have probably heard related terminologies, such as hash value, hashing, hash table, and hashmap. At their core, hashable objects use the same fundamental procedure: *hashing*. Figure 3.6 shows the general process of

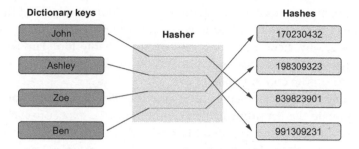

Figure 3.6   The process of hashing, using dictionary keys as an example. A hash function (hasher) hashes the keys of a dictionary, producing hashes as integer values. These hash values are uniquely associated with each of the dictionary keys. Different hashers are expected to produce different hashes.

hashing, using dictionary keys as an example. We start with raw data values: four strings. A hash function, which is often termed a *hasher,* carries out a series of computations by using specific algorithms and outputs the hash values (termed *hashes*) for the raw data values.

Note several key points about the hashing process:

- *A hash function should be so computationally robust that it produces different hash values for different objects.* In rare cases, a hash function can produce the same hash value for different objects—a phenomenon termed *hash collision,* which must be handled according to a specified protocol.

- *A hash function should be so consistent that the same objects always have the same hash values.* When you set a password in an application, the password is hashed by the hasher and stored in a database. When you try to log in again, the entered password string would be hashed and compared with the stored hash value. In these two cases, the same password should produce an identical hash value.

- *For more complicated hashers, hashing is one-way traffic.* By design (such as using a random number), it's almost impossible to reverse-calculate the raw data based on a hash value. This irreversibility is required where cybersecurity is concerned. Even if hackers get a password's hash value, they can't figure out the password from the hash value (at least, not easily).

Python has implemented a hasher that produces hash values for its objects. Specifically, we can retrieve an object's hash value by using the built-in `hash` function. The following code shows some examples:

```
hash("Hello World!")
# output: 9222343606437197585

hash(100)
# output: 100

hash([1, 2, 3])
# ERROR: TypeError: unhashable type: 'list'
```

Expect a different value because some hashers depend on the operating system.

Not every object can produce a hash value by the hash function. Strings and integers are hashable, but lists are unhashable. You may wonder why lists are unhashable or, more broadly speaking, why dictionaries and sets are unhashable too. The reason is simple: these unhashable data types are mutable. By design, the hash function generates a hash value based on the content of an object.

The content of mutable data can change after creation. If we magically make a list hashable, when we update the list with the changed content, we expect to have a different hash value. But a hash function should consistently produce the same hash value for the same object, and in this case, we expect the hash value to stay the same for the list object. Apparently, the list's content change, resulting in a hash-value change, is irreconcilable with the expected consistent hash value for the same list object (figure 3.7).

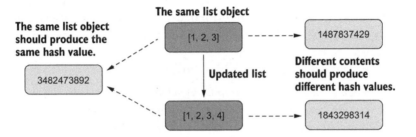

Figure 3.7   Irreconcilability of the hashing process for a mutable object. If a list is hashable, on one hand, you expect the list to produce the same hash value, regardless of its content, as the same object. On the other hand, after the list is updated, the different contents are supposed to produce different hash values. These two scenarios are irreconcilable.

By contrast, for immutable data such as integers, strings, and tuples, the contents stay the same after creation. The consistency of the contents is key to applying a hash function to any object. Thus, all immutable data types are hashable.

You may wonder whether there is a more straightforward way to determine the hashability of an object without using the hash function. Listing 3.8 shows a solution. Everything should be straightforward except the use of Hashable. For simplicity, you can think of Hashable as being a class and every hashable object as being an instance of this class.

Listing 3.8   Checking the hashability of an object

```
from collections.abc import Hashable

def check_hashability():
    items = [{"a": 1}, [1], {1}, 1, 1.2, "test", (1, 2), True, None]
    for item in items:
        print(f"{str(type(item)): <18} | {isinstance(item, Hashable)}")

    print(f"{'Data Type': <18}  {'Hashable'}")
```

Creates a list of objects of varying types

isinstance produces a Boolean value for type checking.

```
check_hashability()

# output the following lines:
Data Type             Hashable
<class 'dict'>       | False
<class 'list'>       | False
<class 'set'>        | False
<class 'int'>        | True
<class 'float'>      | True
<class 'str'>        | True
<class 'tuple'>      | True
<class 'bool'>       | True
<class 'NoneType'>   | True
```

> **TRIVIA** The abc submodule defines a series of abstract base classes (ABCs). It allows you to check whether a class provides a particular interface, such as hashable. In layperson's terms, it helps you check whether an object can do some specific things, such as being hashed.

Consistent with our previous discussion, mutable data—including dictionaries, lists, and sets—is unhashable. By contrast, all other immutable data types are hashable. For built-in data types, immutability is effectively equivalent to hashability. Table 3.1 provides an organized view of the common data types as a function of mutability and hashability.

Table 3.1 Common data types as a function of hashability

Mutability	Hashability	Data types	Allowed as dictionary keys or set items
Mutable	Unhashable	dict, list, set	No
Immutable	Hashable	int, float, str, tuple, bool, NoneType	Yes

In section 3.1, we saw the immutability of tuple objects, and we couldn't assign another value to an item in the tuple object. In table 3.1, notice that strings are also immutable in Python. The indication is that it's impossible to change a character or a substring in a string. The following code shows the immutability of strings:

```
text = "Hello, World."

text[-1] = "!"
# ERROR: TypeError: 'str' object does not support item assignment
```

If you need to replace a substring, don't forget strings' replace method, which creates a new string, as shown in the following code:

```
text.replace(".", "!")
# output: 'Hello, World!'
```

TRIVIA   We know that we can use the id function to check the memory address of an object, which should differ between objects. You can compare the string and its counterpart with a replacement.

3.5.3   Discussion

Hashable is a key programming concept. Under the hood, Python uses hash tables as the storage mechanism for dictionaries and sets. The most significant benefit of using a hash table is that data retrieval has $O(1)$ performance, making it an ideal data model when you want to look up items quickly. We often use set objects to hold data where membership is concerned, for example.

3.5.4   Challenge

Jennifer is learning Python because she's pursuing a data science career. She has learned that a dict object can't have duplicate keys because of the underlying hash table implementation. Suppose that she creates a dict object: numbers = {1: "one", 1.0: "one point one"}. What values do you expect the numbers to have?

HINT   When you intentionally pass duplicate keys, the value of the latter one overrides the value of the first one when you construct a dict object.

3.6   How do I use set operations to check the relationships between lists?

Lists are the go-to data structure for storing homogenous data. Sometimes, we have multiple lists to hold similar items, and we need to determine the relationships between list objects. Suppose that we use an API to retrieve a list of stocks that are recommended by an investment analysis company. Each client's current stocks are also saved as a list object. For simplicity, we have the following data to start with:

```
good_stocks = ["AAPL", "GOOG", "AMZN", "NVDA"]
client0 = ["GOOG", "AMZN"]
client1 = ["AMZN", "SNAP"]
```

One specific functionality of the application is to examine whether all of a client's stocks are contained in the recommended list. Do you know how to address this problem? You can use some list methods to solve it. Like their math counterparts, however, set objects in Python have a series of convenient methods for checking relationships between set objects. In this section, we're going to explore the unique operations of the set class and see how to use these operations to solve problems concerning relationships between lists.

3.6.1   Checking whether a list contains all items of another list

Implementing the preceding feature essentially requires us to address this question: How can we check whether a list object contains all items of another list object? In this section, you'll learn how to use set operations to address this feature. Without using the set operations, a beginner might consider a solution that involves the iteration of the list object. To implement this routine functionality, we create a function that we can call as often as necessary, as shown in the following listing.

> **Listing 3.9   Check whether a list contains the entirety of another list**

```
def all_contained_in_recommended(recommended, personal):
    print(f"Is {personal} contained in {recommended}?")
    for stock in personal:
        if stock not in recommended:        ◄── "not in" checks whether an item
            return False                         isn't contained in the collection.
    return True
```

MAINTAINABILITY   Always think of creating a function when you need to provide a general solution for many similar use cases. When you need to modify the feature, you need to change only this single function instead of separate duplicate functions that do the same job.

The logic of the function in listing 3.9 is that if we can find any case when a stock isn't in the recommended list, we say that the client's list isn't entirely contained in the recommended list. Using this logic, we iterate the items of the client's list. When any stock is found not to be in the recommended list, we exit the function by returning False; otherwise, we return True after iterating the entire list. With this function, we can test a couple of cases:

```
print(all_contained_in_recommended(good_stocks, client0))
# output the following lines:
Is ['GOOG', 'AMZN'] contained in ['AAPL', 'GOOG', 'AMZN', 'NVDA']?
True

print(all_contained_in_recommended(good_stocks, client1))
# output the following lines:
Is ['AMZN', 'SNAP'] contained in ['AAPL', 'GOOG', 'AMZN', 'NVDA']?
False
```

Both use cases are working as expected. But a better solution doesn't require creating a function. One important principle of coding is *Don't reinvent the wheel*. If we can use an available solution, we should use it directly. Thus, the better solution takes advantage of set-related operations:

```
good_stocks_set = set(good_stocks)   ◄─── Creates a set object          Uses the issuperset
                                                                         method
contained0 = good_stocks_set.issuperset(client0)   ◄─────────────┘
print(f"Is {client0} contained in {good_stocks}? {contained0}")
# output: Is ['GOOG', 'AMZN'] contained in
⇒   ['AAPL', 'GOOG', 'AMZN', 'NVDA']? True

contained1 = good_stocks_set.issuperset(client1)
print(f"Is {client1} contained in {good_stocks}? {contained1}")
# output: Is ['AMZN', 'SNAP'] contained in
⇒   ['AAPL', 'GOOG', 'AMZN', 'NVDA']? False
```

To use the issuperset method, we convert the list object good_stocks to a set object good_stocks_set. We call issuperset on the good_stocks_set and pass the list object client0 or client1 as an argument. As expected, we get the desired results. Theoretically, we can use the issubset method to implement this functionality, but it requires creating set objects for each client's list, which is unnecessary repetition. For this reason, issuperset is better than issubset when you share a set object that presumably is the superset. In our case, it's the recommended stock set.

As you can tell, the solution that uses issuperset is more concise than the one that uses a custom function. More importantly, when we use a built-in function instead of a custom function, our program is less prone to bugs.

> **MAINTAINABILITY**   Writing functions to solve problems is great. Using existing functions, such as the built-in ones, is even greater!

3.6.2   *Checking whether a list contains any element of another list*

Another common scenario regarding relationships between lists is whether a list contains any element of another list. This section addresses that problem.

To facilitate the discussion, let's continue the example of stock recommendation. Suppose that we want to check whether a client's list of stocks contains any of the recommended stocks. As shown in section 3.6.1, this functionality is provided by the iteration technique (see the following listing).

Listing 3.10   Checking whether a list contains any item of another list

```
def contained_any_in_recommended(recommended, personal):
    print(f"Does {personal} contain any in {recommended}?")
    for stock in personal:
        if stock in recommended:
            return True
    return False
```

The logic of the function in listing 3.10 is opposite to the one in listing 3.9. If we can find any item of the client's list in the recommended list, our criterion is satisfied, and the function returns True; otherwise, there is no matching record, and the function returns False. The following code snippet shows two use cases:

```
print(contained_any_in_recommended(good_stocks, client0))
# output the following lines:
Does ['GOOG', 'AMZN'] contain any in ['AAPL', 'GOOG', 'AMZN', 'NVDA']?
True

print(contained_any_in_recommended(good_stocks, client1))
# output the following lines:
Does ['AMZN', 'SNAP'] contain any in ['AAPL', 'GOOG', 'AMZN', 'NVDA']?
True
```

The question of whether a list contains any item of another list is essentially a question of whether any overlap exists between them. Unfortunately, there are no built-in methods to check the relationships between two `list` objects. Such methods exist for `set` objects, however. One key set operation creates an intersection between two `set` objects, which is exactly what we need. Here's a solution:

```
good_stocks_set & set(client0)
# output: {'AMZN', 'GOOG'}

bool(good_stocks_set & set(client0))
# output: True

good_stocks_set & set(client1)
# output: {'AMZN'}

bool(good_stocks_set & set(client1))
# output: True
```

Using the intersection operator `&`, we conveniently retrieve the intersection between two `set` objects. If we want to have the Boolean output, we can use the built-in `bool` function, which evaluates any nonempty collection data, such as a `set` here, as `True`.

> **TRIVIA** The `bool` function is the `bool` constructor, which creates a `bool` object by evaluating the item inside the parentheses. `set` objects are evaluated to be `True` if they contain at least one item.

Besides using `&` between two `set` objects, the intersection operation can be performed with the `intersection` method. Like `issuperset`, what makes `intersection` convenient is that it can take any iterable in such a way that we can send the `list` objects `client0` and `client1` directly to the method without converting them to `set` objects first. Observe this feature in the following code snippet:

```
good_stocks_set.intersection(client0)
# output: {'AMZN', 'GOOG'}

good_stocks_set.intersection(client1)
# output: {'AMZN'}
```

In sections 3.6.1 and 3.6.2, we used `set` operations to examine common relationships between `list` objects. Let's step back and take a look at more general operations with `set` objects in Python, particularly for examining the relationships between sets.

3.6.3 Dealing with multiple set objects

As discussed in section 3.5, `set` objects are best for use cases that require membership checking, because this operation has the $O(1)$ complexity. Besides membership testing, when you have multiple `set` objects that are related, you may need to carry out operations between them. In this section, we touch base on operations dealing with multiple `set` objects. Four `set` operations are most common: union, intersection, symmetric difference, and difference (figure 3.8).

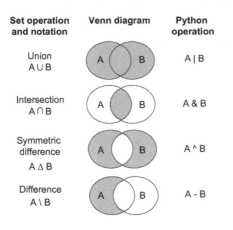

Figure 3.8   **Set operations in Python. Four common set operations are shown with their respective mathematical notations, Venn diagrams, and operations in Python. Union consists of members from A and B. Intersection consists of members common to A and B. Symmetric difference consists of members of one set but not both. Difference consists of members of one set but not both.**

All four operations have corresponding special operators, which simplify the syntax. The following code snippet shows these operations. As you can see, these operations are useful when you try to select the members that fit specific criteria, such as belonging to both sets (intersection) or to either set (union):

```
tasks_a = {"Homework", "Laundry", "Grocery"}
tasks_b = {"Laundry", "Gaming"}

tasks_a | tasks_b          ⬅——————  Union operation with |
# output: {'Laundry', 'Gaming', 'Homework', 'Grocery'}

tasks_a & tasks_b    ⬅———— Intersection operation with &
# output: {'Laundry'}

tasks_a ^ tasks_b          ⬅——————  Symmetric difference operation with ^
# output: {'Homework', 'Grocery', 'Gaming'}

tasks_a - tasks_b               ⬅———— Difference operation with -
# output: {'Homework', 'Grocery'}
```

> **TRIVIA**   You may get the results in a different order. The items stored in a `set` object are unordered because they use hash tables and are not concerned with the item order.

Besides these operations, which create a set from other sets, there are methods `issubset` and `issuperset`, which check the relationships between two sets. `issubset` checks whether the method caller is a subset of the other set (more generally, it can be any iterable), and `issuperset` checks the opposite. Following are some trivial examples:

```
small_set = {1, 2}
large_set = {1, 2, 3, 4}

assert small_set.issubset(large_set) == True
assert small_set.issuperset(large_set) == False

assert large_set.issubset(small_set) == False
assert large_set.issuperset(small_set) == True
```

We have seen the four set-related operations (union, intersection, symmetric difference, and difference), their corresponding methods, and their respective operators. Interestingly, the `issuperset` and `issubset` methods have corresponding operators. These methods and operators are summarized in table 3.2.

Table 3.2   Set operators and their corresponding methods

Set operation	Operator	Method
Union	|	`union`
Intersection	&	`intersection`
Symmetric difference	^	`symmetric_difference`
Difference	–	`difference`
Checks whether one set is a superset of the other	>=	`issuperset`
Checks whether one set is a subset of the other	<=	`issubset`
Checks whether one set is a strict superset of the other	>	N/A but can be achieved by combining `issuperset` and `!=`
Checks whether one set is a strict subset of the other	<	N/A but can be achieved by combining `issubset` and `!=`

Although operators make your code more concise, they work only with set objects. By contrast, all these methods can take iterables as their parameters; thus, they're more flexible. When you deal with iterables that aren't set objects, you should consider using these methods directly, which eliminates the need to convert them to set objects first.

> **READABILITY**   Prefer using the pertinent methods when you perform set operations; they're not only more flexible (because they take any iterables), but also more understandable (because of their names).

3.6.4   Discussion

Set objects are the preferred data model for storing unique members, and Python provides a series of operations to manipulate multiple set objects and examine their relationships. Because lists don't have native methods to check the relationships between lists, we can conveniently convert lists to sets to derive the relationships of the initial list objects.

3.6.5 Challenge

When we perform the union operation between two sets, this operation generates a set consisting of all members from either set. Thus, this operation resembles an OR operation. Do you know what will happen if you use the keyword or between two sets? What result are you expecting for the operation {1, 2, 3} or {4, 5, 6}? In a similar fashion, some people may liken the intersection operation to the AND operation. Can you guess the result of the operation {1, 2, 3} and {4, 5, 6}?

> **HINT** These evaluations are also known as *short-circuit evaluations*. The or operation evaluates to the first object if the first object has a Boolean value of True; otherwise, it evaluates to the second object. For the and operation, it evaluates to the first object if the first object has a Boolean value of False; otherwise, it evaluates to the second object.

Summary

- Lists are a mutable data type, allowing us to add, insert, update, and delete items, whereas tuples are immutable in that you cannot modify them after creation.
- Besides their difference in mutability, lists and tuples are different in terms of the homogeneity of the contained data. We use lists to hold items that are semantically homogeneous, and these items form a linear ordered sequence. We use tuples to hold items that are semantically distinct, and these items form a structural sequence.
- Default sorting can sort a list only by using the numeric or lexicographic order, which is rather limited. Thus, we need to understand how to use a custom function as a key argument to specify the sorting requirement.
- When you need a simple data container, you should consider using named tuples, which allow you to create a class with one line of code. Named tuples have a few advantages, including memory efficiency and dot notation for attribute retrieval.
- When we access all the keys, values, or key-value pairs of a dictionary, we prefer using the dictionary view objects because they will be updated automatically in sync with the underlying dictionary object.
- Only hashable objects can be dictionary keys and set items in Python. Common hashable data types include int, float, str, tuple, bool, and NoneType.
- With the underlying hash implementation, item lookup with dictionaries and sets is efficient, with a time complexity of $O(1)$.
- The get method retrieves a dictionary's item without triggering the KeyError exception. It's the preferred method when you work with dictionaries that other people created.

- If you work with dictionaries that you create, you may want to use subscripting (`dict[key]`), which allows any misspelling of the keys to surface by itself.
- A `set` is a data structure that is specialized to deal with members with unique values. There are multiple operations between `set` objects, such as union and difference. You can take advantage of these operations if you need to check the relationships between other nonset data types, such as lists.

Dealing with
sequence data

This chapter covers

- Using slice objects to retrieve and manipulate subsequences
- Combining the use of positive and negative indexing in item retrieval
- Finding items in a sequence
- Unpacking a sequence
- Considering data models other than lists

In chapter 3, you learned to use lists and tuples to hold data. One shared characteristic of lists and tuples is that the held items have a specific order. These two data structures are examples of the more general data type *sequence*. Python has other sequence data types, such as strings and bytes. These sequence data models are essential data structures that we use in our projects. The reason is simple: we use data to model real life, which is full of ordered objects/events, such as waiting lines, written languages, and house numbers, to name a few. Thus, the effective handling of sequence data is a universal need in programming projects regardless of our business specialty.

From Python's implementation perspective, these sequence data structures share many characteristics, and it's worth discussing them together here. You want to kill two birds with one stone, and you'll find that the skills you may have thought applied only to a specific data model (such as unpacking a `tuple` object) can be applied to all sequence data models. As a related note, even though I'll mostly use lists or strings in the examples in this chapter, don't mistakenly think that these techniques are available only to lists or strings.

4.1 How do I retrieve and manipulate subsequences with slice objects?

When we have sequence data, we may be interested in obtaining a specific subset of the sequence, which we refer to as *subsequence*. The built-in data types include the common sequence data models `str`, `list`, and `tuple`:

```python
# str is a sequence of characters:
text = "Hello, World!"

# list is a mutable sequence of any kinds of objects
fruits = ["apple", "orange", "banana", "strawberry"]

# tuple is an immutable sequence of any kinds of objects
vowels = ("a", "e", "i", "o", "u")
```

When we retrieve a subsequence of a `list` object, we can use slicing. The simplest form of slicing is `list[start:end]`, and the items between the start and end indices (the item at the end index is excluded) are retrieved:

```python
assert fruits[1:3] == ["orange", "banana"]
```

In this section, going beyond the basic form of slicing `list[start:end]`, I'll be discussing more advanced features of slicing, and you'll learn how to use these features to retrieve and manipulate subsequences.

4.1.1 Taking advantage of the full features of slicing

Besides specifying the start and end indices, slicing has a variety of permutations, giving us different ways to retrieve subsequences. We'll discuss the most notable ones here:

- Ignoring the start or the end index
- Not abusing the tolerance of out-of-range slicing indices
- Applying stride to the slicing

IGNORING THE START OR THE END INDEX

By default, the start index is zero, so if you want to retrieve the first *n* items, the Pythonic way is by omitting the start index and using list[:end]. By default, the end index is the length of the list, and slicing selection doesn't include the end index, so if you want to retrieve the last *n* items of a list, you use list[start:]. As you can tell, ignoring the start or end index removes the unnecessary code and improves readability:

```
assert fruits[:3] == ["apple", "orange", "banana"]

assert fruits[1:] == ["orange", "banana", "strawberry"]
```

What if you ignore both the start and end indices? You may have guessed the right answer: list[:] retrieves all the items, which are a copy of the original list. (Section 10.3 discusses copying objects in more detail.) The following code snippet shows you that [:] retrieves all the items of the list object:

```
assert fruits[:] == ["apple", "orange", "banana", "strawberry"]
```

> **READABILITY**   The code is easier to read when you ignore the start or the end index (if possible).

NOT ABUSING THE TOLERANCE OF OUT-OF-RANGE SLICING INDICES

One feature of slicing is the tolerance of out-of-range indices, as Python bounds the slicing with the maximally allowed range. Each item in a sequence has an index to denote its position. When you use an index that matches no items in the sequence, you encounter the IndexError exception, stating that the used index is out of range:

```
fruits[5]
# ERROR: IndexError: list index out of range
```

Notably, Python tolerates the used indices in slicing if they're out of the available range, such as using indices that don't correspond to any item in a sequence. Consider the following examples to observe this feature:

```
numbers = [0, 1, 2, 3, 4, 5]
numbers[:20]                    ⟵——— Uses an index greater than the last item's
# output: [0, 1, 2, 3, 4, 5]

numbers[-10000:2]      ⟵——— Uses an index smaller than the first item's
# output: [0, 1, 2]
```

Although slicing's tolerance of out-of-range indices appears to give us the flexibility of retrieving items, I don't recommend using this feature because it confuses readers. They may wonder whether the code contains a typo or the programmer forgot to update the indices. Either way, your code loses its clarity.

> **MAINTAINABILITY**   When you use out-of-range indices, you're only confusing yourself or your teammates.

APPLYING STRIDE TO THE SLICING

We can apply stride to the slicing to retrieve evenly spaced items. Slicing annotation accepts an optional `stride` parameter: `list[start:end:stride]`, which takes every *n*th item from `start` until it reaches end. When we use `stride` (or `step`, as some users name this parameter), we can still omit the start and end indices, and Python supplies the applicable boundaries for us. Following are some common usages (illustrated in figure 4.1):

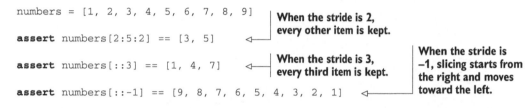

```
numbers = [1, 2, 3, 4, 5, 6, 7, 8, 9]

assert numbers[2:5:2] == [3, 5]

assert numbers[::3] == [1, 4, 7]

assert numbers[::-1] == [9, 8, 7, 6, 5, 4, 3, 2, 1]
```

When the stride is 2, every other item is kept.

When the stride is 3, every third item is kept.

When the stride is −1, slicing starts from the right and moves toward the left.

Using positive strides is straightforward. Notably, slicing also supports negative strides, which can be confusing to many people. One Python trick that many people have seen is reversing a `list` using `list[::-1]`, as shown in the preceding example, but many people don't understand why. The reason is that when the step is negative, the slicing starts from the right side and moves to the left side. Thus, the step of −1 means that we're continuously retrieving the item to the left. Because we didn't specify the start and end indices, the entire list was sliced from the right to the left; thus, it was reversed. Figure 4.1 shows the contrast between positive and negative strides.

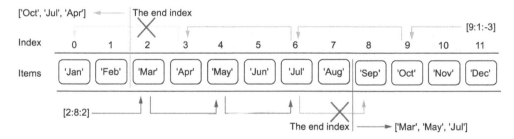

Figure 4.1   Slicing a list with positive and negative strides. When the stride is positive, slicing starts from the left side. When the stride is negative, slicing starts from the right side.

Although slicing supports negative steps, I don't recommend using this feature because it reduces readability. If you want subsequences from the left to the right, you can use the `reverse` method to reverse the `list` in place (calling `reverse` changes the original list), and then perform any slicing operations in the left-to-right direction. This approach requires an extra line of code, but it makes it much easier for readers to understand the slicing operations.

> **MAINTAINABILITY**   Avoid negative steps other than −1 when you use slices. They're not intuitive and can cause great confusion.

4.1.2   *Not confusing slices with ranges*

Under the hood, retrieving a subsequence involves creating a `slice` object. That is, slicing a list `list[start:stop:end]` is equivalent to `list[slice(start, stop, step)]`. But another class, range, has the same calling signature: `range(start, stop, step)`. This similarity confuses some beginners. In this section, I clarify this.

`slice` and `range` are similar, as their constructors take `start`, `stop`, and `step`, creating the three attributes `start`, `stop`, and `step`:

```
slice_obj = slice(1, 10, 2)
range_obj = range(1, 10, 2)

slice_obj.start, slice_obj.stop, slice_obj.step
# output: (1, 10, 2)

range_obj.start, range_obj.stop, range_obj.step
# output: (1, 10, 2)
```

These similarities can be confusing. Slices and ranges differ in two aspects, however, making them not interchangeable. First, ranges are iterables, but slices are not. The implication is that we can use ranges to create a `list` or use them in a `for` loop, whereas we can't use slices in these operations. The following code snippet shows an example:

```
list(range(10))
# output: [0, 1, 2, 3, 4, 5, 6, 7, 8, 9]

list(slice(10))
# ERROR: TypeError: 'slice' object is not iterable
```

Second, we can use a `slice` object to retrieve items in a list or other sequence data. In the following example, we get the odd numbers with the `slice` object, but the same operation is not allowed with a range object:

```
numbers = list(range(10))

odd_slice = slice(1, 10, 2)
numbers[odd_slice]
# output: [1, 3, 5, 7, 9]

odd_range = range(1, 10, 2)
numbers[odd_range]
# ERROR: TypeError: list indices must be integers or slices, not range
```

Figure 4.2 shows you how `slice` and `range` objects differ; it also shows their similarities in constructors and attributes.

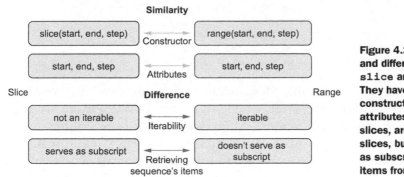

Figure 4.2 The similarities and differences between `slice` and `range` objects. They have a similar constructor pattern and attributes. Ranges, but not slices, are iterables, whereas slices, but not ranges, serve as subscripts for retrieving items from a sequence.

4.1.3 *Using named slice objects to process sequence data*

Most of the time, we use subscript-based slicing to retrieve items: `list[start:stop]`. This approach works when the data in the sequence is straightforward. When the sequence has more complicated data, however, we should use `slice` objects with sensible names to improve our code's readability.

Suppose that we're processing text data generated from an external source for our task management app. Due to some formatting settings, the text data looks like this (the numbers in the text are the indices of the characters):

```
tasks = """
0....5..............20........................48......
1001 Laundry        Wash all clothes          3
1002 Museum Visit   Go to the Egypt exhibit    4
1003 Do Homework    Physics and math           5
1004 Go to Gym      Work out for 1 hour        2
"""
```

In the text, we notice that the same fields of data are aligned vertically in each row. Using `slice` objects is a best practice, and you can find a possible implementation in the next listing.

Listing 4.1 Using named slices in processing data

```
task_id = slice(5)
task_title = slice(5, 20)
task_desc = slice(20, 48)
task_urgency = slice(48, 49)

task_lines = tasks.split("\n")[2:-1]

tasks = []
for line in task_lines:
    task = (line[task_id].strip(), line[task_title].strip(),
➥       line[task_desc].strip(), line[task_urgency].strip())   ⟵— Uses the strip method to get rid of trailing spaces
    tasks.append(task)

print(tasks)
```

```
# output the following lines (re-formatted for clarity):
[('1001', 'Laundry', 'Wash all clothes', '3'),
 ('1002', 'Museum Visit', 'Go to the Egypt exhibit', '4'),
 ('1003', 'Do Homework', 'Physics and math', '5'),
 ('1004', 'Go to Gym', 'Work out for 1 hour', '2')]
```

To separate the task ID, title, description, and urgency level, we create four `slice` objects that extract each corresponding substring. Technically, we can apply slicing directly to the string, such as `line[:5]` for the title. The names of these `slice` objects, however, clearly indicate what data each `slice` obtains. More importantly, from a maintainability perspective, when we're using named slices, if we have formatting changes in the text files, such as extra spaces between data fields, it's easier to modify `slice` objects by updating the indices to reflect the new formatting requirements.

> **MAINTAINABILITY**   Named slices are easy to read and clearly indicate what data they're representing.

4.1.4   *Manipulating list items with slicing operations*

In sections 4.1.1 to 4.1.3, you learned about retrieving subsequences with slicing. These operations are available to all sequence data models, including mutable ones, such as `list` and `bytearray`, and to immutable ones, such as `tuple` and `string` (table 4.1). Mutable sequence data models support another set of operations, which we term *slice surgery*. In this section, you'll learn how to manipulate items in a mutable sequence.

Table 4.1   Common sequence data models as a function of mutability

Mutability	Data types	Allowed for slice surgery
Mutable	`list, bytearray`	Yes
Immutable	`str, tuple, range, bytes`	No

Using lists as an example, slice surgery means that we can manipulate a list's subsequence obtained with a `slice` object. We can do several things with slice surgery to manipulate a subsequence, including replacement, extension, shrinkage, and removal. To replace a subsequence, we assign the same number of items to the subsequence that is retrieved:

```
numbers = [0, 1, 2, 3, 4, 5, 6, 7, 8]
numbers[:3] = [10, 11, 12]
numbers
# output: [10, 11, 12, 3, 4, 5, 6, 7, 8]
```

To extend a subsequence, we assign a longer subsequence to the original subsequence:

```
numbers[3:] = [13, 14, 15, 16, 17, 18, 19, 20]
numbers
# output: [10, 11, 12, 13, 14, 15, 16, 17, 18, 19, 20]
```

To shrink a subsequence, we assign a shorter subsequence to the original one:

```
numbers[:5] = [0, 1]
numbers
# output: [0, 1, 15, 16, 17, 18, 19, 20]
```

Notably, the subsequence doesn't have to be contiguous. Even with a stride in the slice, we can still perform a replacement. As shown in the following example, because the stride is 2, we're updating every second item in the list, using the provided items:

```
numbers[::2] = [0, 0, 0, 0]
numbers
# output: [0, 1, 0, 16, 0, 18, 0, 20]
```

When necessary, you can remove a subsequence by using the del statement. Alternatively, you can assign an empty list to the subsequence so that the corresponding items are removed too:

```
numbers = [0, 1, 0, 16, 0, 18, 0, 20]
del numbers[:4]
print(numbers)
# output: [0, 18, 0, 20]

numbers[-2:] = []
print(numbers)
# output: [0, 18]
```

4.1.5 Discussion

When you use a negative step in slicing, the slicing processes the sequence from right to left. Because people are generally more familiar with left-to-right order, negative striding can be confusing, and you should use it with caution.

When you process a series of sequences in a consistent format, as shown in the example of processing the text data (section 4.1.3), you should use named slice objects, because each name clearly indicates the data that corresponds to that subsequence, improving your code's readability.

4.1.6 Challenge

Jason is learning Python to analyze news about tourism as part of his machine learning interests. In his job, he deals with a variety of sequence data. He wants to try slicing with different sequence data types, such as strings and tuples. Can you help him find the data types for the generated subsequences of these sequence types? Note that as revealed in table 4.1, ranges are also a type of sequence. Please also try to subsequence ranges.

> **HINT**   The generated subsequence should resemble the "parent" sequence in terms of its type.

4.2 How do I use positive and negative indexing to retrieve items?

One shared characteristic of sequence objects is that the stored data follows the linear order, and each data point corresponds to a specific index, so we can use indexing to retrieve the data from the sequence. In most programming languages, the index starts counting from the left. Because we know that lists are a representative sequence data model, we'll use the following `list` object as an example throughout this section. Specifically, this `list` object stores the monthly revenue of a bookstore for the past year:

```
revenue_by_month = [95, 100, 80, 93, 92, 110, 102, 88, 96, 98, 115, 120]
```

Suppose that we want to retrieve November's record. How can we do that? In this section, you're learning about using positive and negative indexing to solve data retrieval questions from a sequence. As you'll see, Python supports indices counting from the right (negative indexing), and you'll learn when to use positive or negative indexing.

4.2.1 Positive indexing starts from the beginning of the list

In section 4.1, you've seen that slices use positive indexing to create a subsequence. From a general perspective, as in most other languages, we retrieve individual items based on their indices, starting with 0 from the left. In this section, we'll review how to use positive indexing. I know that most of you are familiar with this technique, so I'll keep the discussion brief. Using positive indexing, to access January's revenue and the second season's revenue, we can do the following:

```
revenue_jan = revenue_by_month[0]          The first item has
                                            an index of 0.
                                                               Retrieve the fourth,
                                                               fifth, and sixth items
revenue_season2 = revenue_by_month[3:6]                        with indices 3, 4, and 5.
```

What should we do if we retrieve items toward the end? We may want to retrieve November's revenue and the fourth season's revenue, for example. Our first reaction may be the following:

```
                                            November's revenue
                                            has an index of 10.
revenue_nov = revenue_by_month[10]                             Retrieve items starting
                                                               at index of 9 until the
revenue_season4 = revenue_by_month[9:]                         last item.
```

Using positive indexing and slicing, we had to count to 10 and 9, respectively, to retrieve the desired items. Certainly, it is manageable to count the indices if lists contain tens of items. When there are more items, however, getting the correct indices by counting from the beginning can be error-prone. Aren't better ways available? The next section discusses one of them: negative indexing.

4.2.2 Negative indexing starts from the end of the list

Fortunately, Python supports negative indexing. We can count from left to right, and we can also count from right to left. In this section, we'll see how negative indexing improves readability when we're retrieving items near a sequence's end.

In the typical way, the indices of positive indexing start with 0 for the first item and end with the list's length minus 1 for the last item. With negative indexing, we use –1 for the last item, –2 for the last but one, –3 for the last but two, and so on. Thus, the first item has a negative index of -len(list). Negative indexing is a brilliant design, as it's more intuitive. In daily life, we count from 1, with the adjustment of using a negative sign. Figure 4.3 shows both positive and negative indices for a list.

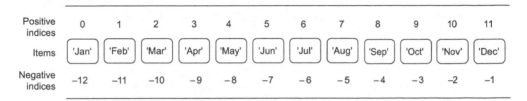

Figure 4.3   Positive and negative indices in a list. Positive indices start the count from the left side with an initial count of 0, whereas negative indices start the count from the right side with an initial count of -1.

Let's apply the feature of negative indexing to the retrieval of November's revenue and the fourth season's revenue for the bookstore:

```
revenue_nov_neg = revenue_by_month[-2]    ◁ ── November has an index of –2.
assert revenue_nov == revenue_nov_neg

revenue_season4_neg = revenue_by_month[-3:]    ◁─┤ The fourth season includes the
assert revenue_season4 == revenue_season4_neg        last three items of the list.
```

As shown in this example, we obtained the same results that we did with positive indexing. But the negative-indexing approach has three advantages:

- *It saves time.* We need to count only a few items from the end of the list.
- *It's straightforward.* We count from the right, and the n-th item has a negative index of -n. We don't have to make a mental adjustment to positive indices starting with 0. We simply negate the number: 2 -> –2.
- *It's clear.* We make it clear to the readers of our code that we are retrieving items toward the end of the list, which is the most important advantage.

Thus, whenever you want to retrieve items that are close to the end of a sequence, using negative indexing is always a good idea.

> **READABILITY**   It's easy to spot the negative index when you're trying to retrieve any items near the end of the sequence.

4.2.3   Combining positive and negative indices as needed

Positive and negative indices aren't mutually exclusive. For each item in the sequence, the positive index and negative index are equivalent despite their different values, and they both refer to the same item, allowing us to combine both kinds of indices whenever applicable.

Suppose that you want to retrieve the items in the middle of a list. You can define the slice by using both positive and negative indexing:

```
revenue_middle = revenue_by_month[1:-1]      ◁──┐  Accesses revenue records
                                                 │  from February to November
print(revenue_middle)
# output: [100, 80, 93, 92, 110, 102, 88, 96, 98, 115]
```

4.2.4   Discussion

When you retrieve items toward the end of a sequence, you should use negative indices. This section may be tedious to some readers, but I decided to include it because sequence data models are used in many projects. It's essential to form the good habit of using negative indexing to denote the last item(s) in a sequence. You not only make it easier to find an index of the last items, but also clearly signal to readers that the code is concerned about items toward the sequence's end. As always, readability is key in any codebase.

4.2.5   Challenge

Jeffrey is a middle-school student who participates on the school's robotics team. He recently learned about positive indexing of a sequence. He knows that he can use the length of the list to compute the positive index of an item toward the end, and he wants to write some code to retrieve November's revenue; this code involves calculating the list's length. Can you help him?

> **HINT**   Remember that positive indexing starts with 0. Therefore, the last item's positive index is off 1 from the sequence's length.

4.3   How do I find items in a sequence?

In sections 4.1 and 4.2, you learned about shared characteristics of sequence data types, such as slicing and indexing. When we have a sequence, we want to know where a specific item is in the sequence. In a `list` object consisting of tasks, for example, we may want to know whether any task deals with completing a survey. As another example, we may want to know whether the text description of a task includes the term *homework*. More generally speaking, finding an item in a sequence is a common task, and this section discusses several approaches that address this need.

4.3.1   Checking an item's presence

The first step in finding an item in a sequence is checking the presence of the item. This section discusses this topic.

Many programming languages, such as JavaScript, check an item's presence in a sequence by implementing a named method: `list.contains(item)`, `list.includes(item)`, or something similar. Python, however, takes a different approach to solving this problem, using the in keyword. The general syntax is item in sequence, which returns a Boolean value to indicate whether the item is present in the sequence. Following are some examples:

```
assert (8 in [1, 2, 3, 4, 5]) == False
```
The parentheses are required. Otherwise, the equality == will be evaluated first.

```
assert ('cool' in 'Python is cool') == True

assert (404 in (404, 'Page Not Found')) == True
```
== True can be omitted. I'm including it here for clarity.

The item in sequence feature is useful when you're interested only in the presence of a specific item in the sequence. But a binary True or False isn't enough in situations when you need to know the exact index of the item. You may need to use the index of the searched item as an anchor and retrieve a subsequence that starts with the anchor, for example. In that case, you need to use the index method, as discussed in the next section.

4.3.2 *Using the index method to locate the item*

Another shared characteristic of sequence data is support for the index method, which returns the item's index in a sequence. In this section, you'll learn how to use the index method to locate a specific item.

The following code snippet shows a few examples of using different types of sequence data. As you can see, all sequence data has the index method:

```
[1, 2, 3, 4, 5].index(4)
# output: 3

(404, 'Page Not Found').index('Page Not Found')
# output: 1

'Python is cool'.index('cool')
# output: 10
```

By default, the index is using the 0-based positive indices. When the checked item is indeed in the sequence, everything works as expected, and we find the item's index.

> **NOTE** When there are duplicate items in the sequence, the index method returns the index of the first matching item.

One caveat of the index method that many people fail to appreciate is that sometimes the item isn't contained in the sequence. Following is an example:

```
[1, 2, 3, 4, 5].index(8)
# ERROR: ValueError: 8 is not in list
```

When an exception is raised—in this case, a ValueError exception—your program crashes if this exception isn't handled. Although you'll learn exception handling in chapter 12, here's a quick peek at a solution that uses the try...except... statement:

```
def process_item_try(item):
    try:
        item_index = the_list.index(item)
    except ValueError:
        # do something when the item isn't present

    # do something with the item_index
```

You can write this code snippet in a different way to perform a presence check before finding the index, as follows:

```
def process_item_check_first(item):
    if item in the_list:
        item_index = the_list.index(item)
        # do something with the item_index
    else:
        # do something when the item isn't present
```

On the surface, both approaches do the same job, but I prefer the first option, as it's more performant than the other. When we use the index method, Python needs to traverse the sequence to check it against each item to identify a match, which is a time-consuming operation. In a similar fashion, when we find whether an item is contained in the sequence, Python needs to traverse the sequence too. Thus, when you use the process_item_check_first approach, the time consumption is expected to double because two traverses are involved, compared to one in the process_item_try approach. Thus, when the sequence is short, either approach is fine, but when the sequence is long, you should use the first approach.

> **EAFP vs. LBYL**
>
> A widely respected principle in Python is EAFP (Easier to Ask for Forgiveness Than Permission). In this pattern, you use try...except... with the assumption that things should work. If something goes wrong, we handle the error accordingly (forgiveness).
>
> By contrast, another principle is known as LBYL (Look Before You Leap). This pattern is more prevalent in other programming languages, such as C. In this pattern, you check the applicable condition first, probably using an if statement (look), and apply the operation (leap) only if the condition is valid.

4.3.3   *Finding substrings in a string*

As a sequence data type, strings support the index method, as you saw in section 4.3.2. Moreover, we addressed the potential ValueError exception associated with the index method. Compared with other sequence types, however, strings are special in that they have two additional item-finding methods: find and rfind.

Both methods return the index of the searched substring. What makes them better than the index method is that they return –1 instead of raising the ValueError exception when the substring isn't found in the string. Thus, I recommend that you use find or rfind when you search any substring, as shown in this example:

```
def find_string(substr):
    str_index = the_str.find(substr)
    if str_index >= 0:
        # do something with the str_index
    else:
        # do something when the substr isn't present
```

Please note that the find method is available only to strings. You can't use it with other sequence data types, although I don't see any technical difficulty in implementing this feature in non-str sequence models.

TRIVIA   You can use find only with strings, not with other sequence data types.

4.3.4   *Finding an instance of custom classes in a list*

When our projects grow in scope, we'll use custom classes as our data models. In our projects, we use lists to store multiple instances of a custom class. Chances are that we want to know whether a specific instance exists in the list. In this section, you'll learn how to locate an instance of a custom class.

Suppose that in our task management application, we use a list object to store a day's tasks. Consider the following listing to be our starting point. For simplicity, the Task class has minimum implementations. To provide a proof of concept, the list object contains four instances.

Listing 4.2   Creating a list of objects of custom classes

```
class Task:
    def __init__(self, title, urgency):
        self.title = title
        self.urgency = urgency


tasks = [
    Task("Laundry", 3),
    Task("Museum", 4),
    Task("Homework", 5),
    Task("Ticket", 2)
]
```

In our application, the interface shows the list of these tasks. One possible feature of our application highlights the row of the task that matches the filtering criterion, such as an urgency level of 5. To implement this feature, we need to know the index of the task that has the desired urgency level. As you may realize, we can't use the index method, as we don't know the task with the needed urgency level beforehand. Thus, we must consider a different approach. Because we're interested in obtaining a task with the desired urgency level, we can iterate the entire list to find the potential match. The following code snippet shows a working solution:

```
                  needed_urgency = 5
                  needed_task_index = None
                                                            See section 4.3.6 for an
                  for task_i in range(len(tasks)):   ◄──┘   alternative technique.
                      task = tasks[task_i]
Uses break           if task.urgency == needed_urgency:
to exit the              needed_task_index = task_i
for loop     └─►         break


                  print(f"Task Index: {needed_task_index}")
                  # output: Task Index: 2
```

We use a for loop to iterate the list to check each instance's urgency attribute against the desired level. When the task is found, we use the break statement (see section 5.4.1) to exit the for loop and complete the search. With the identified index, we can update our application's interface by highlighting the corresponding row of the task.

CONCEPT   The break statement exits the present loop instantaneously.

4.3.5   *Discussion*

Calling index on a sequence returns the index of only the first matching item, so be mindful that the sequence might contain other matching items. Because the index method raises a ValueError exception if the item isn't in the sequence, we can use the try...except... statement (section 12.3) to handle the exception. Although we can check the presence of a specific item, this LBYL approach requires two traverses of the sequence, causing extra time overhead. Thus, it's a good idea to use the EAFP approach for better performance.

MAINTAINABILITY   Prefer adopting the EAFP pattern whenever possible, as it is generally more performant than LBYL.

4.3.6   *Challenge*

In the example of locating an object of custom class, the task with the needed urgency level has an index of 2, which is the object Task("Homework", 5). What happens if you run the code: tasks.index(Task("Homework", 5))? Will you get an index of 2 as the result?

HINT   Even though some objects appear to have the same data, they're distinct objects that have different memory addresses. You can use the id function to explain the findings.

4.4   *How do I unpack a sequence? Beyond tuple unpacking*

Because tuples are immutable data containers, we use them to hold multiple objects without the intention of changing the contents. To retrieve items from the tuple object individually or consecutively, we've learned to use indexing and slicing (sections 4.2 and 4.3):

```
task = (1001, "Laundry", 5)

task_id = task[0]
task_title = task[1]
task_urgency = task[-1]
```

In this example, we used three separate assignments to create three variables, each of which corresponds to one item of the tuple task. If the tuple object has more items, we need to have more assignments, which can be tedious work that can make our code look busy and less readable. Is there a better way to access multiple items with corresponding variables?

The answer is the *unpacking technique*. When it's applied to tuples, it's best known as the *tuple unpacking technique*. The essential idea is that we conceptualize creating tuples to hold data as a process of packing information. Not surprisingly, the reverse process—retrieving the items—is termed *unpacking*. In this section, you'll learn this important technique with a primary focus on tuple objects. Note, however, that unpacking isn't only for tuples; it's also for any iterables, including sequence data types.

4.4.1   Unpacking short sequences with one-to-one correspondence

When we work with tuples that contain a few items and need to use all items, we use one-to-one unpacking, in which each item is assigned to a matching variable:

```
task = (1001, "Laundry", 5)
task_id, task_title, task_urgency = task

print(task_id, task_title, task_urgency)
# output: 1001 Laundry 5

user_data = ("python_user", 35, "male")
username, age, gender = user_data
print(username, age, gender)
# output: python_user 35 male
```

With this one-to-one unpacking technique, we used one line of code to create multiple variables that correspond to each item in the tuple object. Please note that in the preceding examples, the tuples were created first, mimicking the real-life situation in which we obtain tuple objects created by other parts of our projects.

Closely related to one-to-one unpacking is the *multiple-assignment technique,* in which we create multiple variables by sharing a single assignment operator (the equal sign):

```
x0, y0 = (90, 20)
(x1, y1) = 90, 20
(x2, y2) = (90, 20)

assert x0 == x1 == x2 == 90
assert y0 == y1 == y2 == 20
```

The preceding code snippet shows a few varieties of multiple assignments. Although their appearances are different, they perform the same job. On the right side, we create `tuple` objects, and on the left side, we pass the same number of variables in such a way that the items are unpacked on a one-to-one basis. Also, a notable feature to observe in these assignments is the fact that parentheses are optional for creating and unpacking tuples. The following code snippet shows the missing permutation that complements the precedings in string examples:

```
x3, y3 = 90, 20

assert x3 == 90
assert y3 == 20
```

> **READABILITY** Use multiple assignments only if the variables are closely related. Prefer using separate lines of code for assignments when the variables serve different purposes.

4.4.2   *Retrieving consecutive items using the starred expression*

In the preceding section, we retrieved multiple items by using the one-to-one unpacking technique, which works well with tuples that contain a few items. When the tuples have more items, we may want to retrieve some items as separate variables and some consecutive items as a single variable. This section shows you how.

Suppose that we're hosting a gymnastics meet, and each player is scored by eight judges. To calculate a player's final score, we get rid of the lowest and highest scores and then compute the mean of the remaining six scores. For the purpose of data recording, we save the score records for each player: the lowest, middle, highest, and final score. To simplify the example, assume that the scores have already been sorted from low to high. Certainly, we can use indexing to generate these score records, as follows:

```
player_scores = [6.1, 6.5, 6.8, 7.1, 7.3, 7.6, 8.2, 8.9]

lowest0 = player_scores[0]
middles0 = player_scores[1:-1]
highest0 = player_scores[-1]

final0 = sum(middles0) / len(middles0)
```

Instead of using the unpacking technique discussed later in this section, we use multiple lines of code to create these variables one by one. This solution is not the most Pythonic way to create multiple variables from sequence data. Unfortunately, if we try to solve the problem by applying the syntax of the one-to-one unpacking technique, we encounter a problem:

```
lowest1, middles1, highest1 = player_scores
# ERROR: ValueError: too many values to unpack (expected 3)
```

The error message is clear: there are too many values to unpack. Let's take a closer look. On the left side, we have three variables, so Python expects to unpack three items from the tuple. But the tuple object contains eight items, which leads to a mismatch. How can we solve the problem? A *starred expression* comes into play:

```
lowest2, *middles2, highest2 = player_scores    ◄─── Uses a starred expression
final2 = sum(middles2) / len(middles2)

assert lowest0 == lowest2 == player_scores[0]
assert middles0 == middles2 == player_scores[1:-1]
assert highest0 == highest2 == player_scores[-1]
```

You should note several characteristics of a starred expression:

- *A starred expression uses an asterisk as a prefix for the variable* (*var_name). All items that are not denoted by other variables are captured by the variable. In this case, the first and last items go with lowest2 and highest2, respectively. The six items in the middle are captured by middles2. Thus, some Python users refer to the starred expression as the *capture-all asterisk*.
- *A starred expression produces a* list *object of the captured items, regardless of the data type of the original sequence.* We can observe this effect with a str object, as shown in the following code snippet. Don't make the mistake of assuming that the variable b is a str object consisting of all the characters in the middle:

```
a, *b, c = "abcdefg"
assert b == ['b', 'c', 'd', 'e', 'f']
```

- *The number of captured items in the list object can be zero.* If all items are unpacked with the proper number of variables, leaving zero items to account for, the starred expression produces an empty list. Observe this effect:

```
first_score, *scores, last_score = [9.1, 8.9]
assert scores == []
```

- *One assignment can use only one starred expression.* Trying to use two starred expressions is a syntax error. The reason is simple: a starred expression is intended to capture all items that are not accounted for, so when two starred expressions are used, it's impossible to determine which one should capture which items:

```
score0, *scores0, *scores1, score1 = [9.1, 8.8, 9.2, 7.7, 8.4]
# ERROR: SyntaxError: multiple starred expressions in assignment
```

4.4.3   Denoting unwanted items with underscores to remove distraction

We've discussed how to unpack a tuple or a list to access individual or consecutive items. In any unpacking, we must provide a proper number of variables (with a starred expression, if necessary) that corresponds to the items in the sequence. But we don't always use the unpacked items. In this case, we should use underscores in unpacking.

In our task management app, suppose that we have an application programming interface (API) that returns a task saved as a `tuple` object with four items: the task's ID, the task's title, the task's description, and the task's status. As a reminder, the task's ID uniquely identifies a task in our application. We can define a function to update data in our database, as shown in this code:

```
def update_status(t_id, t_status):        ◄──┐  A utility function for
    # use task_id to locate the task in the database and update its status
    pass
                                                  The API returns a
                                                  four-item tuple.
task = (1001, "Laundry", "Wash clothes", "completed")    ◄──┐
task_id, task_title, task_desc, task_status = task    ◄──┐  Unpacks the tuple
                                                          object completely
update_status(task_id, task_status)
```

A utility function for database updating

The API returns a four-item tuple.

Unpacks the tuple object completely

In the preceding code snippet, we unpacked the `tuple` object in such a way that all the items are associated with their respective variables. By doing the one-to-one unpacking, we present a significant implication to readers: we'll use each unpacked item next. As shown in the code, however, we needed to work only on the task's ID and status.

Thus, complete unpacking, which includes the assignment of variables that we don't need, is a distracting signal. To remove such a distraction, we should use the underscores to denote these unwanted items, as follows:

```
task_id, _, _, task_status = task
```

The idea of using underscores is that if we don't need some of the variables, we don't assign them meaningful names. The following features are associated with using underscores in unpacking:

- *You can use as many underscores as applicable.* In our example, the `tuple` object has four items. As we're interested in only two items, we use two underscores plus the `task_id` and `task_status` to unpack these items.
- *The underscores are valid variable names.* More than unpacking, using underscores is a convention among Python users to denote unwanted variables. Even though we give a signal that we don't need these variables, we can refer to them if we choose to do so. In our example, the _ variable holds the task description because the former assignment of the task title (the first _) was overwritten.
- *You can combine an asterisk and underscore in the starred expression.* The following code snippet shows an example:

```
task = (1001, "Laundry", "Wash clothes", "completed")
task_id, *_, task_status = task        ◄──────────
```

Combination of the asterisk and underscore in the starred expression

READABILITY   In sequence unpacking, denote unwanted items with underscores, which signifies that we shouldn't bother using these items.

4.4.4   Discussion

Unpacking is the most readable way to retrieve individual or consecutive items in a sequence. We should have a thorough understanding of the various techniques of unpacking. Notably, I've mostly used tuples to show how unpacking works, but you can apply the same unpacking technique to any iterables. When you learn more about iterables in chapter 5, you can try using the unpacking technique with any iterables.

4.4.5   Challenge

Danny is working on a project in which he uses the unpacking technique to extract data from list objects. What's special about the data is the fact that the list objects in his project have two layers, such as [1, (2, 3), 4]. How can he use one line of code to unpack both layers to extract these four numbers as four variables?

> **HINT**   You can use parentheses to create layers during unpacking.

4.5   When should I consider data models other than lists and tuples?

Of the various sequence data types, the versatility of their features doubtless makes lists and tuples satisfactory data containers in many common situations. When you move on to specific projects, however, you'll find that lists and tuples become less ideal. Thus, you should be open-minded about alternative data structures that can be the correct choice in certain use cases. In this section, I review some common scenarios and recommended alternatives.

4.5.1   Using sets where membership is concerned

We often need to check whether the data container has the specific item under examination, a functionality that is termed *membership checking*. With lists and tuples, we've learned that we can use either item in the_list to check the membership or the index method as an indirect way to determine whether a list contains a specific item. Please note that using index is less desirable because when the item isn't in the list, the ValueError exception is raised.

Although lists support membership testing, you should consider using sets if your application is concerned with membership. As covered in greater detail in section 3.5, Python requires all the items in a set to be unique because under the hood, sets are implemented by means of a hash table, which offers a significant benefit of constant item lookup time, known as O(1) time complexity. By contrast, membership testing lookup time is linear with the length of the list because Python needs to traverse the sequence to find a potential match. The more items a list has, the more time the traverse costs. Thus, you should use sets when your application is concerned with membership testing.

> **QUESTION**   Do you remember the hash table implementation as the storage mechanism for set? See section 3.5.

4.5.2   *Using deques if you care about first-in-first-out*

In certain applications, we want our data to have *first-in, first-out* (FIFO) capability. FIFO emphasizes that the items that are added to the sequence first (first in) are removed from the sequence first (first out). In this section, we'll see a better model when FIFO is concerned.

Suppose that we're building an online customer chat system for an enterprise. Throughout business hours, clients check in, and we use a list to track the order of the check-in sequence. It's reasonable to connect those who check in first with the customer support associates, which represents a FIFO need in the application. One possible solution uses lists, as shown in the following listing.

Listing 4.3   Using lists to create the client queue system

```
clients = list()

def check_in(client):
    clients.append(client)        ◄─┐  Appends a new item
    print(f"in: New client {client} joined the queue.")   to the end of the list

def connect_to_associate(associate):
    if clients:                   ◄────  Examines whether there are items
        client_to_connect = clients.pop(0)    in the list. When the list is empty,
        print(f"out: Remove {client_to_connect}, connecting to    pop results in an IndexError.
{associate}.")
    else:
        print("No more clients are waiting.")
```

Removes the first item in the list

In the snippet, the `check_in` function adds a new client to the end of the waiting queue, which is a `list` object named `clients`. When an associate becomes available, we connect the first client in the queue to the associate. To retrieve the first client, we use the `pop` method of `list` objects. This method doesn't only return the first item in the list, but also removes it.

The removal of the item at the beginning of a `list` object is significant. Under the hood, Python shifts each of the items in the list to adjust the vacancy of the first item in memory, which is an expensive operation with a time complexity of $O(n)$. Given its considerable complexity, we should consider an alternative solution: using deques.

TRIVIA   *Deque* is pronounced "deck," not "dee-queue."

The deque data type is a double-ended queue. Because of its double-ended feature, it supports insertion and removal from both ends, making it a perfect data type for implementing the client chat management system, which requires FIFO. As mentioned previously, the invocation of the `pop` method on a `list` object is an expensive operation in terms of both time and memory. By contrast, because deques' ends are both open, removing the leftmost item from a deque is a computationally trivial operation. Figure 4.4 illustrates the contrast between lists and deques.

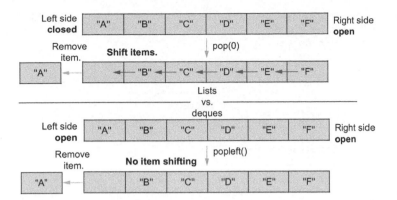

Figure 4.4   Removing the first item in a list vs. a deque. Removing the leftmost item of a list requires the shifting of all remaining items, making it an O(n) operation, whereas removing the leftmost item of a deque requires no actions on the remaining items, making it an O(1) operation.

Let's make a direct comparison between lists and deques for this operation. Consider the following simplified setup for removing the first item from the waiting queue. Please note that the next listing includes the use of a lambda function (chapter 7).

Listing 4.4   Comparing the performance of deques and lists

```
from collections import deque
from timeit import timeit

def time_fifo_testing(n):
    integer_l = list(range(n))
    integer_d = deque(range(n))
    t_l = timeit(lambda : integer_l.pop(0), number=n)
    t_d = timeit(lambda : integer_d.popleft(), number=n)
    return f"{n: >9} list: {t_l:.6e} | deque: {t_d:.6e}"

numbers = (100, 1000, 10000, 100000)
for number in numbers:
    print(time_fifo_testing(number))


# output something like the following lines:
       100 list: 6.470000e-05 | deque: 3.790000e-05
      1000 list: 7.637000e-04 | deque: 3.435000e-04
     10000 list: 1.805050e-02 | deque: 2.134700e-03
    100000 list: 1.641030e+00 | deque: 1.336000e-02
```

The deque data type is available in the collections module in the standard library.

The timeit function calculates the average execution time of an expression.

The popleft method pops the first item from the beginning of the deque.

The performance gain in this trivial example using deques over lists is significant with two orders of magnitude for 100,000 items. For enterprise applications, such improvement in a single aspect can be essential for improving overall user experiences. It's important to note that using the deque data type doesn't involve any complicated implementations. So why not enjoy the performance gain without any cost other than using a built-in data type? The next listing shows the modified implementation using deques.

Listing 4.5   Using lists to create the client queue system

```
from collections import deque

clients = deque()

def check_in(client):
    clients.append(client)
    print(f"in: New client {client} joined the queue.")

def connect_to_associate(associate):
    if clients:
        client_to_connect = clients.popleft()
        print(f"out: Remove {client_to_connect}, connecting to
    {associate}.")
    else:
        print("No more clients are waiting.")
```

4.5.3   *Processing multidimensional data with NumPy and Pandas*

So far, we've focused on linear sequence data structures, such as lists, tuples, and strings. In real life, however, data can take a multidimensional shape, such as images and videos. Images, for example, can be represented mathematically as three layers (red, green, and blue) of two-dimensional pixel panels. It can be a nightmare to try to use basic data models to represent high-dimensional data. Fortunately, Python's open source nature has bolstered the development of many third-party libraries and packages for processing multidimensional large-scale datasets. Thus, instead of using lists, we should consider using alternatives that are designed for computationally heavy jobs.

If you need to work on a large amount of numeric data, for example, you should consider using NumPy arrays, which are the core data type implemented in the NumPy package. It's important to note that lots of related manipulations are available in the package, such as reshaping, transformation, and various arithmetic operations.

If you need to work on spreadsheet-like data with mixed data types (such as strings, dates, and numbers), you should consider using pandas DataFrame, one of the core data types implemented in the pandas packages. If you do machine learning, you need to use tensors, which are the most important data types in major machine learning frameworks, such as TensorFlow and PyTorch. If your applications deal with a large amount of multidimensional data, especially in the form of numeric values, you should take advantage of these third-party libraries, which have specialized data types and associated methods to ease your life.

4.5.4   *Discussion*

Lists and tuples are useful sequence data types for storing ordered items. Now, however, we know essential alternative data models. Certainly, the data models covered here aren't an exhaustive list. Instead, I want to convey only that you should be open-minded about the data model choices. The decision must be driven by the specific business need.

MAINTAINABILITY   Always pick the proper data models for different purposes. Using an improper data model can make your project extremely hard to maintain.

The bottom line in selecting data models is that you should take a *need-driven approach* to choosing the best data model for specific components of your application. In other words, your application should contain as many different data models as possible, with each data model chosen to address specific needs. Figure 4.5 provides an overview of the need-driven approach to data model selection.

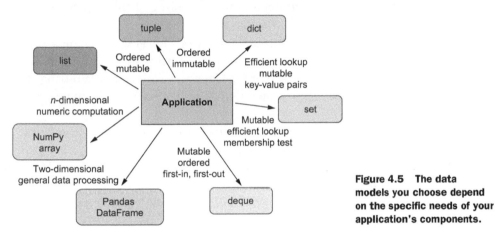

Figure 4.5   The data models you choose depend on the specific needs of your application's components.

4.5.5   *Challenge*

Emma is a beginner data scientist who is starting to use Python for her projects. She understands that she can use lists to store one-dimensional data, such as a `list` of numbers. But her projects involve lists embedded in another list object to hold two-dimensional data that resembles a spreadsheet of four rows and three columns:

```
numbers = [[1, 2, 3], [4, 5, 6], [7, 8, 9], [10, 11, 12]]
```

What should she do if she wants to multiply each item by 3? You may notice that this job is tedious. Can you help her think of another data model that is more appropriate?

HINT   The `array` type in NumPy is specialized for performing operations on multidimensional numeric data.

Summary

- You can use slicing to retrieve a subsequence. With slicing, you can specify `start`, `end`, and `step`. Note that slicing supports a variety of methods of calling, including omission of the `start` and `end` indices.
- We use slices to create subsequences from sequence data, whereas we use ranges for iterations using the specified range and steps.

- Sequence data includes mutable and immutable types. We can manipulate mutable types, such as lists and bytearrays, through slice surgery to replace, expand, shrink, and remove subsequences.

- In a sequence, each item has an index to indicate its position. The positive indices start with 0 from the left with an increment of 1 moving toward the right, and the negative indices start with –1 from the right with an increment of –1 moving toward the left.

- To improve our code's readability, we should form the habit of using a positive index when we refer to items at the beginning of the sequence and a negative index for items toward the sequence's end.

- We need to know the different ways of checking the item's presence in a sequence and understand the limitation of using the `index` method. For strings, we should use the `find` or `rfind` method to locate a substring. For custom instances, we should use iteration to check each of the items for a possible match.

- Tuple unpacking is a notable feature for extracting items from a `tuple` object. This technique is available for all sequence data types and other kinds of iterables. But we should be familiar with different methods of unpacking, including using underscores and starred expressions.

- Lists aren't a one-size-fits-all solution. We should explore alternative data structures that are better for addressing specific business needs, such as NumPy arrays for multidimensional numeric computations.

Iterables and iterations

5

This chapter covers

- Understanding iterables and iterators
- Creating common data containers using iterables
- Using list, dictionary, and set comprehensions for instantiation
- Improving `for`-loop iterations
- Using `continue`, `break`, and `else` in `for` and `while` loops

Previous chapters mentioned iterables several times, and we know that lists, tuples, and many other built-in data types are iterables. But we haven't explicitly defined the concept of iterables. We say that these data types are iterables, but we haven't discussed why. In this chapter, you'll find out how they constitute iterables. More importantly, we'll explore how we can create the most common data models, such as lists and dictionaries, from other iterables by using constructors and comprehensions.

One essential mechanism for Python or any other programming language to perform repetitive work is `for`-loop iterations (or `while` loop, with `for` loops being more prevalent). In each iteration, the same operations can be applied to each item of the iterables. We have a variety of ways to improve the performance of `for` loops by applying built-in functions, such as enumerate and zip, and by using optional statements, including break and continue. In this chapter, you'll learn about these topics.

5.1   *How do I create common data containers using iterables?*

Iterables shouldn't be strangers to you. Chapter 2 reviewed essential techniques of processing strings, and strings are iterables that consist of characters. Chapter 3 discussed several built-in data containers, including lists, tuples, sets, and dictionaries, all of which are iterables that consist of individual items (or key-value pairs). Chapter 4 examined the shared methods among sequence data types, and all sequence data types are iterables. As you can see, iterables are prevalent in Python.

Indeed, iterables are an important base type on which many built-in data structures are built. Consider the following scenario. In the task management app, you have two separate sources of data, with one being the task ID numbers and the other being the task titles. You need to create a dict object that consists of ID-title pairs:

```
id_numbers = [101, 102, 103]
titles = ["Laundry", "Homework", "Soccer"]

desired_output = {101: "Laundry", 102: "Homework", 103: "Soccer"}
```

To create the desired output, beginners might think of using a for loop:

```
desired_output = {}
for item_i in range(len(id_numbers)):
    desired_output[id_numbers[item_i]] = titles[item_i]
```

A seemingly more advanced solution involves dictionary comprehension (section 5.2) and the use of the zip function:

```
desired_output = {key: value for key, value in zip(id_numbers, titles)}
```

These solutions aren't the best, however, because they don't take advantage of the fact that dict, as well as many built-in data containers, takes iterables directly for instantiation. This section first reviews what iterables are and then moves on to discuss one key technique: instantiating common built-in data containers by using iterables.

Instance, instantiation, constructor, and construction

In object-oriented programming (OOP) languages, including Python, the essential data models are classes, including built-in classes such as list, dict, and tuple, and custom classes that we create in our own projects. When we create an object that belongs to the class, such as a dict object—num_dict = dict(one=1, two=2)— we say that we create an instance of the class; thus, num_dict is an instance of the dict class. Relatedly, the process of creating an instance is known as *instantiation*. The same instantiation concept applies to custom classes.

During the instantiation process, we use the `dict` function to create the `dict` object, and this kind of function that creates instances of a class is known as the *constructor*. As you may have seen or known, for custom classes, the constructor is the `__init__` function that you define. Because we use a constructor for instantiation, we can also call the instantiation as construction.

NOTE   Chapter 8 covers instantiation in more detail.

5.1.1   Getting to know iterables and iterators

The use of iterables is not an isolated topic; a key related concept is iterators. *Iterators* are a special data type from which we can retrieve each of their elements via a process known as *iteration*. The key connection between iterables and iterators is that all the iterables are converted to iterators before we can perform any iteration-related operations with them.

Under the hood, two functions are doing the trick for us: `iter` and `next`. Figure 5.1 shows how iterables and iterators work together for iteration in three steps:

1   Create an iterator from an iterable by using `iter`. Iterators are designed to perform iteration of an iterable's elements.

2   Render elements by using `next`. Calling `next` on the iterator retrieves the next element if one is available.

3   Stop the iteration with the `StopIteration` exception. When no more elements are available, calling `next` results in the `StopIteration` exception.

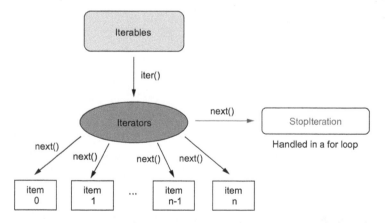

Figure 5.1   The workflow of iteration with iterators. Iterators are created by using the `iter` function from iterables. The iterators use the `next` function to retrieve the next item, if available. When the iterator exhausts its items, the `StopIteration` exception is raised.

To illustrate the iteration process, consider one common iterable, a `list` object, from which we create an iterator by using `iter`:

```
tasks = ["task0", "task1", "task2"]

tasks_iterator = iter(tasks)

tasks_iterator
# output: <list_iterator object at 0x000001F232ACEE50>
```

The memory address will be different on your computer.

We start with a list object, tasks, and create an iterator list_iterator by calling the iter function. We can use the next function to retrieve the iterator's items one by one:

```
next(tasks_iterator)
# output: 'task0'

next(tasks_iterator)
# output: 'task1'

next(tasks_iterator)
# output: 'task2'

next(tasks_iterator)
# ERROR: StopIteration
```

As you can see, every time we call next on the iterator, we retrieve the next item until we exhaust the items of the iterator and encounter the StopIteration exception.

This discussion of using iter and next provides a mechanistic overview of how iteration works. In our code, we rarely need to create an iterator ourselves. Instead, Python does the heavy lifting for us behind the scenes. Take the for loop, the most common form of using iterables and iterators, as an example:

```
for task in tasks:
    print(task)

# output the following lines:
task0
task1
task2
```

We use the list tasks directly in the for loop without worrying about creating an iterator, as it's processed automatically by Python. More importantly, instead of raising the StopIteration exception when the list iterator is exhausted, the for loop is exited safely, as the exception is handled for us.

5.1.2   *Inspecting iterability*

To better use iterables in our code, it's essential for us to know what data types are iterables beyond the ones we've already covered, including str, list, tuple, dict, and set. In this section, you'll find out how to determine whether a specific object is an iterable.

From a practical perspective, any data type that can be used in a for loop is an iterable. What's the formal way to determine an object's iterability? You might infer from the previous section that if the object can be converted to an iterator by means of the iter function, it is an iterable. The following code snippet shows you how objects (an int object versus a list object) behave differently in terms of their iterability:

```
iter(5)
# ERROR: TypeError: 'int' object is not iterable

iter([1, 2, 3])
# output: <list_iterator object at 0x000001F232A44700>
```

> **CONCEPT**   Iterability refers to the characteristic of an object being an iterable, such that it can be converted to an iterator for iteration.

On top of how to inspect an object's iterability, we should be aware of what common data types are iterables besides str, list, tuple, dict, and set. Using iter to determine iterability, we could come up with the solution shown in the next listing. Chapter 12 discusses how try...except... works in greater detail.

Listing 5.1   Checking whether an object is an iterable

```
def is_iterable(obj):
    try:                          Uses an underscore to denote that
        _ = iter(obj)     ◄────   we don't use the return result
    except TypeError:
        print(type(obj), "is not an iterable")
    else:
        print(type(obj), "is an iterable")    ◄───  The else clause executes when
                                                    there is no TypeError exception.

is_iterable(5)
# output: <class 'int'> is not an iterable

is_iterable([1, 2, 3])
# output: <class 'list'> is an iterable
```

In listing 5.1, to test whether an object is iterable, we try to call the iter function directly with the object. When calling this function succeeds, the object is an iterable; when calling fails, the object isn't an iterable. Using the is_iterable function, we can run the test for a series of built-in objects to determine what data types are iterables. Table 5.1 shows common built-in iterables.

Table 5.1   Common built-in iterables with code examples

Data type	Code example	Iterator type
str	"Hello"	str_iterator
list	[1, 2, 3]	list_iterator
tuple	(1, 2, 3)	tuple_iterator

Table 5.1 Common built-in iterables with code examples *(continued)*

Data type	Code example	Iterator type
dict	{"one": 1, "two": 2}	dict_keyiterator[a]
set	{1, 2, 3}	set_iterator
range	range(3)	range_iterator
map	map(int, ["1", "2"])	map
zip	zip([1, 2], [2, 3])	zip
filter	filter(bool, [1, None])	filter
enumerate	enumerate([1, 2, 3])	enumerator
reversed	reversed("Hello")	reversed

[a]When you iterate dict, the default is to iterate its keys. The following two operations are equivalent: for key in dict and for key in dict.keys(). You can iterate the values and the items of a dict object. For more information, see section 5.3.7.

In table 5.1, you'll notice some data types that I haven't covered yet, such as map and zip. Section 5.1.3 discusses some of these iterable types.

5.1.3 *Using iterables to create built-in data containers*

In chapter 2, we learned about collection data types, including lists, sets, tuples, and dictionaries, also known as data containers. In simple scenarios, we can use their respective literal forms to create the data when they involve a small number of elements.

As shown in listing 5.2, we create a few data containers without using their constructors. Instead, we specify the data with its special syntactical requirements, such as square brackets for list objects and curly braces for set objects. This instantiation approach is known as *using literals to create instances*.

Listing 5.2 Using literals for instantiation

```
list_obj = [1, 2, 3]

tuple_obj = (404, "Connection Error")

dict_obj = {"one": 1, "two": 2}

set_obj = {1, 2, 3}
```

When we need to create container data that has many elements, however, it's less convenient to use the literals. Notably, each of these collection data types has its own constructors, using the respective class names, and they can take iterables to create new collection objects. The following listing shows how.

Listing 5.3 Using iterables for instantiation

```
integers_list = list(range(10))                    ◁——— Calls the list constructor
assert integers_list == [0, 1, 2, 3, 4, 5, 6, 7, 8, 9]

integers_tuple = tuple(integers_list)              ◁——— Calls the tuple constructor
assert integers_tuple == (0, 1, 2, 3, 4, 5, 6, 7, 8, 9)

dict_items = [("zero", 0), ("one", 1), ("two", 2)]
integers_dict = dict(dict_items)                   ◁——— Calls the dict constructor
assert integers_dict == {'zero': 0, 'one': 1, 'two': 2}

even_numbers = (-2, 4, 0, 2, 4, 2)
unique_evens = set(even_numbers)   ◁——— Calls the set constructor
assert unique_evens == {0, 2, 4, -2}
```

As shown in listing 5.3, the list, tuple, dict, and set constructors can take an iterable to create a corresponding object. The technique of creating objects from iterables is often used in real-life projects when we deal with many kinds of iterables and the involved data is related. Thus, we often take advantage of this feature to create new data from existing iterables.

> **QUESTION** *Strings* are iterables of characters. Suppose that we have a str object: letters = "ABCDE". What's the best way to create a list of characters, ["A", "B", "C", "D", "E"], from letters?

Suppose that our project has a list object of strings, with each representing a floating-point number: numbers_str = ["1.23", "4.56", "7.89"]. To perform calculations next, we convert strings to floats. We can achieve this conversion by using map, which applies a function to each item of the iterable and creates the map iterator:

```
numbers_str = ["1.23", "4.56", "7.89"]

numbers_float = list(map(float, numbers_str))

assert numbers_float == [1.23, 4.56, 7.89]
```

In the preceding code example, the map function applies the built-in float function (it's the float constructor, to be precise) to each string, and the list constructor takes the created map iterator to create a list object of floating-point numbers.

> **PEEK** The map function is a higher-order function that takes a function as an argument. Find more in section 7.2.

Compared with that of other data containers, the dict type's constructor is special, as it requires each item in the iterable to consist of two items, with the keys and values in a paired manner. Besides using a list of tuples that each have two elements, a common way to create a dict object from existing iterables is to use the zip function to join two iterables. This scenario is the same one that I posed earlier: how to create a `dict` object from two `list` objects. Here's the solution:

```
zipped_tasks = dict(zip(id_numbers, titles))

assert zipped_tasks == {101: "Laundry", 102: "Homework", 103: "Soccer"}
```

The magic of this operation is that the `zip` function joins the id_numbers and titles side by side, forming a `zip` iterator that renders elements consisting of one item from each iterable. Figure 5.2 shows how the `zip` function works.

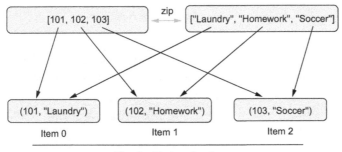

Figure 5.2 The `zip` function creates an iterator from multiple iterables. In the example, we use two iterables. The `zip` function joins the items at the corresponding position from each of the iterables. Please note that the order of the iterables used in the `zip` function matters because the created tuples store the items in the order that matches the iterables' order.

In figure 5.2, the example uses two iterables to create the iterator: a `zip` object that renders two-item `tuple` objects. The two-item tuples are what the `dict` constructor needs, the first item becoming a key and the second item becoming the corresponding value. In real projects, you'll often use the `zip` function to create `dict` objects.

> **This zip and that zip**
>
> The `zip` function joins two or more iterables, with each iterable contributing one item to the `zip` iterator's elements. Most of the time, you use two iterables in a `zip` function, which mimics the action of your real-world jacket's zipper. Thus, if you're confused about what the `zip` function does, think about what your jacket's zipper does: joins two rows of teeth, with the rows alternating to form a pair.
>
> You may know that zipping is a file-compression concept. In Python, the `zipfile` module provides the related functionalities of zipping and unzipping files.

5.1.4 Discussion

Besides Python's standard library, iterables are heavily used in third-party libraries. The `ndarray` in the NumPy and the `Series` in the pandas library, for example, can take an iterable for instantiation. If your work involves data science, you'll find it handy to convert data between different types of iterables.

5.1.5   Challenge

As an aspiring finance analyst, Ava is learning Python for her work. She's fascinated by the `zip` function, which connects multiple iterables. She wonders how `zip` works with multiple iterables. Can you help her write some code to try to zip three iterables? Commonly, the number of items in the iterables differs. Can you find out what happens if you use `zip` to join iterables of different numbers of items?

> **HINT**   Two iterables form two-item tuples after zipping. When one iterable is shorter than others, the shorter iterable has nothing to contribute when its elements are used up first.

5.2   What are list, dictionary, and set comprehensions?

If you ask an intermediate-level Python programmer what feature is one of the most Pythonic, you may get the answer *list comprehension*, a concise way of creating `list` objects. The following code snippet shows what list comprehension looks like:

```
numbers = [1, 2, 3, 4]
squares = [x * x for x in numbers]

assert squares == [1, 4, 9, 16]
```

As you can see, list comprehension doesn't look like literals, as it doesn't list the items directly, but it doesn't look like the constructor approach either, as it doesn't call `list`. List comprehension is a Pythonic feature that you'll use often. *Pythonic* means that it's concise and readable (certainly given that you know the technique). Besides list comprehension, dictionary and set comprehensions are available for creating `dict` and `set` objects, respectively. In the next section, you'll learn about these comprehension techniques and some pitfalls you should avoid.

5.2.1   Creating lists from iterables using list comprehension

We use different kinds of iterables to store a variety of data. Often, we need to convert this data to a `list` object in our projects. In this section, you'll learn to convert iterables to `list` objects by using list comprehension. Suppose that in our task management application, we have a `list` of instance objects of the `Task` class, as shown in the next listing.

Listing 5.4   Creating a list of custom class instances

```
from collections import namedtuple

Task = namedtuple("Task", "title, description, urgency")    ⟵⎯⎯ Custom class using
                                                                 named tuples
tasks = [
    Task("Homework", "Physics and math", 5),
```

```
    Task("Laundry", "Wash clothes", 3),
    Task("Museum", "Egypt exhibit", 4)
]
```

REMINDER A *named tuple* is a lightweight data model used to hold data and support dot notations. See section 3.3 for more details.

In our app, we need a list object to get all the titles for these tasks. A beginner who doesn't know list comprehension might come up with the following solution:

```
task_titles = []
for task in tasks:
    task_titles.append(task.title)

assert task_titles == ['Homework', 'Laundry', 'Museum']
```

We use a for loop to iterate the items in tasks and retrieve their title attributes, and we append them to the list object task_titles. This solution works, but it's not the most efficient or Pythonic. A better approach is to use list comprehension: [expression for item in iterable], in which the expression is a specific operation using each item of the iterable. Expressions are evaluated to become the items in the created list. The following code snippet shows how to use list comprehension to extract the tasks' titles:

```
titles = [task.title for task in tasks]

assert titles == ['Homework', 'Laundry', 'Museum']
```

As shown in this example, by using list comprehension, we create a list object of the desired data. The example highlights the most significant advantage of using list comprehension: *conciseness.* You don't need to use a for loop, and the operation goes into one line of code. Although some beginners may find this technique to be puzzling, when you become more experienced with Python, you'll find list comprehension to be not only concise, but also readable.

List comprehension or map

We use list comprehension to create a list object from an existing iterable. Notably, we can create the same list object by using a list constructor together with the map function. To derive the list of titles, for example, we can use the following alternative solution:

```
def get_title(task):
    return task.title

titles = list(map(get_titles, tasks))
```

As section 7.1 discusses, we can also use a lambda function to eliminate the need to create the get_title function: titles = list(map(lambda x: x.title, tasks)).

As you can see, using `list` and `map` to create a `list` object is usually more verbose than list comprehension; thus, it's generally less readable. I recommend that you use list comprehension instead of the `map` approach. Nevertheless, some people prefer the `map` approach because it represents a coding style termed *functional programming*. The style focuses on writing and using functions instead of focusing on objects, as in OOP languages.

5.2.2   Creating dictionaries from iterables using dictionary comprehension

`dict` is another key data container type in Python. As with `list` objects, we can create `dict` objects by using comprehension: dictionary comprehension. In this section, I quickly go over dictionary comprehension, as it has only a minor difference in syntax from list comprehension. The principle is the same, providing a concise way to create a `dict` object from an existing iterable.

Because dictionaries consist of key-value pairs, dictionary comprehension includes two expressions separated by a colon, as in `{expr_key: expr_value for item in iterable}`, in which `expr_key` evaluates to the key and `expr_value` evaluates to the corresponding value. Another syntactical difference is the use of curly braces in dictionary comprehension, as opposed to square brackets in list comprehension.

Using the same `list` object `tasks` as our starting point, suppose that our application needs a `dict` object in which the titles are the keys and the descriptions are the values. The following code shows how we can address this need by using a `for` loop and dictionary comprehension, providing a head-to-head comparison for readability:

```
title_dict0 = {}
for task in tasks:
    title_dict0[task.title] = task.description

title_dict1 = {task.title: task.description for task in tasks}

assert title_dict0 == title_dict1
```

Compared with the non-Pythonic `for` approach, dictionary comprehension is much more concise. For experienced Python users, it's also more readable, as by reading it, you can tell that the titles become the keys and the descriptions become the values. This clarity is another advantage of comprehension as a concise technique for creating data containers in Python.

5.2.3   Creating sets from iterables using set comprehension

In section 3.5, we learned that `set` objects are the perfect data model when we're concerned about membership testing. Thus, we often need `set` objects that are converted from other iterables. We can achieve such conversion with set comprehension, `{expression for item in iterable}`, in which `expression` evaluates to the set's items. In this section, you'll learn about set comprehension.

REMINDER   Because of the underlying implementation using hash tables, item lookup in a set object takes a constant amount of time, a phenomenon known as *O(1) time complexity.*

Set comprehension uses curly braces instead of square brackets. Across all three comprehension techniques, you may notice that the symbols used are the same as their respective literal forms: [] for list, {:} for dict, and {} for set. Thus, if you're confused about comprehensions' symbols, think of their literal forms.

The following code snippet shows the conciseness of set comprehension for creating a set object from an iterable compared with the for-loop approach. We use task.title to derive each task's title, which goes to the created set object:

```
title_set0 = set()
for task in tasks:
    title_set0.add(task.title)
```

Creating an empty set requires a set constructor, as there is no literal form for an empty set.

```
title_set1 = {task.title for task in tasks}

assert title_set0 == title_set1 == {'Homework', 'Laundry', 'Museum'}
```

One thing to note is that like the set constructor (example: set([1, 1, 2, 2, 3, 3]) = {1, 2, 3}), set comprehension removes duplicates for you automatically, because set objects only store unique items due to the underlying hash implementations. That is, objects that have the same value (and thus the same hash value; remember a hash function's consistency) can have only one copy in the set object, as shown in this example:

```
numbers = [-3, -2, -1, 0, 1, 2, 3]

squares = {x*x for x in numbers}

assert squares == {0, 9, 4, 1}
```

Items in a set object are unordered.

5.2.4   *Applying a filtering condition*

When we iterate through an iterable, sometimes we need to evaluate whether the item meets specific criteria before we perform the operations. In this section, you'll see how to apply a filtering condition to the comprehension technique.

Suppose that for the tasks list, we want to generate a list of the titles only for the tasks whose urgency level is greater than 3. In this case, we should filter the iterable by using the if statement. A beginner who has no knowledge of list comprehension can use a regular for loop to come up with the following solution:

```
filtered_titles0 = []
for task in tasks:
    if task.urgency > 3:
        filtered_titles0.append(task.title)

assert filtered_titles0 == ['Homework', 'Museum']
```

In the for loop, we examine the task's urgency level in each iteration and append the task only if it passes the test. But a Pythonic solution is to integrate the if statement into list comprehension: [expression for item in iterable if condition]. Specifically, we append the if statement following the iterable to filter the applicable elements:

```
filtered_titles1 = [task.title for task in tasks if task.urgency > 3]

assert filtered_titles0 == filtered_titles1
```

Although the pertinent code isn't shown here, the if statement can also be used in dictionary and set comprehensions to filter unwanted items while creating dict and set objects. If you're interested, you can try that feature.

5.2.5 *Using embedded for loops*

When we have nested data, we may need to derive all the elements from each layer of the nested structures. The list object tasks represents a layer of data, for example, and each element is another layer of data, as each task has its own stored data. In this section, you'll learn how to use embedded for loops to derive the innermost items for nested data.

We'll begin with a non-Pythonic approach as a direct comparison. When you use for loops for iteration, you may know that you can embed a for loop in another for loop, as follows:

```
flattened_items0 = []
for task in tasks:
    for item in task:
        flattened_items0.append(item)

assert flattened_items0 == ['Homework', 'Physics and math', 5,
➥ 'Laundry', 'Wash clothes', 3, 'Museum', 'Egypt exhibit', 4]
```

This operation of embedded for loops is valid is because tasks is a list of Task instances, and each Task instance is a named tuple—a kind of iterable too. The same operation is supported by list comprehension. That is, you can have embedded for loops in list comprehension. Observe this feature:

```
flattened_items1 = [item for task in tasks for item in task]

assert flattened_items0 == flattened_items1
```

In this code, the first for loop extracts each task from the list object tasks, and the second for loop extracts each item of the task object. This syntax may confuse some beginners because of the two for loops. My tip is that they read the code as though they're dealing with regular embedded for loops. The first for refers to the outer one, and the second for refers to the inner one: [expression for iterable in iterables for item in iterable].

Theoretically, you can have as many embedded for loops as you want. From a readability perspective, however, I don't recommend using comprehensions with more than two layers of for loops, as I've discussed so far.

READABILITY   Don't use more than two layers of for loops. It's hard to read a list comprehension that has three or more layers of for loops.

5.2.6   *Discussion*

Section 5.2 discussed how to use list, dictionary, and set comprehensions as concise ways to create list, dict, and set objects, respectively. Figure 5.3 summarizes these techniques.

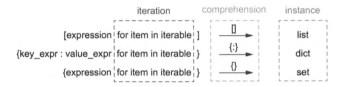

Figure 5.3   The general forms for list, dictionary, and set comprehensions. Each comprehension involves iterating an iterable, uses distinct syntax for comprehension, and creates the respective instance objects.

You should be clear about when you should use comprehensions. That is, when you start with an iterable and want to create an instance of a list, dict, or set class, that scenario probably is the best time to use comprehensions. Do you know why I say *probably*? There are a few exceptions.

First, if you don't need to manipulate the items in the iterable, you should consider using their constructors directly. You start with a list object, numbers = [1, 1, 2, 3], and you want to create a set object, for example. Although it's not wrong to do so, you shouldn't use set comprehension: {x for x in numbers}. Instead, you should use a set constructor, as it takes an iterable directly and creates a set object: set(numbers).

Second, when the comprehension requires complicated expressions or deeply nested for loops, it's better to use the conventional for-loop approach. Suppose that you have the following comprehension:

```
styles = ['long-sleeve', 'v-neck']
colors = ['white', 'black']
sizes = ['L', 'S']

options = [' '.join([style, color, size]) for style in styles
➥ for color in colors for size in sizes]
```

You can't say that this code isn't readable, but you should try your best to make your code readable for most readers. Here's an alternative:

```
options = []
for style in styles:
    for color in colors:
        for size in sizes:
            option = ' '.join([style, color, size])
            options.append(option)
```

Compared with the preceding solution, this one takes a few more lines of code, but it clearly presents the multiple layers of for loops, which are easier to read and understand.

5.2.7 *Challenge*

Lucas is learning Python for his graduate research in the field of physics. He has realized that list, dictionary, and set comprehensions use square brackets and curly braces. He wonders what (expression for item in iterable) can do. Because this expression uses parentheses, which are used in creating tuples, is this approach tuple comprehension? Try running it, and tell Lucas what he'll get.

> **HINT** If the process were tuple comprehension, I would have covered it already. You can check the nature of an object by using the type function. Section 7.4 covers the created object.

5.3 *How do I improve for-loop iterations with built-in functions?*

In our projects, most data is expected to be presented in an organized form. In a discussion forum, for example, we need to lay out the posts with titles on the left side and authors on the right side. To print a receipt in a clear format, we need to list the items one by one together with their respective prices. As you can imagine, you can say that every project uses structured information, and the universal need to store this information justifies the implementation of various kinds of iterables of distinct characteristics in Python.

For the structured information—posts, ordered items, or any applicable data in your projects—most of the time, the data is homogeneous, and we generally apply the same operation. When you try to apply the same operation to an iterable, it's best to use a for loop, which has the following form (and you should be familiar with it):

```
for item in iterable:
    # the same operation goes here
```

Knowing this basic form is a good start toward addressing iteration-related problems. But Python has more features that make for loops work better. In this section, you'll study the Pythonic implementations for the applicable use cases. I'll show you a non-Pythonic solution as a starting point, and then I'll explore the Pythonic solution. Finally, I'll briefly explain the functions and techniques.

5.3.1 Enumerating items with enumerate

Many iterables are sequence data, such as lists and tuples. Each item has a corresponding index—its position in the sequence data. We often want to use an item's position information together with the item's data itself. In this section, I address this need, which is known as *enumeration*.

Suppose that our task management application has a list of instance objects of the Task class. For simplicity, the Task class is implemented by using named tuples, as shown in the following listing.

Listing 5.5   Creating a list of custom class instances

```
from collections import namedtuple

Task = namedtuple("Task", "title description urgency")
tasks = [
    Task("Homework", "Physics and math", 5),
    Task("Laundry", "Wash clothes", 3),
    Task("Museum", "Egypt exhibit", 4)
]
```

The use case is that we want to display these tasks in a numbered list:

```
Task 1: task1_title task1_description task1_urgency
Task 2: task2_title task2_description task2_urgency
Task 3: task3_title task3_description task3_urgency
```

If you think about a solution, you'll probably notice that the only missing information is the counter of each task—that is, the index of the task in the tasks. Thus, you may come up with the following solution:

```
for task_i in range(len(tasks)):
    task = tasks[task_i]
    task_counter = task_i + 1
    print(f"Task {task_counter}: {task.title:<10}
➡ {task.description:<18} {task.urgency}")

# output the following lines:
Task 1: Homework   Physics and math   5
Task 2: Laundry    Wash clothes       3
Task 3: Museum     Egypt exhibit      4
```

> **READABILITY**   In the f-string (covered in section 2.1.4), we apply format specifiers, such as text alignment used in the code, to format the interpolated strings. This structural alignment provides better readability for the string output.

The solution creates a range object using the length of tasks. Note that when you send only one argument (len(tasks), which is 3) to the range constructor, it's parsed as the stop parameter; thus, the range object consists of the indexes of 0, 1, and 2.

Although this solution works for the use case, a more Pythonic solution takes advantage of the enumerate function, which retrieves the items and generates a counter for each one:

```
for task_i, task in enumerate(tasks, start=1):
    print(f"Task {task_i}: {task.title:<10}
    ➥ {task.description:<18} {task.urgency}")
```

The enumerate function takes an iterable and creates an iterator of the enumerate type (table 5.1). This iterator renders a tuple object each time: (item_counter, item), the item's counter, and the item from the original iterable. By default, the counter matches each item's index, so the first item has a counter of 0. Notably, the enumerate function takes an optional argument, start, which allows you to set the number for the first item. In our case, we want to start the counting from 1, so we set start=1 in the enumerate function.

> **REMINDER** We also use tuple unpacking (section 4.4). Each item from the enumerate iterator is a tuple object. One-to-one unpacking creates two variables, task_i and task, to access the counter and the item simultaneously.

5.3.2 Reversing items with reversed

In this section, we start with the same iterable: the list object tasks from section 5.3.1. This time, we want to display the tasks in reverse order while keeping the original data for other purposes. When you see this need, you may think of getting the items from the last to the first one. This thought may lead you to the following solution:

```
for task_i in range(len(tasks)):
    task = tasks[-(task_i + 1)]
    print(f"Task: {task}")

# output the following lines:
Task: Task(title='Museum', description='Egypt exhibit', urgency=4)
Task: Task(title='Laundry', description='Wash clothes', urgency=3)
Task: Task(title='Homework', description='Physics and math', urgency=5)
```

This solution creates a range object by using the length of the tasks. One special thing about this solution involves using negative indexing (section 4.2) to retrieve the items in the reverse order of the original list object. Because negative indexing starts with –1 for the last item, we must add 1 to task_i before we negate the index. As you can tell, figuring out how to create the desired negative indexes from positive indexes isn't straightforward. In this use case, a Pythonic solution takes advantage of the reversed function, as follows:

```
for task in reversed(tasks):
    print(f"Task: {task}")
```

The reversed function takes a sequence data object and returns a reversed object. Notably, the reversed object is an iterator that renders the items in the reverse order of the original `list` object. Compared with the non-Pythonic solution, the solution doesn't need to deal with any indexes. Instead, we use `task` to directly access the items that are rendered by the `reversed` iterator. Such direct access without any index conversion is clean and readable.

5.3.3 *Aligning iterables with zip*

When we have multiple iterables to hold separate pieces of information for the same objects, we want to perform operations that require information from all the iterables. In this case, we need to join these iterables in some way. In this section, you'll learn about joining iterables with the `zip` function.

The description of this use case may be confusing. I'll elaborate it by providing a concrete example. Besides the `list` object `tasks`, our application has two `list` objects—dates, when the tasks are due, and `locations`, where the tasks should be carried out:

```
dates = ["May 5, 2022", "May 9, 2022", "May 11, 2022"]

locations = ["School", "Home", "Downtown"]
```

We want to display the following information to the users: each task's title, its due date, and the task's location. When you see this need, you may think that these iterables contain different aspects of the same items. You may observe that the consistent element across these iterables is that the information at a given index pertains to the same task. Thus, you may come up with the following solution:

```
for task_i in range(len(tasks)):
    task = tasks[task_i]
    date = dates[task_i]
    location = locations[task_i]
    print(f"{task.title}: by {date} at {location}")

# output the following lines:
Homework: by May 5, 2022 at School
Laundry: by May 9, 2022 at Home
Museum: by May 11, 2022 at Downtown
```

Because we know that the indexes are the consistent elements that allow us to refer to the same tasks across these iterables, we create a range object to obtain the indexes. If you recall, however, section 5.1.3 discusses how to use `zip` to join two iterables in creating a `dict` object. As mentioned there, a `zip` object is an iterator that renders `tuple` objects aggregated from aligned iterables. Here's a solution that uses the `zip` function:

```
for task, date, location in zip(tasks, dates, locations):
    print(f"{task.title}: by {date} at {location}")
```

The `zip` function takes multiple iterables (in our case, three) and aligns them side by side. As an iterator, the created `zip` object from this function call renders a `tuple` object consisting of three items that the iterables contribute. Notably, as with the enumerate object, you use one-to-one tuple unpacking to create the task, date, and location at the same time, which significantly improves your code's conciseness and readability. (You'll get used to this feature and find it to be rather readable.)

It's also possible that the related iterables will have different numbers of items. By default, the zip function stops zipping after the iterable with the fewest items is exhausted. But if you want zipping to match the iterable with the most items, you may want to use the zip_longest function, which is available in the itertools module (see the following sidebar).

Zipping iterables of different numbers of items

To show you how zip works, I've used only iterables of the same length. What would happen if the iterables had different numbers of items?

By default, the zip function stops zipping when the iterable with the fewest items is exhausted. If you run zip(range(3), range(4)), for example, you only get three tuple objects. Sometimes, we want to ensure that the iterables have the same numbers of items. To enforce such congruency, Python 3.10 introduced the optional parameter strict, which specifies that there are equal numbers of items when it's set to True. Please note that strict is set to False by default, so previous uses of the zip function still work. Publishing a new software version without affecting the code created using the old version is called *backward compatibility*.

For some use cases, we want to zip until the iterable with the most items is exhausted. In these cases, we should consider using the zip_longest function, which exists in the itertools module in the standard Python library. The following code snippet shows its use. As you can see, when shorter iterables are exhausted, Python uses None as fillers to zip with the remaining items of longer iterables:

```
>>> from itertools import zip_longest
>>> list(zip_longest(range(3), range(4), range(5)))
[(0, 0, 0), (1, 1, 1), (2, 2, 2), (None, 3, 3), (None, None, 4)]
```

5.3.4   Chaining multiple iterables with chain

In the zip function, iterables are aligned side by side before their respective items are zipped. But you may have multiple iterables that you want to join in such a way that you can retrieve their items sequentially. That is, you want to use the iterables consecutively instead of simultaneously. In this section, you'll explore this feature, which is known as *chaining of the iterables*. Suppose that in addition to the list object tasks, you have a list object that saves the tasks you just completed:

```
completed_tasks = [
    Task("Toaster", "Clean the toaster", 2),
    Task("Camera", "Export photos", 4),
    Task("Floor", "Mop the floor", 3)
]
```

The use case is that you want to show all the titles for the completed and pending tasks. When you see this use case, you might create a `list` object that joins `tasks` and `completed_tasks`, resulting in the following solution:

```
all_tasks = tasks + completed_tasks
for task in all_tasks:
    print(task.title)

# output the following lines:
Homework
Laundry
Museum
Toaster
Camera
Floor
```

This solution works, but it involves creating an intermediate `list` object. Although the problem usually doesn't arise when the `list` object isn't big, memory use can be concerning if you must deal with multiple large `list` objects. Thus, a more Pythonic solution involves the use of the `chain` function:

```
from itertools import chain

for task in chain(tasks, completed_tasks):
    print(task.title)
```

Like the `zip_longest` function, the `chain` function is available in the `itertools` module. `chain` takes multiple iterables to create an iterator that aggregates all the items from these iterables. Thus, both `zip` and `chain` can take multiple iterables and join them in different ways. Figure 5.4 shows the differences.

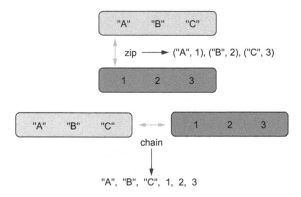

Figure 5.4 **Both `zip` and `chain` take multiple iterables. The `zip` function joins the iterables side by side at each index, and the `chain` function joins the iterables sequentially. The `zip` iterator renders tuple objects with their elements coming from each of the iterables. The `chain` iterator renders the elements sequentially from each of the iterables. The figure uses two iterables as an example, and both functions can take more than two iterables.**

In other words, the iteration of multiple iterables is processed through the `chain` iterator, which doesn't add memory overhead imposed by creating an intermediate `list` object in the non-Pythonic solution.

5.3.5   *Filtering the iterable with filter*

An iterable consists of multiple items. In some cases, however, we want to work with a subset of the items that satisfies our needs. In this section, you'll learn about filtering an iterable with the filter function.

Suppose that we want to display the information of the tasks whose urgency level should be greater than 3. As shown in the comprehension techniques (section 5.2.4), we can apply a filtering condition in a for loop:

```
for task in tasks:
    if task.urgency > 3:
        print(task)

# output the following lines:
Task(title='Homework', description='Physics and math', urgency=5)
Task(title='Museum', description='Egypt exhibit', urgency=4)
```

I should say that this solution is perfectly fine, and I'm happy if you came up with it. But a slightly better way, Pythonic or not (you decide; see section 5.3.6), is using the filter function:

```
for task in filter(lambda x: x.urgency > 3, tasks):
    print(task)
```

The filter function takes a function that is applied to the items of the iterable. Each item is evaluated by the function: if True, the item is kept, and if False, the item is excluded. In our example, we use a lambda function, and x refers to an item from the iterable. Although we saw lambda functions when we discussed sorting lists in section 3.2, they are discussed in detail in section 7.1. For now, you can think of lambda as a regular function that returns a value from the expression—in our case, whether the task's urgency level is greater than 3.

5.3.6   *Discussion*

When you use reversed, you create an iterator that has the same items as the iterable but in reverse order. You shouldn't confuse reversed with the reverse method, which reverses a list object in place. The in-place change implies that this method changes the original list object and returns None. Thus, the following code won't run! The same distinction applies to sorted and sort. The former creates a sorted list object and is compatible with a for loop. The latter returns None and is incompatible with a for loop:

```
tasks = ["task1", "task2", "task3"]
for task in tasks.reverse():
    pass
```

Starting in Python 3.10, zip has an optional strict parameter. Setting strict to True requires the length of the iterables to be the same; otherwise, zip stops when the iterable with the fewest items is exhausted. As you'll see in section 6.1, setting a default value to a parameter allows users to omit the argument during the function call. The most significant implication is that in an old codebase, any call of the zip function, such as zip(list0, list1), still works even if you update your Python to version 3.10. The function will be interpreted as zip(list0, list1, strict=False), which doesn't require the iterables to have the same number of elements, as the old zip function before Python 3.10 did. This brilliant design supports backward compatibility.

> **MAINTAINABILITY**   When you introduce new features to an existing codebase, it's best to have backward compatibility so you don't need to go back to fix code that uses the old features.

For more advanced iteration tools, look at the itertools module, which provides a variety of iteration-related functionalities that you can explore—more than zip_ longest and chain. The range object, for example, is an iterable that renders integers but not decimals. Notably, itertools has a function count that creates an iterator to render evenly spaced values, including decimal values.

For the filter function, some people prefer filter as a Pythonic implementation. But I don't find using the filter function to be a significant improvement on using an if statement. To me, using an if statement is more explicit, as it makes the critical logical operation (the condition evaluation) stand out as a separate line of code. It's up to you whether to use filter or an if statement.

5.3.7 *Challenge*

In section 3.4, you learned that you can use keys(), values(), and items() to access a dictionary's keys, values, or key-value pairs. Do you know whether they'll all be iterables? If you need to iterate the key-value pairs, what's the best way?

> **HINT**   The items function returns key-value pairs as tuple objects, and you can use tuple unpacking to retrieve the key and value from each tuple object.

5.4   *Using optional statements within for and while loops*

So far, I've discussed how for loops help you do repeated work by going over iterables. Besides for loops, we often use another important control flow, while loops, to perform repetitive work. If you aren't familiar with the while loop, see the following example. In essence, you specify a condition after the while keyword, and the code evaluates the condition in every iteration. When the condition is True, the code in the body executes; in the example, it runs when n is 1 and 2. When the condition is False, the while loop is exited; in the example, n becomes 3 after the while loop completes:

```
n = 1
while n < 3:
    print(f"n's value: {n}")
    n += 1
```

```
print(f"n's value after while loop: {n}")

# output the following lines:
n's value: 1
n's value: 2
n's value after while loop: 3
```

These control flows execute the code within the body during the iteration. But you don't always want to complete the iterations for all the elements. Suppose that we have a list of tasks to complete for the week, as shown in the next listing, and we want to prioritize the urgent tasks, so we need to find the first task that has an urgency level of 5.

Listing 5.6   Finding the urgent task by creating a list

```
from collections import namedtuple

Task = namedtuple("Task", "title, description, urgency")    ◁──┐ Task is a class
                                                               │ created by using
tasks = [                                                      │ named tuples.
    Task("Toaster", "Clean the toaster", 2),
    Task("Camera", "Export photos", 4),
    Task("Homework", "Physics and math", 5),
    Task("Floor", "Mop the floor", 3),
    Task("Internet", "Upgrade plan", 5),
    Task("Laundry", "Wash clothes", 3),
    Task("Museum", "Egypt exhibit", 4),
    Task("Utility", "Pay bills", 5)
]
```

If we try to address this need with a for loop, we might come up with the following solution:

```
first_urgent_task0 = None
for counter, task in enumerate(tasks, 1):
    print(f"---checking task {counter}: {task.title}")
    if (task.urgency == 5) and (first_urgent_task0 is None):    ◁──┐ Sets the value
        first_urgent_task0 = task                                  │ when the task is
                                                                   │ urgent and the
print(f"***first urgent task: {first_urgent_task0}")              │ first_urgent_task0
                                                                   │ is not set
# output the following lines:
---checking task 1: Toaster
---checking task 2: Camera
---checking task 3: Homework
---checking task 4: Floor
---checking task 5: Internet
---checking task 6: Laundry
---checking task 7: Museum
---checking task 8: Utility
***first urgent task: Task("Homework", "Physics and math", 5)
```

REMINDER   The enumerate function creates a counter for the iterable.

As you can see, the for loop iterates over the entire list object before it completes the needed job. If you eyeball the list, you'll notice that the task you're looking for is at the beginning; it's highly inefficient if you have to wait for the iteration to complete after the list object is exhausted in the for loop. Why not exit the for loop after the needed task is found? Fortunately, it's possible to change the default iteration behaviors with two optional statements: break and continue. Besides these two statements, Python has a unique feature that allows you to use an else statement with the for and while loops.

In this section, I review how these statements work. More importantly, I use practical examples to show you how these statements improve the readability and efficiency of your for and while loops.

5.4.1   *Exiting the loops with the break statement*

The preceding use case requires a mechanism to exit the for loop before iterating over the entire iterable. We achieve this feature with a break statement, which stops the iteration and makes execution exit the loop immediately. In this section, you'll learn how to use the break statement. To begin, quickly review a simple example to establish a basic understanding of how break works from a technical perspective:

```
for number in range(5):
    print(f"Number: {number}")
    if number == 2:
        print("Breaking at 2")
        break

# output the following lines:
Number: 0
Number: 1
Number: 2
Breaking at 2
```

You can see that the for loop stops running when number is 2, which reflects what break does, exiting the for loop immediately. In case you're wondering, the break statement works the same way in a while loop:

```
number = 0
while number < 100:
    if number == 2:
        print("Breaking at 2")
        break
    else:
        number += 1
        print(f"Number: {number}")

# output the following lines:
Number: 1
Number: 2
Breaking at 2
```

Putting these two examples together, you should observe the general use pattern: we place the break statement within an if statement to check a specific condition. During the iteration, the condition's evaluation may change, and when it evaluates to True, the break statement executes in such a way that the loop terminates instantly. I've used for loops on various occasions. To give you a different taste, figure 5.5 depicts how break works in a while loop.

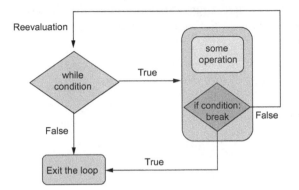

Figure 5.5 How the break statement works in a while loop. The condition in the while loop's head is evaluated in every iteration. When it's True, the execution moves to the body of the while loop. At a certain point, we place an if statement, within which we use break. When this condition evaluates to True, the break statement executes and ends the while loop. If the condition is False, it goes back to the while loop's head and evaluates the condition again to determine whether the while loop ends or continues.

Now that you know how break works, the next step is solving the practical use case introduced earlier. Because you need to find only the first urgent task, retrieving all urgent tasks takes longer because the entire list is iterating. A better solution uses the break statement, as shown in the next listing.

Listing 5.7 Finding the urgent task by using break

```
first_urgent_task1 = None       ⟵──── Sets an initial value

for task in tasks:
    if task.urgency == 5:
        first_urgent_task1 = task
        break

assert first_urgent_task0 == first_urgent_task1
```

As shown in listing 5.7, the for loop iterates the tasks and checks the urgency level for each task. When it finds an urgent task, the iteration ends immediately because we've obtained the needed information; any additional operation wastes time.

> **MAINTAINABILITY** You want to give first_urgent_task1 an initial value, which I set to None. If you don't set an initial value, the only place where first_urgent_task1 is set is within the body of the if statement. Chances are that there are no urgent tasks, in which case first_urgent_task1 is never set. Trying to access a variable that is never set crashes your application.

5.4.2   *Skipping an iteration with the continue statement*

When we work with an iterable, we may need to apply operations only to some elements that meet specific criteria. You've learned that you can filter the iterable (section 5.3.5). But you can also skip the operations for the elements that don't meet the criteria, which can be more readable. In this section, you'll learn how to use `continue` to skip the iterations of specific elements.

Like `break`, the `continue` statement changes the default iteration behavior by skipping the current iteration and moving to the next one. Here's a simple `for` loop that shows the action of `continue`:

```
for number in range(5):
    if number < 3:
        continue
    print(f"Number: {number}")

# output the following lines:
Number: 3
Number: 4
```

For each of the first three iterations with 0, 1, and 2, the `if` condition evaluates to `True`; the `continue` statement gets executed, the code moves to the next iteration, and we don't get any printout. Until the `number` becomes 3, the `continue` statement doesn't run, so the iteration proceeds to the `print` function call. Figure 5.6 shows how `continue` works in general.

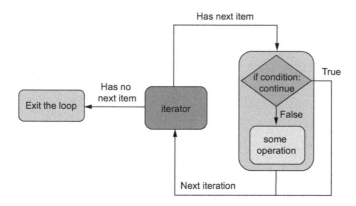

Figure 5.6   How the `continue` statement works in a `for` loop. When the iterator renders an item, the code in the body of the `for` loop executes. In the body, the condition in the `if` statement is evaluated. When the condition is `True`, the continue statement runs and skips to the next iteration. When it's `False`, the execution in the body of the `for` loop moves to some other operations until execution moves to the next iteration. The iteration stops when the iterator exhausts its items and the `for` loop ends.

Consider a more practical example. Suppose that we need to apply a series of functionalities to those urgent tasks. Without using the `continue` statement, we may have the following implementation for an illustration. Please note that the code in the next listing won't run, as we don't define the do_something methods.

Listing 5.8   Applying multiple operations for items when a condition is met

```
for task in tasks:
    if task.urgency > 4:
        result0 = task.do_something0()
        result1 = task.do_something1()
        if (result0 >= 0) and (result1 == "Hello"):
            task.do_something2()
            task.do_something3()
            task.do_something4()
```

In the example, we apply the functions only to urgent tasks. In other words, we don't need to apply any functions to the tasks that have an urgency level equal to or less than 4. Thus, in this kind of situation, you can consider using continue as an alternative implementation, as the following listing shows.

Listing 5.9   Skipping an iteration when a condition is met

```
for task in tasks:
    if task.urgency <= 4:
        continue
    result0 = task.do_something0()
    result1 = task.do_something1()
    if (result0 < 0) or (result1 != "Hello"):
        continue
    task.do_something2()
    task.do_something3()
    task.do_something4()
```

If you compare the implementations in listings 5.8 and 5.9, you'll find that the major difference is using the opposite evaluation conditions in two places. You may wonder what differences these two implementations make. From a performance perspective, they don't make a difference, but their readability may be different. When you have a series of operations to apply to items that meet a criterion, it's usually more readable to use the complementary evaluation criterion together with the continue statement (figure 5.7).

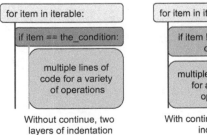
Without continue, two layers of indentation

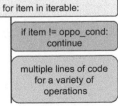
With continue, one layer of indentation

Figure 5.7   Reducing indentation layers with the continue statement. Without continue, the for loop needs two layers of indentation. By contrast, the same for loop needs one layer of indentation when an opposite evaluation condition is used.

As shown in figure 5.7, with `continue`, we reduce the needed level of indentations. Thus, our code has better readability because we removed the deeply nested code. Compare listings 5.7 and 5.8.

5.4.3 Using else statements in the for and while loops

We know that we can use an `else` statement together with an `if` statement. In essence, the `if...else...` statement creates a logical branch by examining a condition. When the condition is evaluated to be true, the operations within the `if` statement execute; otherwise, the operations within the `else` statement execute. Notably, the operations of these two statements are mutually exclusive, meaning that only one of them can run.

In most programming languages, the `else` statement exists only in the `if...else...` statement. Python is unusual in this regard; it allows us to use the `else` statement in `for` and `while` loops. Note that adding an `else` statement to a `for` or `while` loop isn't common practice, and it can confuse many Python programmers, particularly beginners. Although you want to use the `else` statement in a `for` or `while` loop with caution, it's helpful to know and use these features in the desired use scenarios. In this section, you'll explore these use scenarios.

USING ELSE IN A FOR LOOP

When you append an `else` statement to a `for` loop, it forms the following structure:

```
for item in iterable:
    # some operations
else:
    # some other operations
```

Unlike the mutual exclusiveness of execution between `if` and `else` in the `if...else...` statement, the `else` statement doesn't form the opposite branch against the for-loop part (or the iteration part). The execution rule is that the `else` statement runs only one time after completing the iteration, but it's skipped if the iteration is terminated because of the `break` statement. The code in the next listing shows the rule.

Listing 5.10 How the `for...else` statement works

```
def show_for_else_rule(breaking_number):
    for number in range(2):
        print(f"Iteration: {number}")
        if number == breaking_number:
            print(f"Break: {number}; Skip the else statement")
            break
    else:
        print("Running the else statement")
    print("Outside the for...else...")

show_for_else_rule(1)
# output the following lines
Iteration: 0
Iteration: 1
```

```
Break: 1; Skip the else statement
Outside the for...else...

show_for_else_rule(3)
# output the following lines
Iteration: 0
Iteration: 1
Running the else statement
Outside the for...else...
```

As you can see, the factor that determines whether the else statement is skipped is whether the break statement executes. In short: run break -> skip else and no break -> run else. Thus, if the iteration involves no break statements, don't append the else statement because it executes anyway. In other words, a valid use case of the for...else... statement is that you need to include a break statement in the iteration part.

Consider a practical use case. Suppose that we have a list of tasks, and we want to locate the first task with the desired urgency level. We may have a solution that uses a for...else... statement, as shown in the following listing.

Listing 5.11 A practical example of the for...else statement

```
def locate_task(urgency_level):
    for task in tasks:
        if task.urgency == urgency_level:
            working_task = task
            break
    else:
        working_task = None
    print(f"Working Task: {working_task}")

locate_task(1)
# output: Working Task: None

locate_task(4)
# output: Working Task: Task(title='Camera',
  description='Export photos', urgency=4)
```

In listing 5.11, we see that when the iteration finds a task with the desired urgency level, it exits the loop in such a way that the else statement is skipped. When all the iterations complete without triggering the break statement, however, such as when the desired urgency level is 1, the else statement is executed, and we get the printout of None for the task.

USING ELSE IN A WHILE LOOP
When you append an else statement to a while loop, it forms the following structure:

```
while the_condition:
    # some operations
else:
    # some other operations
```

Like the for...else... statement, the while...else... statement has the same execution rule: run break -> skip else and no break -> run else. Figure 5.8 shows the rule for for and while loops.

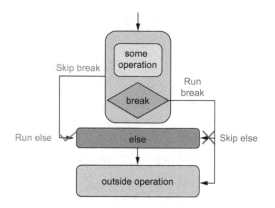

Figure 5.8   How else works in for and while loops. In the iteration loop, if a break statement runs, the iteration ends immediately, and the else statement is skipped. If the loop ends normally without running the break statement, the else statement is executed.

As a practical example, suppose that we want to rest while we complete a series of tasks in each session. To make our work effective in a session, we set a resting threshold as the sum of the total urgency level for the completed tasks. The next listing shows a possible implementation using the while...else... statement.

Listing 5.12   A practical example of the while...else statement

```python
def complete_tasks_with_break(resting_threshold):
    completed_urgency_levels = 0
    while tasks:
        if completed_urgency_levels > resting_threshold:
            print("Coffee break now!")
            break
        next_task = tasks.pop()
        print(f"Completed: {next_task}")
        completed_urgency_levels += next_task.urgency
    else:
        print("Party! Completed all the tasks.")

tasks = [
    Task("Toaster", "Clean the toaster", 2),
    Task("Camera", "Export photos", 4),
    Task("Homework", "Physics and math", 5),
    Task("Floor", "Mop the floor", 3),
    Task("Internet", "Upgrade plan", 5)
]

complete_tasks_with_break(7)
# output the following lines:
Completed: Task(title='Internet', description='Upgrade plan', urgency=5)
Completed: Task(title='Floor', description='Mop the floor', urgency=3)
Coffee break now!
```

A list evaluates to True if it is nonempty.

pop removes and returns the last item from a list object.

```
complete_tasks_with_break(6)
# output the following lines:
Completed: Task(title='Homework', description='Physics and math', urgency=5)
Completed: Task(title='Camera', description='Export photos', urgency=4)
Coffee break now!

complete_tasks_with_break(5)
# output the following lines:
Completed: Task(title='Toaster', description='Clean the toaster', urgency=2)
Party! Completed all the tasks.
```

> **READABILITY** When you examine the emptiness of a data container or a sequence object, such as str, list, or dict, it's preferred that you use the object itself, such as if tasks and while tasks. In these cases, if the tasks has any items, it's evaluated to be True. By contrast, a non-Pythonic or less-readable approach involves examining the length of these objects, such as if len(tasks) > 0.

The first two calls on the complete_tasks_with_break function involve running the break statement so that the else statement is skipped. By contrast, the third call completes the iterations without running the break statement so that the else statement runs.

5.4.4 Discussion

You should be clear about when to use for and when to use while for iterations. Use for loops when you have an iterable to begin with and the number of iterations depends on the number of items that the iterable can render. By contrast, use while loops when you're not sure how many iterations you will run, as the while loop consistently checks against a specific criterion to determine when to end.

Avoid using else with for and while loops because this practice is unfamiliar to most people and thus confuses many programmers. I don't recommend using this feature in your codebase. I showed you the technique only in case you see other programmers use it.

> **MAINTAINABILITY** Avoid using else with for and while loops, which can be confusing.

5.4.5 Challenge

Listing 5.7 set an initial value of None to the first_urgent_task1 variable. As mentioned, setting this initial value is important because there's no guarantee that an urgent task can be found if you deal with a different set of tasks. Suppose that you don't set an initial value and use a list of tasks that doesn't contain any urgent task. See what happens if you try to access the first_urgent_task1 variable.

> **HINT** If a variable hasn't been assigned, Python has no way to figure out what you mean by that variable.

Summary

- Iterables can be converted to iterators by means of the `iter` function. The iterators are data objects that can render their elements one by one by using the `next` function.

- Common data containers such as `list`, `dict`, `set`, and `tuple` can take iterables to create their respective instance objects using their respective constructors. Thus, whenever you have iterables of any type, if you need to create data containers from the existing iterables, think about using these constructors first.

- List, dictionary, and set comprehensions are concise ways to create `list`, `dict`, and `set` objects, respectively. They eliminate the need to use a regular `for` loop for instantiation. If you don't manipulate the items, however, it's likely that you can use the constructor directly for instantiation.

- We use `for` loops to perform iterations on iterables, and they constitute an essential way of applying the same operations to a group of items stored in an iterable. To make `for` loops more effective, you need to remember the advanced approaches to manipulating existing iterables, such as `enumerate`, `reversed`, `zip`, `chain`, and `filter`. Among these functions, `chain` is part of the `itertools` module, which has additional advanced operations with iterations.

- Both `for` and `while` loops can include three optional statements: `break`, `continue`, and `else`. `break` exits the loop instantly, `continue` skips the current iteration, and `else` runs when there is no `break` in the iteration loop. You need to know the proper use cases for these statements.

Part 2

Defining functions

In part 1, we learned about using built-in data models to represent real-life problems in our application. Converting real-life problems to proper abstract data models, however, is only the first step in building our application. This data is like raw material, and we must use appropriate equipment to process this raw material, following a specific protocol to make the desired product. In our application, the functions serve as the equipment, and the algorithms of the functions define the protocol. As you can imagine, we can't process any raw material (the data) if we don't have the necessary equipment and protocol (the functions and their implementation details). In this part, you'll learn various techniques for writing functions—the driving forces behind any application's data flow.

Defining
user-friendly functions

This chapter covers

- Setting proper default arguments for a function
- Setting and using the return value for a function
- Applying type hints to the parameters and the return value
- Defining functions with a variable number of positional and keyword arguments
- Creating proper docstrings for a function

In previous chapters, you've seen several examples of functions. Broadly speaking, no matter what our applications are about, we define a wide range of functions to perform various operations, such as making calculations and formatting strings. When you work in a team environment, you often need to define functions that allow your team members to reuse your code. When you publish a Python package, the package should include well-defined functions for users like the built-in functions provided by the standard Python library. Thus, it's an essential skill to define user-friendly functions; even if you work on your own, you don't want functions to be hard to use.

When I say *user-friendly functions,* I mean functions that are easy to understand, with proper type hints for the arguments, and that are convenient to call, possibly using default arguments. For functions that are self-explanatory, users can locate the needed help information, usually in the form of docstrings.

In this chapter, you'll learn the key techniques underlying user-friendly functions. When we build our own task management app in chapter 14, you'll see the usage of all these techniques, highlighting the importance of functions in any project.

6.1 How do I set default arguments to make function calls easier?

Depending on the specific requirements, functions may take zero to multiple arguments. For functions, it's easier to call those with fewer arguments; ideally, a function is easiest to call if it doesn't require any arguments. When a function has multiple arguments, we can reduce the number of arguments needed for function calls by setting default arguments.

The biggest advantage of setting default arguments in a function is *convenience.* We don't need to set parameters when the default arguments are exactly what we need. Moreover, the function needs *flexibility* so we can still override the default values by setting the applicable arguments. In this section, you'll learn about setting default arguments.

6.1.1 Calling functions with default arguments

Setting default arguments in functions is a common technique for making function calls easier and is prevalent in the standard Python library. In this section, let's take a quick look at some use cases to gain firsthand experience with the convenience of calling functions with default arguments.

Although we didn't explicitly discuss default arguments in previous chapters, we have taken advantage of this feature several times. Section 3.2, for example, discusses how to use the sort method on list objects, as in the following code snippet:

```
numbers = [4, 5, 7, 2]

numbers.sort()

assert numbers == [2, 4, 5, 7]
```

When we want to sort the numbers list in descending order, we call the sort method by setting the reverse parameter:

```
numbers.sort(reverse=True)

assert numbers == [7, 5, 4, 2]
```

Let's examine the head of the sort method: sort(*, key=None, reverse=False). You'll notice that the parameters key and reverse have default values: None and False. The default values for these parameters are often known as *default arguments*.

> **TRIVIA** The asterisk in the sort method dictates that all the arguments following the asterisk should be set with their parameter names, such as numbers .sort(reverse=True). By contrast, numbers.sort(True) is an invalid call. This technique is known as *setting keyword-only arguments*. See section 6.4.1 for more about it.

When Python's core developers defined the sort method, they knew that when we sort a list object, in most cases we use the lexicographic or numeric order, and we want the items in ascending order so that they supply None and False as the default arguments to the key and reverse parameters. When we use sort on a list object, we typically use the_list.sort(), which is interpreted as the_list.sort(key=None, reverse=False) because of the default arguments that are set in the function definition.

6.1.2 *Defining functions with default arguments*

Functions with default arguments are not only easy to call, but also flexible, supporting multiple use scenarios. In this section, you'll study the general process of defining functions with default arguments.

When we initially define a function, it usually serves one specific purpose by taking one or multiple arguments. Suppose that in our task management app, we update the task's status when the user completes a task. We can have the following function: complete_task. Note that this function should have been defined as an instance method (section 8.2). Here, I'm defining it outside the Task class for the purpose of calling it conveniently:

```
                          Defines a custom class
class Task:          ⟵
    def __init__(self, title, description, urgency):
        self.title = title
        self.description = description
        self.urgency = urgency


def complete_task(task):
    task.status = "completed"
    print(f"{task.title}'s status: completed")


task = Task("Homework", "Physics and math", 5)
complete_task(task)
# output: Homework's status: completed
```

> **PEEK** We use a custom class instead of a named tuple-based data model here. A custom class gives us the flexibility of changing the instance object's attributes, which we can't do with a named tuple model (section 3.3). Defining custom classes is covered in chapter 8.

When the user completes the task, we update its status to "completed," which is one thing the function does. Later, we realize that we may want the user to add a completion note for the task—that is, we need to expand the function's functionality. With this added functionality, our function has evolved to the following version:

```
def complete_task(task, note):
    task.status = "completed"
    task.note = note
    print(f"{task.title}'s status: completed; note: {note}")
```

After updating this function, we're happy about our decision, but we recognize two problems. First, we need to update our old code where we call `complete_task(task)`, as it's missing an argument. Second, in most other places, we need to update the status without worrying about setting any note, as follows:

```
# Use case 1
complete_task(task1, "")

# Use case 2
complete_task(task2, "")

# Use case 3
complete_task(task3, "")
```

As you can see, we're using the function in a pattern that sends an empty string as the note, which may remind you of the DRY (Don't Repeat Yourself) principle: when you repeat something, chances are that you should refactor your code. In this case, we mostly set the note to be an empty string, which is a perfect usage for setting default arguments in function definitions, handling automatic argument setting for most use cases:

```
def complete_task(task, note=""):
    task.status = "completed"
    task.note = note
    print(f"{task.title}'s status: completed; note: {note}")
```

With the updated function, when we don't need to set the note, we can simply run

```
complete_task(task)
```

Besides the convenience of omitting an argument, the most important thing is that updating the function doesn't break any old code that calls the same function with only the `task` argument. Because of the default argument in the updated function definition, this function call in your old code `complete_task(task)` is automatically interpreted as `complete_task(task, "")`.

> **MAINTAINABILITY**   When you update your functions, it's best to keep the same calling signature so that existing code will still work without any update.

To provide a systematic overview, figure 6.1 shows the general process of evolving a function with a single functionality to one with multiple functionalities by using default arguments. In the figure, we define two roles: application programming interface (API) developer, who defines the function, and API consumer, who uses the function in building the application. Certainly, depending on the size of a team, these roles can be handled by different people. On smaller projects, however, it's likely that the same person will play both roles.

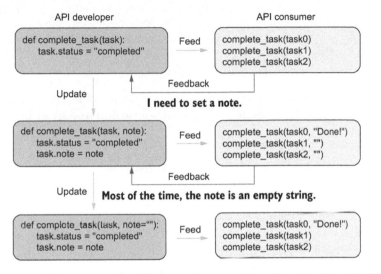

Figure 6.1 An example of the general process of creating a function with default arguments. When API developers receive feedback from the consumers, they add the needed parameter so that consumers can set the note. Later, consumers realize that it's tedious to set an empty string to the note and ask the developer to change the API. The developer uses the default-arguments feature to update the API, eliminating the need to set the `note` parameter when the empty string is the desired argument.

From the consumer's perspective, calling a function with default arguments allows them to omit setting the arguments, which automatically default to the preset values. From the developer's perspective, when you simplify the calling of the defined function, consumers are less likely to make mistakes because of the reduced number of parameters. Thus, you're improving consumers' experience in two aspects:

- *You're providing an additional feature to the existing function.* The function is more flexible with multiple functionalities.
- *You're making sure that the existing code that uses the old calling signature still works.* The missing argument will be interpreted with the default value.

6.1.3 *Avoiding the pitfall of setting default arguments for mutable parameters*

In section 6.1.2, you learned the rationale for setting default arguments and the evolving process of a function that uses default arguments. Our examples involved setting a default argument of the `str` type. As discussed in chapter 3, strings are immutable.

Another category of data models is the mutable ones, such as lists and dictionaries. In this section, you'll learn about setting the correct default arguments for mutable parameters.

What's the correct term: Arguments or parameters?

The terms *arguments* and *parameters* appear to be used interchangeably to refer to the variables used in a function. A minor nuance exists, however. When we define functions, we refer to the variables specified in the function head as *parameters*. When we call functions, we refer to the variables we use as *arguments*. In other words, parameters are the variables used in a function's definition. By contrast, arguments are the variables used in a function's invocation.

Suppose that when we complete a task, we can optionally add the task to a group of tasks that we track. We may have the following working version to start with:

```python
def complete_task(task, grouped_tasks=[]):
    task.status = "completed"
    grouped_tasks.append(task.title)    ◁──── Use the titles only
    return grouped_tasks                       for simplicity.
```

We set an empty list object to the grouped_tasks parameter as the default argument. Our intention is that if we call this function by omitting the grouped_tasks argument, an empty list object will be created. You can observe the result in the next listing.

Listing 6.1   Using functions with mutable default arguments

```python
task0 = Task("Homework", "Physics and math", 5)
task1 = Task("Fishing", "Fishing at the lake", 3)

work_tasks = complete_task(task0)
play_tasks = complete_task(task1)

print("Work Tasks:", work_tasks)
print("Play Tasks:", play_tasks)

# output the following lines:
Work Tasks: ['Homework', 'Fishing']
Play Tasks: ['Homework', 'Fishing']
```

As shown in listing 6.1, for each invocation of the complete_task function with the omission of grouped_tasks, we wanted to have a new list object that holds the completed task. Quite surprisingly, however, both list objects have the same items, although we were expecting work_tasks and play_tasks to be ['Homework'] and ['Fishing'], respectively. If you take a closer look at these two list objects, you'll find that they're the same object:

```
assert work_tasks == play_tasks
                                        ⎤ is compares whether two variables
assert work_tasks is play_tasks  ◄──────⎦ refer to the same object.
```

The underlying reason for this phenomenon is that Python evaluates the function when it's defined. The evaluation has a side effect: any mutable default arguments are created during evaluation and become part of the function. In our example, a list object is created when the function is evaluated. Now that specific list object is used as the grouped_tasks argument whenever the function is called without a grouped_tasks argument being provided, as the code in the next listing shows.

Listing 6.2   Using the same mutable object defined in the function

```
def append_task(task, tasks=[]):            ⎤ An id function returns the memory
    tasks.append(task)                      ⎥ address, which uniquely identifies
    print(f"Tasks: {tasks}; id: {id(tasks)}")  ◄──⎦ an object.

                                 ⎤ __defaults__ retrieves the default
append_task.__defaults__  ◄──────⎦ objects associated with the function.
# output: ([],)

id(append_task.__defaults__[0])
# output: 4356663616

append_task("Homework")
# output: Tasks: ['Homework']; id: 4356663616

append_task("Laundry")
# output: Tasks: ['Homework', 'Laundry']; id: 4356663616

append_task.__defaults__
# output: (['Homework', 'Laundry'],)
```

In listing 6.2, we use the built-in id function to check an object's memory address. When we work with the same object, the id function returns the same memory address. As you can see, when we call the function without specifying the tasks argument, we're getting the same object that is created from the function definition.

CPython and the id function

When you write Python code, the code gets executed on your computer (the machine). Notably, the Python code itself doesn't talk to your machine directly. Instead, the code must be compiled into bytecode before it can be executed. There are different implementations for compiling Python code. Among them, the most prevalent is CPython, which is the original Python implementation and the one you can download from Python's official website. Other implementations such as Jython compile Python code to Java bytecode.

> **(continued)**
> In CPython, the `id` function returns the memory address of the object at that moment. Thus, if you run the `id` function in the same code at different times or on different machines, you should expect the memory addresses to be different. In a related note, other Python implementations may use different identities for the `id` function.

If we can't use `[]` or `list()` as the default value for a `list` parameter, what can we use? Does this mean that we can't set a default value for a mutable parameter? The answer is no. The common practice is to use `None` as the default argument for mutable parameters. The next listing shows the desired pattern.

Listing 6.3   Using `None` as the default value for mutable parameters

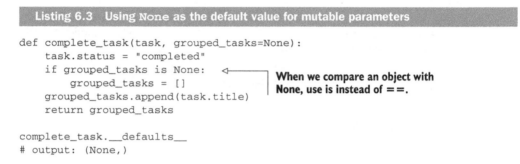

```
def complete_task(task, grouped_tasks=None):
    task.status = "completed"
    if grouped_tasks is None:           ◄──────┐ When we compare an object with
        grouped_tasks = []                      │ None, use is instead of ==.
    grouped_tasks.append(task.title)
    return grouped_tasks


complete_task.__defaults__
# output: (None,)
```

As you can see, the default argument for the function is `None`. In the function body, we check whether the `grouped_tasks` argument is `None`, and when it is true, we create a new `list` object. Every time we call this function with the omission of the `grouped_tasks` arguments, the function creates a new `list` object for us, which is the desired behavior.

> **MAINTAINABILITY**   When you set a default argument for a mutable parameter in a function, set it to `None`.

6.1.4   *Discussion*

Setting default arguments in function definitions is a widely used pattern in Python's standard library. Besides the `sort` method, many built-in functions, such as `sorted` and `print`, include default arguments. With default arguments, these functions are easy to call; they also maintain flexibility if we set different arguments. You should be mindful of the difference between mutable and immutable parameters. When you set a wrong default argument for a mutable parameter, you can introduce bugs into your codebase.

6.1.5   *Challenge*

Cory teaches Python coding in college. He wants to show his students that the default arguments are evaluated when a function is defined, not when the function is called. Can you help him think of another approach to support this claim?

HINT   Create a timestamp to check what happens during function definition and calls. The following code allows you to retrieve a timestamp:

```
from datetime import datetime
timestamp = datetime.today()
```

6.2   *How do I set and use the return value in function calls?*

We define functions to perform specific operations. To use these functions, we call them by sending the applicable arguments, which are a function's input. When the function completes its operation, it returns a value, which is a function's output. By now, you should know the importance of functions in your applications; thus, it's critical to have not only the skills to deal with the input (such as setting a default argument, covered in section 6.1), but also the skills to deal with the output. In this section, we'll focus on studying how to set the return value and how to use it.

6.2.1   *Returning a value implicitly or explicitly*

We have used many built-in and custom functions in our examples. Some functions return a value; others don't appear to return a value. In this section, I show that every Python function returns a value, although sometimes implicitly.

The built-in sum function calculates the summation value of an iterable. Not surprisingly, the returned value is the sum of the items of the iterable:

```
numbers = list(range(5))

sum_numbers = sum(numbers)

print(f"Sum of {numbers} is {sum_numbers}")
# output: Sum of [0, 1, 2, 3, 4] is 10
```

In section 3.2, we learned about using sort to order the items of a list object. Notably, the sort method sorts a list object in place, which means that sort changes the original list object. Relatedly, if you check sort's return value, you'll find that it is None:

```
primes = [5, 7, 2, 3, 11]

sort_return_value = primes.sort()

print(f"Return value of sort: {sort_return_value}")
# output: Return value of sort: None
```

Through these two examples, we should be aware that every function returns a value, and we should be clear about what a function returns: None or something else. Don't assume what a function returns because you can make silly mistakes when you try to chain method calls. The following problematic code is trying to sort the primes list and append 13 to the end:

```
primes.sort().append(13)
```

QUESTION   Do you know why this code won't run? Check what `sort` returns.

6.2.2   *Defining functions returning zero, one, or multiple values*

The best way to understand how functions return values is to define functions so that you have granular control of their behavior. In general, there are three scenarios in terms of how many values a function returns: zero, one, and multiple.

RETURNING ZERO VALUES

Strictly speaking, we can't define functions that return no values. As discussed in section 6.2.1, every function has a return value, implicitly or explicitly. When we define a function that doesn't return anything, it is still evaluated to return None. Consider the following example:

```
def append_task(task, grouped_tasks):
    grouped_tasks.append(task)

appended_no_return = append_task("Homework", [])

print(f"Appended: {appended_no_return}")
# output: Appended: None
```

As we can see, the function definition doesn't have a `return` statement. But when we check the return value, the `appended_no_return` value is None. This result is consistent with the discussion in section 6.2.1. Figure 6.2 shows a general pattern for defining a function without returning a variable explicitly.

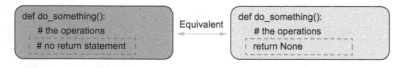

Figure 6.2   The implicit return of a function. When a function doesn't have a return statement, it's equivalent to a function that returns None.

QUESTION   What's the return value of a function when it has a bare return statement?

RETURNING ONE VALUE

Returning a value is the most common form for functions. As you should be aware, functions are defined to perform a specific operation. Typically, we expect to have one output value from an operation, as it eliminates ambiguity about the function's purpose. Thus, in most cases, you should aim for your functions to return only one value.

It's time for a quick review of the process of assigning a function's return value to a variable—the most common form of calling a function. Consider the following scenario:

```
def say_hello(person):
    hello = f"Hello, {person}!"
    return hello

greeting = say_hello("Rocky")
```

This code snippet shows a common use case: calling the function say_hello and assigning its return value to the variable greeting. Do you know exactly what's happening behind the scenes? If so, you can skip to the next section; otherwise, see figure 6.3.

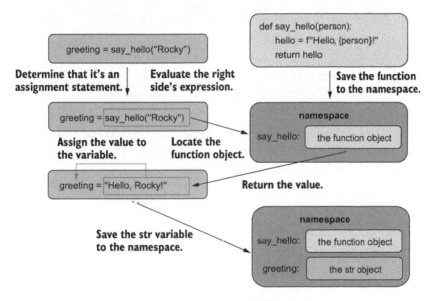

Figure 6.3 The process of creating a variable from a function call. When you define a function, the function is saved to the namespace. When you call the function, it looks up the namespace to locate the function and calls the function with the supplied arguments. When the function call is complete, the returned value is sent back and assigned to the variable. When the assignment is complete, the new variable is loaded into the same namespace so that it can be looked up for later use.

> **CONCEPT** A *namespace* is a collection of defined variables that you can look up and use. You can think of it as a dictionary object: the identifiers, such as a function's name, are the keys, and their corresponding objects are the values. Section 10.2 discusses namespaces in detail.

When you create a variable from a function call, you're using an assignment statement. An assignment statement evaluates the right side's expression; in our case, it's calling the function, which is looked up from the current namespace. After completing the operation defined in the function, execution returns the value and assigns it to the greeting variable.

RETURNING MULTIPLE VALUES

When your function performs complicated operations, these operations may generate two or more objects, and you'll need all objects for subsequent processing. In this case, you should consider returning all these objects as the function's output.

As you probably know, it's standard for scientists to report the mean and the standard deviation of all the measures in an experiment. Suppose that you're defining a function to help scientists complete this job. The next listing shows a possible solution.

Listing 6.4   Returning multiple values from a function

```python
from statistics import mean, stdev

def generate_stats(measures):
    measure_mean = mean(measures)
    measure_std = stdev(measures)
    return measure_mean, measure_std
```

The `generate_stats` function returns the mean and the standard deviation simultaneously, which simplifies your codebase. A non-Pythonic approach might use two separate functions if each function returns only one value:

```python
def calculate_mean(measures):
    measure_mean = mean(measures)
    return measure_mean

def calculate_std(measures):
    measure_std = stdev(measures)
    return measure_std
```

Notably, you don't always want to return multiple values. In listing 6.4, the values `measure_mean` and `measure_std` are closely related, and they constitute the statistical reports of these experimental measures; thus, the listing is a valid example of returning two values from a function.

By contrast, when you're trying to return two values that are unrelated, your function is likely to consist of mixed operations that serve separate purposes. The following code snippet is an example of a poorly defined function:

```python
def process_data(measures):
    formatted_measures = [f"{x} mg/L" for x in measures]
    measure_mean = mean(measures)
    return formatted_measures, measure_mean
```

As you can see, in the `process_data` function, the returned values aren't related. Thus, when some other people use this function, it's hard for them to figure out what's coming from this function call because the function serves two distinct purposes: formatting the measures and calculating the measures' mean. A more readable approach would define separate functions for each purpose. More important, these functions should be named in a way that clearly reflects their purposes:

```
def format_measures(measures):
    formatted_measures = [f"{x} mg/L" for x in measures]
    return formatted_measures

def calculate_mean(measures):
    measure_mean = mean(measures)
    return measure_mean
```

MAINTAINABILITY   Functions should serve single purposes. When you think that you're "refactoring" or "saving" lines of code by combining functions that serve different purposes, you're making the code harder to use and read, which can cause confusion for yourself and your teammates.

6.2.3   *Using multiple values returned from a function call*

When a function returns `None` or any other single value, using the return value is straightforward. But a function can return multiple values in some cases. In this section, we'll discuss how to use multiple values returned from a function call.

Although I've been saying that we can define a function that returns multiple values, in fact, we can return only one object in any function. Check the use of the `generate_stats` function that we defined in listing 6.4:

```
measures = [5.6, 7.0, 5.7, 5.8, 4.3, 5.2]

measures_stats = generate_stats(measures)

print(type(measures_stats), measures_stats)       ◁——  The type function checks
# output: <class 'tuple'> (5.6, 0.8786353054595518)      the data type of the object.
```

The returned value from calling `generate_stats` is a `tuple` object, although it appears that we're returning two values in the function definition. These two values are packed into a single `tuple` object. In other words, strictly speaking, when we appear to return multiple values in a function definition, we're returning a single variable that is a `tuple` object consisting of these values. Please note that as discussed regarding tuple unpacking (section 4.4), parentheses are optional for creating a `tuple` object.

You can apply the tuple unpacking technique to using the multiple values returned from a function, which is a concise, Pythonic way to access the individual items of the returned `tuple` object, as shown in the next listing.

Listing 6.5   Unpacking the return `tuple` object

```
m_mean, m_std = generate_stats(measures)

print(f"Mean: {m_mean}; SD: {m_std}")
# output: Mean: 5.6; SD: 0.8786353054595518
```

QUESTION   What should you do if you want to use only the mean from calling the `generate_stats` function?

6.2.4   *Discussion*

Your functions should serve a single purpose, so returning only one value is the preferred form of output. Although you can return as many values as you want from a function, it's not a good idea to return too many, because it is confusing for the function's users to figure out what each of the values stands for. As a rule of thumb, it's best to have your function return one value. In some cases, using two to four values is fine, but using five or more probably means that something is wrong with your function, such as serving multiple purposes.

6.2.5   *Challenge*

Zoe continues to work on her location-centered application (section 3.1.4). She defines multiple functions that return a place's latitude and longitude:

```
def locate_me():
    # look up the user's current location
    return latitude0, longitude0

def locate_home():
    # look up the user's home location
    return latitude1, longitude1

def locate_work():
    # look up the user's work location
    return latitude2, longitude2
```

When you see the pattern repetition of return values, you realize that she should refactor her code. What suggestion can you give her to make these functions return one value?

> **HINT**   Named tuples (section 3.3) are a lightweight data model that you can use to hold data.

6.3   *How do I use type hints to write understandable functions?*

When we define functions, Python doesn't require that we specify the types of the arguments and the return value. In most cases, our functions accept only specific data types. Consider this function from listing 6.4:

```
def generate_stats(measures):
    pass
```

If users don't know what kind of data types they need to use, they might call the function as follows:

```
generate_stats({"measure0": 7.9, "measure1": 6.8, "measure2": 7.0})
```

This function call doesn't work because the function assumes that the argument `measures` is a `list` or `tuple` object. Thus, to reduce the possibility that others will use our functions incorrectly, we should consider using type hints in our function definitions. Proper *type hints* tell users what kinds of arguments our functions take and what value our functions return, making our functions more understandable. In the next section, you'll learn how to write user-friendly functions with type hints.

6.3.1 *Providing type hinting to variables*

In chapters 1–5, you learned about common data models such as str, list, tuple, and dict. When we define a variable of a particular type, we create it without worrying about specifying the data type. But we can indicate the data type of the variable, which is the basis of applying type hints to functions. In this section, we'll review the essential skills for providing type hints to variables. Here's a simple example of creating an int variable:

```
number = 1

print(type(number))
# output: <class 'int'>
```

> **TRIVIA**   The built-in type function allows us to inspect an object's type.

As expected, the variable number has a data type of int. If we decide to assign this variable with a different value, such as a string, to number, we can do the following in Python:

```
number = "one"

print(type(number))
# output: <class 'str'>
```

In the code snippet, we assign a string literal to the variable number, which makes its data type str. In other words, we're working with the same variable, number, but its data type has been converted from int to str with a simple reassignment. Using programming terminology, we say that Python is *dynamically typed*—the type of variables can change after their creation.

By contrast, some other programming languages won't let you change the type of a variable after it's defined; these languages are *statically typed*. Swift, the recommended language for developing iPhone apps and other Apple-related systems, is a statically typed language. In Swift, we can't reassign a string value to a variable that is initially defined as an integer. When a variable has a specific type, you can't use a value of a different type for reassignment, as shown in the next listing.

Listing 6.6   An example of static typing in Swift

```
var number = 1

number = "one"
error: cannot assign value of type 'String' to type 'Int'
```

Even though Python is a dynamically typed language, we can provide type hints to the variables that we create in Python. This feature, known as *type hinting*, was added to Python 3.6. To provide a type hint, you use a semicolon after the variable name, after which you specify the type of the variable. Following are some examples:

```
number: int = 3

name: str = "John"

primes: list = [1, 2, 3]
```

It's important to know that type hinting doesn't make Python a statically typed language and that it doesn't enforce the typing of the variable. (If you're wondering about the point of using type hints, see the next section.) You can still assign a value of a different type to a variable that you create with type hinting and run the following two lines of code without problems:

```
numbers: tuple = (1, 2, 3)

numbers = [1, 2, 3]
```

6.3.2 *Using type hinting in function definitions*

In section 6.3.1, you learned to provide type hinting to individual variables. In this section, we'll apply this technique to a function definition to see the benefits of defining functions with type hints.

Using type hinting in a function definition is no different from using it to create variables except for one thing: providing hints to the return value. We'll use the example in the next listing (a modified version of the generate_stats function defined in listing 6.4) to see how type hinting with functions works.

Listing 6.7   Using type hints in a function

```
from statistics import mean, stdev

def generate_stats(measures: list) -> tuple:
    measure_mean = mean(measures)
    measure_std = stdev(measures)
    return measure_mean, measure_std
```

Adding type hints to a function's parameters is the same as creating variables, and both usages take the form param: data_type. Adding type hints to the return value is different because in the function head, we don't have an explicit variable for the return value. Instead, we use -> data_type to indicate the type for the return value. There are two major reasons to use type hints in the function definitions:

- *Type hints make it clear to users what parameters the function takes and what it returns.* If you call help(generate_stats), for example, you'll be able to see the function's signature and use it correctly:

```
>>> help(generate_stats)
Help on function generatate_stats in module __main__:

generate_stats(measures: list) -> tuple
```

- *Type hints facilitate coding efficiency by allowing you to check the proper types while you're coding.* This advantage is not obvious if you use the console or a plain-text editor because real-time code analysis is provided by the leading Python integrated development environments (IDEs), either natively or through the installation of plugins, also known as extensions.

Suppose that you define a function that accepts integers, and you specify this requirement by using type hints. Figure 6.4 shows how code analysis can result in meaningful pop-up menus that help you ensure code quality.

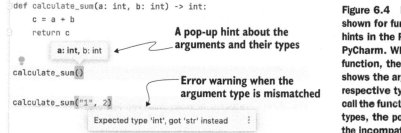

Figure 6.4   Pop-up menus are shown for functions with type hints in the Python editor PyCharm. When you call the function, the pop-up menu shows the arguments and their respective types. When you call the function with the wrong types, the pop-up menu shows the incompatible types.

6.3.3   Applying advanced type-hinting skills to function definitions

In section 6.3.2, you learned about the syntax of using type hints in a function definition. In several situations, however, you'll find that the basic usage isn't enough. In this section, you'll learn about some advanced uses for type hinting:

- Arguments with default values
- Custom classes
- Container objects
- Multiple data types

USING ARGUMENTS WITH DEFAULT VALUES

I've covered how to set a default value for a parameter in a function definition. When this feature is combined with type hints, all we need to know is the order of the sequence: type hint first and then the default value. The following code snippet shows an example:

```
def calculate_product(a: int, b: int, multiplier: int = 1) -> int:
    c = a * b * multiplier
    return c
```

The parameter `multiplier` has a default value of 1 with the `int` type. Please note that the spaces used in specifying the parameter's default value and type are necessary because they help improve the readability of the code. Specifically, you should have spaces before and after the type and the = sign.

> **READABILITY**   Spaces and empty lines are necessary in many places to improve code readability by creating visual separators for distinct components.

WORKING WITH CUSTOM CLASSES

When our project grows, we introduce new classes to manage the data. These classes are new types, and we can use them as we do built-in data types such as `int`, `tuple`, and `dict`. The following listing shows how to include custom classes in function definitions by using type hints.

Listing 6.8   Using type hints with custom classes

```
from collections import namedtuple

Task = namedtuple("Task", "title description urgency")

class User:          Uses the pass statement
    pass         ←───  as a placeholder

def assign_task(pending_task: Task, user: User):
    pass
```

> **TRIVIA**   The pass statement is used where code is required to fulfill syntactical requirements. As a placeholder, the pass statement does nothing. In the body of a class definition, we're required to write code to implement the class. In this case, however, we can use `pass` to validate the class definition.

As shown in listing 6.8, we define two classes: `Task` (using the named tuple technique) and `User` (using a typical class definition). When these classes are defined, we can use them immediately. Python knows these classes are types and that they can be used to indicate the types of the arguments in a function definition.

WORKING WITH CONTAINER OBJECTS

We have learned that several built-in data types, such as `list` and `tuple`, are containers because they can hold other objects. When it comes to type hints for these containers, you may notice that providing a type for the container itself isn't always meaningful enough. Suppose that we have a function for completing several tasks, as shown in the following listing.

Listing 6.9   Type hints using a container type

```
def complete_tasks(tasks: list):
    for task in tasks:
        pass
```

The function definition shows that the `tasks` argument is a `list` object, but it doesn't specify what objects go into the `list`. Thus, people may use a `list` of `str` objects or a `list` of `Task` objects:

```
complete_tasks(["Laundry", "Museum"])

complete_tasks([Task("Laundry", "Wash clothes", 5),
⇒ Task("Museum", "Egyptian exhibit", 4)])
```

It's true that when you add specific operations to the function, you make either `str` or `Tasks` objects compatible, but it's more user-friendly to provide specificity to the tasks argument. Is it a `list` of `str` or `Task` objects? The next listing shows a modified version of the function.

Listing 6.10   Type hints using a container of specific content types

```
def complete_tasks_hinted(tasks: list[Task]):
    for task in tasks:
        pass
```

TRIVIA   The type-hinting feature is evolving in recent Python versions. Some features may be not available if you don't use the latest version of Python.

Instead of using only `list`, you can use a pair of brackets following `list` to include the expected data type of the contained objects. In our case, we expect the `list` object to contain `Task` objects but not `str` objects. With this change, you'll notice that the IDE can give you a warning when you use a `list` object of an incompatible data type, such as strings, as shown in figure 6.5.

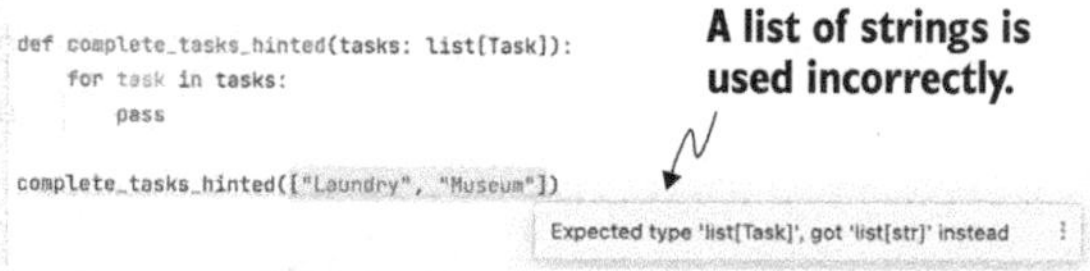

Figure 6.5   Displaying a warning when the container holds objects of an incompatible data type. The screenshot was taken from the Python IDE PyCharm. Because of the IDE's real-time code analysis, after you specify the argument that is incorrect according to the type hints, the IDE displays a warning pop-up menu.

Besides `list`, the most common container data types are `dict`, `tuple`, and `set`. Table 6.1 summarizes the respective type hints for the contained objects.

Table 6.1   Type hints for common built-in container objects

Container type	Code examples	Explanation
list	list[str]	A list of str objects
	list[int]	A list of int objects
tuple	tuple[float, int]	A tuple of a float object and an int object
	tuple[float, ...]	A tuple of multiple float objects

Table 6.1   Type hints for common built-in container objects *(continued)*

Container type	Code examples	Explanation
dict	`dict[int, str]`	A `dict` of keys using `int` objects and values using `str` objects
	`dict[int, list[int]]`	A `dict` of keys using `int` objects and values using `list` objects of `int` objects
set	`set[int]`	A `set` of `int` objects
	`set[str]`	A `set` of `str` objects

TAKING MULTIPLE DATA TYPES

It's possible for a function to take different data types for a specific parameter. In listing 6.6, the `generate_stats` function's measures parameter is a `list` of numbers. But this function would work the same way if we used a `tuple` of numbers. In this case, we should use type hinting to indicate that a parameter can be of multiple types, as show in the next listing.

Listing 6.11   Specifying multiple types

```
from statistics import mean, stdev


def generate_stats(measures: list[float] | tuple[float, ...])
    -> tuple[float, float]:
    measure_mean = mean(measures)
    measure_std = stdev(measures)
    return measure_mean, measure_std
```

To specify multiple types for a parameter, we use the vertical bar | to separate types. Notably, if you have more than two types, you can use more than one bar:

```
para0: int | float | str | list
```

6.3.4   *Discussion*

Python didn't support type hints in its early days but gradually became equipped with type-hinting features. One major addition to Python's standard library is the `typing` module for advanced type hinting. What you've learned in this chapter will make you ready to learn anything new in the `typing` module. To give you a head start, the following code shows how to make type hints clearer with the `typing` module, as it includes higher-level typing information (such as `Sequence`, which can capture any sequence data types):

```
from statistics import mean, stdev
from typing import Sequence


def generate_stats(measures: Sequence[float]) -> tuple[float, float]:
```

```
measure_mean = mean(measures)
measure_std = stdev(measures)
return measure_mean, measure_std
```

6.3.5 Challenge

Andrew is building a Python package to process finance data. He uses type hints in the package to make it easier for users. How can he write type hints when the parameter for a function is a `list` of `int` or a `list` of `str`?

> **HINT** The vertical bar indicates *or*, which doesn't have to be between the type annotations. In other words, it can be used within a type annotation, such as `set[int | str]`.

6.4 How do I increase function flexibility with *args and **kwargs?

When we define functions, we want them to solve specific problems. To call these functions, we send the applicable arguments so they can perform the desired operations. So far, all the functions that we have defined accept a preset number of arguments, but sometimes the desired use case requires more than a preset number of arguments. Consider the head for the built-in `print` function:

```
print(*objects, sep=' ', end='\n', file=sys.stdout, flush=False)
```

On the surface, it appears that the `print` function takes five arguments, with the last four having default values. As you may have noticed, however, we can print as many objects as we want by using `print`, as the next listing shows.

> **Listing 6.12   Using the built-in `print` function**

```
word = "Hello"
numbers = [1, 2, 3]
prime_number = 11

print(word, numbers, prime_number)
# outprint: Hello [1, 2, 3] 11
```

The reason why `print` can accept multiple objects is that `*` is used before the `objects` parameter, which means a variable number (zero or more) of positional arguments. This parameter specification technique is commonly denoted as `*args`. Using `*args` makes the `print` function flexible enough to accept any number of objects. Notably, there is another closely related technique for specifying a variable number of keyword arguments, which is denoted as `**kwargs`. In the next section, you'll learn how to use `*args` and `**kwargs` to define functions that have good flexibility. Moreover, we'll introduce some key concepts in terms of arguments' categories.

6.4.1   *Knowing positional and keyword arguments*

You may have noticed that when we call functions, in the parentheses, we sometimes use the arguments directly, and at other times, we use identifiers preceding the specified arguments. We have different terms for these two types of arguments.

When the arguments have associated identifiers, they're *keyword arguments,* and these identifiers are used in the function body to refer to these arguments. When the arguments don't have associated identifiers, they're *positional arguments.* In other words, Python processes these arguments based on the arguments' positions according to the sequence in the function definition. To understand the distinction between keyword and positional arguments, consider a simple function:

```
def multiply_numbers(a, b):
    return a * b
```

For a typical function like `multiply_numbers`, we can set the parameters as either positional or keyword arguments. Figure 6.6 shows a few ways to call this function with two parameters.

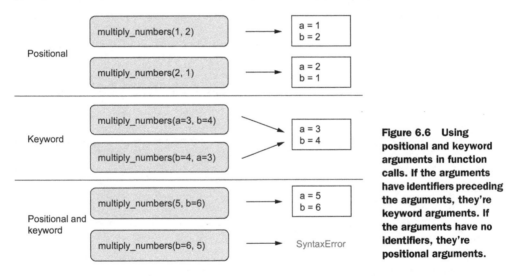

Figure 6.6   **Using positional and keyword arguments in function calls. If the arguments have identifiers preceding the arguments, they're keyword arguments. If the arguments have no identifiers, they're positional arguments.**

From the various examples shown in figure 6.6, we can summarize the following key points regarding the use of positional and keyword arguments:

- *When you use positional arguments, the order of these arguments matters.* The arguments will be matched with the original parameters in the function head.
- *When you use keyword arguments, the order of these arguments doesn't matter.* The arguments will be used according to the supplied keywords/identifiers.
- *When you use both positional and keyword arguments, you have to place positional arguments before any keyword arguments.* Otherwise, you'll raise a `SyntaxError`.

Now that you know the distinction between positional and keyword arguments, we're ready to discuss defining a variable number of positional and keyword arguments.

> ### Positional-only and keyword-only arguments
>
> Figure 6.6 shows that arguments can be set as either positional or keyword when you call the function. That is, when you call a function with arguments, Python follows a specific order to figure out what the arguments are against the function's definition. If the arguments are keyword, Python matches them with the corresponding parameters in the definition. If the arguments are positional, Python processes them based on their positions. In general, we don't restrict how the arguments, either positional or keyword, are set.
>
> There are two more advanced ways to specify how the arguments should be set: *positional-only arguments* can be set only positionally, and *keyword-only arguments* can be set only with identifiers. If you recall, the sort method has the following head: sort(*, key=None, reverse=False). The * specifies that all the arguments behind it should be set only as keyword-only arguments.
>
> By reinforcing keyword-only arguments, you're forcing readers to use keyword arguments, so they know exactly what parameters they're setting. You can use this feature if you want some arguments to be set only as keyword arguments.
>
> For positional-only arguments, look at the sum function: sum(iterable, /, start=0). The / specifies that the arguments before it should be set only as positional arguments. This feature can be useful, but in your code, you rarely need to set arguments that can be used only as positional arguments.

6.4.2   Accepting a variable number of positional arguments

In the print function (listing 6.12), *objects allows us to print as many objects as we want, which improves its flexibility. In this section, you'll learn how to define a function that accepts a variable number of positional arguments.

To facilitate the discussion, I'll begin with a simple function, the purpose of which is to convert any number of objects to their corresponding string representations. Apparently, we don't know how many objects will be sent to the function call. Thus, we want this function to be flexible, like the print function. The following code snippet shows the function:

```
def stringify(*items):
    print(f"got {items} in {type(items)}")
    return [str(item) for item in items]
```

USING *ARGS AS A TUPLE

In the function's head, we use *items to indicate that the function can take a variable number of positional arguments. In essence, you use the asterisk (*) symbol to precede the argument name. Now that we know that with this function head, the user can call it with an arbitrary number of positional arguments, the next question is how we can use these positional arguments in the function body.

Because we've included a line of code to print the arguments, `print(f"got {items} in {type(items)}")`, we can call `stringify` to inspect what items is:

```
>>> stringify(1, "two", None)
got (1, 'two', None) in <class 'tuple'>
['1', 'two', 'None']
```

The return value of the function is printed in the console.

From the output, we know that all the positional arguments are packed into a `tuple` object named `items`. Thus, we can apply any `tuple`-related techniques to `items`. In the example, we use the list comprehension technique to iterate the `items` object.

PLACING *ARGS AS THE LAST POSITIONAL ARGUMENT

When you expect the user to call a function that accepts other specified positional arguments besides *args, you should place *args at the end. Consider a modified version of the `stringify` function:

```
def stringify_a(item0, *items):
    print(item0, items)
```

When we call `stringify_a`, Python knows to parse the positional arguments accordingly. The first argument goes to `item0`, and the remaining arguments go to `items`:

```
>>> stringify_a(0)
0; ()
>>> stringify_a(0, 1)
0; (1,)
```

Apparently, the `stringify_a` function is valid. Now look at an invalid modification:

```
def stringify_b(*items, item0):
    print(item0, items)
```

When we call `stringify_b` with positional arguments, it is impossible for Python to figure out which argument goes to which parameter. `items` means any number of positional arguments, and Python doesn't know where to stop, as in this example:

```
stringify_b(0, 1)
# ERROR: TypeError: stringify_b() missing 1 required keyword-only argument:
     'item0'
```

When we call `stringify_b` with only positional arguments, we encounter the Type-Error, and the error message tells us that we're missing the keyword-only argument `item0`. Thus, we could use `stringify_b` if we set `items` as a keyword argument:

```
>>> stringify_b(0, item0=1)
1 (0,)
```

Although the function call works, our original intention was to define a function that could be called only with positional arguments. With that assumption, we should remember to place *args at the end of the list of positional arguments.

6.4.3 Accepting a variable number of keyword arguments

In section 6.4.2, we learned to create a function that accepts any number of positional arguments. As a counterpart, we can define a function that accepts any number of keyword arguments. As a convention, we use **kwargs to denote the variable number of keyword arguments. In this section, you'll learn about **kwargs.

To facilitate the discussion, I'll start with a simple function that involves **kwargs. Using the function as an example, here are the key points of using **kwargs:

```
def create_report(name, **grades):
    print(f"got {grades} in {type(grades)}")
    report_items = [f"***** Report Begin for {name} *****"]
    for subject, grade in grades.items():
        report_items.append(f"### {subject}: {grade}")
    report_items.append(f"***** Report End for {name} *****")
    print("\n".join(report_items))
```

USING **KWARGS AS A DICT

We know that the variable number of positional arguments is packed as a tuple object. In a similar fashion, the variable number of keyword arguments is packed into a single object: dict. Let's see whether that's the case by calling the create_report function:

```
create_report("John", math=100, phys=98, bio=95)
# output the following lines:
got {'math': 100, 'phys': 98, 'bio': 95} in <class 'dict'>
***** Report Begin for John *****
### math: 100
### phys: 98
### bio: 95
***** Report End for John *****
```

From the printout, you can easily see that these keyword arguments form a dict object. With this dict object, we can use applicable dict-related methods. In this example, we iterate all the key-value pairs by using items.

PLACING **KWARGS AS THE LAST PARAMETER

When you use **kwargs in a function, you should remember the syntax rule that **kwargs should be placed after all the other parameters. Related to this rule, positional arguments should be placed before all the keyword arguments. Figure 6.7 shows the general order of these kinds of arguments.

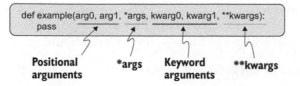

Figure 6.7 The order of placing positional and keyword arguments in a function definition. In general, positional arguments should always precede keyword arguments. `*args` should be the last positional argument, and `**kwargs` should be the last keyword argument.

6.4.4 *Discussion*

Although using `*args` and `**kwargs` helps improve the flexibility of the defined functions, it's less explicit to the function's users regarding the applicable parameters. Thus, we shouldn't abuse this feature. Only when you can't know how many positional or keyword arguments you expect the function to accept should you consider using `*args` and `**kwargs`. In general, it's preferred to use explicitly named positional and keyword arguments in a function definition, because these argument names clearly indicate what the parameters are presumed to be doing.

6.4.5 *Challenge*

Let's continue the story about Cory, who teaches Python coding in college. The students know that a function with `**kwargs` accepts a variable number of keyword arguments, as in the following example:

```
def example(**kwargs):
    pass
```

To test the students' knowledge of calling functions, he creates a list of ways to call the preceding `example` function:

```
example(a=1, b=2)
```

```
example(1, 2)
```

```
example(2a=1, 2b=2)
```

```
example()
```

If you were one of the students, would you know which techniques are valid and which are not? What makes some calls invalid?

> **HINT** The keyword arguments use identifiers. Python has specific rules about identifiers. They can't start with a number, for example.

6.5 *How do I write proper docstrings for a function?*

When we come across a new function, it's common to look up its documentation to figure out how to use it. You can use the built-in `isinstance` function to check whether an object belongs to a specific type, for example. But you don't know how to call this function. Besides looking up the information online, is there any way to get the pertinent information? The answer is yes—with the help of the built-in `help` function, as the following listing shows.

Listing 6.13 Getting the docstring by using `help`

```
>>> help(isinstance)
Help on built-in function isinstance in module builtins:

isinstance(obj, class_or_tuple, /)
Return whether an object is an instance of a class or
    of a subclass thereof.

A tuple, as in ``isinstance(x, (A, B, ...))``, may be given as the
    target to check against. This is equivalent to
    ``isinstance(x, A) or isinstance(x, B) or ...`` etc.
```

As shown in listing 6.13, we use the `help` function to retrieve the docstrings for the `isinstance` function. Although this technique is less commonly known, you can also retrieve a function's docstring by accessing its special attribute __doc__:

```
>>> print(isinstance.__doc__)
Return whether an object is an instance of a class or
    of a subclass thereof.

A tuple, as in ``isinstance(x, (A, B, ...))``, may be given as the
    target to check against. This is equivalent to
    ``isinstance(x, A) or isinstance(x, B) or ...`` etc.
```

If you didn't know, Python uses docstrings to refer to the documentation of a function, a class, or a module to explain the functionalities of these things. In our case, we're viewing the docstrings for the function `isinstance`, which provides specific instructions on how to use `isinstance`. More importantly, you can conveniently access the docstrings with a simple `help` call in a Python console without relying on any external resources. In this section, you'll learn to write proper docstrings for a function.

> **CONCEPT**　A *docstring* is a string that documents a module, class, function, or method in such a way that users know how to use them properly.

6.5.1 *Examining the basic structure of a function's docstring*

A function's docstring is a multiline string below the function's head. As a convention, we use triple quotes to enclose the string. You can use double or single quotation marks to form the triple quotes as long as they're matched. In this section, we review the basic structure of a function's docstring.

For this multiline string, as a best practice, three key elements are required: a summary of the function, parameters, and a return value. If your function can raise one or multiple exceptions, you want to specify them too, as a fourth element. Figure 6.8 shows the building elements of a function's docstring.

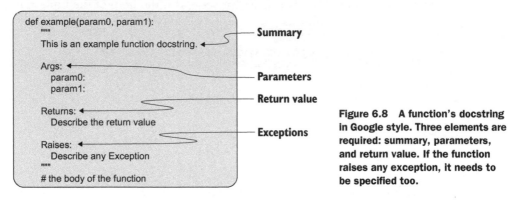

Figure 6.8 A function's docstring in Google style. Three elements are required: summary, parameters, and return value. If the function raises any exception, it needs to be specified too.

Notably, Python programmers haven't reached a consensus regarding docstring style. The docstring shown in figure 6.8 is called Google style because it's officially recommended by Google. Multiple styles have been adopted by different Python users and IDEs. As one of the most common Python IDEs, PyCharm uses the so-called *reStructuredText (reST)* style as the default option for docstrings; figure 6.9 shows an example.

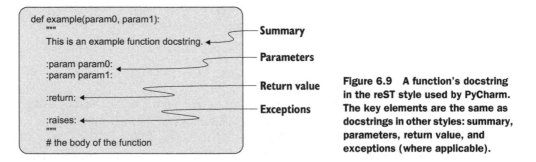

Figure 6.9 A function's docstring in the reST style used by PyCharm. The key elements are the same as docstrings in other styles: summary, parameters, return value, and exceptions (where applicable).

Although Python programmers generally agree on what elements should be included in a function's docstring, it's up to each individual programmer to choose a preferred style or follow the company's convention. In this section, we'll stick to the reST style. In the next sections, we'll discuss the proper ways to define each element.

> **MAINTAINABILITY**   It's important to stick to a specific docstring style in the project. Consistency in documentation is essential for both readability and maintainability.

6.5.2   *Specifying the function's action as the summary*

The first element in a function's docstring is the summary of the function. The summary should be concise, occupying only one line if at all possible. It provides a high-level description of the action that the function performs.

In listing 6.13, for example, we saw the docstring for the built-in `isinstance` function. Its summary clearly indicates the function's action: `Return whether an object is an instance of a class or of a subclass thereof`. We should use the same philosophy in creating our own summary. Notably, for some simple functions, it's possible to need only one line as the docstring. In this case, the summary constitutes the entire docstring. The following simple function represents such a scenario:

```python
def doubler(a):
    """Return the number multiplied by 2"""
    return a * 2
```

6.5.3 Documenting the parameters and the return value

After providing the summary for the function, the next step in creating a function's docstring is documenting each of the parameters used by the function. In reST style, each parameter starts with `:param`, and different parameters are listed as separate lines. For each parameter, we need to provide the following information:

- *Parameter name*—It should match exactly what is used in the function's head.
- *Parameter type*—What type of data are you expecting for the parameter? Specify it.
- *Description*—Depending on how intuitive the parameter is, provide a useful description to help users understand what this parameter is or why it's needed if its purpose isn't clear.
- *Default value* (optional)—If the parameter has a default value, specify it. Notably, if it's ambiguous why you choose a specific value as the default value, you need to provide a brief justification.

You can see these guidelines in action in the following listing.

Listing 6.14   Docstring example of a simple function

```python
def quotient(dividend, divisor, taking_int=False):
    """
    Calculate the product of two numbers with a base factor.

    :param dividend: int | float, the dividend in the division
    :param divisor: int | float, the divisor in the division
    :param taking_int: bool, whether only taking the integer part of
        the quotient; default: False, which calculates the
        precise quotient of the two numbers

    :return: float | int, the quotient of the dividend and divisor
    """
    result = dividend / divisor
    if taking_int:
        result = int(result)
    return result
```

The example in listing 6.14 provides the needed docstring for the three parameters, including parameter name, type, and explanation. In addition, because `taking_int` has a default value, it's mentioned in the docstring. When one parameter's docstring expands more than one line, remember to insert some indentation for the second line and later lines so that the delineation between different parameters is clear.

From a readability perspective, we use sensible names for the function itself (quotient) and all the parameters (dividend, divisor, and taking_int). Using sensible names is key in a function definition because these names can provide intuitive information about the function. If they're named well, users probably don't even need to check the docstring to understand the function.

> **READABILITY** Everything should be named sensibly for best readability. It's OK to use long names because autocompletion is a feature in common IDEs. After you write the first couple of letters, you can select the needed name.

In other words, your goal in defining a function is to make it easy for users to understand and use, minimizing the possibility that they must refer to the function's docstrings. Keep in mind that the docstring should be a backup source of information for your functions.

For a function's return value, the docstring uses :return to indicate the return value's type and explanation. The explanation should be concise and easy to understand.

6.5.4 *Specifying any exceptions possibly raised*

When your function could raise any exceptions, you should specify them in the docstring so that when users read the docstrings, they know the possible exceptions to expect and can avoid or handle them.

Let's consider the quotient function, which includes the division operation dividend / divisor. We know that a division is undefined if the divisor is 0, and we can see what will happen if we're trying to divide a number by 0:

```
1 / 0
# ERROR: ZeroDivisionError: division by zero
```

Thus, we should specify such an exception in the docstring, as shown in the next listing.

Listing 6.15 Specifying the possible exception in the docstring

```
def quotient(dividend, divisor, taking_int=False):
    """
    Calculate the product of two numbers with a base factor.

    :param dividend: int | float, the dividend in the division
    :param divisor: int | float, the divisor in the division
    :param taking_int: bool, whether only taking the integer part of
        the quotient; default: False, which calculates the
        precise quotient of the two numbers

    :return: float | int, the quotient of the dividend and divisor
```

```
:raises: ZeroDivisionError, when the divisor is 0
"""
if divisor == 0:                                          Raises ZeroDivisionError
    raise ZeroDivisionError("division by zero")    ←——   explicitly
result = dividend / divisor
if taking_int:
    result = int(result)
return result
```

In listing 6.15, we explicitly examine whether divisor is 0 and raise the ZeroDivision-Error when it's 0. Please note that even if we don't raise this exception explicitly, such an exception can still be raised when we call something like quotient(1, 0) because Python raises ZeroDivisionError whenever applicable. Here, I explicitly raise this exception because I want to show you how an exception raised by a function should be documented in the docstring.

On a related note, when we create our own Python modules, we often need to define custom exceptions ourselves to explicitly raise these custom exceptions in the functions we create. I cover custom exceptions in section 12.5.

6.5.5 Discussion

There are different styles in which to create a function's docstrings. The key is sticking to a specific style consistently. If you work on a team, use the style that your team has agreed on. If you write functions/modules only for yourself, adopt the style you're most used to. Please remember that consistency in coding is key to sustained maintainability of any project.

6.5.6 Challenge

Jerry used to adopt the reST style for his docstrings, as shown in listing 6.15. He's joining a company that uses Google style for all the documentation. As a best practice, what would the docstring look like if he rewrote the docstrings in listing 6.15 by using Google style?

HINT   Figure 6.8 shows a docstring that uses Google style.

Summary

- You should consider setting default values for the arguments whose values are the same for most calls. The users don't need to set them anymore when the default values are used, making it easier to read these function calls with fewer arguments.
- When you set default values for mutable arguments, such as list, don't use the constructor list(), because a function is evaluated when it's defined, including the default arguments. Using the constructor will result in different function calls manipulating the same mutable object and producing undesired side

effects. To avoid this pitfall, you should use None as the default value of mutable arguments.

- Every Python function has a return value—either the explicitly returned value or the implicitly returned None.

- A function can return multiple values that form a single tuple object. You can use the tuple unpacking technique to retrieve individual items after the function call. That way, it's clearer to the readers how you're going to use the return value.

- Although Python is a dynamically typed language, we can use type hints to provide useful typing information on the arguments and return value for a function. When you incorporate type hinting into a function definition, you make your functions more readable, making it easier for users to understand your function. More important, modern IDEs can take advantage of a function's type hints and provide real-time warnings if an incompatible type of object is used for an argument.

- When we call a function, we often pass the needed arguments. When the arguments use identifiers, they're called keyword arguments. By contrast, arguments that have no identifiers and are parsed based on their positions are positional arguments. Positional arguments should always be placed before keyword arguments.

- Most of the time, it's best to define a fixed number of positional and keyword arguments. In certain situations, however, it's necessary to define functions that accept a variable number of positional and/or keyword arguments, which are denoted as *args and **kwargs, respectively.

- You need to provide documentation, called docstrings, if your functions are to be used publicly. A function's docstring should include the function's summary, all the parameters, the return value, and the possible exceptions (if any).

- Developers use different styles for docstrings. When you write docstrings for your functions, be sure to adopt a specific docstring style and use it consistently. When you apply a docstring consistently, it's easy for you to develop and maintain your code (you need to be savvy about only one style), and you also make things easy for readers.

7

Using functions beyond the basics

This chapter covers

- Using lambda functions for a small job
- Working with higher-order functions
- Creating and using decorators
- Using generators to obtain data
- Creating partial functions

You may have realized that in every project, the greatest amount of time that you spend in development is devoted to writing functions. In chapter 6, we focused on the fundamentals of writing and using functions. After covering these topics, you're able to write user-friendly functions to serve your work needs. Python knows the integral role of functions in any project; thus, it has advanced features that you can take advantage of to make functions serve your work better.

In this chapter, you'll learn about more-advanced function topics. You'll find that the pertinent concepts may sound advanced, but the pragmatic techniques are not hard to apply to your daily coding work.

7.1   *How do I use lambda functions for small jobs?*

When we define functions, we use the def keyword and then give the name to the function, which serves as the identifier for the function. Although the terminology isn't common, we can refer to these functions as *named functions* because they have associated identifiers.

By contrast, you can define another type of function without specifying names in Python. These functions are called *anonymous functions*. More formally, these functions are known as *lambda functions*. When we discussed advanced sorting with custom functions (section 3.2), we used an example involving setting a lambda function to the key parameter in the sort method:

```
tasks.sort(key=lambda x: x['urgency'], reverse=True)
```

In this section, you'll learn everything you need to know about using lambda functions: the components and the best practices.

> **TRIVIA**   Calling anonymous functions *lambda functions* or *expressions* exists not only in Python, but also in many other languages, such as Java. This name is derived from the lambda calculus in mathematics.

7.1.1   *Creating a lambda function*

You may have seen some examples of lambdas but haven't formally learned about creating them. First, let's review the key elements that constitute a lambda function.

Creating lambdas doesn't involve using the def keyword and supplying an identifier, as we do for a regular function. Instead, we use the lambda keyword to signal that we're creating a lambda function. Figure 7.1 shows the components of a lambda function.

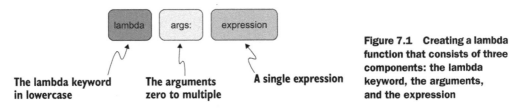

The lambda keyword   The arguments   A single expression
in lowercase   zero to multiple

Figure 7.1   Creating a lambda function that consists of three components: the lambda keyword, the arguments, and the expression

As shown in figure 7.1, after the lambda keyword, we provide the arguments and a single expression that uses the arguments to produce a value. Don't forget that you need to append a colon to the arguments. Please note that you can use zero for multiple arguments in a lambda function. When the lambda function contains no arguments, the colon is still required before you specify the expression.

> **CONCEPT**   *Keywords* are special words reserved by Python for performing predefined operations, such as def for creating a function, class for creating a class, and lambda for creating a lambda function.

Unlike regular functions, which may return an object, lambda functions don't return anything. When they do, you get a syntax error:

```
lambda  x: return x * 2

# ERROR: SyntaxError: invalid syntax
```

The SyntaxError is expected because lambdas use expressions as opposed to statements, and return x * 2 is a kind of statement.

> **REMINDER** An expression evaluates to a single value or an object, whereas a statement performs a specific action without evaluating to any object.

Now we know how to create a lambda function, and it's time to give it a try:

```
doubler = lambda x: x * 2
```

This lambda function multiplies a number by 2. For demonstration purposes, we assign the lambda function to a variable doubler, which allows us to inspect a lambda function in greater detail. As you'll see in the next section, however, it's not good practice to assign a lambda function to a variable. When you inspect the lambda function's type, you'll see that it is indeed a kind of function:

```
print(type(doubler))
# output: <class 'function'>
```

Lambda functions are functions at their core, so we can call them as regular functions. When you call a lambda function, you send the needed arguments as you normally do with a regular function:

```
>>> doubler(5)
10

>>> doubler(8)
16
```

7.1.2 *Using lambdas to perform a small one-time job*

In section 7.1.1, I mentioned that you shouldn't assign a lambda function to a variable. The major reason is that a lambda function is supposed to perform a small job, and it's used a single time. In this section, I discuss what I mean by *a small job*.

You may wonder what kind of use case a small job is. If you recall, you learned to perform more complicated sorting with a custom function (listing 3.3) in section 3.2.1. For your quick reference, the code is shown in the next listing.

Listing 7.1   Sorting a list with a custom function

```
tasks = [
    {'title': 'Laundry', 'desc': 'Wash clothes', 'urgency': 3},
```

```
        {'title': 'Homework', 'desc': 'Physics + Math', 'urgency': 5},
        {'title': 'Museum', 'desc': 'Egyptian things', 'urgency': 2}
]


def using_urgency_level(task):
    return task['urgency']


tasks.sort(key=using_urgency_level, reverse=True)
```

We define the using_urgency_level function and set it to the key argument in the sort method call. Notably, this using_urgency_level function performs a small job to get a dict object's value. Moreover, this function is used only once as the key argument in the sort method. By using the single-use lambda function part of calling sort as the key argument, you're not creating extra "noise" (the explicitly defined function), making your code cleaner. Thus, this example is a perfect scenario for the use of a lambda function:

```
tasks.sort(key=lambda x: x['urgency'], reverse=True)
```

This lambda function takes one parameter, which stands for each dict object of the list object, as in the using_urgency_level function.

> **REMINDER**   Calling both regular and lambda functions is an expression, taking input and generating output.

7.1.3   *Avoiding pitfalls when using lambda functions*

After you learn about lambda functions, you may think that they're cool advanced features for a variety of reasons. The name—lambda!—is cool. A lambda function is concise—one line of code. Also, many Python beginners don't know lambda functions well, and they think that if they use this advanced feature, they're no longer beginners. If you have any of these thoughts, chances are that you'll run into one of the following pitfalls.

ASSIGNING A LAMBDA TO A VARIABLE

I have mentioned a couple of times that we don't assign a lambda function to a variable. Our reasoning (implied in the preceding section) is that we use a lambda function only once. From a readability perspective, however, it appears to be good practice to assign a lambda function to a variable so that we can name the variable sensibly and tell readers more about the lambda function. Consider the following example:

```
using_urgency_level = lambda x: x['urgency']

tasks.sort(key=using_urgency_level, reverse=True)
```

In this example, we use using_urgency_level to refer to the lambda function, and it does give us some information about the sorting algorithm. The more important reason to avoid assigning a lambda function to a variable, however, is that debugging is harder if the function goes wrong, as the next listing shows.

```
using_urgency_level0 = lambda x: x['urgency0']

tasks.sort(key=using_urgency_level0, reverse=True)
# ERROR:
Traceback (most recent call last):
  File "<stdin>", line 1, in <module>
  File "<stdin>", line 1, in <lambda>
KeyError: 'urgency0'
```

For a direct comparison, apply the same error (using a wrong key to access the value) to a named function. The following listing shows what happens.

```
def using_urgency_level1(task):
    return task['urgency1']

tasks.sort(key=using_urgency_level1, reverse=True)
# ERROR:
Traceback (most recent call last):
  File "<stdin>", line 1, in <module>
  File "<stdin>", line 2, in using_urgency_level1
KeyError: 'urgency1'
```

Between listings 7.2 and 7.3, I've highlighted the most significant difference, although both code snippets show the same `KeyError`. When we use a named function, the error message clearly shows where things went wrong: in the `using_urgency_level1` function. By contrast, when we use a lambda function that uses a wrong key, the error message tells us only that something is wrong with a `<lambda>` function. Such an error message is unclear about where you can fix the problem, particularly if you're using a lambda function defined elsewhere.

> **MAINTAINABILITY**   Don't assign a lambda function to a variable; the code will be hard to debug if things go wrong.

USING BETTER ALTERNATIVES

We understand that lambda functions are intended to perform a small job. A common use scenario is to set a lambda function as the key parameter in functions, such as `sort`, `sorted`, and `max`. In some situations, however, better alternatives exist.

Suppose that we have a list of numbers, and we want to create a new `list` object that has these numbers ordered based on their absolute values. You might come up with the following solution:

```
integers = [-4, 3, 7, 0, -6]

sorted(integers, key=lambda x: abs(x))
# output: [0, 3, -4, -6, 7]
```

In the lambda function, we use the built-in abs function, which calculates the absolute value of the item. A more Pythonic solution is to use the abs function directly as the key parameter:

```
sorted(integers, key=abs)
```

For another example, suppose that we have a list of tuples, with each tuple recording a student's scores in math, science, and art, and we want to find out what tuple object has the highest total score. Consider the following solution:

```
scores = [(93, 95, 94), (92, 95, 96), (94, 97, 91), (95, 97, 99)]

max(scores, key=lambda x: x[0] + x[1] + x[2])
# output: (95, 97, 99)
```

In this lambda function, we use indexing to retrieve each of the three scores and add them to obtain the total score. But we know that the built-in sum function can take any iterable to generate the sum for its items. Thus, we should take advantage of the sum function directly. As a side note, you can call max(scores) to produce the same result. Here, I'm including key=sum to be explicit regarding how the maximal item should be selected:

```
max(scores, key=sum)
```

> **READABILITY**   Prefer using built-in functions or applicable alternatives, which are generally more concise, to creating lambda functions.

7.1.4   *Discussion*

Lambda functions should perform only a small job for one-time use, such as serving the key argument in built-in functions such as sorted, max, and min. Notably, lambda functions are widely used in third-party libraries, such as pandas, a popular data science library. In pandas, for example, we can use the apply function to create new data from the existing DataFrame. The apply function takes a key parameter, which specifies how you create the new data from existing data. Thus, lambda functions are a universal technique that you can use to specify a small job in terms of data extraction or conversion.

7.1.5   *Challenge*

High-school student Linda is learning Python to batch-process her pictures and video files. She knows that Python functions have a special attribute called __name__. She tried to access this attribute for a lambda function and a named function. What do you think the values should be?

> **HINT** Go back to listings 7.2 and 7.3 to see what the error message says about the named function and the lambda function.

7.2 *What are the implications of functions as objects?*

We know that Python is an object-oriented programming (OOP) language at its core. From a general perspective, when we talk about objects, we're usually referring to an object as an entity that represents specific data. In the first five chapters, we focused on a variety of topics related to data models, such as `str`, `list`, `tuple`, `dict`, and `set`. These classes and their respective instances are examples of objects. An essential implication of being an object is that we can manipulate the represented data by sending it to a function. The following code snippet shows that we can use `int` and `str` instance objects in functions:

```
def add_three(number):
    return number + 3

add_three(7)    ⟵  Uses an int object in a function

def greeting_message(person):
    return f"Hello, {person}!"

greeting_message("Zoe")    ⟵  Uses a str object in a function
```

Notably, in the preceding section, we mentioned that we could pass a named or lambda function to the `sort` method:

```
tasks.sort(key=lambda x: x['urgency'], reverse=True)
```

Being able to set a function as an argument seems to imply that lambda functions, or functions in general, represent some data, like other data models such as `int` and `str`. If you go a step further, you may wonder whether functions are also objects. Indeed, there is a saying that everything is an object in Python: *Python treats functions like objects too.* In this section, I'll cover the most significant implications of functions being objects and present some practical use cases.

7.2.1 *Storing functions in a data container*

We know that basic data models can be interwoven to create enormous possibilities. Particularly, we can use data containers to store almost any kind of data model. You can have a `list` of `int`, `str`, `dict`, and `set`. In a `dict`, you can store `int`, `str`, `list`, and `dict` as its values. In this section, you'll learn about the first implication of functions as objects: using functions with other data models. Specifically, we'll see how we can take advantage of storing functions in a data container.

Suppose that we have an application programming interface (API) that allows users to send a list of numbers and specify the needed action for the data. For simplicity, let's say the action is to calculate the mean, min, or max. The API function looks like this:

```python
def get_mean(data):
    return "mean of the data"

def get_min(data):
    return "min of the data"

def get_max(data):
    return "max of the data"

def process_data(data, action):
    if action == "mean":
        processed = get_mean(data)
    elif action == "min":
        processed = get_min(data)
    elif action == "max":
        processed = get_max(data)
    else:
        processed = "error in action"

    return processed
```

In this code snippet, `get_mean`, `get_min`, and `get_max` represent the functions that perform the respective calculations. As you may notice, the `process_data`'s body is rather cumbersome. Instead, if we save functions as values in a `dict` object, we'll have a better solution, as shown in the following listing.

Listing 7.4   **Saving functions in a `dict` object**

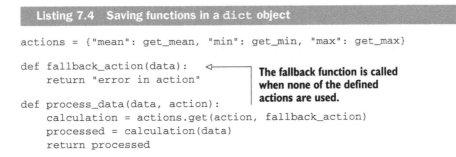

```python
actions = {"mean": get_mean, "min": get_min, "max": get_max}

def fallback_action(data):          ◁─────────    The fallback function is called
    return "error in action"                      when none of the defined
                                                   actions are used.
def process_data(data, action):
    calculation = actions.get(action, fallback_action)
    processed = calculation(data)
    return processed
```

In listing 7.4, we have the `actions` dict, which saves all the needed actions. When the user specifies an action, we can look up the `dict` object to locate the needed function. By doing so, we eliminate the use of multiple branches of the `if...elif...else...` statement. If you have more actions, you can improve readability significantly by saving functions in a `dict` object.

READABILITY   Code is less readable if you have a complicated structure for an `if...elif...else...` statement. Consider other alternatives whenever possible.

7.2.2 Sending functions as arguments to higher-order functions

The second implication of using functions as objects is that we can use functions as arguments when we call other functions. When functions can accept other functions as input (arguments) or return a function as output, we refer to these functions as *higher-order functions*—functions on top of other functions. In this section, we'll focus on one notable higher-order function, map, to illustrate how to send a function as data (argument) to another function.

Higher-order functions

Higher-order functions take functions as arguments or return functions as output, as shown in the following figure. Please note that if a function takes one or more functions as parameters, it's a higher-order function, and if a function returns a function as its output, it's a higher-order function too. If a function does both things, it's certainly a higher-order function.

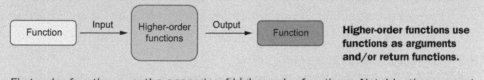

First order functions are the opposite of higher-order functions. Notably, the concept of higher-order functions is prevalent in many modern languages, such as JavaScript, Kotlin, and Swift. Knowing this concept can benefit you if you ever need to use other languages.

In section 5.1, I briefly mentioned the map function, which has the calling signature map(func, iterable), in which func is a function object, often called the mapping function. The map function creates a map iterator, and I've shown you how to construct a list object from the map iterator, as follows:

```
numbers_str = ["1.23", "4.56", "7.89"]

numbers = list(map(float, numbers_str))

assert numbers == [1.23, 4.56, 7.89]
```

> **TRIVIA** The map function can take more than one iterable. When there are multiple iterables, the items from each iterable are sent to the mapping function based on the order of the iterables. The most common use case of the map function deals with one iterable, so it can be confusing for some beginners if you use multiple iterables in map. Use this feature with caution.

Notably, from the perspective of writing Pythonic code, if you're trying to create a list object from the map iterator, it's best to use the list comprehension technique instead:

```
numbers_list = [float(x) for x in numbers_str]
```

Using a higher-order function, however, represents the functional coding style (formally known as functional programming), as opposed to the more prevalent OOP style in Python. In the functional coding style, we focus on applying and composing functions. By contrast, in the OOP style, we focus on working with a variety of objects. Because of list comprehension and generator expression (section 7.4), you can replace most map-related usages with these two techniques, which are respected as being more Pythonic. Because the map object can be an iterator, a valid use case is to implement it in a for loop when the involved operations are complicated:

```
for number in map(float, numbers_str):
    # operation 1
    # operation 2
    # operation 3
    # operation 4
    ...
```

In this example, the for loop includes multiple operations that don't fit into a list comprehension. In this case, you should take advantage of the map iterator, which renders its items one by one without the need for you to construct a list object.

7.2.3 *Using functions as a return value*

In the preceding section, we focused on how to use functions as objects by sending them as parameters to higher-order functions, such as map. In this section, we'll focus on the third implication of using functions as objects. Specifically, I'll show you how to create a higher-order function that returns a function.

We use def to signify that we're creating a function. You may not know that we can embed the definition of a function inside another function, following this general format:

```
def outside(x):
    def inside(y):
        pass
    pass
```

> **REMINDER**   We use the pass statement to satisfy the syntactic requirements where statements are expected.

Suppose that we want to create a higher-order function. With this new function, we can create incrementing functions that add a predefined number. Applying the preceding syntax, we can come up with the solution shown in the next listing.

Listing 7.5   Creating a function that returns a function

```
def increment_maker(number):
    def increment(num0):
        return num0 + number

    return increment
```

READABILITY   Add a blank line between the inner function and the outer function's return statement to improve readability. As a general rule, spaces and empty lines are natural separators between different logical components.

As shown in listing 7.5, the outside function, known as the *outer function,* takes the number parameter. Within the increment_maker function, we define an *inner function:* the increment function, which takes another number (the num0 parameter). Unlike first-order functions, which return None or some form of data, the higher-order function increment_maker returns the increment function as its output. Now we can see how useful this higher-order function is because it allows us to create a series of incrementing functions, as shown in the next listing.

Listing 7.6   Creating functions by calling a higher-order function

```
increment_one = increment_maker(1)
increment_three = increment_maker(3)
increment_five = increment_maker(5)
increment_ten = increment_maker(10)

increment_one(99), increment_three(88), increment_five(80),
➥ increment_ten(100)
# output: (100, 91, 85, 110)
```

As shown in listing 7.6, we can create multiple functions conveniently by specifying the desired incrementing values. When we call these functions, we obtain expected results.

7.2.4   *Discussion*

As an OOP language, Python gives us additional flexibility to use functions by treating them as regular objects. You may wonder whether the example shown in listing 7.5 and 7.6 is too trivial to be practical, and I absolutely agree. Here, I'm using this simple example to provide a proof of concept. In section 7.3, I'll talk about using decorators, a practical technique built on creating a higher-order function.

7.2.5   *Challenge*

In listing 7.4, we saved functions in a dict object. Besides these functions, do you understand the rationale for creating the fallback_action function? On a related note, why do we use the get method instead of subscript notation?

HINT   You can never predict how users will call a function that you define. How do you handle a possible call like process_data([1, 2, 3], "maxx")?

7.3   *How do I check functions' performance with decorators?*

Functions are integral components of any application. Your application's performance, particularly its responsiveness, depends largely on how fast your functions can process the data. Thus, during development, we often want to record the speed of our functions. Using a naïve approach, we may create the solution shown in the next listing.

Listing 7.7   Recording a function's performance

```
import random
import time

def example_func0():
    print("--- example_func0 starts")
    start_t = time.time()
    random_delay = random.randint(1, 5) * 0.1      Injects a random delay (0.1–0.5
    time.sleep(random_delay)                       second) to mimic actual operations
    end_t = time.time()
    print(f"*** example_func0 ends; used time: {end_t - start_t:.2f} s")

def example_func1():
    print("--- example_func1 starts")
    start_t = time.time()
    random_delay = random.randint(6, 10) * 0.1     Injects a random delay (0.6–1
    time.sleep(random_delay)                       second) to mimic actual operations
    end_t = time.time()
    print(f"*** example_func1 ends; used time: {end_t - start_t:.2f} s")
```

In listing 7.7, we calculate the time difference between when the function starts running and when it ends so that we know how long it takes. When this function is called, we can observe its performance:

```
example_func0()
# output the following lines:
--- example_func0 starts
*** example_func0 ends; used time: 0.20 s


example_func1()
# output the following lines:
--- example_func1 starts
*** example_func1 ends; used time: 0.70 s
```

> **READABILITY**   It's a good idea to have some patterned prefix if you expect many lines of output that have similar words. These prefixes serve as distinct visual cues.

You won't have only one or two functions in your application that you need to observe. Chances are that you'll need to monitor the performance of tens or hundreds of functions. It could be tedious to add the pertinent lines of code in listing 7.7 (highlighted in bold) to all these functions. If you recall the DRY (Don't Repeat Yourself) principle, if there are significant repetitions, it's almost guaranteed that we'll need to refactor our code. In this section, I'll show you how to use decorators to solve this kind of problem: applying a shared action to multiple functions.

7.3.1   *Decorating a function to show its performance*

I've mentioned decorators a few times, but you may not know what this term means. *Decorators* are functions that provide additional functionalities to the decorated functions. It's important to note that decorators don't change the way the decorated functions work; thus, we call this process *decoration*. In this section, we'll build a decorator to track a function's performance.

Without introducing the mechanisms, I'll show you some code before I explain how things work. For now, you can skim the `logging_time` function and start to read the code from the line `@logging_time` in the next listing.

Listing 7.8   Using a performance-logging decorator

```
import random
import time


def logging_time(func):
    def logger(*args, **kwargs):
        print(f"--- {func.__name__} starts")
        start_t = time.time()
        value_returned = func(*args, **kwargs)
        end_t = time.time()
        print(f"*** {func.__name__} ends; used time: {end_t - start_t:.2f} s")
        return value_returned

    return logger


@logging_time
def example_func2():
    random_delay = random.randint(3, 5) * 0.1
    time.sleep(random_delay)


example_func2()
# output the following two lines:
--- example_func2 starts
*** example_func2 ends; used time: 0.40 s
```

As you can see in listing 7.8, when we call the `example_func2` function, we get the output showing its performance. No code does such a thing in the body of `example_func2`, however. So what makes `example_func2` output its performance data?

The magic results from the `@logging_time` right above `example_func2`'s head. This special syntax is about decoration; it means that the function defined below will be decorated by the decorator function `logging_time`. We can apply this decorator function to as many functions as we like, as in this example:

```
@logging_time
def example_func3():
    pass

@logging_time
```

```
def example_func4():
    pass

@logging_time
def example_func5():
    pass
```

> **MAINTAINABILITY**   Decorators extract the shared utility functionalities that can be used by multiple functions. You need to maintain only the decorator functions, not all individual decorated functions.

We've seen that we can apply the decorator function to multiple functions to perform the shared functionalities. But we haven't discussed what constitutes a decorator, which is the topic of the next section.

7.3.2   *Dissecting the decorator function*

In section 7.2, I mentioned that a decorator is a kind of higher-order function. As shown in listing 7.8, the `logging_time` function is a decorator—a form of closure. (See the following sidebar for additional information.) Using this example, we'll dissect the decorator by identifying its key elements in this section.

Behind decorators: Closures

Decorators are a form of closure. From a broad perspective, closures represent an advanced programming concept in many modern languages, including Kotlin, Swift, and certainly Python. A *closure* is an inner function that is created and returned from the outer function. Moreover, it requires the inner function to use the variable(s) in the outer function's scope, a technique called *nonlocal variable binding*.

As you will notice, several new terminologies are involved, including scopes and non-local variable binding. Explaining this concept fully would require a whole section, if not more. Nevertheless, this topic is an important one that can help you understand related techniques, particularly decorators. Thus, I'm providing a figure to show the essential components of a closure. Please note that you can use closures' applications, such as decorators, without fully understanding closures, so don't worry if the concept doesn't make sense to you.

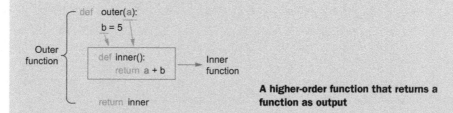

In this figure, note three things: In the body of the outer function, we create an inner function; the inner function uses parameters that belong to the outer function; and the outer function returns the inner function as its output.

When we create a function by calling the outer function, we're creating a closure. If you inspect the closure, you see that it is indeed the `inner` function created in the `outer` function, and you can call the closure too:

```
>>> closure = outer(100)
>>> closure
<function outer.<locals>.inner at 0x7f89a812d5a0>
>>> closure()
105
```

There are even more ways to inspect the closure on a more in-depth level. We can check, for example, what variables the closure binds:

```
>>> closure.__closure__[0].cell_contents
100
>>> closure.__closure__[1].cell_contents
5
```

ESSENTIAL STRUCTURE: A CLOSURE-GENERATING FUNCTION

If we leave out the implementation details of the `logging_time` function, we can have the following backbone structure:

```
def logging_time_backbone(func):
    def logger(*args, **kwargs):
        # covering the body's details later
        pass

    return logger
```

If you recall, this structure represents a higher-order function, taking a function as input and returning a function as output. In essence, a decorator processes a function, and we call this process *decoration*. But what's happening to the decoration process behind the scenes? To illustrate the underlying mechanism, I'll show you this code snippet first:

```
def before_deco():
    pass

after_deco = logging_time(before_deco)

after_deco()
# output the following lines:
--- before_deco starts:
*** before_deco ends; used time: 0.00 s
```

It's interesting to observe that calling the `after_deco` function results in the same performance-related output as that of other previously decorated functions using `@logging_time`. If you go back one step, you see that the `after_deco` function is created by calling the decorator function `logging_time` and passing in the `before_deco` function. Thus, as you may have figured out, decoration is a process of creating a closure by sending an existing function to the decorator. Figure 7.2 shows this process.

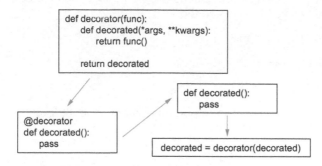

Figure 7.2   Applying a decorator is the process of creating a closure from the decorator function. The decorator function is a higher-order function that takes a function (the to-be-decorated function) and returns a function (the decorated function, a closure). Please note that we can use the same variable name in an assignment statement. The Python interpreter will evaluate the right side first and assign the evaluated value to the left side. Because the name is the same, the old variable's value is replaced by the new value.

*ARGS AND **KWARGS IN THE INNER FUNCTION

In section 6.4, you learned the concepts of *args and **kwargs and saw how to use them to allow users to pass any number of positional and keyword arguments, respectively. The rationale of using *args and **kwargs in the inner function is the same: you want the decorator to be compatible with all functions, regardless of their calling signatures.

To illustrate the necessity of using *args and **kwargs, consider a decorator that doesn't use them to see the problem we may run into. For simplicity, the decorator monitor reports when a function is called:

```
def monitor(func):
    def monitored():
        print(f"*** {func.__name__} is called")
        func()

    return monitored
```

If we use this decorator for a function that doesn't take any parameters, everything works out fine:

```
@monitor
def example0():
    pass

example0()
# output: *** example0 is called
```

If we use this decorator for a function that takes one or multiple parameters, however, we're running into a TypeError:

```
@monitor
def example1(param0):
    pass

example1("a string")
# ERROR: TypeError: monitor.<locals>.monitored() takes 0 positional
➡ arguments but 1 was given
```

The error message tells us where the problem is. In the fourth line of the decorator function `monitor`, we call the decorated function by using `func()`, which doesn't specify any parameters! But the decorated `example1` function expects one positional argument. As you can imagine, such incompatibility significantly restricts where you can use decorators. Thus, to maximize decorators' flexibility, it's essential to include `*args` and `**kwargs` in the inner function, because the created inner function will be the decorated function, and using `*args` and `**kwargs` makes the inner function compatible with any calling signature.

> **MAINTAINABILITY** Use `*args` and `**kwargs` in the inner function of a decorator to provide maximum flexibility to the decorator.

THE RETURN STATEMENT IN THE INNER FUNCTION

Section 6.2 mentions that every Python function returns a value either implicitly as `None` or as an explicitly returned value. Thus, when we define the inner function, we shouldn't forget to add the `return` statement. Specifically, the return value should be the one that you get by calling the decorated function.

On a related note, be cautious about where you place the `return` statement. As you may know, any code below the `return` statement can't be executed because `return` means that the current execution is done, and we're giving the control back to the caller where the execution was initiated. Thus, when we want to apply operations after calling the decorated function, we use a temporary variable to store the return value. After the extra operations, we return this variable. This is exactly what we did for the `logging_time` function in listing 7.8. Figure 7.3 shows the contrast.

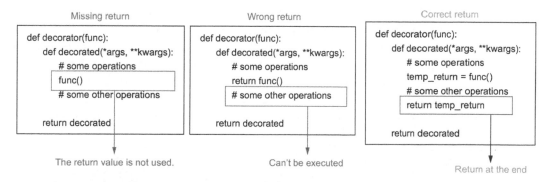

Figure 7.3 Place the return statement at the end of the inner function. First, we shouldn't forget to add the return statement. Otherwise, we're changing how the decorated function behaves, as the expected return value vanishes in the inner function. Second, we should place the return value at the end of the inner function instead of somewhere in the middle.

7.3.3   *Wrapping to carry over the decorated function's metadata*

So far, I've introduced the core features of decorators and how to create a `logging_time` decorator to monitor the performance of any function through decoration. But the decoration process may make the decorated function lose its metadata, such as its docstring. In this section, we'll see how to keep the decorated function's metadata. Before you jump into the solution, examine the following code for potential problems that might arise after decoration:

```
def say_hi(person):
    """Greet someone"""
    print(f"Hi, {person}")

@logging_time
def say_hello(person):
    """Greet someone"""
    print(f"Hello, {person}")

print(say_hi.__doc__, say_hi.__name__, sep="; ")
# output: Greet someone; say_hi

print(say_hello.__doc__, say_hello.__name__, sep="; ")
# output: None; logger
```

As shown in this code, without decoration, we retrieved the say_hi function's docstring by accessing its __doc__ attribute. By contrast, after decoration, we lost say_hello's docstring. In a similar manner, the decoration changed the function's name (accessible with the __name__ attribute). These function attributes, including __doc__ and __name__ (known as its metadata), are affected by the decoration process. Why? Give yourself a few seconds to think about it before moving on.

> **HINT**   Decoration converts the original function to a closure, which is an inner function created from the decorator.

When we define a function without a decorator, the identifier (function name) represents the defined function and its associated operations. By contrast, when we define a function with a decorator, the decorated function is more than a function, as it appears to be. Instead, the inner function is created and returned by the decorator function, and is known as a *closure*. Thus, accessing say_hello's __doc__ attribute is equivalent to accessing the __doc__ attribute of logging_time's inner function, logger. To prove it, we can run an experiment by adding some docstring to the inner function:

```
def logging_time_doc(func):
    def logger(*args, **kwargs):
        """Log the time"""
        print(f"--- {func.__name__} starts")
        start_t = time.time()
        value_returned = func(*args, **kwargs)
        end_t = time.time()
```

```
        print(f"*** {func.__name__} ends; used time:
        ➥ {end_t - start_t:.2f} s")
        return value_returned

    return logger

@logging_time_doc
def example_doc():
    """Example function"""
    pass

print(example_doc.__doc__)
# output: Log the time
```

The output supports our prediction, as it is indeed the docstring of the decorator's inner function. If we use this decorator for multiple functions, all the decorated functions will have the same docstring and name that matches the inner function! We can't make things happen this way. Fortunately, Python provides a solution: we can use the wraps decorator in the functools module, which takes care of keeping the correct metadata for the decorated function. Observe this effect in the next listing.

Listing 7.9   Wrapping the decorated function

```
import functools

def logging_time_wraps(func):
    @functools.wraps(func)
    def logger(*args, **kwargs):
        """Log the time"""
        print(f"--- {func.__name__} starts")
        start_t = time.time()
        value_returned = func(*args, **kwargs)
        end_t = time.time()
        print(f"*** {func.__name__} ends; used time:
        ➥ {end_t - start_t:.2f} s")
        return value_returned

    return logger

@logging_time_wraps
def example_wraps():
    """Example function"""
    pass

print(example_wraps.__doc__, example_wraps.__name__, sep="; ")
# output: Example function; example_wraps
```

We use the wraps decorator (boldface in listing 7.9) to decorate the inner function logger. Notably, this decorator is different from what you've learned; it takes the decorated function (func) as a parameter besides performing its decoration of the logger function. In other words, the wraps decorator uses both func and logger as its arguments.

This feature is valid, as decorators are higher-order functions at their core, and they can accept as many functions as applicable to use as arguments. More generally, this feature—a decorator accepting parameters—is more advanced, and typically, we don't need to use it. But I do want to challenge you on it at the end of this section!

MAINTAINABILITY   Don't forget to use the `wraps` decorator to keep the decorated function's metadata, particularly its docstring and name.

7.3.4   *Discussion*

This section's topic probably represents one of the hardest that I've covered so far. Nevertheless, after learning the material, you should feel accomplished; we conquered some complicated concepts and made a useful logging decorator. You should know what constitutes a closure and why a decorator is an application of the closure technique. In terms of best practices, when you define a decorator, it's important to use the `wraps` decorator to carry over the decorated function's metadata.

7.3.5   *Challenge*

Mike is a web developer using Python as his work language. His work requires him to define a few decorators that can take arguments. As a best practice, can you help him write a decorator function—say, one named `logging_time_app`—that accepts an argument? The decorator performs the same job as the `logging_time` decorator. The parameter is a string to denote the application's name, which serves as the prefix for all the output strings in the `print` function. When we use the decorator, we want to achieve the following effect:

```
@logging_time_app("Task Tracker")
def example_app():
    pass

example_app()
# output the following lines:
Task Tracker --- example_app starts
Task Tracker *** example_app ends; used time: 0.00 s
```

HINT 1   When a parameter is used in `@decorator(param)`, we call the higher-order function `decorator` with the `param` first, which subsequently returns another decorator, perhaps called `true_decorator`. Next, the `true_decorator` is applied to the to-be-decorated function as though we'd used `@true_decorator`.

HINT 2   Don't be afraid to create a higher-order function within another higher-order function when both higher-order functions are decorators!

7.4   How can I use generator functions as a memory-efficient data provider?

The core of any application is data. With the advent of data science and machine learning, many users have used Python to process enormous amounts of data—gigabytes or more. When you deal with this magnitude of data, it can take minutes or even hours to load all the data into memory. When multiple data processing steps are involved, each step can take a long time, and the code is hard to debug if any step goes wrong. Besides the extended wait time throughout processing, probably the biggest limitation is the fact that some computers don't have sufficient memory to handle so much data.

As an illustration, consider a simple example that involves a large amount of data. (Please note that I could have used a larger number, but the example might not have been easy to run on a regular computer, so I used a moderately large number.) Suppose that we need to calculate the sum of perfect squares that are generated for 1 to 1,000,000. Using a typical approach, we create a list object to hold these numbers and then calculate their sum:

```
upper_limit = 1_000_000

squares_list = [x*x for x in range(1, upper_limit + 1)]    ◀── The stop index isn't used. Correct it by I.

sum_list = sum(squares_list)
```

> **QUESTION**   Can you write a function that is decorated by logging_time to see the time cost of running this sum operation?

If you run the code, you'll notice that it takes quite some time to obtain the result. And note that the object consumes considerable memory:

```
print(squares_list.__sizeof__())

# output: 8448712    ◀── Different computers may produce varied results due to different storage mechanisms.
```

In this section, you'll learn how to use generator functions to provide the needed data in a memory-efficient approach.

7.4.1   Creating a generator to yield perfect squares

As a special kind of iterator, a *generator* is created from a generator function. Because a generator is an iterator, it can render its items one by one. A generator is special because it doesn't store its items, and it retrieves and renders its items when needed. This characteristic means that it's a memory-efficient iterator for data rendering. In this section, we'll focus on generators.

First, let's solve the problem with the new technique: using generators to compute the sum of perfect squares. The code in the next listing shows a solution.

Listing 7.10   Creating a generator to calculate the sum of perfect squares

```
def perfect_squares(limit):
    n = 1
    while n <= limit:
        yield n * n
        n += 1

squares_gen = perfect_squares(upper_limit)

sum_gen = sum(squares_gen)

assert sum_gen == sum_list == 333333833333500000
```

The perfect_squares function is a generator function. By calling this function with upper_limit, we're creating a generator named squares_gen. This generator renders perfect squares: 1^2, 2^2, 3^2, 4^2, ... until $1,000,000^2$. As expected, the sum of these perfect squares obtained from the generator is the same as the result obtained from the list object squares_list.

The reason why this generator works resides in the body of the generator function. The most significant feature to observe is the yield keyword, which is the hallmark of a generator function. Whenever the operation executes to the yield line, it provides the item n * n. The coolest thing about a generator is the fact that it remembers which item it should yield next. Figure 7.4 shows how a generator works.

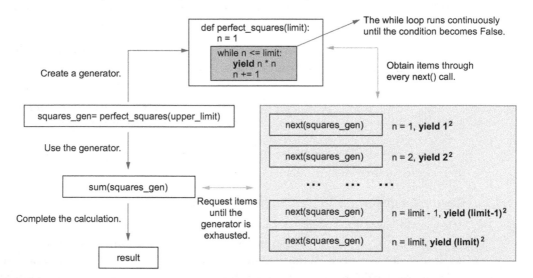

Figure 7.4   The flow of creating and using a generator. Calling a generator function creates a generator. When we use the generator, it iterates its applicable items by going through the while **loop. Every time it encounters the** yield **keyword, it yields an item by calling** next **behind the scenes, as shown in the gray box. When the condition (**n <= limit**) is no longer satisfied, the** while **loop ends, and there is no more chance to encounter the** yield **keyword, so iteration ends.**

As shown in figure 7.4, a generator is an iterator at its core, so using a generator involves invoking the next function. Every next(squares_gen) call reinstates the execution of the generator, starting from where it was left: the line following the last yield execution. As the yield statement is part of the while loop, the loop runs continuously, and each loop encounters the yield term once. When the loop is terminated, all the items are yielded, the generator is exhausted, and we're done with the iteration.

> **REMINDER** When you call next on iterators manually, you'll encounter the StopIteration exception.

As an important conception, yield is different from return, which terminates the current execution and gives control back to the caller. By contrast, yield pauses the current execution and gives control back to the caller temporarily. When requested, it continues the execution. The scenario is like driving a car on a two-lane road. You can yield to other cars when necessary, and after the yield, you go back to the original lane.

7.4.2 Using generators for their memory efficiency

In the preceding section, you learned how to create a generator from a generator function. But why do we bother using generators? In this section, we'll find out.

The most important feature of a generator is that it renders an item when it's asked to do so. Related to this feature is a computer programming concept called *lazy evaluation*, in which specific operations or variables aren't evaluated until the need arises. In terms of generators, they don't create all the items in the first place. Instead, a generator creates the next item only when it's called on.

> **Lazy evaluation**
> Lazy evaluation exists in various forms in different programming languages, such as Kotlin and Swift. An object can have an attribute that has a significant amount of data, but this attribute is not an essential one. When we create such an object, it can take a long time to prepare the attribute before we can use the object. Instead, we can make this attribute "lazily" evaluated, which means that we'll make the object without having that attribute. The first time it's called, we'll prepare the attribute.

Because they yield their items once upon request, generators are memory-efficient. By contrast, we've seen that the list object of the perfect squares of 1 to 1 million consumes more than 8 MB (converted from 8,448,712 bytes). Now, it's time to observe how much memory a generator, which can render the same amount of data, costs:

```
squares_gen = perfect_squares(upper_limit)

print(squares_gen.__sizeof__())        Your computer may
# output: 88              ◄──────────  show a different value.
```

The size of the generator is only 88 bytes, which is about 0.001 percent of the `list` object. The reason why it's much smaller is that it needs to know only its current state; when it needs the next item, it can start from its current state and create the next item. By contrast, the `list` object needs to load all its items up front before it can use the items.

7.4.3   *Using generator expressions where applicable*

We've seen how useful a generator is. But we need to create a generator function before we can use it, which can be tedious. In this section, you'll learn an alternative way to create a generator: using an expression in a process called *generator expression*.

When you learned about comprehensions in section 5.2, I mentioned that there is no tuple comprehension, which otherwise could have used the following syntax: (expression for x in iterable). In fact, this expression is the syntax for generator expression. Now let's rewrite the `perfect_squares` function as a generator expression:

```
>>> squares_gen_exp = (x * x for x in range(1, upper_limit))
>>> squares_gen_exp
<generator object <genexpr> at 0x7f89a8111f50>
```

Instead of using the `yield` keyword in a generator function, a generator expression uses an expression directly to denote what the data should render. From the syntax perspective, you must pay attention to using parentheses; otherwise, you'll produce a `list` instead if you accidentally use square brackets. To show that a generator is an iterator, you can use the next function to retrieve items from the generator one at a time:

```
>>> next(squares_gen_exp)
1
>>> next(squares_gen_exp)
4
>>> next(squares_gen_exp)
9
```

Let's calculate the sum for the generator expression:

```
>>> sum_gen_exp = sum(squares_gen_exp)
>>> sum_gen_exp
333332833333499986
```

It's working! But wait a second—why is the sum off by 14 compared with the sum that we calculated previously?

QUESTION   What did we do before using the `squares_gen_exp`?

As I mentioned before, a generator is lazily rendering its items by remembering its state. The first next call retrieves 1, the second next call retrieves 4, and the third next call retrieves 9. When we call sum(`squares_gen_exp`), the generator still remembers its state, so it starts to render the next item, which is 16. As you should have noticed, the difference of the sums results from being unable to use the first three items, which have already been consumed by invoking `next` manually three times.

From a syntax perspective, we can call the sum function with a generator expression directly, which eliminates the need to create an intermediate variable. When a generator is straightforward, it's the preferred approach:

```
>>> sum(x*x for x in range(4))
14
```

Please note that in this expression, we omit the parentheses for the generator expression, as it's optional if it's used within another pair of parentheses.

7.4.4 Discussion

Under the hood, the implementation of generators involves using the `yield` keyword. Besides generators, an advanced technique, coroutines, also uses `yield`, and these coroutines are called *generator-based coroutines*. These coroutines, however, are being phased out of Python, and you may see this technique only in legacy projects that use older versions of Python. So don't worry if you don't know generator-based coroutines well.

7.4.5 Challenge

James teaches introductory Python programming to undergraduates in the mathematics department. To use a familiar concept, he thought about Fibonacci numbers—a sequence of numbers whose value is the sum of the previous two numbers, as in 0, 1, 1, 2, 3, 5, 8, 13. He challenged his students to write a generator function with an upper limit to produce a generator that renders Fibonacci numbers until it reaches the specified limit.

> **HINT** You can define the first two numbers yourself and then build the formula by using the definition $value_{n+2} = value_n + value_{n+1}$.

7.5 How do I create partial functions to make routine function calls easier?

Functions aren't isolated from other components of your application. Instead, they interact with other entities by taking the input and returning the processed output. To increase a function's flexibility, we often define multiple parameters in a function so that it can handle different forms of input to derive the needed results for different scenarios.

Suppose that you use Python for your data science work. You have the following function to perform statistical modeling using the specified dataset:

```
def run_stats_model(dataset, model, output_path):
    # process the dataset
    # apply the model
    # save the stats to the output path
    calculated_stats = 123          Nominal value to
    return calculated_stats         make the code run
```

This function is so important and universal that you use it in multiple projects. In each of your projects, you use the same model and output to the same folder on different datasets. The following code snippet may reveal what you may be doing across projects:

```
# Project A
run_stats_model(dataset_a1, "model_a", "project_a/stats/")
run_stats_model(dataset_a2, "model_a", "project_a/stats/")
run_stats_model(dataset_a3, "model_a", "project_a/stats/")
run_stats_model(dataset_a4, "model_a", "project_a/stats/")
```

As you may realize, there is a repetition pattern here because the same parameters are used across multiple function calls. Your first reaction may be to apply the default parameters to the run_stats_model function. This solution is not optimal, however, as you may still have to specify these parameters for other projects:

```
# Project B
run_stats_model(dataset_b1, "model_b", "project_b/stats/")
run_stats_model(dataset_b2, "model_b", "project_b/stats/")
run_stats_model(dataset_b3, "model_b", "project_b/stats/")
run_stats_model(dataset_b4, "model_b", "project_b/stats/")

# Project C
run_stats_model(dataset_c1, "model_c", "project_c/stats/")
run_stats_model(dataset_c2, "model_c", "project_c/stats/")
run_stats_model(dataset_c3, "model_c", "project_c/stats/")
run_stats_model(dataset_c4, "model_c", "project_c/stats/")
```

In the next section, you'll learn about a new technique called partial functions, and we'll see how to use partial functions to simplify function calls when common parameters are shared within each project.

7.5.1   *"Localizing" shared functions to simplify function calls*

For this business need, we use the same model and output path for the run_stats_model function in each project. Because the run_stats_model is shared across multiple projects, using this function within each project is local. Thus, we can operationalize the need as a localization question. This section discusses a working solution that uses our existing knowledge.

Because each project uses the same model and output path, we could create a variation version of the shared function for each project. At the top of the Project A file, for example, we might create a function like this one:

```
def run_stats_model_a(dataset):
    model_stats = run_stats_model(dataset, "model_a", "project_a/stats/")
    return model_stats
```

READABILITY Even though I can write return run_stats_models(dataset, "model_a", "project_a/stats/"), I want to use an intermediate variable to denote the exact nature of the return value from the function call. In general, it's a good idea to return a clearly-defined variable instead of returning something directly from another function call.

The run_stats_model_a function is rather straightforward. It provides a convenience function call wrapped around the run_stats_models function. With this localized function, all the original calls to run_stats_models become the following:

```
# Project A
run_stats_model_a(dataset_a1)
run_stats_model_a(dataset_a2)
run_stats_model_a(dataset_a3)
run_stats_model_a(dataset_a4)
```

7.5.2 *Creating a partial function to localize a function*

The preceding section defines a regular function to localize the shared function. It works. But it reinvents the wheel, as Python has already implemented such functionality for us. The more Pythonic solution is to use the partial function to localize a shared function:

```
from functools import partial

run_stats_model_a = partial(run_stats_model, model="model_a",
    output_path="project_a/stats/")

run_stats_model_a("dataset_a")
# output: 123
```

The partial function exists in the functools module, which has a collection of advanced function-related tools in the standard Python library. In the partial function, we specify the shared function and any additional parameters that we want to set—in this case, the project-specific model and output path.

REMINDER We previously used wraps to keep a function's metadata during decoration. The wraps function is also in the functools module.

The created function run_stats_model_a is known as a *partial* function. When we call it, we no longer need to specify the shared parameters, which have already been taken care of. Using the partial function technique, we can create separate partial functions for each project, and they can significantly simplify the calling signature, making your code more readable.

7.5.3   *Discussion*

This entire section (7.5) is brief. I use a simple example to show you a useful technique: partial functions. When you accumulate your codebase, you'll find that you often need to use some functions across multiple locations. In this case, you can create partial functions from existing functions. These partial functions freeze the shared parameters in a location, and you can omit these parameters to improve the clarity of your code.

7.5.4   *Challenge*

Partial functions are created from other functions. How can you find out which function a partial function is created from?

> **HINT**   A partial function has extra attributes compared with a regular function. You can check its attributes by calling `dir(partial_function_created)`. Inspect the list to see which attribute is relevant.

Summary

- Lambda functions are intended to perform a small job for one-time use, which implies that you don't assign a lambda function to a variable.
- Although lambda functions are handy, don't reinvent the wheel. Where applicable, use built-in functions to perform the same job without defining a lambda function, such as using the built-in `int` instead of `lambda x: int(x)`.
- Functions are first-class citizens in Python, as they're other objects. Any operations that you can do with an object can be applied to functions too.
- Higher-order functions take functions as input and/or return functions as output. Some notable built-in higher-order functions include `sorted`, `map`, and `filter`.
- Using decorators, we can apply additional functionalities to other functions without changing the decorated functions' original functionalities.
- Although not introduced formally in this chapter, closures are an essential programming concept. They're inner functions created and returned by higher-order functions, and they also bind variables defined by the higher-order function. Decorators are an application of the closure technique.
- We can create generators from a generator function, which uses the `yield` keyword to yield an item and gives up control temporarily. When it's called again, it remembers its state and continues the execution by rendering the next applicable item or completing iteration.
- Compared with other iterators, generators are more memory-efficient, as they don't load all their elements up front, unlike conventional iterators such as lists and tuples, which must load all their items before they can be iterated.
- We use partial functions to freeze some parameters of a shared function so that we have a localized version of the function that specifically serves the project. A partial function eliminates the need to specify the frozen parameters, which makes your code cleaner.

Part 3

Defining classes

Built-in data structures are the most generic data types, and we can use them no matter what kind of application we're building. Despite the prevalence of these data types, their generic nature doesn't allow us to define customized data and operations for these objects. Thus, we must almost always define our own classes. In these classes, we define a variety of attributes, giving us compartments to store customized data and a series of methods to perform customized operations. With the increasing complexity of our application, we define multiple classes, and we need to ensure that these classes work coherently and collectively. As you can imagine, defining well-behaved classes to serve an application is a challenging task. In this part, you'll learn the essential techniques for defining custom classes.

Defining
user-friendly classes

This chapter covers

- Defining the initialization method
- Creating instance, static, and class methods
- Applying encapsulation to a class
- Creating proper string representations
- Defining a superclass and subclasses

The core of any application is data. Although built-in data types are useful for managing data, you'll find them to be limited because they only have attributes and methods that are designed to address the most generic functionalities, including named tuples (section 3.3). You may have noticed that you don't have useful methods to manipulate tasks with named tuples. But the task management app (like all applications in general) addresses specific business needs, which require data models that can handle those needs. Thus, custom classes are irreplaceable elements in your application. By defining proper attributes for the class, you can better capture the data needed in your application. By defining proper methods, you can better process the data in your application.

In this chapter, I focus on how to define attributes and different kinds of methods for your class, mostly using the `Task` class as part of the task management app to discuss the pertinent topics. The goal of defining a good custom class is to make it user-friendly—not only robust in terms of its attributes and methods (what should be available), but also maintainable in terms of implementing its functionalities in a clear organization (how they are structured).

8.1   *How do I define the initialization method for a class?*

When we use built-in classes, such as `list` and `dict`, we can use their constructors to create instance objects (or instances) of these classes. The process of creating an instance is known as *instantiation:* you create the instance object. Under the hood, creating an instance object involves calling the __init__ method, as shown in the next listing.

> **Listing 8.1   Creating a `Task` class with no meaningful initialization**

```
class Task:
    def __init__(self):
        print("Creating an instance of Task class")


task = Task()
# output: Creating an instance of Task class
```

As you can see, we call the constructor `Task()` to create an instance, which triggers calling the __init__ method. If you're wondering what the name of this method (init) means, it stands for *initialization,* setting the initial states for the instance object. Thus, this method is the most essential method that you almost always define in a custom class. In this section, you'll learn the best practice for defining the initialization method: __init__.

8.1.1   *Demystifying self: The first parameter in __init__*

In listing 8.1, although we don't have any implementation for the __init__ method, the method still has one parameter: `self`. More broadly, if you've ever read someone else's code, you should see that their __init__ method also uses `self` as its first parameter. If you've wondered what `self` is, this section demystifies it by addressing four questions:

- What does `self` stand for?
- Why don't we need to send an argument for `self`?
- Is `self` a keyword?
- Do we have to use `self` as the parameter name?

SELF: THE INSTANCE OBJECT

The first question is what `self` stands for. When you define methods in a class, most of the time, the methods are intended to manipulate instance objects, such as __init__, which sets the initial attributes for the new instance object. Thus, we need a convenient way to refer to the instance object. If you happen to know other object-oriented programming (OOP) languages, you know that these languages may use this, that, self, or it to refer to the instance object. Python uses self to refer to the instance objects in the method definitions. To prove the claim that self refers to the newly created instance object, we can use the built-in id function, which uniquely identifies an object in the memory, as follows:

```python
class Task:
    def __init__(self):
        print(f"Memory address (self): {id(self)}")

task = Task()
# output: Memory address (self): 140702458470768

task_address = f"Memory address (task): {id(task)}"
print(task_address)
# output: Memory address (task): 140702458470768
```

> **Expect a different value on your computer, and each run can have a new value.**

The printout reveals that the self's and task's memory addresses are the same, meaning that they're the same object—the newly created instance object of the Task class.

> **REMINDER** The id function checks an object's memory address. Because each object has a unique memory address, when objects have the same memory address, they're the same object.

SETTING SELF IMPLICITLY

When we create an instance object by calling the constructor Task(), we don't use any arguments. But the underlying __init__ method does require one argument: self. How can you explain this apparent conflict? The reason is that the self argument is set, however implicitly, by Python. As you'll see, Python creates the instance object by calling __new__ and sends it to __init__ as the self argument. To understand the implicit setting of the self argument, observe the following code snippet:

```python
class Task:
    def __init__(self):
        print(f"__init__ gets called, creating object at {id(self)}")

    def __new__(cls):
        new_task = object.__new__(cls)
        print(f"__new__ gets called, creating object at {id(new_task)}")
        return new_task


task = Task()
# output the following lines:
__new__ gets called, creating object at 140702458469952
__init__ gets called, creating object at 140702458469952
```

In this code, we call the constructor Task(). Note that the construction involves the sequential automatic invocation of two special methods under the hood: __new__ and __init__. The __new__ method creates and returns (boldfaced) the new instance object, and the __init__ method doesn't return anything. The reason for this difference in returning a value is that after you call __new__, you need to refer to the instance object that you just created. Thus, if the __new__ method doesn't return that new instance object, you can't access and use it. By contrast, the __init__ method takes self as an argument; it refers to the new instance and manipulates the instance in-place.

To simulate the fact that the instance construction is a two-step process that calls __new__ and __init__, we can call these two methods manually. Please note that this simulation is meant to demonstrate the underlying machinery and is rarely used in a codebase:

```
task = Task.__new__(Task)
# output: __new__ gets called, creating object at 140702458476192


Task.__init__(task)
# output: __init__ gets called, creating object at 140702458476192
```

First, we use __new__ method to create an instance object: task. Then we can set task as the self argument in the __init__ method. As you can tell from the memory address, we're manipulating the same instance object. Figure 8.1 summarizes the process.

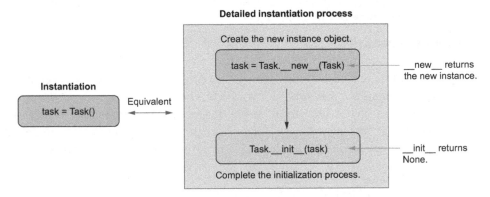

Figure 8.1 The detailed instantiation process behind the scenes. When you create an instance object by calling the constructor, the instance object is created first by the __new__ method. When it's created, it's sent to the __init__ method to complete the initialization, where the instance's attributes are set.

Because of the equivalence between the call to the constructor and two-step instantiation, you can think of using the constructor directly as being syntactic sugar for the two-step process. Moreover, using the constructor for instantiation is more concise and readable.

SELF IS NOT A KEYWORD

In Python, we use def to signify that we're creating a function, and we use for to signify that we're running a for loop. def and for are examples of keywords in Python, meaning that they're reserved by the language for special operations. Because we use `self` to refer to the instance in Python, which appears to be a special operation, this may lead some people to think that `self` is a keyword. As you'll see, however, `self` is not a keyword. One rule of keywords is that you can't use keywords as a variable name, as shown in this example:

```
def = 5
# ERROR: SyntaxError: invalid syntax

class = 7
# ERROR: SyntaxError: invalid syntax

self = 9
# Works!
```

We can't assign any value to `def` or `class`, but we can assign a value to `self`, clearly indicating that `self` is qualitatively different from other keywords. In fact, a more formal way to check whether a word is a reserved keyword is to take advantage of the keyword module, which provides the convenient `iskeyword` function:

```
import keyword

words_to_check = ["def", "class", "self", "lambda"]
for word in words_to_check:
    print(f"Is {word:^8} a keyword? {keyword.iskeyword(word)}")

# output the following lines:
Is   def    a keyword? True
Is   class  a keyword? True
Is   self   a keyword? False
Is   lambda a keyword? True
```

As shown in the preceding code snippet, `def`, `class`, and `lambda` are identified as keywords by the `iskeyword` function. By contrast, `self` isn't a keyword.

TRIVIA You can get the entire list of keywords by calling the `kwlist` function in the `keyword` module.

PREFERRING USING SELF AS THE PARAMETER NAME

We know that `self` refers to the instance object in `__init__` and that it's not a keyword. We may have seen that the first argument in `__init__` is always `self`; thus, we may assume that it must be named `self`. We're not required to use `self` as the parameter name, however. We can use any legitimate variable name (but it can't be a keyword). The following code snippet shows the use of `this` instead of `self` in `__init__`:

```
class Task:
    def __init__(this):
        print("An instance is created with this instead of self.")

task = Task()
# output: An instance is created with this instead of self.
```

As you can see, we can still create an instance object of the Task class without any problems when we use this. From the syntax perspective, we're not obligated to use self in __init__. But we should use self anyway; using self in __init__ is a convention, and every Python programmer should respect this convention.

> **READABILITY** Follow the common conventions, such as using self in __init__. When you follow the convention, it's easier for others to read your code because they know exactly what you mean.

8.1.2   Setting proper arguments in __init__

In the examples I've shown, I don't include arguments other than self in the __init__ method. This section shows what considerations we should give to the arguments we use in the __init__ method.

The __init__ method is intended to complete the initialization process for the new instance object, particularly setting the essential attributes to the instance. The discussion of named tuples in section 3.3 mentions that the Task class should handle three attributes for each task: title, description, and urgency level. The following code snippet shows the data model created with named tuples:

```
from collections import namedtuple

Task = namedtuple("Task", "title desc urgency")

task = Task("Laundry", "Wash clothes", 3)

print(task)
# output: Task(title='Laundry', desc='Wash clothes', urgency=3)
```

As you can see, using the named tuples-based data model, we create the instance object by specifying all three attributes. Thus, when we're creating a custom class other than named tuples, we should have the same mechanism that allows the users to set these attributes, adding the necessary arguments to the __init__ method:

```
class Task:
    def __init__(self, title, desc, urgency):
        self.title = title
        self.desc = desc
        self.urgency = urgency
```

By taking arguments, __init__ can perform an additional initialization procedure: setting the initial attributes from the arguments for the instance. It's important to note that the arguments should be related to the attributes of the instance object. In the body of the __init__ method, we're setting the instance's attributes with the arguments. With this updated __init__ method, we can create an instance object by supplying the arguments:

```
task = Task("Laundry", "Wash clothes", 3)
```

When the instance is created, it has all the needed attributes set up. To inspect the new instance's attributes, you can check the instance's special attribute __dict__. As you can see, the new instance task has these attributes stored as a dict object:

```
print(task.__dict__)
# output: {'title': 'Laundry', 'desc': 'Wash clothes', 'urgency': 3}
```

For the Task class, this specific example applies to the task management application, but your project uses different custom classes that address your data modeling needs. Thus, the question is what considerations you should use for the arguments in the __init__ method when you build your own custom class. In general, I recommend the following rules of thumb:

- *Identify the required arguments.* When you construct an instance, you want the new instance to have all the attributes set up and ready for use. Thus, you need to identify the arguments that are required to set the instance's attributes.
- *Prioritize key arguments.* Your custom class may require ten initial attributes that need to be set for a new instance object. Some attributes are always more important than others, however. You want to list the more important ones before the less important ones.
- *Use key arguments as positional.* This requirement is more of a style convention than a rule. You want users to be able to set important arguments as positional arguments, because calling a constructor without specifying keyword arguments is cleaner than using keyword arguments.
- *Limit the number of positional arguments.* This point is related to the preceding one. Although we prefer using positional arguments for the __init__ method, when there are too many positional arguments, readers may not know which is which. Thus, as a rule of thumb, I recommend using no more than four positional arguments. You can make additional arguments keyword-only (section 6.4.1).
- *Set applicable default values.* At its core, __init__ is a function. Thus, to make calling this function easier, you want to set default values for the arguments that most users don't bother changing. Of the ten initial attributes, it's likely that seven are the same in most use cases; thus, you can set default values for these seven attributes.

8.1.3 Specifying all attributes in __init__

In section 8.1.2, we discussed setting arguments in the __init__ method. With these arguments, we set the corresponding attributes for an instance object in the body of the __init__ method. An instance object can have more attributes than those created from __init__'s arguments. Although you can set an instance's attributes anywhere in the class's body, the best practice is to specify all attributes of an instance object in the body of the __init__ method. This section discusses this practice.

First, consider the next listing, in which the instance's attributes are initialized in multiple places. Please note that I don't recommend this pattern, as it's unclear about what attributes an instance can have.

Listing 8.2   Setting attributes elsewhere other than __init__

```
class Task:
    def __init__(self, title, desc, urgency):
        self.title = title
        self.desc = desc
        self.urgency = urgency

    def complete(self):
        self.status = "completed"

    def add_tag(self, tag):
        if not self.tags:
            self.tags = []
        self.tags.append(tag)
```

PEEK   The methods whose first parameter is `self` are known as *instance methods,* which are intended to be called by the instance objects of the class. We'll discuss them in section 8.2.

In listing 8.2, besides the `title`, `desc`, and `urgency` attributes, we set the attributes `status` and `tags` in the `complete` and `add_tag` methods, respectively. You don't want to adopt the pattern of initializing instance attributes everywhere (other than inside the `__init__` method) for two reasons:

- When you try to access these attributes, you encounter an `AttributeError` unless you've called these two methods, which set these attributes accordingly. In other words, if you access these attributes accidentally without calling the related methods, your application will crash:

```
task = Task("Laundry", "Wash clothes", 3)
print(task.status)

# ERROR: AttributeError: 'Task' object has no attribute 'status'

task.complete()
print(task.status)
# output: completed
```

- It's hard for users to know what attributes an instance object of the class can have. Particularly when your application is complicated, it's likely that your class has many functionalities. If you set attributes in these methods, users have a nightmare of a time trying to figure out the attributes of an instance object.

For these two reasons, we should specify all the attributes in `__init__`, even though some attributes are to be updated through a specific method call. In these cases, these attributes should have a reasonable initial value. The next listing shows the desired pattern.

Listing 8.3 Setting all attributes in __init__

```
class Task:
    def __init__(self, title, desc, urgency):
        self.title = title
        self.desc = desc
        self.urgency = urgency
        self.status = "created"
        self.tags = []

    def complete(self):
        self.status = "completed"

    def add_tag(self, tag):
        self.tags.append(tag)
```

With the updated pattern, after you create an instance object, it has all the attributes assigned properly, and we can inspect them by accessing the __dict__ special attribute:

```
task = Task("Laundry", "Wash clothes", 3)
print(task.__dict__)
# output: {'title': 'Laundry', 'desc': 'Wash clothes',
➥ 'urgency': 3, 'status': 'created', 'tags': []}
```

MAINTAINABILITY By placing all the attributes in __init__, you make it clear to your teammates what attributes an instance object of the class can have. When you access any attribute, it always has a value, so no AttributeError will be raised.

Now you can access the status and tags attributes without calling the complete and add_tag methods first. More importantly, readers can scan the __init__ method to know an instance's available attributes instead of looking for attributes buried in various methods (listing 8.2). Figure 8.2 shows the contrast between the two patterns.

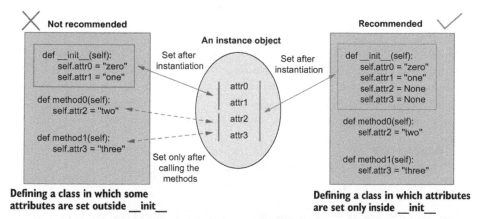

Figure 8.2 The contrast between two patterns that differ in where they specify the attributes for the instance object. In the unrecommended pattern, you initialize the attributes in various places. In the recommended pattern, you initialize the attributes only in the __init__ method, making it clear to readers what attributes an instance object has.

8.1.4   Defining class attributes outside the __init__ method

The initialization method should provide initialization for an instance object by defining its attributes on a per-instance basis. Notably, there can be shared attributes for all instance objects. In this case, you should not include them as instance attributes and should consider class attributes instead. This section discusses this feature.

> **CONCEPT**   *Class attributes* are those attributes that belong to the class (as an object), and all the instance objects of the class share the attributes through the class.

For simplicity, suppose that each task has an attribute user who creates the task. Theoretically, you can make user an instance attribute by using the following __init__ method:

```
def __init__(self, title, desc, urgency, user):
    self.title = title
    self.desc = desc
    self.urgency = urgency
    self.user = user
```

Because user is an instance attribute, you expect your application to need more memory, as you need to save user data for every instance. But it's important to know that in the application, after the user login, there will be only one user who will create all the tasks. Thus, all the instances should share the attribute user. To help reduce the memory cost of saving user for each instance, you should create a class attribute in this case:

```
class Task:
    user = "the logged in user"

    def __init__(self, title, desc, urgency):
        pass
```

Depending on the data model, you may need to define additional class attributes for your class. Defining class attributes is an important technique for saving memory, as the instances share the same attributes by referencing the same underlying object in memory. From a readability perspective, it's essential to know that you place the class attributes below the class definition head and above the __init__ method.

> **READABILITY**   All the class attributes should be explicit and clear. Place them right below the class definition head.

8.1.5   Discussion

You almost always implement the __init__ method in your custom class. The __init__ method should include all the attributes for an instance object so that readers don't have to guess what attribute the instances have. Also, place the __init__ method before any other methods in the body of the class. Why? From a readability perspective, we want to know what data a class can hold; the instance's attributes represent the data that the class holds. Defining a proper __init__ method is the first thing you want to work on in a custom class.

8.1.6   Challenge

Leah is working on the task management app to learn coding in Python. She suggested allowing users to specify tags during instantiation. So, she needed to add tags as an argument in the __init__ method (listing 8.3). In most cases, she expected users to set an empty list to the tags argument. What default value should she set for tags in this case?

> **HINT**   At its core, __init__ is a function. You may recall from section 6.1 that we should set a default value for a mutable argument in a function.

8.2   When do I define instance, static, and class methods?

After we set proper attributes for the instance objects, it's time to provide functionalities to the class. In listing 8.3, the class has two functions: complete and add_tag. These functions are known as *instance methods*. Besides instance methods, you can define static and class methods. These methods are intended for different use cases. This section explores situations in which you need to define instance, static, or class methods.

8.2.1   Defining instance methods for manipulating individual instances

An instance method is intended to be called on an instance object of the class. Thus, when you want to change the data of an individual instance object or run operations that rely on an individual instance object's data, such as attributes or other instance methods, you need to define instance methods.

> **REMINDER**   Syntactically, you're allowed to use a different parameter name for the self argument, but it's a convention to use self as the name.

The hallmark of an instance method is that you set self as its first parameter. As discussed extensively in section 8.1.1, self refers to the instance object in the __init__ method, which is true for all instance methods. In listing 8.4, we verify that the self argument in instance methods also refers to the instance object with a simple modification of the Task class's complete method from listing 8.3. Please note that to save space, I don't include other implementation details of the Task class, such as __init__.

Listing 8.4   Creating and using an instance method

```
class Task:
    def __init__(self, title, desc, urgency):
        self.title = title
        self.desc = desc
```

```
        self.urgency = urgency
        self._status = "created"

    def complete(self):
        print(f"Memory Address (self): {id(self)}")
        self.status = "completed"


task = Task("Laundry", "Wash clothes", 3)
task.complete()
# output: Memory Address (self): 140508514865536


task_id = f"Memory Address (task): {id(task)}"
print(task_id)
# output: Memory Address (task): 140508514865536
```

As you can see, self in the complete method has the same memory address as the task instance, which indicates that self is indeed the instance object on which we call the method. Under the hood, an instance method is invoked by the class calling the method with the instance as an argument, as illustrated in figure 8.3.

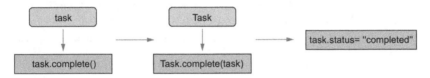

Figure 8.3   The underlying action for calling an instance method. When you use an instance object to call an instance method, it's processed as using the class to call the method with the instance object as an argument. At the end, the function's operations are applied to the instance object that calls the instance method.

The single purpose of an instance method is to manipulate a specific instance object. That is, you always take the following calling pattern to use an instance method: instance.instance_method(arg0, arg1, arg2).

In the body of the instance method, the operations should be about manipulating the instance object that we call the method on. Therefore, if you find out that the method doesn't manipulate the instance or doesn't rely on the instance-related data, it's likely that the method shouldn't be implemented as an instance method to begin with. Instead, you may need to implement the method as a static method.

8.2.2   *Defining static methods for utility functionalities*

When you implement utility-related functions that are not specific to any instance, you need to define a static method. This section discusses how to define a static method.

Unlike an instance method, which uses self as its first parameter, a static method doesn't use self, as it's intended to be independent of any instance object, and there is no need to refer to a specific instance. To define a static method, we use the static-method decorator for the function within the body of the class. Consider the example in listing 8.5.

REMINDER   Decorators add additional functionalities to the decorated function without changing its original functionality.

Listing 8.5   Creating a static method

```
from datetime import datetime

class Task:
    @staticmethod
    def get_timestamp():
        now = datetime.now()
        timestamp = now.strftime("%b %d %Y, %H:%M")
        return timestamp
```

In listing 8.5, get_timestamp is a static method defined with the @staticmethod decorator. In this static method, we create a formatted timestamp string, which we can use whenever we need to show users the exact time. To call this method, we use the following pattern: CustomClass.static_method(arg0, arg1, arg2). We can try this pattern with the get_timestamp static method:

```
refresh_time = f"Data Refreshed: {Task.get_timestamp()}"

print(refresh_time)
# output: Data Refreshed: Mar 04 2022, 15:43
```

As you can see, we use the static method by calling Task.get_timestamp(), which retrieves the current timestamp in the desired format. This operation represents a general utility need; as you can imagine, there are multiple scenarios in which a timestamp should be displayed. Providing utility functionalities is the main purpose of static methods. That is, when you need to define utility-related methods that are independent of any instance object, you should use the @staticmethod decorator to create static methods. When you read someone else's custom class and notice any use of @staticmethod, you know that it's a static method, as the staticmethod decorator is a hallmark of a static method.

8.2.3   Defining class methods for accessing class-level attributes

In section 8.2.2, you learned about defining static methods that are utility methods without the need to access individual instance objects. It's possible that some methods may need to access the attributes of the class. In this case, you need to define a class method.

The first hallmark of a class method is that you use cls as its first parameter. Like self in an instance method, cls is not a keyword, and you can give this argument other applicable names, but it's a convention to name it cls, and every Python programmer should respect this convention.

READABILITY You name the first parameter as `cls` in a class method. When other programmers see `cls`, they know that it's referring to the class.

The implementation of static methods requires the `staticmethod` decorator. A class method also uses the `classmethod` decorator—the second hallmark of a class method. The method is called a *class method* because it needs to access the attributes or methods of the class. Consider an example. Suppose that in our task management application, we obtain data in the form of a `dict` object, which stores the data for a task:

```
task_dict = {"title": "Laundry", "desc": "Wash clothes", "urgency": 3}
```

To construct an instance object of the `Task` class from this `dict` object, we may have to do the following:

```
task = Task(task_dict["title"], task_dict["desc"], task_dict["urgency"])
```

But because we may often obtain this kind of `dict` data and create a corresponding `Task` instance, we should provide a more convenient way to address this need. Fortunately, a class method is a good solution, as the following listing shows.

Listing 8.6   Creating a class method

```
class Task:
    def __init__(self, title, desc, urgency):
        self.title = title
        self.desc = desc
        self.urgency = urgency
        self._status = "created"

    @classmethod
    def task_from_dict(cls, task_dict):
        title = task_dict["title"]
        desc = task_dict["desc"]
        urgency = task_dict["urgency"]
        task_obj = cls(title, desc, urgency)
        return task_obj
```

As you can see in listing 8.6, we define a class method called `task_from_dict` with `@classmethod`. In the body of this method, because `cls` stands for the class that we're working with (`Task`), we can use the class's constructor directly—`cls(title, desc, urgency)`—to create an instance object. With this class method, we can conveniently create a `Task` instance object from a `dict` object:

```
task = Task.task_from_dict(task_dict)

print(task.__dict__)
# output: {'title': 'Laundry', 'desc': 'Wash clothes',
➥ 'urgency': 3, 'status': 'created', 'tags': []}
```

From a general perspective, a class method is used mostly as a *factory method,* meaning that this kind of method is used to create an instance object from a particular form of data. Section 4.5 mentions that DataFrame is a spreadsheet-like data model in the pandas library. It has a couple of class methods—from_dict and from_records—that you can use to construct instance objects of the DataFrame class.

8.2.4   *Discussion*

Of the three kinds of methods, instance and class methods are the most straightforward. Static methods are a little trickier. Because they're intended to provide utility functionalities, it's generally acceptable to define them outside a class; after all, they don't need to manipulate any instance or the class. In general, I recommend that you place a static method outside a class if it addresses a more general utility functionality than a class should handle. Taking the data processing library pandas as an example, the core data models are Series and DataFrame classes. One utility function, to_datetime, converts data to a date object. This function addresses a more general need; thus, it's not implemented as a static method within Series or DataFrame.

8.2.5   *Challenge*

While Leah continues to work on the task management app, she realizes that she needs to create an instance of the Task class from a tuple object: ("Laundry", "Wash clothes", 3). What kind of method should she implement to address this need in the class?

> **HINT**   We implement a method that creates an instance object from a dict object in listing 8.6.

8.3   *How do I apply finer access control to a class?*

In a custom class, you may define tens of methods. Some methods are for internal use by you (the developers of the class), whereas other methods are for other developers that use your class. Consider the following scenario. In the Task class, another method formats the note for the complete method:

```
class Task:
    def __init__(self, title, desc, urgency):
        self.title = title
        self.desc = desc
        self.urgency = urgency
        self._status = "created"
        self.note = ""

    def complete(self, note = ""):
        self.status = "completed"
        self.note = self.format_note(note)

    def format_note(self, note):
        formatted_note = note.title()
        return formatted_note
```

When the user calls the `complete` method, this method sets a formatted note to the `note` attribute by calling the `format_note` method. Notably, the user can also call `format_note` directly. This behavior isn't the desired behavior, as one key principle of OOP is encapsulation: you expose only attributes and methods that users need to access and nothing more. The implication of encapsulation is that you apply finer access control to the class. In this section, we'll talk about some key access control techniques.

CONCEPT   *Encapsulation* refers to a coding principle that is widely adopted in OOP languages, in which you bundle data and methods into a class and allow access to only the part of the data relevant to users.

Public, protected, and private

In a typical OOP language, to restrict access to a specific attribute or method, many languages use `protected` or `private` as a keyword. The opposite of `protected` and `private` is `public`, meaning that the attributes and methods are available to all users both outside and inside a class. *Protected* means that the attributes and methods are available to the class and its subclasses but not outside the class. *Private* means that the attributes and methods are only available to the class itself, not to its subclasses or outside the class. Because of their restrictive access to the inside, *private* and *protected* are also referred to as *nonpublic*.

8.3.1   *Creating protected methods by using an underscore as the prefix*

At its core, Python is an OOP language. Unlike other OOP languages that use `private` and/or `protected` for access control, however, Python has no formal mechanism that restricts access to any attribute or method. In other words, everything in a class is public, and Python doesn't have `protected` or `private` as a keyword. The convention in creating an access-control mechanism is to use underscores as the prefix for the attribute or method. A one-underscore prefix means protected, and a double-underscore prefix means private (as discussed in section 8.3.2). In this section, you'll learn about defining protected methods. Notably, the same mechanism applies to creating protected and private attributes.

When I talked about named tuples in section 3.3, I mentioned that creating a named tuple data model allows us to take advantage of an integrated development environment's (IDE's) autocompletion hints by populating the available attributes after you enter the dot following the object. This approach can be inconvenient, however, if the populated list includes the methods you're not going to use. As a user, you're not going to call the `format_note` method yourself; thus, it's ideal for the autocompletion suggestion not to show `format_note` (figure 8.4).

Apparently, by hiding the functions you don't need in the autocompletion hint list, you can have higher coding efficiency. But how does the IDE know what functions to hide? The magic is in using an underscore as a prefix for the method's name, which

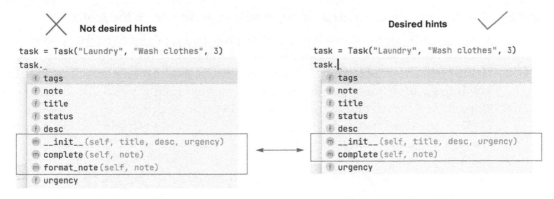

**Autocompletion hints
include format_note.**

**Autocompletion hints don't
include format_note.**

Figure 8.4   Different autocompletion hints provided for the instance object. It's less desirable if the autocompletion hints include functions that users don't need to use—in this case, the `format_note` method.

indicates that it's a protected method. Instead of format_note, we can name the method _format_note. The significance of the underscore prefix is twofold:

- This method is not intended to be used outside the class, so it's not prompted in the autocompletion hints when you work outside the class, as shown in the right panel of figure 8.4.
- This method is still available as part of the autocompletion hints when you work inside the class, as shown in figure 8.5.

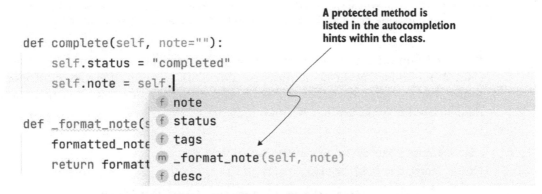

Figure 8.5   The availability of a protected method within the class. After you enter the dot, the available attributes and methods for the instance object appear in the list, and the list includes the protected method.

These two implications are in line with the encapsulation principle. You restrict outside users' access to the functions they don't need and keep the same functions available to users who do need them.

8.3.2 *Creating private methods by using double underscores as the prefix*

In section 8.3.1, you learned how to define protected methods to restrict public access to the methods you don't want users to see. Besides using protected methods, you can define private methods, which achieve the same encapsulation effect. In this section, you'll learn to define a private method. More importantly, you'll see why it's sometimes a good idea to define a private method instead of a protected method.

You've learned that defining a private method requires two underscores as the prefix. Let's continue using the `format_note` method as an example. To make the method private, change the name to `__format_note`. With this name change, the method's access is consistently restricted to the internal of the class (figure 8.6).

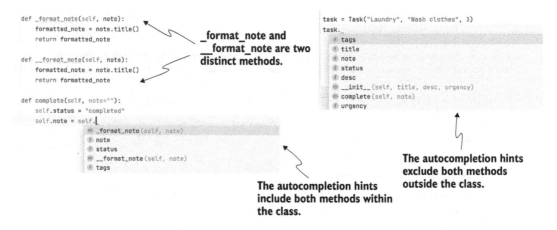

Figure 8.6   Internal but no external access to private methods. The `__format_note` method starts with double underscores, meaning that it's private. A private method is available only within the class.

Protected and private methods are similar in terms of their availabilities inside the class. As mentioned at the beginning of section 8.3.1, however, there are no strict non-public methods in Python. If you want to access protected methods, you can, although many IDEs display a warning, as shown in figure 8.7.

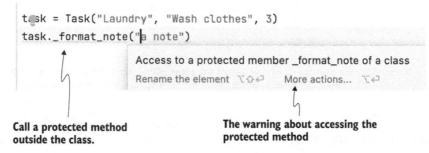

Call a protected method outside the class.

The warning about accessing the protected method

Figure 8.7   Calling a protected method outside a class is technically allowed, but a warning appears in response to this unintended behavior, as protected methods are not intended for outside use.

What happens when someone is trying to access a private method outside a class? A seemingly strange thing happens. As shown in the following code snippet, no such method or attribute exists:

```
task.__format_note("a note")
# ERROR: AttributeError: 'Task' object has no attribute '__format_note'.
```

This "inaccessibility" of __format_note outside the class marks a major difference between private and protected methods, as it seems to be more private than a protected method such as _format_note. Thus, if you want to have more restrictive access to nonpublic methods, you should use double underscores as the prefix to create private methods instead of using one underscore to create protected methods.

> **MAINTAINABILITY** Because of the differential public access rule between protected and private methods, use private methods if you want to have restrictive access.

I said that Python has no real nonpublic methods, which is why I put quotation marks around *inaccessibility* earlier in this section. But the question is how to access a private method if you need to. You may want to manipulate some code within a package developed by others, for example. As shown in the following code snippet, you can access the private method by calling _Task__format_note("a note"):

```
task._Task__format_note("a note")
# output: 'A Note'
```

This technique is called *name mangling*, which converts a private method to a differently named method, allowing a private method to be called outside the class. Specifically, the name mangling follows the rule __private_method -> _ClassName__private_method. Thus, __format_note becomes _Task__format_note, and we can call this private method outside the Task class.

> **CONCEPT** *Name mangling* is the process of converting a private method name to a different name by using _ClassName as a prefix. Then the private method can be accessed outside the class.

In addition to having different public access rules, protected and private methods have different rules for accessing them within the subclass where these methods are defined. I'll review this topic in section 8.5.

8.3.3 *Creating read-only attributes with the property decorator*

One major reason for implementing a custom class is that you can define as many attributes as you need so that the custom class, as a cohesive entity, can bundle all related data through well-defined attributes and methods. Notably, a custom class is *mutable*, meaning that you can change the attributes of the instance objects. But you may not want users to change some attributes. In that case, you should consider another access control technique: *read-only attributes*. Users can read these attributes but can't change them. In this section, you'll learn how to define read-only attributes.

For the `Task` class, consider the `status` attribute. For now, users can freely change the status attribute for an instance:

```
print(task.status)
# output: created

task.status = "completed"
print(task.status)
# output: completed
```

For encapsulation purposes, we don't allow users to set the `status` attribute freely. To update a task's status to `completed`, for example, they should call the `complete` method. So the question is how to prevent users from setting `status` manually. The solution is to take advantage of the `property` decorator. The next listing shows the technique.

Listing 8.7   Using the `property` decorator

```
class Task:
    def __init__(self, title, desc, urgency):
        self.title = title
        self.desc = desc
        self.urgency = urgency
        self._status = "created"

    @property
    def status(self):
        return self._status

    def complete(self):
        self._status = "completed"
```

In listing 8.7, we keep only the code that is relevant to defining a read-only attribute technique. In the code, we should note three significant things:

- The instance has a protected attribute _status.
- We define an instance method `status`, which is decorated by the `property` decorator.
- In the `complete` method, we update the _status attribute.

We know that when we call a method on an object, we use the call operator—the parentheses following the method name. But the `property` decorator makes a method accessible as though it's an attribute. For simplicity, you can refer to a method with the `property` decorator as a property, and you don't need to use the call operator to access a property:

```
task = Task("Laundry", "Wash clothes", 3)

print(task.status)
# output: created
```

Notably, a property represents a read-only attribute. You can read it as shown in the preceding code snippet. You can't set it, however, which is exactly what you want: to prevent users from setting `status` directly, as shown in the following listing.

Listing 8.8   Read-only property

```
>>> task.status = "completed"
# ERROR: AttributeError: can't set attribute 'status'
```

> **MAINTAINABILITY**   Creating read-only properties can prevent users from changing a specific attribute, maintaining data stability.

In a more general scenario, when you define a read-only property, it's common to create a protected attribute designed to handle the corresponding data internally. `status`, for example, is a read-only property, and we use `_status` to handle status-related data inside the class.

> **QUESTION**   Why do we want to use a protected attribute instead of a private attribute? Think about the difference between them in terms of access from a subclass.

8.3.4 *Verifying data integrity with a property setter*

In section 8.3.3, we introduced the `property` decorator, which we used to create the read-only property `status` for the `Task` class. The implication of the read-only property is that we can't set a value for it. That behavior isn't always the desired behavior, however. Sometimes, we want to have a mechanism to set a value for a property. One useful scenario for setting a property is verifying data integrity, as discussed in this section.

> **CONCEPT**   In a conventional OOP language such as Java, two concepts are related to a property: getter and setter. The *getter* is the method that allows you to retrieve the property's value, and the *setter* is the method through which you set the value for the property. The `property` decorator creates a getter, and in the following paragraphs, we're creating a setter.

Suppose that we allow users to set the `status` property directly. The value must be a valid one, however. Consider that a task's status can be `created`, `started`, `completed`, or `suspended`. How can we ensure that the set value is one of them? This kind of data verification of property can be best addressed with the property setter technique, as shown in the next listing.

Listing 8.9   Creating a setter for a property

```
class Task:
    # __init__ stays the same

    @property
    def status(self):
        return self._status

    @status.setter
    def status(self, value):
        allowed_values = ["created", "started", "completed", "suspended"]
        if value in allowed_values:
            self._status = value
            print(f"task status set to {value}")
        else:
            print(f"invalid status: {value}")    ◁──┐
```

The best practice is to raise an exception (see section 12.4).

In listing 8.9, after creating the status property, we create a setter for this property by using @status.setter, which adopts the general form @property_name.setter. This setter is an instance method, which takes a value argument that stands for the value we want to assign to the property. In the body of the setter, we verify that the value is one of the four possibilities. With this setter, we're able to set the status property:

```
task = Task("Laundry", "Wash clothes", 3)
task.status = "completed"
# output: task status set to completed

task.status = "random"
# output: invalid status: random
```

As you can see, we can directly set the status to completed. More important, when we're trying to set an invalid value, we're notified of this error. Although we can create getters and setters to convert attributes to properties, we don't want to, because they complicate the class. Unless you implement properties for reasons such as read-only or data verification, you should access and set the attributes directly instead of going through properties. This pattern of direct access and manipulation separates Python from other OOP languages, making Python code more concise in general.

8.3.5   *Discussion*

Defining private and protected methods is an essential technique for implementing encapsulation for the class; it helps minimize the public attributes of a class. When users work with the classes, they'll be given the autocompletion hints for these public attributes, making their work more efficient. Don't try to encapsulate everything by creating setters and getters as some other OOP languages do; that practice isn't Pythonic. In most cases, you should use direct accessing and setting of attributes instead of properties, because the former technique is more straightforward and requires less implementation code.

8.3.6 Challenge

Suppose that the urgency attribute should have an integer value between 1 and 5. Can you convert it to a property with a setter? The setter allows you to check the value.

> **HINT** You can use a protected attribute, such as _urgency, as the internal representation of the urgency data, and create a property called urgency.

8.4 How do I customize string representation for a class?

In section 8.1, we studied the initialization method __init__. This kind of method, the name of which is surrounded by two sets of double underscores, is known as a *special method*. Special methods carry special operations, such as __init__, which is invoked when we create an instance object using the constructor. Notably, when we implement a special method in a class, we can say that we're overriding this method, as all Python classes are subclasses of the object class, which implements these special methods.

> **CONCEPT** In an OOP language, overriding means that a subclass provides different implementations for a method that is defined in its parent class.

In this section, I'll show you two other special methods: __str__ and __repr__, which provide customized string representations for a class.

8.4.1 Overriding __str__ to show meaningful information for an instance

In many places, we need to inspect the instance objects that we're working with. One common method is the print function, which shows the string representation of the object. Using this method, we can see what an instance of the Task class looks like:

```
print(task)
# output: <__main__.Task object at 0x7f9f280d6800>
```

The information includes the instance's class and its memory address, but nothing else. In other words, we don't see anything more meaningful about the instance, such as its attributes. In this section, we'll see how we can show more meaningful information of an instance with the print function.

When you use print with a custom class instance, the special method that is invoked is __str__, which defines the string representation of the instance. To provide customized string representation other than the default one shown in the preceding code snippet, we can override __str__ in our Task class, as the next listing shows.

> **Listing 8.10 Overriding __str__ in a class**

```
class Task:
    def __init__(self, title, desc, urgency):
        self.title = title
        self.desc = desc
        self.urgency = urgency

    def __str__(self):
        return f"{self.title}: {self.desc}, urgency level {self.urgency}"
```

When you override __str__ in a class, you should note three things:

- It's an instance method, as it's intended to provide a string representation for an instance object.
- It should return a str object as its return value.
- The returned string should provide descriptive information for the instance. In our case, we want to show the key attributes of the instance, including title, desc, and urgency.

After overriding the __str__ method, we can see what we observe with the print function:

```
task = Task("Laundry", "Wash clothes", 3)

print(task)
# output: Laundry: Wash clothes, urgency level 3
```

Besides print, we also often use an f-string to prepare string output for data display. When you include an instance object in curly braces, the interpolation of the instance calls the __str__ method under the hood. Observe this behavior:

```
planned_task = f"Next Task - {task}"

print(planned_task)
# output: Next Task - Laundry: Wash clothes, urgency level 3
```

If you want to invoke the __str__ method on an instance explicitly, the preferred approach is str(instance), although we can call Class.__str__(instance) directly:

```
str(task)
# output: Laundry: Wash clothes, urgency level 3
```

8.4.2   Overriding __repr__ to provide instantiation information

Many people like to use Python in an interactive Python console, particularly when they're learning Python, as the console provides real-time output of the code. In the console, if you enter a str variable, you see its string value:

```
>>> planned_task
'Next Task - Laundry: Wash clothes, urgency level 3'
```

If you try to do that with the task instance, you'll see something like this:

```
>>> task
<__main__.Task object at 0x7f9f280d6f80>
```

We've already implemented the __str__ method, which doesn't change the displayed information for the instance in an interactive console. In this section, we'll see how to change the string representation displayed in a console.

When the interactive console shows the string representation for the instance, the special method that is invoked is __repr__. First, I'll show you how to implement __repr__ in a class (see listing 8.11) and explain key things to note:

- It's an instance method, as it provides string representation information on an instance-specific basis.
- It returns a string value.
- The string should provide information about the instantiation. Specifically, if other users type the string as code, it should create an instance object that has the same attributes as the current instance object.

Listing 8.11   Overriding `__repr__` in a class

```
class Task:
    def __init__(self, title, desc, urgency):
        self.title = title
        self.desc = desc
        self.urgency = urgency

    def __str__(self):
        return f"{self.title}: {self.desc}, urgency level {self.urgency}"

    def __repr__(self):
        return f"Task({self.title!r}, {self.desc!r}, {self.urgency})"
```

> !r requests the __repr__ method to be used for string interpolation.

After implementing __repr__, we can inspect the instance of the Task class in an interactive Python console:

```
>>> task = Task("Laundry", "Wash clothes", 3)
>>> task
Task('Laundry', 'Wash clothes', 3)
```

To call __repr__ on an instance, you should use repr(instance) instead of Class.__repr__(instance):

```
repr(task)
# output: Task('Laundry', 'Wash clothes', 3)
```

8.4.3   Understanding the differences between __str__ and __repr__

In sections 8.4.1 and 8.4.2, you learned about __str__ and __repr__, both of which are designed to provide string representation for instances of a custom class. This section addresses their differences.

DIFFERENT PURPOSES

The first difference, which is also the biggest, is that the methods serve different purposes. The string provided by __repr__ is intended for debugging and development, so it's for developers. Specifically, developers should be able to construct an instance literally from the string. As mentioned in section 2.2, we can use the built-in function eval to evaluate a string literal to derive the underlying object. We can do the same thing here:

```
task = Task("Laundry", "Wash clothes", 3)

task_repr = repr(task)

task_repr_eval = eval(task_repr)

print(type(task_repr_eval))
# output: <class '__main__.Task'>

print(task_repr_eval)
# output: Laundry: Wash clothes, urgency level 3
```

By contrast, the string provided by __str__ is intended to show descriptive information and is for regular users of the code. Thus, the string is less formal than that provided by __repr__, which shows the instantiation information.

DIFFERENT USAGES

Although both methods provide string representation for a class, __str__ is the method that underlies both the print function and the interpolation in an f-string. By contrast, __repr__ is the method to use when you try to inspect an instance in an interactive console.

In listing 8.11, you may notice that we append !r to the interpolation of self.title. !r is known as a *conversion flag*, which requests that the interpolated string of the object call __repr__ instead of __str__ to create the string representation. By default, interpolating an instance of a custom class uses the string created from __str__. To override this default behavior, you use the conversion flag following the instance: f"{instance!r}". Relatedly, the default conversion flag for an instance is !s, which uses the string created from __str__. In other words, the expressions f"{instance}" and f"{instance!s}" are equivalent.

You may wonder why we need to use the !r flag for title and desc but not for urgency. The reason is that both title and desc are str objects. Their string representations from __str__ have no quotation marks. Thus, if we use their default interpolation, the string from __repr__ can't be used to construct an instance object, as follows:

```
class Task:
    def __init__(self, title, desc, urgency):
        self.title = title
        self.desc = desc
        self.urgency = urgency

    def __str__(self):
        return f"{self.title}: {self.desc}, urgency level {self.urgency}"

    def __repr__(self):
```

```
            return f"Task({self.title}, {self.desc}, {self.urgency})"


task = Task("Laundry", "Wash clothes", 3)

print(repr(task))
# output: Task(Laundry, Wash clothes, 3)
```

In the revised class, we omit the !r conversion flag for `title` and `desc`. From the printout, we can see that there are no more quotation marks for `Laundry` and `Wash clothes`. As you can expect, we can't construct a `Task` instance from this string:

```
eval(repr(task))
# ERROR: SyntaxError: invalid syntax. Perhaps you forgot a comma?
```

By contrast, the string representation from __repr__ does have quotation marks, as quotation marks are required for string literals, such as `"Laundry"` as opposed to `Laundry`. The former is a valid `str` object, but the latter is not. (It will be treated as a variable named `Laundry`, but it can't be used because we never define a variable called `Laundry`.)

8.4.4   Discussion

The essential purpose of the __repr__ method is to explain what the object is in an unambiguous way. Because the string generated from the `repr` method (note that calling `repr` invokes the __repr__ method in the class) should represent a text that we can use to reconstruct a similar object, any strings generated by `repr` should have quotes to make them valid Python string literals. Don't forget to use the !r conversion flag if you use an f-string. I recommend that you implement both the __str__ and __repr__ methods for custom classes. If you prefer to implement only one method, override __repr__, because Python uses __repr__ when __str__ isn't implemented.

8.4.5   Challenge

For the `Task` class, we return `f"Task({self.title!r}, {self.desc!r}, {self.urgency})"` for the __repr__ method, in which we hardcode the class name `Task` in the f-string. A general programming principle is that we minimize hardcoded data. Do you know how we can retrieve the class name programmatically?

> **HINT**   An instance has a special attribute __class__ to identify its class, and a class has a special attribute __name__ to retrieve the class's name.

8.5   Why and how do I create a superclass and subclasses?

An essential concept in OOP is *inheritance,* which generally refers to the process of creating a child class that can reuse the implementations, or part of them, of a parent class. In the meantime, you can apply customized implementations to the child class, which becomes better at addressing specific questions than the parent class. The child class is also known as a *subclass,* and the parent class is also known as a *superclass.*

TRIVIA   Subclasses and superclasses are relative. A subclass is its own subclass's superclass.

Creating a subclass is a more advanced topic than many others that we have discussed so far. As you'll find out in this section, it's less straightforward to manage a superclass with multiple subclasses than distinct unrelated classes. Thus, a rule of thumb is that you justify the use of subclasses before you commit to implementing subclasses. In this section, we'll review what constitutes good justification and examine the technical details of implementing a subclass.

8.5.1   Identifying the use scenario of subclasses

When your project's scope grows, you'll define more classes to deal with increased data. At this stage, all classes have no inheritance relationships. You notice, however, that some classes are similar in their functionalities; a level of code repetition exists. If you recall the DRY (Don't Repeat Yourself) principle, you may realize that it's time to refactor these classes. One essential approach is creating subclasses to reduce the overlapped implementations between classes. In this section, we'll see when to use subclasses.

> **Top-down (superclass to subclasses) or bottom-up (subclasses to superclass)?**
>
> When you try to implement subclasses in a project, two common scenarios can happen. In the first scenario, you start with one class as a data model, and you realize that you need to create subclasses from this class to form more specific data models. In the second scenario, you start with multiple classes as separate data models, and you realize that a considerable number of functionalities are similar between these classes. In this case, you can create a superclass from which the current class can inherit.
>
> Both scenarios can happen in a project. In this section, we'll focus on the second scenario: the bottom-up one. Based on my experience, a project typically starts with a flat data model structure—multiple classes for each model. When you implement these classes, you recognize similarities between them, making it necessary to create a superclass.

Suppose that our task management application supports user registration. There are two kinds of users: supervisors and subordinates. When we start to develop our application, we've created two separate classes, `Supervisor` and `Subordinate`, to manage the data for supervisors and subordinates, respectively. Figure 8.8 provides a visual overview of the attributes and methods of these two classes.

As you can see, these two classes are similar, sharing most attributes and methods. In this case, you should consider creating a superclass that handles the shared functionalities. To handle the distinct functionalities for each type, you can inherit the

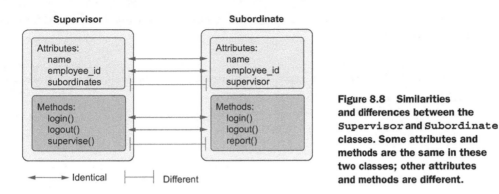

Figure 8.8 Similarities and differences between the `Supervisor` and `Subordinate` classes. Some attributes and methods are the same in these two classes; other attributes and methods are different.

superclass to create two subclasses. Figure 8.9 provides a visual overview of the inheritance structure.

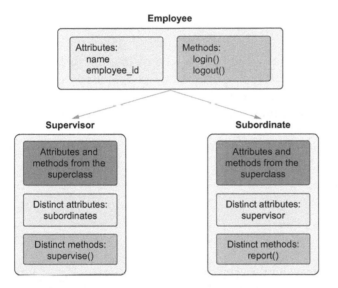

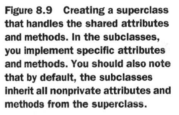

Figure 8.9 Creating a superclass that handles the shared attributes and methods. In the subclasses, you implement specific attributes and methods. You should also note that by default, the subclasses inherit all nonprivate attributes and methods from the superclass.

As shown in figure 8.9, when we create a superclass, we move all the shared attributes and methods from the subclasses to the superclass. In the subclasses, you implement specific attributes and methods. These instructions may sound too abstract. Let's see more implementation code in the next section.

8.5.2 *Inheriting the superclass's attributes and methods automatically*

Earlier, I mentioned that overlapping of functionalities between classes is the basis of creating a superclass, which helps reduce code repetition. In this section, you'll learn why we need less code with the inheritance.

To see how superclass and subclass work together, let's continue with the `Employee-Supervisor` example. Please read the code in the next listing first. We don't implement the customized __init__ in the Supervisor class; I leave that task for section 8.5.6 instead.

> **Listing 8.12   Basic structure of a superclass and subclasses**

```
class Employee:
    def __init__(self, name, employee_id):
        self.name = name
        self.employee_id = employee_id

    def login(self):
        print(f"An employee {self.name} just logged in.")

    def logout(self):
        print(f"An employee {self.name} just logged out.")


class Supervisor(Employee):
    pass
```

When you define a subclass, you specify the superclass in parentheses following the class's name. Here, the superclass is Employee, so we place it after Supervisor. Notably, the subclass Supervisor automatically inherits everything from its superclass Employee, including its initialization and other methods. We can observe this feature in the following code snippet:

```
supervisor = Supervisor("John", "1001")

print(supervisor.name)
# output: John

supervisor.login()
# output: An employee John just logged in.
```

As you can see, we create an instance by calling Supervisor("John", "1001"). The body of the Supervisor class uses only the pass statement. Supervisor supports instantiation, but the created instance object has attributes and methods because the Supervisor class inherits from the Employee class.

From a general perspective, when your subclasses have the same attributes and methods as the superclass, you don't need to provide any implementation in the subclass, as the subclass automatically gains all the attributes and methods from the superclass.

8.5.3   *Overriding the superclass's methods to provide customized behaviors*

In section 8.5.2, you learned that subclasses automatically inherit all attributes and methods from the superclass. Sometimes, however, you want to provide customized behaviors to a subclass. In this section, you'll learn how to override a superclass's method to provide specific implementations to a subclass.

OVERRIDING A METHOD COMPLETELY

You can override a superclass's method completely. Unlike some OOP languages, in which you may have to use the override keyword, Python allows you to define the same method with a distinct implementation from the superclass. Let's use the login method as an example:

```
class Supervisor(Employee):
    def login(self):
        print(f"A supervisor {self.name} just logged in.")
```

With this updated login method in the subclass, we can see that the instance of the Supervisor class will call the login method of the subclass instead of that of the superclass:

```
supervisor = Supervisor("John", "1001")

supervisor.login()
# output: A supervisor John just logged in.
```

We don't have a customized implementation for the logout method. As you can expect, if we call logout on the instance, the Employee class's logout implementation will be triggered. How does Python determine which implementation it should use? The answer pertains to an important concept: *method resolution order* (MRO), which dictates the order of using a specific implementation of a method in a hierarchical class structure.

> **CONCEPT**   MRO determines how a method or an attribute of an instance is evaluated in an inherited class structure.

Because Python supports multiple inheritance—a class inherits from multiple classes—the MRO in multiple inheritance is more complicated. Here, let's focus on the most common scenario: a subclass with only one superclass. Figure 8.10 illustrates how the MRO works. Please note that when you define a class that has no explicit superclass, Python uses the object class as its superclass—in the case of Employee, a subclass of object.

When you call a method on an instance, the instance object has an established MRO through its class, which you can inspect with the mro method:

```
Supervisor.mro()

# output the following line:
[<class '__main__.Supervisor'>, <class '__main__.Employee'>,
➥ <class 'object'>]
```

As you can see, the resolution order is Supervisor -> Employee -> object. That is, following this order, if the method is found to be implemented in any class, it's resolved

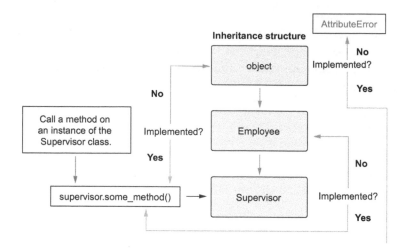

Figure 8.10   MRO in a hierarchical class structure. When you call a method on an instance, Python checks the method with its class first. If the method is resolved, apply the implementation. If not, move up to its superclass. If it's still not, move up to the object superclass, trying to resolve the method. If the method is still not resolved, raise the `AttributeError` exception. If there are more levels for the class inheritance structure, every level is checked.

and evaluated. If all the classes are examined without resolving the method, the `AttributeError` exception is raised.

OVERRIDING A METHOD PARTIALLY

You don't always want a different implementation for a method from the superclass. Instead, you want to keep the implementation of the superclass, on top of which you apply additional customization. In this case, we're saying that we're overriding a method partially.

This time, consider the `logout` method. Besides the superclass's implementation, we want to apply a customized behavior that is specific to a supervisor—for simplicity, showing the message `Additional logout actions for a supervisor`. The following code snippet shows how we should implement this behavior:

```
class Supervisor(Employee):
    def logout(self):
        super().logout()
        print("Additional logout actions for a supervisor")
```

The most significant thing to note is that we use `super()` as a reference to the superclass to create a proxy object of the superclass. From a conceptual perspective, you can think of `super()` as being a temporary instance object of the superclass, allowing us to call the superclass's `logout` method on this object. With this partially overridden `logout` method, what output do you expect? The following is the result:

```
supervisor = Supervisor("John", "1001")

supervisor.logout()
# output the following lines:
An employee John just logged out.
Additional logout actions for a supervisor
```

From the output, we can see that calling `logout` on the `supervisor` instance invokes not only the `Employee` class's logout method through `super().logout()`, but also the additional customized implementation in the `Supervisor`'s `logout` method.

8.5.4   *Creating non-public methods of the superclass*

In section 8.3, we introduced two nonpublic attributes/methods: `protected` and `private`. Besides their naming difference (prefix with one underscore versus two underscores), we also mentioned that they differ in their accessibility in a subclass. In this section, we'll observe this difference and see when to create a protected or a private method from the class inheritance perspective.

To begin, assume that our superclass `Employee` has the following implementation. Besides the initialization method, we define one protected method, `_request_vacation`, and one private method, `__transfer_group`:

```
class Employee:
    def __init__(self, name, employee_id):
        self.name = name
        self.employee_id = employee_id

    def _request_vacation(self):
        print("Send a vacation request to the employee's supervisor.")

    def __transfer_group(self):
        print("Transfer the employee to a different group.")
```

We are ready to create a subclass `Supervisor` that inherits from `Employee`. To illustrate the difference between `protected` and `private` in terms of accessibility within a subclass, let's try accessing these nonpublic methods within `Supervisor`:

```
class Supervisor(Employee):
    def do_something(self):
        self._request_vacation()
        self.__transfer_group()
```

In this subclass, we define an instance method `do_something`, within which we call `_request_vacation` and `__transfer_group`. What do you expect will happen if you call `do_something`? Give yourself a few moments to think. Remember that subclasses inherit protected methods. If you're ready, here's the answer:

```
supervisor = Supervisor("John", "1001")
supervisor.do_something()

# output the following lines:
Send a vacation request to the employee's supervisor.
# ERROR: AttributeError: 'Supervisor' object has no attribute
➥ '_Supervisor__transfer_group'
```

As you can see, _request_vacation is successfully invoked, which is expected. But __transfer_group can't be invoked because using the double underscores as the prefix triggers name mangling. Instead of trying to call __transfer_group, Python tries to call _Supervisor__transfer_group, a method that is not defined in Supervisor!

Given their different accessibility within subclasses, you should define nonpublic methods based on this principle: if you expect that the subclasses should have access to the nonpublic methods, you should define protected methods, which the subclasses can inherit. If you expect that the subclasses should have no access to the nonpublic methods, you should define private methods.

8.5.5   *Discussion*

Creating a hierarchical class structure is an essential technique in the OOP world, and it's a critical skill for building a clean, maintainable codebase. The superclass is responsible for handling attributes and methods that are shared among its subclasses. Instead of handling methods in multiple locations if you define the same methods in similar classes, you need to maintain these methods in only one place: the superclass.

You should realize that creating a hierarchical class structure has a price. Because subclasses depend on the behaviors of the superclass, this interrelationship or tight coupling can make it tricky or hard to update your codebase. When you want to add something to a subclass, you may also need to update its superclass. Thus, in your project, it's better to use flatter data models. If you notice overlapping functionalities between classes, however, don't hesitate to implement superclasses and subclasses.

8.5.6   *Challenge*

In section 8.1, we studied how to implement the __init__ method in a custom class. If the subclass has the same implementation as the superclass, you don't need to override __init__ at all. But if you need customized initialization, as in the case of Supervisor, you want to override __init__. How can you override __init__ in the Supervisor class?

> **HINT** Overriding __init__ isn't different from overriding other methods. You use super() to create a proxy object to use the constructor of the superclass.

Summary

- Your class should have __init__ as the first method, and it should initialize all attributes of an instance, even if some attributes have a value of None.
- The initialization method __init__ is an instance method, which uses self as its first parameter. You should know how things work behind the scenes—how an instance is created from calling the constructor.
- When all the instances share the same attribute values, you should define them as class attributes, which helps save memory.
- In general, you can define three kinds of methods in a class: instance (note that the first parameter is self), static (using the @staticmethod decorator), and class (using the @classmethod decorator). You should know how these methods differ and when to use which.
- When you define a class, consider minimizing the attributes and methods that the users need access to. By "hiding" them, such as by defining protected and private methods, you help users increase their coding efficiency because they don't need to bother with these nonpublic methods in the autocompletion hint list.
- The property decorator allows you to create a read-only property, which helps you create data integrity by disallowing data change. If you want to allow users to change the property, you can create a setter for the property, which is also an opportunity for you to verify data integrity in the setter.
- When you define a class, you want to override both __str__ and __repr__ so that you can provide proper string representations for users and developers.
- Creating a hierarchical class structure helps you manage your data when there are similarities between data models. The shared data can go to the superclass, making it easier to develop and maintain your codebase.
- Think twice before you create a hierarchical class structure because you may overcomplicate your data models by dealing with superclasses and subclasses.

Using classes
beyond the basics

This chapter covers

- Creating enumerations
- Eliminating boilerplate of a custom class
- Processing JSON data
- Creating lazy attributes
- Refactoring a cumbersome class

Python is an object-oriented language at its core. The hallmark of an object-oriented language is using objects to preserve data and provide functionalities, which generally requires you to implement well-defined custom classes. In chapter 8, you learned the essential techniques for defining a class. But many other techniques can help us define more robust custom classes so that we can build a more maintainable codebase with well-defined data models.

Custom classes typically require implementation of several special methods, for example, including __init__ and __repr__. As you code more, you may find it tedious to write these methods, as they can be boilerplate. Did you know that you can use the `dataclass` decorator to remove boilerplate?

In this chapter, you'll learn advanced techniques. Some of these techniques, such as creating enumerations, have a specific use case (when you need enumerations, for example, such as the task status in our task management application). Other techniques are more fundamental, such as refactoring a cumbersome class and creating lazy attributes, which you'll find useful no matter what application you're making. Please pay special attention to these project-agnostic techniques.

9.1 How do I create enumerations?

In our applications, some data is naturally connected within the same concept umbrella. Consider the four directions—north, east, south, and west—all of which belong to the direction category. When we represent this data in our application, the simplest way is to use strings: `"north"`, `"east"`, `"south"`, and `"west"`. When we write a function that expects a direction, however, it may be unclear to the users what data they should provide, even if we supply type hints to the function, as in this example:

```
def move_to(direction: str, distance: float):
    if direction in {"north", "south", "east", "west"}:
        message = f"Go to the {direction} for {distance} miles"
    else:
        message = "Wrong input for direction"
    print(message)
```

Because strings lack inherent semantics, when users call this function, they have no clue about what they should provide and may use a semantically meaningful string that is incompatible with the function:

```
move_to("North", 2)

# output: Wrong input for direction
```

As you might expect, if we can provide more specific type information about the direction parameter, it'll be clear to users what they should enter. Also, when you define a type that has discrete members, such as weekdays and seasons, you have a perfect use case for enumerations. This section explores that feature.

9.1.1 Avoiding a regular class for enumerations

Some people's first thought about implementing enumerations may involve a regular custom class. As discussed in this section, however, you may encounter a few drawbacks if you use a regular class for enumerations. To begin, let's see what a possible implementation looks like using a custom class:

```
class Direction:
    NORTH = 0
    SOUTH = 1
    EAST = 2
    WEST = 3
```

From the style perspective, two things are noteworthy:

- Because these four directions are constants, it's common to use all capital letters.
- In most programming languages, enumerations use whole integers as the values of the enumerated members.

Besides these two style notes, this implementation is a bit hacking by defining class attributes in the `Direction` class. You can use these "enumerations" (they're not true enumerations, as you'll see in section 9.1.3) by accessing these class attributes:

```
print(Direction.NORTH)
# output: 0

print(Direction.SOUTH)
# output: 1
```

You may notice a couple of drawbacks. First, the type for these members isn't `Direction`, which prevents you from using the members when you use `Direction` in a function (figure 9.1).

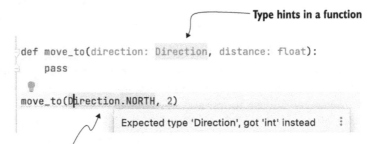

Figure 9.1   **Incompatible type when class attributes in a class are used as enumerations. You can use a custom class as the type hint for the argument, but you can't use a member in the function call.**

The value of the member `Direction.North` is 0, which is an integer instead of an instance of the `Direction` class. When you use enumerations, you should expect each member to be an instance of the enumeration class.

The other drawback is that you can't iterate the class to go over each member, as the "members" are class attributes; they don't form a united entity and can't represent the enumeration concept. By contrast, a true enumeration class should support iteration of each member. These drawbacks undermine a regular class for the purpose of enumerations, which is a non-Pythonic implementation. As revealed in the next section, we'll use the `enum` module to address these drawbacks.

9.1.2 Creating an enumeration class

You learned about subclasses in section 8.5. Creating an enumeration class is the process of creating a subclass of the built-in Enum class in the enum module. In this section, you'll learn to implement an enumeration class for directions. The next listing shows the code.

> **Listing 9.1 Implementing an enumeration class**

```
from enum import Enum

class Direction(Enum):
    NORTH = 0
    SOUTH = 1
    EAST = 2
    WEST = 3
```

Compared with a custom class implementation, a true enumeration class is a subclass of the Enum class. By subclassing Enum, the enumeration class converts the seemingly class attributes to discrete members. Within the body, we specify the members and their associated values. Notably, we can also create the enumeration class as a one-liner:

```
class DirectionOneLiner(Enum):
    NORTH = 0; SOUTH = 1; EAST = 2; WEST = 3
```

Although you can declare the members in the enumeration class by using semicolons to separate them on a single line, I recommend using the former style—defining each member on its own line—because it has better readability.

> **READABILITY**   Each member in an enumeration class should occupy one line so that it's easier to see what the members are and to count the number of members.

In many use cases, you don't care about the raw values of the members. In our examples, we've been using small integers incrementally, but you can use any integers:

```
class DirectionRandomInt(Enum):
    NORTH = 100
    SOUTH = 200
    EAST = 300
    WEST = 400
```

In addition, Python doesn't restrict what data you use for the members' raw values. You can also use strings instead of integers, as in this example:

```
class DirectionString(Enum):
    NORTH = "N"
    SOUTH = "S"
    EAST = "E"
    WEST = "W"
```

9.1.3   *Using enumerations*

After we define the enumeration class, it's time to explore how we use enumerations from the class. This section covers that topic.

CHECKING AN ENUMERATION MEMBER'S TYPE

The first usage of enumerations pertains to checking the type of an enumerated member. From section 9.1.1, we know that when we use a regular class, the enumerations using class attributes don't have the type of the class. Everything works differently in a true enumeration class, as shown in this example:

```
north = Direction.NORTH

print("north type:", type(north))
# output: north type: <enum 'Direction'>

print("north check instance of Direction:", isinstance(north, Direction))
# output: north check instance of Direction: True
```

As you can see, the "attributes" of the enumeration class are of the type of the class: the north variable has the type of the Direction class. That is, each member represents a predefined instance of the class.

USING AN ENUMERATION MEMBER'S ATTRIBUTES

As the members are essentially the enumeration class's instances, it's no surprise that each member has instance attributes. Among those attributes, the most important are name and value, which are the enumerated member's name and its associated value:

```
print("north name:", north.name)
# output: north name: NORTH

print("north value:", north.value)
# output: north value: 0
```

The value of a member is useful in a variety of use cases. Suppose that we receive an application programming interface (API) response in which an integer number indicates the direction in which the user should go. The following code snippet shows this scenario:

```
direction_value = 2

direction = Direction(direction_value)

print("Direction to go:", direction)
# output: Direction to go: Direction.EAST
```

As you can see, we construct the enumerated member by supplying an applicable value to the constructor. Because EAST has a value of 2 in the Direction class, calling the constructor with 2 creates the EAST direction. If you're trying to create a member with a value that isn't among the defined values, you encounter an exception:

```
unknown_direction = Direction(8)
# ERROR: ValueError: 8 is not a valid Direction
```

ITERATING ALL ENUMERATION MEMBERS

The major reason that we define enumerations is to group related concepts in the form of members in the enumeration class. When users want to find out what these members are, they can iterate the enumeration class—a feature that isn't available for a regular class. This section shows how to iterate the members of an enumeration class.

The enumeration class Direction, as a subclass of Enum, is by design an iterable that consists of its members. Thus, we can use the iteration techniques on the Direction class, as follows:

```
all_directions = list(Direction)

print(all_directions)
# output: [<Direction.NORTH: 0>, <Direction.SOUTH: 1>,
    <Direction.EAST: 2>, <Direction.WEST: 3>]
```

This code shows how to create a list object containing all the directions. As discussed in section 5.1, we create the list by using the list constructor with the iterable: the Direction class. Because Direction is an iterable, you can also use it in a for loop:

```
for direction in Direction:
    pass
```

9.1.4   Defining methods for the enumeration class

At its core, an enumeration class is still a Python custom class, so we can define applicable methods to add more versatile functionalities to the class. We have learned how to create an enumeration and know that the enumeration class is an iterable. We're ready to update the move_to function, as shown in this code snippet:

```
def move_to(direction: Direction, distance: float):
    if direction in Direction:
        message = f"Go to the {direction} for {distance} miles"
    else:
        message = "Wrong input for direction"
    print(message)
```

One significant thing to note is that we use direction in Direction to determine whether the supplied direction argument is appropriate. When we call this function, we get the desired type hints. The output doesn't look perfect, however:

```
move_to(Direction.NORTH, 3)
# output: Go to the Direction.NORTH for 3 miles
```

The output isn't human-friendly, as the shown direction is `"Direction.NORTH"` instead of `north`, as you would expect. To solve this problem, we can define a custom instance method to show proper human-readable output for the members, as shown in the next listing.

Listing 9.2   Adding a custom method

```
class Direction(Enum):
    NORTH = 0
    SOUTH = 1
    EAST = 2
    WEST = 3

    def __str__(self):
        return self.name.lower()


def move_to(direction: Direction, distance: float):
    if direction in Direction:
        message = f"Go to the {direction} for {distance} miles"
    else:
        message = "Wrong input for direction"
    print(message)

move_to(Direction.NORTH, 3)
# output: Go to the north for 3 miles
```

In listing 9.2, two important things are noteworthy:

- We overrode the __str__ method in the `Direction` class. As covered in section 8.4, __str__ determines an instance's string representation.
- In the f-string for the message, the curly braces enclose `direction`, which calls the __str__ method behind the scenes. From the printout, you see that we get the human-readable output for the `direction` argument.

The code snippet in listing 9.2 shows that you can override special methods in the enumeration class. You can also define other methods as you need them. You could define the `move_to` function as an instance method in the `Direction` class, for example; I'll leave that task as a challenge for you in section 9.1.6.

9.1.5   *Discussion*

Enumeration is the most common technique to use when you have related concepts that fall into the same category. To use enumerations, create an enumeration class by subclassing the `Enum` class in the `enum` module. When you need to add customized behaviors to the enumeration class, you can define methods as you normally do with a regular class.

9.1.6   *Challenge*

Zoe is building a location-based application in which she defines a `Direction` class, as shown in the preceding sections. In listing 9.2, the `move_to` function is defined outside the Direction class, but she thinks that it makes more sense for this function to be an instance method. Can you help her make the conversion?

> **HINT**   Place the move_to function within the body of the Direction class. For an instance method, don't forget that the first argument is self and that it refers to the instance object.

9.2   How do I use data classes to eliminate boilerplate code?

Data is the core element of any programming project. All programs have a place for data. In section 3.3, you learned about creating a lightweight data model by using named tuples. Named tuples, however, are best used as data holders because of their immutability. If you want data mutability and greater flexibility in data manipulation, you need to create a custom class, as discussed in chapter 8. In a custom class, best practices include the implementation of special methods such as __init__ and __repr__:

```
class CustomData:
    def __init__(self, attr0, attr1, attr2):
        self.attr0 = attr0
        self.attr1 = attr1
        self.attr2 = attr2

    def __repr__(self):
        return f"CustomData({self.attr0}, {self.attr1}, {self.attr2})"
```

In the __init__ method, we assign all the arguments to each of the instance's attributes, whereas in the __repr__ method, we create an f-string that mimics a string literal for instantiation. The code for these methods is boilerplate, which means that everything follows a predefined template. If you define many other classes, you'll do pretty much the same thing for these methods. Why can't we eliminate this boilerplate? In this section, we're going to discover how to use data classes to create a class without all the boilerplate.

> **CONCEPT**   In programming, *boilerplate* means code that is used without any significant modification in places where highly similar (or identical) code is required. Boilerplate is a pattern of repetition, although at a higher level.

9.2.1   Creating a data class using the dataclass decorator

Section 7.3 introduced decorators, which provide additional functionalities to the decorated function without modifying the original function's performance. Decorators can do more than decorate just functions, however; when they're defined properly, they can also decorate classes. One such special decorator is dataclass, which addresses the boilerplate by decorating the class, as discussed in this section.

The dataclass decorator is available in the dataclasses module. Before I discuss how to use this decorator, examine the code in the next listing, which creates a data class that models bill management for a restaurant.

Listing 9.3   Creating a data class

```
from dataclasses import dataclass

@dataclass
class Bill:
    table_number: int
    meal_amount: float
    served_by: str
    tip_amount: float
```

Observe three things in listing 9.3:

- *We import the* `dataclass` *decorator from the* `dataclasses` *module, which is part of the standard Python library.* If you install Python from the official Python website, the `dataclasses` module should already be on your computer.
- *As with using a decorator with a function, you place the decorator above the class's head in the form of* `@dataclass`.
- *In the body of the class, you specify the attributes with their respective types.* Note that specifying the types is required for a data class.

At the beginning of this section, I mentioned that we can use data classes to get rid of some boilerplate, including __init__ and __repr__. In other words, the `dataclass` decorator has taken care of the boilerplate:

```
bill0 = Bill(5, 60.5, "John", 10)

bill_output = f"Today's bill: {bill0}"

print(bill_output)
# output: Today's bill: Bill(table_number=5, meal_amount=60.5,
➥ served_by='John', tip_amount=10)
```

As you can see, we create an instance object of the `Bill` class, although the __init__ method is never explicitly defined in the class. In a similar fashion, without implementing the __repr__ method, we get the string representation for the instance in the correct form, which mimics the string for instantiation.

9.2.2   *Setting default values for the fields*

Setting default values for some attributes in the initialization method keeps the code clean and saves users' time. Data classes support default values for the attributes. In this section, you'll learn the rules for setting default values in data classes.

Before I jump into the technicalities, I need to clarify one key concept. In a custom class, below the head, we list the class attributes. In a data class, the `dataclass` decorator converts these attributes to instance attributes, which are known as *fields*. I mentioned that type annotations are required for these fields. Why? Mechanistically speaking, the `dataclass` decorator takes advantage of the class's annotations to locate the fields:

```
print(Bill.__annotations__)
# output: {'table_number': <class 'int'>, 'meal_amount':
➥ <class 'float'>, 'served_by': <class 'str'>,
➥ 'tip_amount': <class 'float'>}
```

As you can see, we retrieve all the fields of the class by accessing the __annotations__ special attribute. Conversely, if you don't annotate some attributes, they can't be part of the __annotations__ attribute, preventing the dataclass decorator from locating these fields. Thus, the dataclass decorator can't help construct the data class properly. Figure 9.2 summarizes the underlying process of creating a data class.

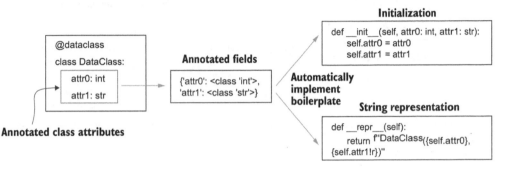

Figure 9.2 The underlying workflow of creating a data class using the dataclass decorator. The dataclass decorator takes advantage of the type annotations for the fields to create the boilerplate, including __init__ and __repr__.

In figure 9.2, using the annotated fields, the dataclass decorator creates the applicable __init__ method. When you set default values for the fields, they become part of the __init__ method too. Setting default values for the fields involves using the syntax described in chapter 6: you specify the default value after the type annotation, as the following listing shows.

Listing 9.4 Setting a default value for fields

```
@dataclass
class Bill:
    table_number: int
    meal_amount: float
    served_by: str
    tip_amount: float = 0
```

Because you specify the default value for the tip_amount field, when you create an instance object of the Bill class, you can omit this field, which will be filled with the default value instead:

```
bill1 = Bill(5, 60.5, "John")

print(bill1)
# output: Bill(table_number=5, meal_amount=60.5,
➥ served_by='John', tip_amount=0)
```

When I discussed setting default arguments for a function in section 6.1, I emphasized that an argument with a default value can't precede arguments without default values. The same rule applies to a data class. When you set a field with a default value that precedes other fields that have no default values, you encounter a TypeError. If you use an integrated development environment (IDE) such as PyCharm, a warning is displayed when you do (figure 9.3).

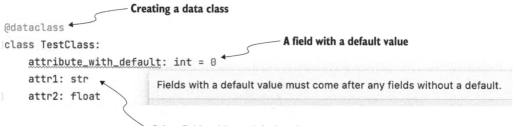

Figure 9.3   Warning about placing a field with a default value before fields that have no default values in a data class definition

9.2.3   *Making data classes immutable*

Compared with immutable named tuples, the fields of data classes can be modified for each instance; thus, data classes are mutable. Depending on the specific use case, however, mutability may be not desired for the data. In this section, you'll learn to make data classes immutable.

The dataclass decorator cannot only be used by itself without any arguments, in the form of @dataclass, but it can also take additional arguments to provide customized decoration behaviors. Some notable arguments include init and repr, which are set to True by default, meaning that we request that the dataclass decorator implement __init__ and __repr__. Among other arguments, one pertains to mutability: frozen. When you want your data class to be immutable, you should set frozen to True. The following code snippet shows the usage:

```
@dataclass(frozen=True)
class ImmutableBill:
    meal_amount: float
    served_by: str


immutable_bill = ImmutableBill(50, "John")
immutable_bill.served_by = "David"

# ERROR: dataclasses.FrozenInstanceError: cannot assign
➥ to field 'served_by'
```

As you can see for the data class `ImmutableBill`, after the instance is created, we can't update its fields anymore. Such immutability protects you from unintended data changes—a feature that you can obtain from named tuples, which are defined to be immutable.

> **MAINTAINABILITY**   If you don't want your data classes to change their data, consider making their fields frozen to prevent unintended changes.

9.2.4   Creating a subclass of an existing data class

At its core, a data class has the same extensibility as other regular custom classes. As covered in section 8.5, we can create a class hierarchy. In terms of data classes, we can also create a subclass. But several aspects of the `dataclass` decorator make subclassing a data class different from subclassing regular classes (defined without a `dataclass` decorator), as discussed in this section.

INHERITING THE SUPERCLASS'S FIELDS

We know that in a data class, its attributes become data fields. When you create a subclass of an existing data class, all the fields of the superclass automatically become part of the subclass's fields:

```
@dataclass
class BaseBill:
    meal_amount: float

@dataclass
class TippedBill(BaseBill):
    tip_amount: float
```

> **QUESTION**   Can you try subclassing a frozen dataclass?

As shown in this example, we created the `TippedBill` class as a subclass of `BaseBill`. Both classes should use the `dataclass` decorator to make them data classes. The subclass `TippedBill`'s constructor includes both the fields of the superclass and its own fields:

```
tipped_bill = TippedBill(60, 10)

print(tipped_bill)
# output: TippedBill(meal_amount=60, tip_amount=10)
```

When you create an instance of the subclass, remember that the superclass's fields come first, followed by the subclass's fields. The order matters!

AVOIDING DEFAULT VALUES FOR THE SUPERCLASS

We have seen that a subclass of a data class uses all the fields from its superclass and its own fields, following the order superclass -> subclass. In section 9.2.2, however, you learned that fields with default values must come behind those that don't have default values. This requirement has an important implication: if a superclass has fields with default values, you must specify default values for each subclass's fields. Otherwise, your code won't work, as shown in this example:

```
@dataclass
class BaseBill:
    meal_amount: float = 50

@dataclass
class TippedBill(BaseBill):
    tip_amount: float

# ERROR: TypeError: non-default argument 'tip_amount'
➥ follows default argument
```

Thus, in most cases, you may want to avoid setting default values for the superclass so that you'll have more flexibility to implement your subclasses. If you do set default values for the superclass, you must specify default values for the subclasses too:

```
@dataclass
class BaseBill:
    meal_amount: float = 50

@dataclass
class TippedBill(BaseBill):
    tip_amount: float = 0
```

9.2.5   *Discussion*

Using the `dataclass` decorator, you can easily convert a regular class to a data class, which helps eliminate a lot of boilerplate that you would have to write otherwise. Compared with named tuples, which are a lightweight data model, we use data classes because they're mutable data models and because they support extensibility by defining customized functionalities, like regular custom classes. If necessary, we can freeze the attributes to prevent unwanted data changes—an advantage that named tuples also have.

9.2.6   *Challenge*

Bradley works on the analysis team of a website company. He uses data classes in his project. He knows that when he sets default values for a mutable argument in a function (section 6.1), the convention is to use `None` as the default value. But he's not sure what value he should use for a mutable data class's field, such as `list`. Can you figure out what default value he should set?

> **HINT**   The `dataclass` module has a function called `field`, which is designed to set a default value for a mutable field.

9.3 How do I prepare and process JSON data?

When your application has interactions with outside entities, such as other websites, there should be a mechanism for data exchange. You may need to download data from another server, for example, usually in the form of APIs. JavaScript Object Notation (JSON) is one of the most popular formats for data interchanges between different systems. Suppose that our task management application gets the following JSON data from a server using one API, which resembles a `dict` object in Python:

```
{
  "title": "Laundry",
  "desc": "Wash clothes",
  "urgency": 3
}
```

For another API, we may get the following data, which resembles a `list` object consisting of two `dict` objects in Python. Please note that I've formatted the strings by using proper indentation to make them easier to read:

```
[
  {
    "title": "Laundry",
    "desc": "Wash clothes",
    "urgency": 3
  },
  {
    "title": "Homework",
    "desc": "Physics + Math",
    "urgency": 5
  }
]
```

When you receive this data as strings, to further manipulate the data, you want to convert it to the proper classes (discussed in chapter 8). More generally, JSON's remarkable readability and its object-like structure make it a universal data format in any application you may work on. In this section, you'll learn about the essential techniques for processing JSON data in Python.

9.3.1 Understanding JSON's data structure

Before you learn to process JSON data, you need to know the structure of JSON data and its relationship with Python's data types. This section is devoted to introducing JSON data. If you know the topic well, please feel free to skip to the next section.

JSON data is structured as JSON objects in the form of key-value pairs scoped by a pair of curly braces, such as `{"title": "Laundry", "desc": "Wash clothes", "urgency": 3}`. JSON objects require their keys to be only strings, and this requirement allows the standard communication between different systems. The values shown include strings and integers, but JSON supports other data types, including Boolean, arrays (like `list` in Python), and objects, as summarized in table 9.1.

Table 9.1   JSON data types

Data type	Data content
String	String literals enclosed in double quotes
Number	Number literals, including integers and decimals
Boolean	Boolean values, true or false (all lowercase)
Array	A list of supported data types wrapped in square brackets
Object	Key-value pairs surrounded by curly braces
Null	A special value (`null`) representing an empty value for any valid data type

We know that we can use single or double quotes for Python strings. But JSON strings must be enclosed only in double quotes. The improper use of single quotes creates invalid JSON data that can't be processed by a common JSON parser.

NOTE   You can use only double quotes to enclose strings in JSON.

It's important to know that JSON supports nested data structures. A JSON object can hold another JSON object, for example. An array can be a list of any supported data types, including objects. Following are some examples:

```
embedded object:   {"one": {"one": 1}, "two": {"two": 2}}
array of strings:  ["one", "two", "three"]
```

The flexibility of mixing different data types in JSON allows us to construct complicated data with clear structural information, all in the form of key-value pairs.

9.3.2   *Mapping data types between JSON and Python*

When you use Python to make applications, and your applications have interactions with other systems via JSON, you must know how to convert data between JSON and Python. At a high level, the conversion is about how different JSON data types are mapped to the corresponding Python data types.

Because both JSON and Python are used for general purposes, it's no surprise that JSON data types have corresponding native Python data structures. Figure 9.4 shows these conversions. Most of the conversions are straightforward. But Python doesn't have a native data type that matches numbers in JSON objects, which don't differentiate integers from floating-point numbers and refer to them as numbers collectively. By contrast, Python uses `int` and `float` to represent JSON numbers when they're integers or real numbers.

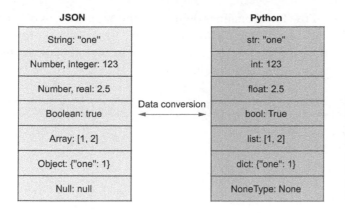

Figure 9.4 **Data conversion between JSON and Python with supporting examples. Please note that these types have different names in JSON and Python, such as String vs. str, due to the different terminologies used by these two languages.**

9.3.3 *Deserializing JSON strings*

When we read JSON data into data structures of other programming languages, such as Python, we *decode* or *deserialize* JSON data. A more formal term for the reading-and-decoding process is *deserialization*. In this section, you'll learn how to read JSON data into Python.

I've mentioned that it's common for web services to use JSON objects as API responses and that these responses take the form of text to facilitate intersystem data exchange. Consider a response expressed as a Python string object:

```python
tasks_json = """
[
  {
    "title": "Laundry",
    "desc": "Wash clothes",
    "urgency": 3
  },
  {
    "title": "Homework",
    "desc": "Physics + Math",
    "urgency": 5
  }
]
"""    ◁──── Uses triple quotes for multiline strings
```

The standard Python library contains the `json` module, which is specialized for deserializing JSON data. To read this JSON string, we use the `loads` method. As shown in the following code snippet, we obtain a `list` object that consists of two nicely formatted `dict` objects, which represent the two JSON objects originally saved in the JSON array:

```python
import json

tasks_read = json.loads(tasks_json)

print(tasks_read)
# output: [{'title': 'Laundry', 'desc': 'Wash clothes', 'urgency': 3},
➡ {'title': 'Homework', 'desc': 'Physics + Math', 'urgency': 5}]
```

We can't take advantage of the functionalities defined in the Task class, as discussed in chapter 9, if the data is in the form of dictionaries. Thus, we need to convert these dict objects to instances of the Task class. This conversion highlights a perfect use case for class methods, as shown in the following listing.

Listing 9.5   Converting `dict` objects to instances of a custom class

```
from dataclasses import dataclass

@dataclass
class Task:
    title: str
    desc: str
    urgency: int

@classmethod
def task_from_dict(cls, task_dict):
    return cls(**task_dict)

tasks = [Task.task_from_dict(x) for x in tasks_read]

print(tasks)
# output: [Task(title='Laundry', desc='Wash clothes', urgency=3),
⮡ Task(title='Homework', desc='Physics + Math', urgency=5)]
```

In listing 9.5, we successfully converted the list of dict objects to a list of Task instance objects, as we planned. Notably, we used several techniques that we've learned so far. As mentioned in chapter 1 (section 1.4), we're trying to synthesize a variety of techniques along the way. Here are the key takeaways:

- We use the dataclass decorator (section 9.2) on the Task class so that we don't have to implement the boilerplate for __init__ and __repr__.
- The cls argument in the class method (section 8.2.3) task_from_dict refers to the class Task.
- We know that **kwargs refers to the variable number of keyword arguments (section 6.4) and is packed as a dict object. Conversely, to access the key-value pairs, the ** operator converts the dict object to keyword arguments, which the constructor uses to create a new instance of the Task class.

We've seen how to convert a JSON array to a list object in Python. The loads method is flexible. The method does more than convert JSON arrays; it can also parse any JSON data types other than objects. Following are a few examples:

```
json.loads("2.2")
# output: 2.2

json.loads('"A string"')
# output: 'A string'
```

```
json.loads('false')      ◁——— Boolean value
# output: False

json.loads('null') is None      ◁——— JSON null to Python None
# output: True
```

These strings represent JSON data, including floating-point number, string, Boolean, and Null, and they're all converted by `loads` without any customization. All the conversion happens automatically, which highlights Python's power as a general-purpose language.

9.3.4 Serializing Python data to JSON format

When you process JSON data from external entities, you're building an incoming communication route. In the meantime, you may need to build an outgoing route so that your application can send applicable information to the outside world.

As illustrated in figure 9.5, the opposite of deserializing JSON data is creating JSON data from other data, a process called *serialization*. Thus, when we convert Python data to JSON data, we serialize Python objects to JSON data. This section addresses JSON serialization.

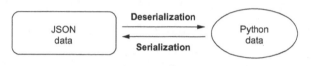

Figure 9.5   Data conversion between JSON and Python. When you convert JSON to Python, the process is *deserialization*; when you convert Python to JSON, the process is *serialization*.

Like the `loads` method, the `json` module has the `dumps` method to handle JSON data serialization. For the basic built-in data types, the conversions are straightforward:

```
builtin_data = ['text', False, {"0": None, 1: [1.0, 2.0]}]

builtin_json = repr(json.dumps(builtin_data))      ◁——┐ To show the quotes for
                                                        a string, use repr.
print(builtin_json)
# output: '["text", false, {"0": null, "1": [1.0, 2.0]}]'
```

In this example, notice that the `dumps` method creates a JSON array that holds different kinds of JSON data. The most significant observation is that although the original `list` object uses native Python data structures, the generated JSON string has the respective JSON data structures. Note the following conversions:

- The string enclosed in single quotes (`'text'`) now uses double quotes (`"text"`).
- The Python `bool` object `False` becomes `false`.
- The object `None` becomes `null`.
- Because only strings can be JSON keys, the number 1 is automatically converted to its string counterpart, `"1"`.

What happens if you try to serialize an instance object of a custom class, like `Task`? Here's the result:

```
json.dumps(tasks[0])

# ERROR: TypeError: Object of type Task is not JSON serializable
```

As you can see, we can't serialize a custom class instance. The major reason is that for a custom class, an instance object may contain many attributes and other metadata, so without a proper instruction, Python can't know what data should be serialized. Thus, to make a custom class serializable, we must provide instructions for serialization. Here is one possible solution (please note that alternative solutions exist):

```
dumped_task = json.dumps(tasks[0], default=lambda x: x.__dict__)

print(dumped_task)
# output: {"title": "Laundry", "desc": "Wash clothes", "urgency": 3}
```

The most significant change we made to the `dumps` function call uses the `default` argument. This argument instructs what object (as a fallback) the encoder (the underlying object that makes the encoding or serialization) should use when it can't serialize the object. In this case, because we know that the encoder can't serialize the `Task` class instance object, we instruct the encoder to use its `dict` representation instead. The encoder knows how to convert the built-in `dict` class.

We often use two other features during conversion. First, to create JSON objects in a more readable format, we can set the `indent` argument to have proper indentation:

```
task_dict = {"title": "Laundry", "desc": "Wash clothes", "urgency": 3}

print(json.dumps(task_dict, indent=2))
# output the following lines:
{
  "title": "Laundry",
  "desc": "Wash clothes",
  "urgency": 3
}
```

Every level is nicely indented to indicate the relative structure of JSON objects and their key-value pairs.

READABILITY   Use proper indentation to improve the readability of JSON data. Readability is especially relevant if you're creating a JSON string.

The other useful feature is setting the `sort_keys` argument. Because we set it to `True`, the created JSON string has its keys sorted alphabetically, making it easier for us to look up information, particularly for multiple items. Observe this feature:

```
user_info = {"name": "John", "age": 35, "city": "San Francisco",
➥ "home": "123 Main St.", "zip_code": 12345, "sex": "Male"}

print(json.dumps(user_info, indent=2, sort_keys=True))
# output the following lines:
{
  "age": 35,
  "city": "San Francisco",
  "home": "123 Main St.",
  "name": "John",
  "sex": "Male",
  "zip_code": 12345
}
```

9.3.5   Discussion

JSON is probably the most popular data format used in data exchange between different systems. You should know how to deserialize and serialize JSON data by using native Python objects. One important thing to note is that instances of custom classes in Python are not JSON-serializable by default, so you should specify custom encoding behavior. Besides working on JSON strings, the `json` module has the `dump` and `load` methods to process JSON files directly. The calling signatures of these methods are almost identical to those of `dumps` and `loads`, respectively.

9.3.6   Challenge

Lucas is building a social media web app as his summer intern project. In his app, he uses named tuples in the data models. Suppose that the project has the following named-tuples class:

```
from collections import namedtuple

User = namedtuple("User", "first_name last_name age")
user = User("John", "Smith", "39")
```

What happens if he tries to serialize the user object?

> **HINT**   A `tuple` object is JSON-serializable and becomes a JSON array after serialization.

9.4   How do I create lazy attributes to improve performance?

Lazy evaluation is a general programming implementation paradigm that defers evaluating operations until it's requested to do so. Usually, lazy evaluation is the preferred evaluation pattern when the operation is expensive, requiring extensive processing time or memory. Generators (section 7.4), for example, are applications of lazy evaluation, which delays retrieving and yielding the next item. Lazy evaluation is also a relevant topic in custom classes. Specifically, you can define lazy attributes for instance objects to save time or memory. In this section, you'll learn about defining lazy attributes.

9.4.1 *Identifying the use scenario*

Let's start by identifying a proper use scenario. Suppose that our task management app is a social media app in which a user can follow other users. One functionality is to view a user's followers. In the app, we can further view a user's detailed profile by tapping the user's thumbnail image. Consider the implementation in the next listing.

Listing 9.6 Creating the `User` class

```
class User:
    def __init__(self, username):
        self.username = username
        self.profile_data = self._get_profile_data()
        print(f"### User {username} created")

    def _get_profile_data(self):
        # get the data from the server and load it into memory
        print("*** Run the expensive operation")
        fetched_data = " Extensive data, including thumbnail,
        ➥ followers, etc."
        return fetched_data


def get_followers(username):
    # get the followers from the server for the user
    usernames_fetched = ["John", "Aaron", "Zack"]
    followers = [User(username) for username in usernames_fetched]
    return followers
```

We define the `User` class to manage user-related data, and the `get_followers` function fetches the followers for a user. When we call this function, we observe the following output:

```
followers = get_followers("Ashley")
# output the following lines:
*** Run the expensive operation
### User John created
*** Run the expensive operation
### User Aaron created
*** Run the expensive operation
### User Zack created
```

As you can see, when we get a user's followers, we're creating multiple instance objects for each user. This process requires an expensive operation to get the profile data, as the application must connect to the remote server to download the data and load it into memory. The profile data isn't needed, however, because we need to display only followers' usernames unless a user taps a follower; then the follower's profile data becomes relevant. It's an unnecessary operation to load data for all users up front, so we should consider using the lazy evaluation technique to avoid the heavy lifting. The following sections explore two ways to implement lazy attributes.

9.4.2   Overriding the __getattr__ special method to implement lazy attributes

In a custom class, we can override several special methods other than __str__ and __repr__ to define customized behaviors (section 8.3). One such method, __getattr__, pertains to retrieving an instance's attributes. In this section, we'll see how to implement lazy attributes by overriding __getattr__.

For custom classes, instance objects have their attributes saved in a dict object, which is accessible through the special attribute __dict__. This dict object uses the attribute names as the keys and the attribute values as the corresponding values. When you access an instance object's attribute by using dot notation, if the dict object contains the attribute, it returns the value. If the dict object doesn't contain the attribute, the special method __getattr__ gets called as a fallback mechanism and tries to provide a value for the requested attribute. Figure 9.6 depicts the order of resolving an instance's attribute that pertains to accessing __dict__ and __getattr__.

> **NOTE** The attribute resolution order is more complicated than what's shown in figure 9.6. An instance's attribute can also use the class's attribute as a fallback, for example. Figure 9.6 is a simplified version that applies to common scenarios.

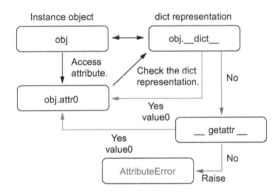

Figure 9.6   The order of resolving an instance object's attribute. Python first checks whether the dict object of the instance object contains the attribute. If the dict object doesn't contain the attribute, Python checks whether it can return a value by calling the __getattr__ special method.

Now that we understand how __dict__ and __getattr__ work together to provide the needed attributes for an instance object, we're ready to see the specific implementation of overriding __getattr__ for a lazy attribute, as shown in the next listing.

Listing 9.7   Overriding __getattr__ in a class

```python
class User:
    def __init__(self, username):
        self.username = username
        print(f"### User {username} created")

    def __getattr__(self, item):
        print(f"__getattr__ called for {item}")
        if item == "profile_data":
            profile_data = self._get_profile_data()
```

```
        setattr(self, item, profile_data)
        return profile_data

def _get_profile_data(self):
    # get the data from the server and load it into memory
    print("*** Run the expensive operation")
    fetched_data = "Extensive data, including thumbnail,
    ➥ followers, etc."
    return fetched_data
```

Compared with listing 9.6, there are two significant changes in listing 9.7:

- *The* __init__ *method removes setting the* profile_data *attribute.* This removal is necessary because if it's set, even with None, the profile_data attribute and its value are stored in the object's __dict__ attribute. The special method __getattr__ can't be called, defeating the purpose of implementing a lazy attribute with __getattr__.

- *In the* __getattr__ *method, we specify that when the* profile_data *attribute is accessed, we'll run the expensive operation to get the profile data for the user.* It's important to note that we also set the fetched data by using setattr; when the profile_data attribute is accessed again, it will become available immediately.

With these changes, we expect the following actions:

- *Action 1*—When a user is created, there is no profile data, preventing the expensive operation up front.
- *Action 2*—When we do access the attribute, the expensive operation can be triggered to provide the requested attribute.
- *Action 3*—When we access the attribute for the second time, there's no need to run the expensive operation again.

Let's see whether our expectation is met:

```
followers = get_followers("Ashley")     ◀──── Action 1
# output the following lines:
### User John created
### User Aaron created
### User Zack created

follower0 = followers[0]
follower0.profile_data                  ◀──── Action 2
# output the following lines:
__getattr__ called for profile_data
*** Run the expensive operation
'Extensive data, including thumbnail, followers, etc.'

follower0.profile_data        ◀───┐ Action 3
'Extensive data, including thumbnail, followers, etc.'
```

For Action 1, when we get one user's followers, the created User instance objects contain only usernames, which saves memory! For Action 2, when we access profile_data for the first time, the expensive operation runs to fetch the data. For Action 3, when we access profile_data for the second time, we get the data without triggering the expensive operation, which saves time!

9.4.3   *Implementing a property as a lazy attribute*

In section 8.3, you learned to use the property decorator to create read-only properties as a finer access-control approach. Because the property decorator allows us to "intercept" how an attribute is accessed, we can use it to implement the lazy attribute feature, as discussed in this section. Please note that a property isn't strictly an attribute, but properties and attributes are similar in terms of supporting dot notation.

By now, you should be familiar with using the property decorator. You can jump directly into the next listing to see how to create a lazy attribute involving @property.

Listing 9.8   Creating a decorator for a lazy attribute

```python
class User:
    def __init__(self, username):
        self.username = username
        self._profile_data = None
        print(f"### User {username} created")

    @property
    def profile_data(self):
        if self._profile_data is None:
            print("_profile_data is None")
            self._profile_data = self._get_profile_data()
        else:
            print("_profile_data is set")
        return self._profile_data

    def _get_profile_data(self):
        # get the data from the server and load it into memory
        print("*** Run the expensive operation")
        fetched_data = "Extensive data, including thumbnail,
➥ followers, etc."
        return fetched_data
```

Compared with listing 9.6, there are two significant changes in listing 9.8:

- *In the* __init__ *method, we set the* _profile_data *attribute as* None. The _profile_data is the internally managed counterpart of the profile_data property; setting it to None saves memory compared with getting the data during instantiation.
- *We implement* profile_data *as a property.* In this method, we check whether _profile_data is set, and we run the expensive operation only when _profile_data isn't set. If it's set, we return the value.

As discussed in section 9.4.2, we expect the same three actions from the User class implemented in listing 9.8:

```
followers = get_followers("Ashley")
# output the following lines:
### User John created
### User Aaron created
### User Zack created

follower0 = followers[0]
follower0.profile_data
# output the following lines:
_profile_data is None
*** Run the expensive operation
'Extensive data, including thumbnail, followers, etc.'

follower0.profile_data
# output the following lines:
_profile_data is set
'Extensive data, including thumbnail, followers, etc.'
```

Consistent with our expected actions, users don't have their profile data loaded when they're created. Instead, the expensive operation is run when a user's profile data is requested, which is exactly what lazy evaluation is all about—delaying evaluation until we must do it, thereby saving time (not running the time-consuming operation) and memory (not using any memory to store a large amount of data).

9.4.4 *Discussion*

You can override __getattr__ or implement a property to provide lazily evaluated attributes to a custom class. I recommend using the property approach; it's more straightforward, and all the implementations are explicit. By contrast, overriding __getattr__ requires knowledge of how a Python instance object's attribute resolution order works.

9.4.5 *Challenge*

Tim is updating a Python package that his company has published. An API in the package accesses an object's attribute, such as user.initials. With recent updates, he needs to have finer control of this attribute. How can he create a property to maintain the API?

> HINT   Both properties and attributes support dot notation. You can convert a previously defined attribute to a property in the updated codebase.

9.5   *How do I define classes to have distinct concerns?*

As you develop your project, you'll find that you must deal with more data. Suppose that you start with one class to manage the data. To accommodate the increasing data volumes, your class can become cumbersome if you're sticking to a single class. One underlying cause of the problem is the fact that the class may have mixed concerns; a single class models different kinds of data, which can make your project hard to maintain.

Imagine the two scenarios shown in figure 9.7. In the first scenario, one large box (your class) holds two kinds of objects (the data). In the second scenario, you have

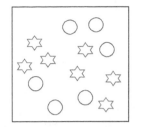

One large box consists of two kinds of objects.

VS.

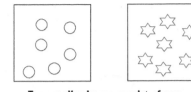

Two smaller boxes consist of one kind of object each.

Figure 9.7 Better organization when objects are handled by their own type in separate boxes as opposed to a large box that stores mixed objects

two smaller boxes (two separate classes), each of which holds only one kind of object. You can tell which scenario is better for managing the objects.

In this section, I show you how to define classes that have distinct concerns, which is a vital form of refactoring your project. This topic is important for improving the long-term maintainability of your project, as it's easier to move multiple lighter boxes than to move a gigantic heavy box. You'll find it manageable to maintain and update the data models when each class focuses on one purpose.

9.5.1 Analyzing a class

In an ideal project, we have an experienced leader who can design the perfect data structures for our project: our project has multiple small classes, each of which addresses a specific data model. Suppose, however, that you're assigned to update and maintain a legacy project in your company. You find that the essential data model is a single gigantic class, making this project almost impossible to update. In this section, you'll see what the cumbersome class might look like and how to analyze it.

Suppose that this project involves a program that a school district uses to manage data. One key class is `Student`, which stores all student-related data. This class has the structure shown in the following listing. Please note that for simplicity, I'm showing only part of the `Student` class.

Listing 9.9 A class with mixed purposes

```python
class Student:
    def __init__(self, first_name, last_name, student_id):
        self.first_name = first_name
        self.last_name = last_name
        self.student_id = student_id
        self.account_number = self.get_account_number()
        self.balance = self.get_balance()
        age, gender, race = self.get_demographics()
        self.age = age
        self.gender = gender
        self.race = race
```

```
def get_account_number(self):
    # query database to locate the account number using student_id
    account_number = 123456
    return account_number

def get_balance(self):
    # query database to get the balance for the account number
    balance = 100.00
    return balance

def get_demographics(self):
    # query database to get the demographics using student_id
    birthday = "08/14/2010"
    age = self.calculated_age(birthday)
    gender = "Female"
    race = "Black"
    return age, gender, race

@staticmethod
def calculated_age(birthday):
    # get today's date and calculate the difference from birthday
    age = 12
    return age
```

Before you do anything with the existing class, it's a good idea to generate a diagram to inspect its components. Although you can create such a diagram in different ways, the key is to view the structure at a high level. For this purpose, use the Unified Modeling Language (UML) diagram (figure 9.8).

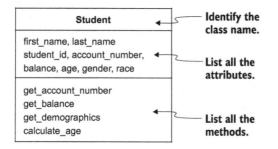

Figure 9.8   The UML diagram (version 0) of the `Student` class. In the diagram, we list all the attributes and the methods for the class.

CONCEPT   UML is a standard way to visualize a system's design, showing a system's components and their connections.

In version 0 of the UML diagram, you're not judgmental and are listing only the structural components of the `Student` class. To help view the data, you list the names of the methods without any implementation details. After you obtain the class's structural information, the next step is inspecting its functional components (figure 9.9).

In the UML diagram (version 1), the methods that collectively fulfill the same functionality are grouped together. Here, we have two functional components: one that handles a student's lunch account and one that handles the student's demographics. In addition, each functional component has related attributes.

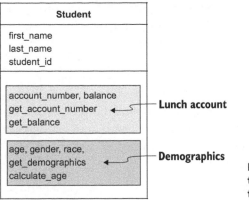

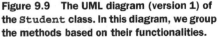

Figure 9.9   The UML diagram (version 1) of the Student class. In this diagram, we group the methods based on their functionalities.

9.5.2   Creating additional classes to isolate the concerns

Figure 9.9 shows part of the Student class. In an actual project, this class might contain many other functionalities, and functionalities such as lunch account and demographics might include other methods. The function for managing lunch accounts, for example, might have many additional operations, such as suspending a lost card and consolidating multiple accounts. Implementing these operations makes the Student class complicated. As discussed in this section, we should create additional classes that have separate concerns.

When we analyzed the Student class, we recognized two major functional components: lunch account and demographics, which represent concerns distinct from the Student class. Thus, these two functional components can form their own classes. Before we write any code, we can continue to work on our UML diagram (figure 9.10), an updated version of which reflects the additional structural components of our application.

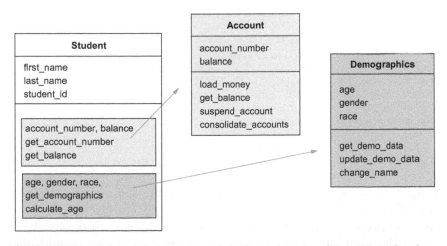

Figure 9.10   Isolate the functionalities of handling Account and Demographics to form separate classes (UML diagram version 2). Please note that I list some other attributes and methods that could exist in each class.

The updated UML diagram depicts two additional classes: `Account` and `Demographics`. The `Account` class has the attributes and methods for managing a student's lunch account, and the `Demographics` class has the attributes and methods to handle a student's demographic information.

9.5.3 *Connecting related classes*

When we created the `Account` and `Demographics` classes, the process was one-way; we extracted information from the existing `Student` class. These two classes are still standalone and don't work with the `Student` class yet. In this section, we'll connect them so that they work together in a neat way.

CONNECTING THE DATA USING ATTRIBUTES

One thing you may have noticed is that the `Account` and `Demographics` classes have the `student_id` attribute. Because of the uniqueness of student identification numbers, all the data of a specific student can be connected via the unique `student_id`. To create two-way traffic between `Student` and `Account/Demographics`, an instance object of the `Student` class should have access to account and demographic information via the `student_id`. The next listing connects the instance objects.

Listing 9.10   **Separating classes to have distinct concerns**

```python
class Account:
    def __init__(self, student_id):
        # query the database to get additional information using student_id
        self.account_number = 123456
        self.balance = 100

class Demographics:
    def __init__(self, student_id):
        # query the database to get additional information using student_id
        self.age = 12
        self.gender = "Female"
        self.race = "Black"

class Student:
    def __init__(self, first_name, last_name, student_id):
        self.first_name = first_name
        self.last_name = last_name
        self.student_id = student_id
        self.account = Account(self.student_id)
        self.demographics = Demographics(self.student_id)
```

In listing 9.10, we define `Account` and `Demographics` classes implementing only the initialization method. Notably, we update the `Student` class's initialization method by adding two attributes: `account` and `demographics`, which are instance objects of the `Account` and `Demographics` classes, respectively. By doing so, we connect these three classes. We can now inspect the attributes of an instance of the `Student` class:

```
student = Student("John", "Smith", "987654")
print(student.account.__dict__)
# output: {'account_number': 123456, 'balance': 100}

print(student.demographics.__dict__)
# output: {'age': 12, 'gender': 'Female', 'race': 'Black'}
```

As you can see, the instance student has the correct account and demographic information because it has the instances of Account and Demographics as its attributes. Note that we can save student_id as an attribute for the instance objects of the Account and Demographics classes. We don't have to do so, however, because an instance object of Student has attributes of account and demographics; the connections have been established.

CONNECTING THE METHODS

Connecting the data between these three classes is straightforward. The fun part is connecting the methods.

The purpose of creating additional classes isn't only about having them hold a specific attribute. The more important part is using these classes to provide the dedicated functionalities. Specifically, our plan is to move all the implementations of account management to the Account class and to move all the implementations of demographics to the Demographics class. The following listing shows updated versions of the Account and Demographics classes.

Listing 9.11 The updated Account and Demographics classes

```
class Account:
    def __init__(self, student_id):
        self.student_id = student_id
        # query the database to get additional information using student_id
        self.account_number = self.get_account_number_from_db()
        self.balance = self.get_balance_from_db()

    def get_account_number_from_db(self):
        # query database to locate the account number using student_id
        account_number = 123456
        return account_number

    def get_balance_from_db(self):
        # query database to get the balance for the account number
        balance = 100.00
        return balance


class Demographics:
    def __init__(self, student_id):
        self.student_id = student_id
        # query the database to get additional information
        age, gender, race = self.get_demographics_from_db()
        self.age = age
```

```
        self.gender = gender
        self.race = race

    def get_demographics_from_db(self):
        # query database to get the demographics using student_id
        birthday = "08/14/2010"
        age = self.calculated_age(birthday)
        gender = "Female"
        race = "Black"
        return age, gender, race

    @staticmethod
    def calculated_age(birthday):
        # get today's date and calculate the difference from birthday
        age = 12
        return age
```

> **QUESTION** If the database operations are expensive, such as hosting the data-base in the cloud, they may be implemented as lazy attributes. Can you recall how? See section 9.4.

In our application, whenever we want to show the student's account information, we can take advantage of the Account class directly. We can show the student's balance by running the following code:

```
balance_output = f"Balance: {student.account.balance}"

print(balance_output)
# output: Balance: 100.0
```

In a similar manner, we can show the student's demographics by running the following code:

```
demo = student.demographics

demo_output = f"Age: {demo.age}; Gender: {demo.gender}; Race: {demo.race}"

print(demo_output)
# output: Age: 12; Gender: Female; Race: Black
```

Note that some users may prefer working with methods from fewer classes, so they might create some methods in the Student class:

```
class Student:
    def __init__(self, first_name, last_name, student_id):
        self.first_name = first_name
        self.last_name = last_name
        self.student_id = student_id
        self.account = Account(self.student_id)
        self.demographics = Demographics(self.student_id)
```

```
def get_account_balance(self):
    return self.account.balance

def get_demographics(self):
    demo = self.demographics
    return demo.age, demo.gender, demo.race
```

We can get the account balance and the demographics by calling the get_account_ balance and get_demographics methods on the Student instance. I don't recommend this pattern, however. It makes the connection between the Student and Account/Demographics classes too tight—a problem known as *tight coupling*. When you update your Account class, you may also have to update the Student class because its functionality (get_account_balance) depends on Account.

MAINTAINABILITY Don't introduce tight coupling between related classes. The classes should be in a loosely coupled state for best maintainability.

9.5.4 *Discussion*

Before you start your project, it's a good habit to use a UML diagram to lay out the necessary classes for data management. Don't expect that work to be a one-time deal, however. As your project progresses, you may realize that some classes are becoming more complicated. It's a great habit to think about your data models from time to time throughout the project's development process. The single objective is to make the classes slim and loosely connected—that is, related classes work together but don't depend heavily on one another, making refactoring hard in such a tight-coupling design.

9.5.5 *Challenge*

In this section's code snippets, I intentionally made all the methods in the classes public. As discussed in section 8.3, however, it's a best practice to make methods that users don't need to access nonpublic. As a challenge, can you make the applicable methods in listing 9.11 nonpublic?

HINT If you want to define a nonpublic method, prefix the method name with an underscore.

Summary
- Create an enumeration class by subclassing Enum when you need to group related concepts.
- The enumeration class makes iteration over possible values and membership checking convenient.
- Use the dataclass decorator to create classes to avoid boilerplate, such as implementing __init__ and __repr__. When you use this decorator, remember to use the type annotations to create the applicable fields.

- JSON data is the universal data exchange format for different systems. We can use the `json` module to convert JSON to native Python data structures (JSON deserialization) and the other way around (JSON serialization).

- An instance object of a custom class usually isn't JSON-serializable. You should provide specific encoding instructions for JSON serialization of the class.

- You can use `__getattr__` to implement lazy attributes, but you must understand that `__getattr__` is a fallback mechanism when an attribute isn't contained in the object's `__dict__` attribute.

- Implementing a property allows you to have finer control of specific attributes. In the case of lazy attributes, you can set None to an internally managed counterpart. When the attribute is requested, you can set the counterpart attribute.

- Classes should be kept for a single purpose. When your class grows in its scope and you realize that it has mixed purposes, you should refactor your class to create distinct classes, each of which addresses a specific need.

- Use a UML diagram to analyze a class's structure, which allows you to have a clear understanding of the class at a high level.

## Part 4

Manipulating objects and files

Python is an object-oriented programming language by design. Its modules, packages, and built-in data types, as well as functions and custom classes and their instances, are all objects. Thus, the common characteristics of objects are an essential topic that every Python user should know well. In this part, we focus on the fundamentals of using objects in Python.

In addition to objects, this part covers reading and processing files, which are the most common data storage mechanisms. As a general-purpose language, Python makes it possible for us to do the following:

- Read data stored in a file, either as pure text or as comma-delimited data
- Write data to a file
- Move, delete, and copy files
- Obtain the metadata of files, such as modification times

Fundamentals of objects 10

This chapter covers

- Inspecting objects
- Illustrating an object's lifecycle
- Copying an object
- Resolving a variable: the LEGB rule
- Understanding an object's callability

Objects are everywhere in Python, as Python is an object-oriented programming (OOP) language by design. We work with objects constantly in our applications. Thus, it's important to know the fundamentals of using objects, particularly instance objects of a custom class, as they're the most prevalent data model in applications. In a function, for example, we expect that users may send different types of data, and we can add this flexibility by handling applicable data types accordingly. As another example, copying an object is necessary when we have a working copy to update while keeping the original object intact in case we need to revert our update. In this chapter, I'll cover the fundamentals of objects. Certainly, this chapter isn't intended to be exhaustive, as everything is an object in Python, and I can't cover all the aspects of how objects are used. Another thing to note is that some sections address a specific problem (section 10.4, for example, is about changing a variable in a different

273

scope), but I'll use addressing the specific problem to cover a more general topic (such as the variable lookup order).

10.1   *How do I inspect an object's type to improve code flexibility?*

We always work with a variety of objects, such as functions, classes, and instances. Let's use custom functions as an example. Most of our coding work involves writing functions: defining the input, performing the operations, and providing the output. A function's input usually has a specific type requirement; accordingly, users must use one specific type of data to call a function. Consider the following function, which filters the list of tasks (the `tasks` argument) based on their urgencies in our task management app:

```
def filter_tasks(tasks, by_urgency):
    pass
```

Our first thought may be that the `by_urgency` argument should be an integer, such as 4 and 5 as possible arguments. Thus, the function may have the following implementation:

```
def filter_tasks(tasks, by_urgency):
    filtered = [x for x in tasks if x.urgency == by_urgency]
    return filtered
```

> **REMINDER**   To use this function, you need to create the `Task` class (chapter 8) and create some instances to be used as the `tasks` argument.

In the function's body, we use a list comprehension to select the tasks whose urgency level matches that supplied by the `by_urgency` argument. It's entirely plausible, however, to have a feature that allows users to filter tasks with multiple urgency levels like this: `filter_tasks([4, 5])`. For this feature, the function should have the following implementation instead:

```
def filter_tasks(tasks, by_urgency):
    filtered = [x for x in tasks if x.urgency in by_urgency]
    return filtered
```

Instead of comparing the integer values, now we use `item in list` to check whether a task's urgency level is in the provided urgency values.

To accommodate these two cases, we should have a mechanism to check the `by_urgency` argument and filter the tasks accordingly. This form of checking an object's type is an example of object *introspection*—inspecting an object to find out its characteristics, such as type, attributes, and methods. In this section, we'll review the key techniques of object introspection and their use scenarios with a primary focus on improving code flexibility. Using the `filter_tasks` function as our work subject, we'll write a single function that can take different kinds of input.

> **CONCEPT**   *Introspection* is the act of examining an object's type or properties, such as attributes, during the execution of the program.

10.1.1 Checking an object's type using type

In the code example in section 10.1, to provide flexibility in handling an int or a list as an argument in the filter_tasks function, we need to check the argument's type. In this section, we'll see what built-in functions we can use to check an object's type.

The first function that may come to your mind is type. Calling type on an object returns its type, and you've seen this usage several times. The following code snippet shows some examples as a quick refresher:

```
print(type(4))
# output: <class 'int'>

print(type([4, 5]))
# output: <class 'list'>
```

As expected, 4 has a type of int, and [4, 5] has a type of list. We know how to obtain an object's type information, so the next question to ask is how we can compare the type of an object against the desired type. If you overthink the comparison, you may not get the answer, which is to compare the object's type with the class:

```
assert (type(4) is int)

assert (type([4, 5]) is list)
```

> **QUESTION**   When you compare two objects, are == and is the same?

Based on these comparisons, we can now update the filter_tasks function to handle both calling scenarios, as shown in the next listing. Please note that we simplify the condition by assuming that there are only two possibilities for the by_urgency argument: int and list.

Listing 10.1   Comparing an object's type with a class

```
def filter_tasks(tasks, by_urgency):
    if type(by_urgency) is list:
        filtered = [x for x in tasks if x.urgency in by_urgency]
    else:
        filtered = [x for x in tasks if x.urgency == by_urgency]
    return filtered
```

As shown in this listing, when by_urgency is a list, we check the presence of the urgency in the list, and when by_urgency is an int, we compare each task's urgency level with the number.

10.1.2   *Checking an object's type using isinstance*

Another useful introspection function is isinstance, which checks whether an object is an instance of the specified class. As you'll see in this section, isinstance does a similar job to type, but it's the preferred approach for checking an object's type.

When you learned about creating proper docstrings for a function (section 6.5), you used help on the isinstance function, but I didn't expand the discussion of its usage. Now it's time to learn formally what we can do with isinstance:

```
assert isinstance(4, int)

assert isinstance([4, 5], list)
```

The first argument is the object, and the second argument is the specific class. In fact, the second argument can also be a tuple of classes, allowing you to check an object flexibly against multiple classes. Observe this feature:

```
passed_arg0 = [4, 5]
passed_arg1 = (4, 5)

assert isinstance(passed_arg0, (list, tuple))
assert isinstance(passed_arg1, (list, tuple))
```

If your function takes either list or tuple, for example, you can combine the test in a single isinstance call, as shown in the preceding code snippet. Note that the relationship between these classes is equivalent to an "or" evaluation:

```
assert isinstance([4, 5], list) or isinstance([4, 5], tuple)
```

Using the isinstance function, we can update the filter_tasks function to handle by_urgency as int or list, as the following listing shows.

Listing 10.2   Checking an object's type using `isinstance`

```
def filter_tasks(tasks, by_urgency):
    if isinstance(by_urgency, list):
        filtered = [x for x in tasks if x.urgency in by_urgency]
    else:
        filtered = [x for x in tasks if x.urgency == by_urgency]
    return filtered
```

When you compare listings 10.1 and 10.2, you may notice that both type and isinstance determine whether an object is of a specific type. But they're not the same.

When we use type to determine an object's type, we're doing a one-to-one comparison: the object's type against the specified type. By contrast, isinstance is more flexible, and it's a one-to-many comparison; it checks against not only a class, but also its superclass. That is, isinstance considers class inheritance, but type doesn't. Sound confusing? Here's a general example:

```
class User:
    pass

class Supervisor(User):
    pass

supervisor = Supervisor()

comparisons = [
    type(supervisor) is User,
    type(supervisor) is Supervisor,
    isinstance(supervisor, User),
    isinstance(supervisor, Supervisor)
]

print(comparisons)
# output: [False, True, True, True]
```

From the first and second comparisons, you can tell that when you use type, the obtained type information is specific to the immediate class: Supervisor. By contrast, although supervisor is an instance of the Supervisor class, not the User class, isinstance also uses the information that Supervisor is a subclass of User, and it returns True even if you check the instance against the superclass User.

This flexibility is important, as even if our function checks a specific type using isinstance, such as User, it's still valid if we call the function by sending an instance of Supervisor (an argument named user), which passes the isinstance(user, User) check.

> **MAINTAINABILITY** To improve the robustness of type checking, you should use isinstance when you're checking an object's type, as this function considers not only the object's immediate class, but also the class's subclasses.

10.1.3 Checking an object's type generically

In listings 10.1 and 10.2, we assumed that the passed by_urgency argument is either int or list. But it's not user-friendly if another user tries to call the filter_tasks function as filter_tasks(tasks, (4, 5)). That is, instead of using list, the user calls the function with a tuple object. As you can see, to provide greater flexibility to our function, it's rather restrictive to check only the argument's type against a specific kind. In this section, we'll see how we can obtain an object's type information more generically.

We know that isinstance is preferred over type in checking an object's type. Moreover, we can specify multiple classes in isinstance. Thus, the next listing shows a working solution for checking by_urgency in the filter_tasks function against multiple classes.

Listing 10.3 Checking an object's type against multiple classes using `isinstance`

```
def filter_tasks(tasks, by_urgency):
    if isinstance(by_urgency, (list, tuple)):
        filtered = [x for x in tasks if x.urgency in by_urgency]
    else:
        filtered = [x for x in tasks if x.urgency == by_urgency]
    return filtered
```

As you might expect, the updated `filter_tasks` function can handle `list` and `tuple` for the `by_urgency` argument. But it's also possible that a user may want to call this function with a `set` object: `filter_tasks(tasks, {4, 5})`. The current implementation can't handle this call. Theoretically, we can add `set` to the `isinstance` function call. The problem is that many other `list`-like data types, such as `Series` in the pandas library, can be used for `by_urgency`. Thus, it's impossible to list all these types one by one, considering that you can also define custom classes. We should have a mechanism to check an object's type generically.

In the standard library, the `collections.abc` module defines several *abstract base classes* (where the name abc comes from), which can be used to test whether a specific class has attributes or methods, a concept known as *interface* in programming.

> **CONCEPT** In OOP, *interface* represents the defined attributes, functions, methods, classes, and other applicable components of an entity (such as a class or a package) that developers can use.

Relevant to the present topic is the `Collection` abstract class, which requires three key special methods: `__contains__` (to check whether an item exists: `item in obj`), `__iter__` (convertible to an iterator: `iter(obj)`), and `__len__` (to check the number of items: `len(obj)`). `list`, `tuple`, `set`, and many other types of data containers, including `Series`, implement these methods, and all of them are concrete (as opposed to abstract) classes of `Collection`. Thus, we can update the `filter_tasks` function to be more generic in terms of checking the `by_urgency` argument's type, as the next listing shows.

Listing 10.4 Checking an object's type against an abstract class

```
from collections.abc import Collection

def filter_tasks(tasks, by_urgency):
    if isinstance(by_urgency, Collection):
        filtered = [x for x in tasks if x.urgency in by_urgency]
    else:
        filtered = [x for x in tasks if x.urgency == by_urgency]
    return filtered
```

By using the abstract `Collection` class, we can accommodate all the collection-like data types without identifying the variety of classes that a user may send, which helps improve our code's flexibility.

As you can see from these sections, we're gradually improving the flexibility of our function by checking the type of the argument by using type and isinstance with one type, isinstance with multiple definite types, and isinstance with a generic type. Figure 10.1 provides a visual summary of these usages.

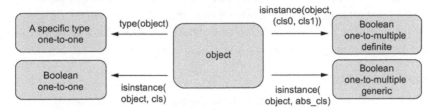

Figure 10.1 Checking an object's type information using type **and** isinstance. cls, **as well as** cls0 **and** cls1, **refer to specific classes, whereas** abs_cls **refers to an abstract class that might represent an unlimited number of classes that use the interface.**

10.1.4 Discussion

Checking an object's type is an essential aspect of object introspection. There are too many other introspection techniques to cover comprehensively. As a developer, when you're using a new library that you're not familiar with, instead of looking up the information online, you can run dir(obj), which returns all the available attributes and methods for the object.

The collections.abc module has many other abstract base classes. One abstract class is Sequence, and list is a concrete class of Sequence. Another abstract class is Iterable, which defines the __iter__ interface.

10.1.5 Challenge

In listing 5.1, we defined the following function to check whether an object is an iterable:

```
def is_iterable(obj):
    try:
        _ = iter(obj)
    except TypeError:
        print(type(obj), "is not an iterable")
    else:
        print(type(obj), "is an iterable")
```

We mentioned that Iterable is an abstract class in the collections.abc module. Can you rewrite the is_iterable function by taking advantage of the Iterable class?

> **HINT** If an object is an iterable, its class must have implemented __iter__ and have the corresponding interface for the Iterable class.

10.2 What's the lifecycle of instance objects?

When a project grows in its scope, you define your own custom classes. When you learn to implement custom classes (chapters 8 and 9), you come across various terms related to the creation of custom class instances. Understanding the lifecycle of these instances is a fundamental skill that enables you, the Python developer, to manipulate these instances properly.

In this section, I'll review the key events of an instance object by going through specific examples. During this process, you'll see terms describing essential programming concepts that you need to know to communicate with other developers effectively. Some of these terms are covered in chapter 8; I'll briefly review them here and place the discussion in the context of an object's lifecycle.

10.2.1 Instantiating an object

The life of an instance object starts with its creation, known as *instantiation*. This section reviews the instantiation process.

> **REMINDER** *Instantiation* is the process of creating an instance object of a specific class.

For some built-in data types, such as str and list, we can use literals to create an instance, such as "Hello, World!" for a str instance and [1, 2, 3] for a list instance. Other than these literals for creating built-in data types, a more general situation is calling the constructor of a class. Consider the following Task class (and note that I'm keeping its implementation minimal so that I can focus on showing you the most relevant content):

```python
class Task:
    def __new__(cls, *args):
        new_task = object.__new__(cls)
        print(f"__new__ is called, creating an instance at {id(new_task)}")
        return new_task

    def __init__(self, title):
        self.title = title
        print(f"__init__ is called, initializing an instance
        ➥ at {id(self)}")
```

In the Task class, besides the __init__ method, we implement the __new__ method. Note that we typically don't implement __new__, as there isn't much we need to worry about in this method. Here, in both __new__ and __init__, we add two print function calls, allowing us to see when each function is called. More importantly, the printed message will inform us of the memory address of the instance (using the id function), allowing us to know the identity of the object for tracking purposes. With this class, let's see what happens when we create an instance object:

```python
task = Task("Laundry")

# output the following lines:
__new__ is called, creating an instance at 140557771534976    ◁
```

> **Expect a different memory address on your computer.**

```
__init__ is called, initializing an instance at 140557771534976
```

```
print("task memory address:", id(task))
# output: task memory address: 140557771534976
```

When we call the Task's constructor, __new__ is invoked first, creating the instance without assigning any attributes; at this stage, it's a brand-new object, as indicated by the method name. The purpose of this step is to allocate a specific slot in the memory to save the object. This is also why we can obtain the instance's memory address.

The next step is invoking the __init__ method, in which the newly created instance gets its attribute assignment to complete the initialization process. As indicated by the same memory address, we're constantly dealing with the same object in __new__, in __init__, and in the created task variable. Putting all these observations together, figure 10.2 shows the instantiation process.

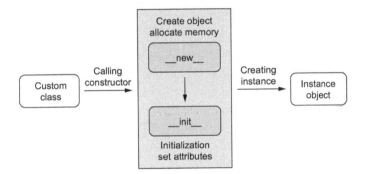

Figure 10.2 The instantiation process of a custom class. After we call the constructor of a custom class, behind the scenes, the __new__ and __init__ methods are invoked sequentially, with __new__ creating the new object and __init__ completing the initialization process. In the end, the construction results in the creation of an instance object.

10.2.2 Being active in applicable namespaces

You create an instance by calling the class constructor. Next, you use the created instance. This section introduces the namespace concept. You'll see that the created instance is active in an applicable namespace, allowing it to be used.

We created an instance object of the Task class by running task = Task ("Laundry"), in which the variable task represents the instance object. Later in our code, we may want to retrieve the task's title attribute, as follows:

```
title_output = f"Title: {task.title}"
```

When we write this line of code, we implicitly assume that the task variable refers to the variable that we've defined: an instance of the Task class. When Python tries to run this line of code, however, it doesn't know our assumption; instead, it needs a mechanism to locate the `task` variable so that it can create the f-string. The mechanism for looking up variables involves *namespaces,* which track the variables that have been defined.

> **CONCEPT** Working as a dictionary, a *namespace* tracks variables that have been defined within its space. When you use a variable, the namespace can help locate the variable's information.

Suppose that the `Task` class is defined and the `task` instance is created in the same Python file, which forms a module. In this module, we have a *global namespace* that tracks all the variables, and we can check these variables by calling the `globals` function:

```
print(globals())
# output the following data:
{'__name__': '__main__', '__doc__': None, '__package__': None,
    '__loader__': <class '_frozen_importlib.BuiltinImporter'>,
    '__spec__': None, '__annotations__': {}, '__builtins__':
    <module 'builtins' (built-in)>, 'Task': <class '__main__.Task'>,
    'task': <__main__.Task object at 0x7fd6280af280>}
```

You can think of namespaces as being dictionaries in which the active variables are the keys and the corresponding values (objects) are the values. The preceding example highlights two variables: the `Task` class and the instance `task`. After we define the class and create an instance, both objects enter the namespace, and they can be located whenever we use these variables. As a quick reference, the following identity comparison shows that the values of `'Task'` and `'task'` are indeed the class and the instance object:

```
assert Task is globals()["Task"]
```

```
assert task is globals()["task"]
```

After we create the instance, we can use it, as it can be resolved by looking up the global namespace, which has registered the created instance.

10.2.3 *Tracking reference counts*

When an object is active in the namespace, Python tracks how many other objects hold references to it for memory management purposes. This important event is happening behind the scenes, and many modern OOP languages have a similar feature. In this section, we'll discuss the mechanism of tracking reference counts.

A computer has a fixed amount of memory. When our applications are running, we create objects that consume memory. The more objects we add, the more memory our application uses. If we keep creating objects, our computer may run out of memory, causing our applications to crash and maybe even freezing up the computer. Thus, our applications should have a mechanism for removing objects from memory when we're no longer using them. *Reference counting* is such a mechanism.

UNDERSTANDING THE DISTINCTION BETWEEN OBJECTS AND VARIABLES

To understand how reference counting works, we first need to understand the distinction between objects and variables. When we run task = Task("Laundry"), two distinct things happen:

- An instance object is created, creating the actual object and its related data stored in memory.
- The object is referenced by the variable task, using a label to refer to the underlying object in memory.

Notably, the relationship between the object and the label can change. In Python, which is a dynamically typed language, we can assign a different object to the same label; the object that was associated with the label still exists in memory, but now the label references the new object (figure 10.3).

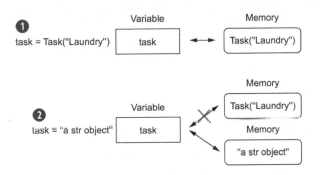

Figure 10.3 The relationship between objects and variables. In the assignment statement, an instance object of the Task class is created in memory, and this object is associated with the task variable. Later, we assign a str object to the task variable. This reassignment disrupts the previous association between task and the actual Task("Laundry") object and creates a new association between task and the str object.

As shown in figure 10.3, we create a variable named task by assigning it to an instance of the Task class so that the variable task is referencing the Task instance object. When we assign the same variable task to another str object, task no longer references the Task instance object; instead, it references the str object.

INCREMENTING AND DECREMENTING REFERENCE COUNTS

Now we understand the distinction between objects and variables, and we know that a variable represents a reference to the underlying object in memory. Such a reference to the object is counted as 1 to start with the initial assignment statement. This section shows how we can change the reference counts.

Before we try to change an object's reference count, we should find a way to track the reference count. In Python, we can use the getrefcount function in the sys module:

```
import sys

task = Task("Laundry")

assert sys.getrefcount(task) == 2
```

The preceding example has two references to the Task instance object. Wait a second. Shouldn't there only be one reference—the task variable in the assignment? It's an awesome question. The answer is that using the variable in the getrefcount function call creates another reference to the object, making the current reference count 2. More generally, using a variable in a function increments the underlying object's reference count.

   We know how to track an object's reference count, and we can do some experiments to manipulate the count for an object. To increase this count, one common approach is to include the variable in a data container, such as a dict or a list object:

```
work = {"to_do": task}
assert sys.getrefcount(task) == 3

tasks = [task]
assert sys.getrefcount(task) == 4
```

In both cases, using task in a dict and a list object increments the reference count by 1. We've seen how reference counting increments, and it's time to see how we can decrement the count. The common way is to use the del statement:

```
del tasks

assert sys.getrefcount(task) == 3
```

After removing tasks, we remove a reference to the instance object; thus, the reference count drops by 1. We can also delete work to reduce the reference count by 1, but doing the same thing all the time is boring. Instead of deleting the dict object, we can manipulate the work objectby replacing task with a different value, in which case we also remove a reference to the Task instance:

```
work["to_do"] = "nothing"

assert sys.getrefcount(task) == 2
```

You can see how responsively and instantaneously Python tracks the reference count for us. But what does reference counting end up with? Let's continue exploring the lifecycle of the instance object.

10.2.4 *Destructing the object*

Section 10.2.3 discussed how Python tracks reference counts. The key is that when an object's reference count reaches zero, Python destructs the object so that the memory that it occupied can be released for the system to use. In this section, we take a closer look at the destruction process.

Like the construction process, the destruction process is typically handled in Python through automatic reference counting. To zoom in on the destruction process, we can override __del__, the special method related to object destruction, as shown in the next listing.

Listing 10.5 Overriding __del__ in a class

```
class Task:
    def __init__(self, title):
        print(f"__init__ is called, initializing an instance
        ➥ at {id(self)}")
        self.title = title

    def __del__(self):
        print(f"__del__ is called, destructing an instance at {id(self)}")
```

With this updated Task class, let's write some code to review initialization and the global namespace processes:

```
task = Task("Homework")
# output: __init__ is called, initializing an instance at 140557504542416

assert "task" in globals()
```

To set the reference count to zero manually so that we can trigger the destruction process, we can use the del statement:

```
del task
# output: __del__ is called, destructing an instance at 140557504542416

assert "task" not in globals()
```

As you can see, calling del on task invokes the __del__ special method. By cross-checking the memory address, we're indeed removing the same instance that we created. Notably, after the destruction, "task" is also removed from the namespace, and we can no longer access the task variable. If you insist on trying, you'll see an error:

```
title_output = f"Title: {task.title}"

# ERROR: NameError: name 'task' is not defined. Did you mean: 'Task'?
```

10.2.5 Discussion

This section discusses the major events in the lifecycle of an object, using an instance object of a custom class as an example. Putting all the key points together, figure 10.4 shows the big picture of an object's lifecycle.

The great thing about working with Python is that these events are largely automatic; Python does the heavy lifting behind the scenes. Unless you're building a

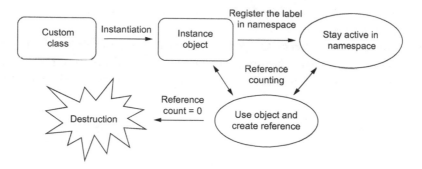

Figure 10.4   The key events in an object's lifecycle. An object starts with the construction and becomes active in an applicable namespace. During its usage, Python tracks its reference count. When there are no references to the object, Python destructs it to make its occupied memory available again.

memory-intensive application, you don't need to worry about these underlying events. Nevertheless, these concepts are fundamental to OOP, and if you're also learning another OOP language, this knowledge can expedite your learning process.

A key module that I haven't mentioned is gc, the name of which stands for *garbage collection*. This module has advanced algorithms to handle memory management while working with the reference counting mechanism. Reference counting can't destruct objects when cyclic referencing happens, for example. This problematic scenario arises when two or more objects reference each other, and their reference counts can never reach 0. Interested readers can explore the gc module to find out how this kind of problem (cyclic referencing) is handled.

10.2.6   Challenge

As a Python beginner, James is particularly interested in how reference counting works for custom class instances. He has a question. Suppose that he creates an instance variable, such as task = Task("Homework"), and he knows that the reference count for the underlying object is 1—the task variable. Does using the task variable in a function increment its reference counts? Write some code to tell him what happens.

> **HINT**   You can check the reference count of an argument by including get-refcount in the function.

10.3   *How do I copy an object?*

When we work with an object, we can modify its attributes, but we may also want to keep its original attributes in case we need to cancel the modification. This need is common in many applications. In our task management application, one feature allows users to edit an existing task. After the user makes some changes, they can either save the update or cancel the edits. In this use case, we create a copy of the original task so we have the new copy for tracking the updates and the original one as the backup. In this section, you'll learn the proper way to copy an object.

10.3.1 Creating a (shallow) copy

In Python, the copy module provides copy-related functionalities for objects. This section shows how to make a copy. More precisely, it discusses creating a shallow copy as opposed to a deep copy; section 10.3.2 distinguishes between those two processes.

Suppose that we've created the following class Task for our application. For simplicity, the class has implemented only __init__ and __repr__:

```
class Task:
    def __init__(self, title, desc):
        self.title = title
        self.desc = desc

    def __repr__(self):
        return f"Task({self.title!r}, {self.desc!r})"

    def save_data(self):
        # update the database
        pass
```

In the application, the user can view the list of tasks and can edit a specific task if they want. They may want to edit the following instance of Task, for example:

```
task = Task("Homework", "Math and physics")
```

If the user is happy with the edit, the updated task is saved, and if the user cancels the edit, everything in the original task is kept. Because an instance of the Task class has a dict representation, a naïve solution to creating a copy may use the dict object as an "informal" copy of the original instance:

```
task_dict = task.__dict__

task_dict_copied = task_dict.copy()

print(task_dict_copied)
# output: {'title': 'Homework', 'desc': 'Math and physics'}
```

As shown in this example, we obtain the dict representation using __dict__. For this dict object, we can create a copy using its instance method copy. When the user edits the task, we use the dict object to track the changes. This solution has a complicating factor, however: after the dict object is updated, we must revert the dict object to an instance of Task so that we can use additional functionalities implemented by the Task class. Otherwise, we can't do much with a dict object because we have no access to task-related functionalities such as save_data.

Instead of making a copy of the instance's dictionary representation, we can copy it directly by using the functionalities available in the copy module. The following code snippet shows a better solution that makes a real copy of the instance:

```
from copy import copy

task_copied = copy(task)

print(task_copied)
# output: Task('Homework', 'Math and physics')
```

TRIVIA   Note that the function copy has the same name as the module copy. This example isn't the only case in which a function has the same name as its module. The datetime module has a function called datetime, for example, so you'll sometimes see from datetime import datetime.

We import the copy function from the copy module, and we can send the instance task to the copy function. The printout shows that the copied variable task_copied holds the same data as task and confirms that it's a copy of the original task. With this copied task, after the user makes the edits, we run task_copied.save_data() to update our database.

10.3.2 *Noting the potential problem of a shallow copy*

At the beginning of section 10.3.1, I mentioned that there are two kinds of copies: shallow and deep. The copy function is creating a shallow copy. But what's a shallow copy, and what's a deep copy? In this section, I'll show how these types of copies differ and discuss a potential problem that might arise from a shallow copy.

For our task management application, suppose that we can have tags for each task. To address this need, our Task class may look like this:

```
class Task:
    def __init__(self, title, desc, tags = None):
        self.title = title
        self.desc = desc
        self.tags = [] if tags is None else tags     ◁─── Ternary assignment

    def __repr__(self):
        return f"Task({self.title!r}, {self.desc!r}, {self.tags})"

    def save_data(self):
        pass
```

CONCEPT   A *ternary expression* is evaluated based on a logical condition and has the format value_when_true if condition else value_when_false. When you use a ternary expression to assign a value, the process is called ternary assignment.

With this updated class, let's create an instance and make a copy using the copy function in the next listing.

> **Listing 10.6 Creating a copy of an existing task**

```
task = Task("Homework", "Math and physics", ["school", "urgent"])

task_copied = copy(task)

print(task_copied)
# output: Task('Homework', 'Math and physics', ['school', 'urgent'])
```

In the application, the user starts to update the task. Specifically, the user adds another tag to the task:

```
task_copied.tags.append("red")

print(task_copied)
# output: Task('Homework', 'Math and physics', ['school', 'urgent', 'red'])
```

As you can see, we're able to update the copied task's tags. But the user decides to cancel this edit. In this scenario, we still use the original task's data. Because we haven't touched the original task, its data should stay the same:

```
print(task)
# output: Task('Homework', 'Math and physics', ['school', 'urgent', 'red'])
```

We're sure that the original task has the tags: `['school', 'urgent']`, but why has it been changed? Specifically, it's been changed to match the `list` object in the copied task. This situation can't be a coincidence, as you should suspect. It seems that `task` and `task_copied` have the same `list` object for tags. This hypothesis is easy to test:

```
assert task.tags is task_copied.tags

assert id(task.tags) == id(task_copied.tags)
```

> **Checking equality with `is` or `==`**
>
> When I compare two objects in Python, you may notice that sometimes I use `is`, and at other times I use `==`. `is` compares whether two objects are the same object, so it's also known as the *identity test*. By contrast, `==` compares whether two objects have the same value. Because they're intended for different comparisons (identity versus value), they should be used differently. In the common use case of comparing an object against `None`, for example, you should use `is`, although you may have seen people use `==`. `None` is a singleton object, meaning that only one object holds `None` in an application. Whenever you use `None`, it's the same object accessed from the memory. Thus, a comparison of an object with `None` should use `is`, as the comparison is supposed to be an identity test. The same identity test is intended to be used to compare `task.tags` and `task_copied.tags`.

(continued)
On the other hand, if we want to compare the memory addresses of the two list objects, we should use == instead. Every time we call the id function on an object, it creates an int object to denote the object's memory address. Thus, calling id two times creates two distinct int objects, and we're only comparing whether these two int objects have equal values.

As shown in the preceding example, both equality comparisons (identity and memory address) support our hypothesis that the list object of task_copied's tags is the same as task's. Why could that happen? This unexpected sharing of the list object highlights the difference between shallow and deep copies. In a shallow copy, we copy the outmost data container. Between copies, we share the contained mutable objects, such as the list object for tags. By contrast, in a deep copy, we copy not only the outmost container, but also recursive copies of the interior objects. Both types of copies leave the contained immutable objects (such as strings and tuples) alone, as they have no way to manipulate those objects anyway. Figure 10.5 shows the differences between deep and shallow copies.

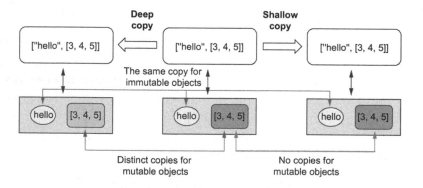

Figure 10.5   **The distinction between shallow and deep copies. In a shallow copy, the outmost data container (or any noncontainer object, such as a string) and its immutable contained objects are copied, but not the interior mutable objects, such as a list. By contrast, in a deep copy, the outmost container and all its interior objects have distinct copies. The gray boxes represent objects in memory.**

In figure 10.5, we use a list object, which contains a str "hello" and a list [3, 4, 5]. When we make a shallow copy, we copy only the outermost list object. The interior list object [3, 4, 5] and the immutable str object "hello" are shared by the shallow copy and its original list. By contrast, when we make a deep copy, the outmost container and its mutable item, the interior list object, are copied distinctly for each object.

Because of the differences in the way the two types of copies deal with interior mutable objects, if you make only a shallow copy, you can overwrite the data in the original object accidentally. Thus, if you want two real copies of independent objects, you should create a deep copy, as shown in the next section.

10.3.3 *Creating a deep copy*

Now that we know the difference between shallow and deep copies, we can revisit the task editing feature of our application. For this feature, we want the original task and the copied task to be distinct, sharing no interior mutable objects—in our case, the tags attribute—so that we're free to update the mutable attribute tags without affecting the original task. Based on the distinction between shallow and deep copies, this feature requires us to create a deep copy.

Besides the copy function, the copy module has a deepcopy function. That function is specifically designed to create a deep copy of an object:

```
from copy import deepcopy

task = Task("Homework", "Math and physics", ["school", "urgent"])

task_deepcopied = deepcopy(task)

print(task_deepcopied)
# output: Task('Homework', 'Math and physics', ['school', 'urgent'])
```

In this code, we use the deepcopy function to create a copy of the original task. At this stage, we shouldn't expect a difference between a shallow copy and a deep copy because we haven't manipulated the interior mutable object yet. Next, it's time to see the usefulness of a deep copy:

```
task_deepcopied.tags.append("red")

print(task_deepcopied)
# output: Task('Homework', 'Math and physics', ['school', 'urgent', 'red'])

print(task)
# output: Task('Homework', 'Math and physics', ['school', 'urgent'])
```

In this code snippet, we update the data for the deep copied task's tags attribute. Notably, this change exists in task_deepcopied but not in task—the expected behavior, because the deep copy creates a distinct copy of each interior object, including the mutable list object tags.

10.3.4 *Discussion*

Shallow and deep copies differ in their behaviors when they copy the interior mutable objects, usually in the form of data containers, such as list, dict, and set. Shallow copies don't create a copy for these interior data containers, which can save memory if you're not concerned about the shared interior objects. By contrast, when you expect to create a copy with distinct data, such as when you edit a task and want to keep its original data, you should use a deep copy instead.

10.3.5 Challenge

In the examples, we use `copy` and `deepcopy` functions in the `copy` module. Calling these functions creates a shallow copy and a deep copy, respectively. Notably, you can override two special methods, `__copy__` and `__deepcopy__`, in a custom class, which will be triggered when you use the `copy` and `deepcopy` functions. In the case of overriding `__copy__`, suppose that we change the title for the copied task: `"Homework"` -> `"Copied: Homework"`. We also want the copy to have a distinct copy of the `tags` attribute, making it like a deep copy. Can you implement this feature?

> **HINT** Copying an instance is supposed to be instance-specific, so `__copy__` should be an instance method. In the body, you should return a new instance with the updated task's `title` and a new `list` object for `tags`.

10.4   How do I access and change a variable in a different scope?

Section 10.2 introduced the concept of namespaces. When we define a class, such as `Task`, in a Python module (a `.py` file), the class is registered in the global namespace, which takes the form of a dictionary: the identifiers are the keys, and the corresponding objects are the values. Suppose that in our task management app, we have a module with the filename of `task.py`. This file contains the code shown in the next listing.

Listing 10.7   Attempting to change a global variable

```
db_filename = "N/A"

def set_database(db_name):
    db_filename = db_name

set_database("tasks.sqlite")

print(db_filename)
# output: "N/A"
```

In listing 10.7, we have the variable `db_filename`, which is the file path of our task management app. By calling the `set_database`, we set the `db_name` to `db_filename`. In the printout, however, `db_filename` has a value of `"N/A"`. This result is unexpected, as we thought we'd changed it. What happened?

In this section, I'll show you how to access and change a variable in this scenario. More generally, this kind of problem pertains to manipulating variables in a different scope, with a special emphasis on cases involving two keywords: `global` and `nonlocal`. Through the examples, you'll learn how to access variables, which are resolved by applying the LEGB rule.

10.4.1 *Accessing any variable: The LEGB rule for name lookup*

Scopes and namespaces are closely related. *Scopes* form the boundaries for namespaces, and *namespaces* constitute the contents of scopes. Using a Python module as an example, figure 10.6 shows the relationship between namespaces and scopes.

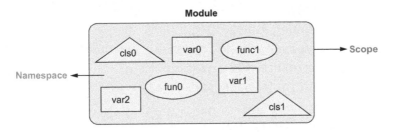

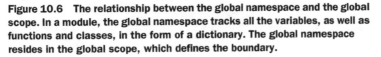

Figure 10.6   The relationship between the global namespace and the global scope. In a module, the global namespace tracks all the variables, as well as functions and classes, in the form of a dictionary. The global namespace resides in the global scope, which defines the boundary.

As shown in figure 10.6, the namespace tracks all the objects, each of which has its own identifier in the module. Thus, we can think of a namespace as being a container whose internal space is filled with different objects. The scope is the container's entire enclosing structure, defining the boundary of the module.

   To interpret code from Python's perspective, when Python encounters a variable, it's trying to resolve that variable, meaning that it needs to find the variable's referenced object. Section 10.2.2 mentioned that Python looks up variables in a namespace that is associated with a scope. There are different levels of scopes for the lookup order, known as the LEGB rule.

> **CONCEPT**   The *LEGB rule* dictates the order of resolving a variable in Python, from local (L), to enclosing (E), global (G), and built-in (B).

The acronym *LEGB* stands for *local, enclosing, global,* and *built-in* scopes in an incremental order in terms of scale. A module forms a global scope. Above the global, the built-in scope holds the namespaces for all the built-in functions and classes. In the module, you can define a class or a function, each of which forms a local scope.

> **TRIVIA**   It may sound weird to refer to a module's scope as global. But if you recall that a function within a module creates a local scope, it's not too surprising to call a scope global when it's larger than local. This logic may help you remember the distinction.

But what about the enclosing scope? When I introduced decorators in section 7.3, I nested a function within another function. For the inner function, the local scope of the outer function is known as the *enclosing scope.* Figure 10.7 shows how variables/functions (referred to as names in general) are resolved by looking up a specific scope.

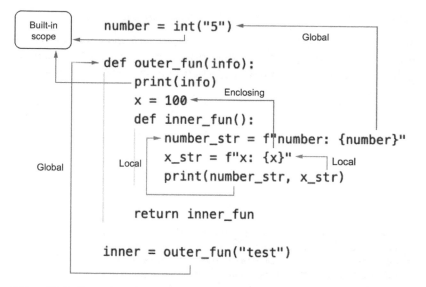

Figure 10.7   Examples of variable resolution. Functions such as `int` and `print` are built-in functions, and they're resolved by looking up the built-in scope. The variable `number` and the function `outer_fun` are resolved in the global scope. The variable `x` is used in `inner_fun`, which is resolved in the enclosing scope. `number_str` and `x_str` are resolved in the local scope.

The LEGB rule applies in the sequential order for variable resolution. As shown in figure 10.8, for a variable (or a name in general, or a name as an identifier, which can refer to a function, a list, or even a class), Python first searches its local scope. If the name is resolved, the corresponding value is used. If not, Python continues searching the enclosing scope. If the name is resolved, the value is used—and so on for the global and built-in scopes sequentially. If a name can't be resolved after Python checks all these scopes, a `NameError` is raised.

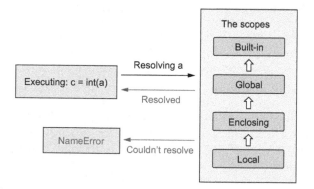

Figure 10.8   The general process of resolving a variable: the LEGB rule. When Python encounters a variable, it tries to resolve it by looking up the local, enclosing (if applicable), global, and built-in scopes sequentially. If the variable is resolved, Python uses the value; otherwise, it raises a `NameError`.

10.4.2 *Changing a global variable in a local scope*

At the beginning of this section, I presented a problem in which we failed to change the variable `db_filename` by calling the `set_database` function. In section 10.4.1, you learned that db_filename represents a global variable, whereas the set_database function forms a local scope. Thus, the problem is generalized as changing a global variable in a local scope, which is the topic of this section.

Before I show you the solution, focus on part of the code in listing 10.7. Note that I'm calling the print function to show you what's available in the function's local scope:

```
db_filename = "N/A"

def set_database(db_name):
    db_filename = db_name
    print(list(locals()))
```

For the first assignment statement (db_filename = "N/A"), we create a variable named db_filename in the global scope. Then we define the set_database function in the next several lines. If we check the global namespace, we expect it to include both db_filename and set_database:

```
print(list(globals()))
# output: ['__name__', '__doc__', '__package__', '__loader__', '__spec__',
➥ '__annotations__', '__builtins__', 'db_filename', 'set_database']
```

In the body of the set_database function, the code that requires our special attention is db_filename = db_name, the intention of which is to update the global variable db_filename. But the printout in listing 10.7 shows that it doesn't work.

Let's observe one more thing before we find the explanation. You may have noticed that I also included an extra line of code: print(list(locals())), which generates the registered objects in the local scope of the set_database function. When we call this function, we should be able to observe the local namespace's content:

```
set_database("tasks.sqlite")
# output: ['db_name', 'db_filename']
```

The set_database function's local namespace has two variables: db_name and db_filename. When Python executes the line of code db_filename = db_name, how does the LEGB rule play out in resolving db_filename and db_name, respectively?

The variable db_name exists only in the local scope, and it's resolved to be the argument that we use for the function call. For db_filename, both local and global scopes have a variable with such a name, but according to the LEGB rule, the one in the local scope is used. As the one in the local scope has no registered value, Python interprets this line of code as an assignment statement to create a new variable instead of updating the existing global variable.

Now that we know what happened, it's easier to understand the solution: using the global keyword to denote that a specific variable is global instead of local, as the next listing shows.

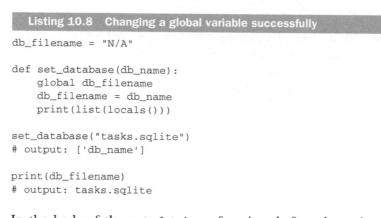

Listing 10.8 Changing a global variable successfully

```
db_filename = "N/A"

def set_database(db_name):
    global db_filename
    db_filename = db_name
    print(list(locals()))

set_database("tasks.sqlite")
# output: ['db_name']

print(db_filename)
# output: tasks.sqlite
```

In the body of the set_database function, before the assignment, we denote that db_filename is global so that the local scope won't register this name again. Next, we run the assignment. Python knows that it's updating the db_filename in the global scope. We can observe the updated value (tasks.sqlite) by printing db_filename, which no longer has the initial value "N/A".

Please note that you use the global keyword only when you attempt to change a global variable in a local scope. If you use the global variable without any assignment or update, you don't need to use global, as it'll be resolved through accessing the global scope.

10.4.3 *Changing an enclosing variable*

In section 10.4.2, you learned about using global to change a global variable in a local scope. Another keyword, nonlocal, changes an enclosing variable in a local scope. nonlocal is used less often than global, as global scopes are everywhere, but enclosing scopes exist only in functions that have nested functions. Thus, I'll briefly introduce changing an enclosing variable in this section. To help explain this feature, I'll use the simple code example in the following listing.

Listing 10.9   Changing a nonlocal variable

```
def change_text(using_nonlocal: bool):
    text = "N/A"
    def inner_fun0():
        text = "No nonlocal"

    def inner_fun1():
        nonlocal text
        text = "Using nonlocal"

    inner_fun1() if using_nonlocal else inner_fun0()
    return text


change_text(using_nonlocal=False)
```

```
# output: 'N/A'

change_text(using_nonlocal=True)
# output: 'Using nonlocal'
```

In the `change_text` function, we define a local variable `text`. The two inner functions form their own local scopes; to them, the `change_text` function's scope is the enclosing scope. These two functions differ in whether they declare `text` as a nonlocal variable by using the `nonlocal` keyword. When you use the `nonlocal` keyword, you're telling Python to use the variable `text` in the enclosing scope.

From the printout, we can see that calling the inner function `inner_fun1` changes the nonlocal variable `text` successfully. Calling `inner_fun0` has no effect on the nonlocal variable `text`, however, because Python interprets `text = "No nonlocal"` as a regular assignment statement instead of updating the nonlocal variable.

10.4.4 Discussion

Section 10.4 covers how Python resolves variables, as well as functions and classes, by following the LEGB order (Local -> Enclosing -> Global -> Built-in). When you write code that involves multiple scopes, remember what scopes are expected to resolve specific variables. Because of the complication of the LEGB order, remember to use the `global` keyword if you need to update a global variable in a local scope. Don't make a silly mistake by assuming that you can make the update by calling a function, as we attempted in listing 10.7.

10.4.5 Challenge

John has a programming background in Swift, the language used for creating macOS and iOS apps. In Swift, an `if...else...` statement can form a scope separate from the global scope. How can he find out whether the `if...else...` statement has its local scope in Python?

> **HINT** Create a global variable and attempt to change it in the `if...else...` statement. If a local scope does exist, you can't change its value if you don't use the `global` keyword.

10.5 What's callability, and what does it imply?

As an OOP language, Python organizes its building blocks—such as packages, modules, classes, functions, and data—as different kinds of objects. Thus, understanding the characteristics of objects is essential to writing better Python code. In section 3.1, when we discussed choosing between lists and tuples, we discussed hashability and mutability, which refer to an object's capability to be hashed and mutated, respectively.

Besides hashability and mutability, a key characteristic of objects is *callability*—whether an object can be called. As in most modern languages, we call an object in Python by using a pair of parentheses (the call operator). Thus, if an object can be used with the call operator, we say that it's callable; if an object can't be used with the call operator, it's not callable. In fact, Python has a built-in function, `callable`, that can check an object's callability. We know that we can call a function, and we should expect it to be callable, as follows:

```
def doubler(x):
    return 2 * x

assert callable(doubler)
```

The concept of callability seems to be straightforward, but callability is an underlying mechanism for several key features in Python. This section reviews the important practical implications of an object's callability.

10.5.1 *Distinguishing classes from functions*

We can call a class, such as `Task("Homework", "Math and physics")`, to create an instance object of the `Task` class. We can also call a function, such as `print("Hello, World!")`, to perform a defined operation. Thus, both classes and functions are callable, and the same callability can make it hard to distinguish classes from functions. You may often hear people say that Python has many useful built-in functions, such as `list`, `range`, and `sum`, but not all of them are functions. The first implication of callability involves the nuances between classes and functions.

> **CONCEPT** *Callable* means an object that can be called. When a function expects a callable, such as the `sorted` function's `key` argument, you can pass a function or a class. If you have a custom class that implements `__call__`, you can use an instance of that class as a callable too!

Many of these "functions" are not functions. Instead, they are classes, such as `bool`, `int`, and `dict`, as opposed to `callable` and `hash`, which are functions. The major reason why they're not easy to differentiate is their shared callability, but the difference is notable from a semantic perspective. When we call these classes, we obtain an instance object of the class, such as calling `bool` to obtain a `bool` object, and calling `dict` returns a `dict` object.

> **TRIVIA** These built-in classes have their names in lowercase, as opposed to the camel naming convention for custom classes. Naming these built-in types in lowercase is for historic reasons: they were named that way in early versions of Python.

By contrast, real functions aren't directly associated with any underlying classes. Thus, we don't get an instance object of the same name by calling these functions. We don't expect to get a `sum` object by calling `sum` or a `hash` object by calling `hash`, for example. By contrast, we do obtain a `range` object by calling `range` or a `slice` object by calling `slice`.

10.5.2 Revisiting the higher-order function map

One manifestation of Python's functional programming is *higher-order functions:* functions that take other functions as an argument or return functions as the output. Section 7.2 introduced one higher-order function, map, but is it a real function? Your intuition may tell you that it is. Intuition can be wrong, however. We'll revisit map in this section.

The easiest way to inspect an object is to call it with the print function. We expect a custom or built-in function to be a function:

```
def do_something():
    pass

print(do_something)
# output: <function do_something at 0x7fe8180f30a0>

print(sum)
# output: <built-in function sum>
```

If map is indeed a function, we should expect a printed message telling us that it's a built-in function, such as sum. Let's see whether that's the case:

```
print(map)
# output: <class 'map'>
```

Unlike what you may have thought, map isn't a function. Instead, it's a class: the map class. Consistent with map's being a class, calling map creates a map object, like built-in classes such as list and dict:

```
print(map(int, ["1", "2.0", "3"]))
# output: <map object at 0x7fe8180df700>
```

The misconception that map is a function may result from the assumption that classes usually take nonfunction objects for instance construction. Don't forget, however, that all of Python's functions are objects. Thus, the map class is special in the sense that the construction involves accepting functions as an argument.

10.5.3 Using callable as the key argument

Several Python functions include a parameter called key that's used when functions perform sorting, such as sorted, or comparison, such as max. In section 3.2, the list's sort method uses a function as key; we may have an assumption that we can use only a function for the key argument. But any callable can be the key argument, as discussed in this section.

The easiest scenario for using a class instead of a function as the key argument in sorted is using the built-in str class. Suppose that we want to sort a list of poker cards. Without setting a key argument, the sorting fails due to the inability to compare integers and strings:

```
cards = [10, 1, "J", "A"]

print(sorted(cards))
# ERROR: TypeError: '<' not supported between instances of 'str' and 'int'

print(sorted(cards, key=str))
# output: [1, 10, 'A', 'J']
```

Because str is used as the key, the sorting can happen, but the order isn't right: A should be greater than J. Let's solve the problem by creating a class, PokerOrder, as shown in the next listing.

```
class PokerOrder(int):
    def __new__(cls, x):
        numbers_mapping = {'J': 11, 'Q': 12, 'K': 13, 'A': 14}
        casted_number = numbers_mapping.get(x, x)
        return super().__new__(PokerOrder, casted_number)
```

> **REMINDER**   When we're trying to retrieve a value from a dict object, the get method can include a fallback value when the key doesn't exist.

In the PokerOrder class, we override the __new__ method so that we can modify the default behavior when we construct an instance of the PokerOrder, which is a subclass of int. Notably, as covered in section 8.1, super() creates a proxy object that refers to the superclass int, which expects to take a number (the casted_number in our implementation) to construct an instance. Specifically, if the card is between 2 and 10, we use the number. If the card is J, Q, K, or A, we cast it to its corresponding integers so the class can map the non-number cards to the correct numeric values. Let's sort them now:

```
print(sorted(cards, key=PokerOrder))
# output: [1, 10, 'J', 'A']
```

10.5.4 *Creating decorators as classes*

In section 7.3, you learned about creating decorators, which are higher-order functions that modify decorated functions without affecting the intended operations of the decorated functions. Behind the scenes, the decoration process sends the to-be-decorated function to the decorator. That is, the decoration process essentially calls a higher-order function. Because classes are also callable, this characteristic allows us to create decorators in the form of a custom class, as shown in this section. To refresh your memory, the following code snippet shows how to create a decorator that can log a function's execution time:

```
import time

def logging_time(func):
    def logger(*args, **kwargs):
```

```
        start = time.time()
        result = func(*args, **kwargs)
        print(f"Calling {func.__name__}: {time.time() - start:.5f}")
        return result

    return logger
```

Please note that I use only the minimum elements for a decorator. If you're unfamiliar with decorators, refer to section 7.3 for best practices in creating a decorator. To convert this function to a class, bear in mind that the constructor for the class expects to take a function as its argument. We may have the following solution:

```
import time

class TimeLogger:
    def __init__(self, func):
        def logger(*args, **kwargs):
            start = time.time()
            result = func(*args, **kwargs)
            print(f"Calling {func.__name__}: {time.time() - start:.5f}")
            return result
        self._logger = logger

    def __call__(self, *args, **kwargs):
        return self._logger(*args, **kwargs)
```

Notice two things in this code snippet:

- The protected attribute _logger is used to store the created inner function internally, as we know that the decoration process is creating a closure, which is an inner function.
- We override the special method __call__, which is invoked when we try to call an instance of the class. That is, when we call the decorated function, we should call the closure instead, which is the _logger attribute. Note that by implementing __call__ in a custom class, we make the instances of the class callable. Thus, as shown in figure 10.9, we should know that besides functions and classes, instance objects of a class that implements __call__ are also callable, as in the case of the TimeLogger class.

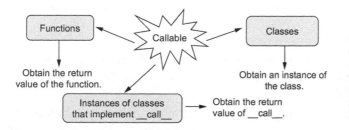

Figure 10.9   Three types of callable objects and their expected results after calling. You call functions to get their return values. You call classes to get instance objects. And you call a callable instance to get the result of the __call__ method.

With this class, we can use the same syntax to decorate a function:

```
@TimeLogger
def calculate_sum(n):
    return sum(range(n))

result = calculate_sum(100_000)
# output: Calling calculate_sum: 0.00181
```

Note, however, that the decorated function is no longer a function. Instead, it's an instance object of the TimeLogger class:

```
print(calculate_sum)

# output: <__main__.TimeLogger object at 0x7fe8180de710>
```

By default, we can't call an instance object. We can't write [1, 2, 3]() or "Hello, World!"(), for example. To make this instance object behave like a function, we override the __call__ special method, which returns the _logger attribute—a function and therefore callable. In other words, we pass the call operation of an instance object to its function attribute (_logger) to make this instance object callable.

10.5.5 *Discussion*

This section focuses on Python objects' callability—their ability to be called by the call operator (). In essence, both classes and functions are callable, which creates a lot of crosstalk possibilities, such as serving as the key argument and creating a decorator by using a custom class. Particularly in the latter case, you can implement complicated decorators that take parameters. Using a class makes it easier to offer this flexibility, as you can add other attributes to the instance object.

10.5.6 *Challenge*

Ruby creates the TimeLogger class as a decorator to log the functions' performance in her project. As discussed in section 7.3, one best practice for implementing a decorator is using the wraps decorator from the functools module. How should she use the wraps in the TimeLogger class?

HINT   We wrap the decorated function before we define the inner function.

Summary

- We can check the type of an object by using the built-in type function. Obtaining the type information during the run time of our program makes it possible for us to write flexible code.
- The isinstance function can check whether an object is an instance of a class or a tuple of classes. isinstance is also more flexible than type, as it gives us a valid result if the checked class has a superclass.

- The collections.abc module allows us to check an object's generic type to apply the same operations to multiple classes that implement the same interface.

- An instance object of a class goes through this process: Instantiation -> active in a namespace -> being tracked regarding the reference counts (happening simultaneously with its activeness in a namespace) -> destruction.

- When you make a copy of an object, the default copying behavior is copying only the outmost data container, termed a shallow copy.

- When you need the copy to have distinct copies for the contained mutable objects, you should create a deep copy, allowing you to manipulate the inner mutable objects without affecting the original one.

- The built-in copy module is designed to copy objects in a standard way. But you can override __copy__ and __deepcopy__ if you want to define customized copying behaviors for your class.

- When Python needs to resolve a variable or a name in general, it uses the LEGB rule (Local -> Enclosing -> Global -> Built-in) to find a value for the used name.

- When you want to change a variable in a local scope, dependent on where the variable is initially defined, you need to use the global or nonlocal keyword, the former for a globally defined variable and the latter for a variable in the enclosing scope, which exists only for a nested function.

- Both classes and functions are callable natively. Despite the shared callability, you need to know the distinction between classes and functions for the built-in functions. Because of the shared callability, you can use classes and functions in some common scenarios, such as using them as a key argument or creating a decorator.

Dealing with files

Files are integral to any computer system or application. We use files to store data. We share data with our teammates by using files. When we obtain a file from others, we need to open the file, read its content, process the data, and write some data to another file or append data to the same file. These operations are concerned with the contents of the files. Our application can use hundreds of different Python objects, and some objects require excessive calculations or other processing steps, so it's ideal that we can save these objects as files. When we need to use these objects again, we can load them from files, which can save lots of processing time.

Files are everywhere in any computer system, and our job can include many kinds of file manipulations, such as moving files to a destination, extracting files of a specific kind, and finding out the files that we've modified in the last week. Adequate knowledge of performing these operations in a programmatic way allows us to perform jobs that we can't do easily in a manual way and track any changes that we've made to the files. In this chapter, we'll cover important topics concerning files—not only reading and writing from a content perspective, but also common file operations such as moving and copying files.

11.1   How do I read and write files using context management?

Our projects can involve a variety of file types, such as tabulated data, media, and pure text files. When we work with these files, the first step is to read them to process the contained data. Although we can use special software to manipulate files, our projects often require that we process files programmatically, particularly when we process many files. To take advantage of Python tools such as pandas to process tabulated data, we must also read files programmatically. As you can imagine, dealing with files programmatically is an essential operation for general data processing. In this section, you'll learn how to read and write files in Python. As textual data is the most common form, we'll use text files in our examples. The general techniques, however, apply to other file formats, such as binary files that store byte data.

11.1.1   Opening and closing files: Context manager

The most basic file-handling operations are opening and closing files. In this section, we'll see how to open and close files in two ways: using the basic approach and using a context manager (which we'll discuss soon).

Suppose that we use text files to store the data for our task management application. To start, we can create a text file named tasks.txt, which has the following data:

```
1001,Homework,5
1002,Laundry,3
1003,Grocery,4
```

Each row of the data represents a task's information: the ID number, the title, and the urgency level. For simplicity, we have three rows of data. We can open this file by using the built-in open function:

```
text_file = open("tasks.txt")

print(text_file)
# output: <_io.TextIOWrapper name='tasks.txt' mode='r' encoding='UTF-8'>
```

We inspect the text_file object by using the print function and get four pieces of information:

- This object is an instance of the _io.TextIOWrapper, the class that creates a buffered text stream providing higher-level access to the underlying text data in the file. This kind of object is also known as a *stream* or *file object*.
- name tells you the file's name.

- mode indicates how the file is read. `'r'` means read mode, in which we only read the file. In read mode, you can't perform nonread operations, such as writing data to the file.
- The encoding indicates how the text file is encoded. In most cases, you don't need to worry about it, because most data is encoded with UTF-8 (it also has backward compatibility with ASCII encoding, if you've heard about ASCII), which is the most common form of encoding in the Unicode system.

With the created file object, we can read the data. We have different ways to read the data (section 11.1.2), but the most straightforward one is the read method shown in the next listing.

Listing 11.1 Reading data as a string

```
text_data = text_file.read()

print(type(text_data))   ◁─── Checks with type
# output: <class 'str'>

print(text_data)
# output the following lines:
1001,Homework,5
1002,Laundry,3
1003,Grocery,4
```

The read method reads all the text data in the file as a string, and we can print out the string to make sure that it indeed matches the text in the file. We can apply additional processing steps to this string, such as splitting each row to extract the underlying data (section 2.3). When we're done with the processing, we can close the file by using the close method. After we close the file, we can verify the status by accessing the closed attribute, which should be True:

```
text_file.close()

assert text_file.closed
```

You should always close the file when you're done with it. As files are shared resources in your computer, if you forget to close them, any changes you've made with the file object may get lost in the actual file. After you close the file, all the updates to the file are saved, and when other processes access the file, they have the latest data.

To prevent us from losing data due to forgetting to close a file, we can use the *context management* technique: the with statement, which is the Pythonic way to read files, as shown in the next listing.

Listing 11.2 Using with to open a file

```
with open("tasks.txt") as file:   ◁─── The with statement
    print(f"file object: {file}")
    data = file.read()
```

```
    print(data)

# output the following lines:
file object: <_io.TextIOWrapper name='tasks.txt' mode='r' encoding='UTF-8'>
1001,Homework,5
1002,Laundry,3
1003,Grocery,4
```

The syntax of using the with statement is with open("filepath") as file, which is the head, and which creates the file object and assigns it to the variable file. Then we create an indentation to indicate the body in which we define the applicable operations. As you can see in listing 11.2, we obtain the same output that we got in listing 11.1. The most significant advantage of using the with statement is that we no longer need to close the file explicitly. When the with statement is complete, the file closes automatically:

assert file.closed

The automatic closing of the file results from using the with statement, which is known as the context management technique. A context manager establishes a connection to the applicable resource object in the with statement's head, and in the body, you manipulate the object. When you complete the body and exit the with statement, the context manager automatically closes the connection to the resource. For a file, the manager releases the file object. Figure 11.1 shows how a context manager works, using the file object as a concrete example.

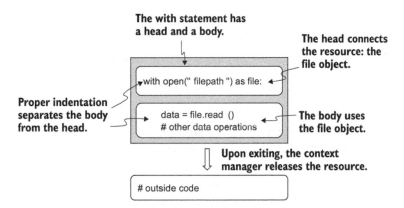

Figure 11.1   The flow of a context manager using file management as an example. The with statement consists of the head and the body. The head connects the resource, and the body uses the resource. When you exit the with statement, the context manager releases the resource.

11.1.2 *Reading data from a file in different ways*

Listing 11.1 shows the read method, which obtains the entire text data. When the text file is large, it can take considerable time to load all the data, and sometimes, a computer may not have enough memory to hold that much data. Thus, we must use other ways to read data depending on specific use cases, as we'll discuss in this section.

READING LINES AS A GENERATOR

In section 7.4, you learned about generators, which are memory-efficient data providers because they yield items individually upon request. A file object represents a stream of data, and we can use the file object as though it's a generator, yielding each line of data one at a time.

The most common way to process the file as a generator is to read the lines one by one using the for loop so that we process each line of data, as the next listing shows. To add some flavor to the file reading, I include some code that converts each line to an instance of the Task class.

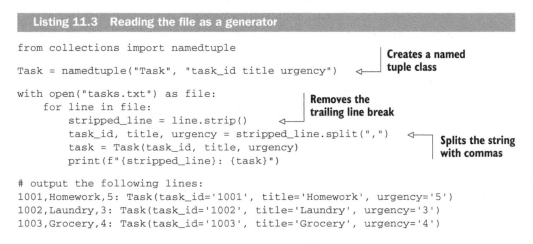

Listing 11.3   Reading the file as a generator

```
from collections import namedtuple

Task = namedtuple("Task", "task_id title urgency")     ← Creates a named
                                                           tuple class
with open("tasks.txt") as file:
    for line in file:
        stripped_line = line.strip()     ← Removes the
                                             trailing line break
        task_id, title, urgency = stripped_line.split(",")     ← Splits the string
        task = Task(task_id, title, urgency)                       with commas
        print(f"{stripped_line}: {task}")

# output the following lines:
1001,Homework,5: Task(task_id='1001', title='Homework', urgency='5')
1002,Laundry,3: Task(task_id='1002', title='Laundry', urgency='3')
1003,Grocery,4: Task(task_id='1003', title='Grocery', urgency='4')
```

As you can see, we use the file as the iterator in the for loop, which yields each of the lines. Please note that each line ends with an "invisible" line break, and you should use strip to remove it. We use the split elements to create an instance of the Task class.

QUESTION   What happens if you don't remove the line break?

READING LINES TO FORM A LIST

If the file doesn't have too much data, we can read the lines to form a list object using the readlines method. Because list objects are mutable, it'll be easier to change the data and save it for other purposes.

Suppose that we want to extract all the data from the text file tasks.txt as a list object, and we want to add a row number to each row. Here is the desired output:

```
desired_output = [
    '#1: 1001,Homework,5',
    '#2: 1002,Laundry,3',
    '#3: 1003,Grocery,4'
]
```

Because the expected output is a list object, we can take advantage of readlines to create a list object, which allows us to manipulate the data due to its mutability, as shown in the next listing.

Listing 11.4   Reading the lines as a list

```
with open("tasks.txt") as file:
    lines = file.readlines()
    updated_lines = [f"#{row}: {line.strip()}" for row, line
    in enumerate(lines, start=1)]
```
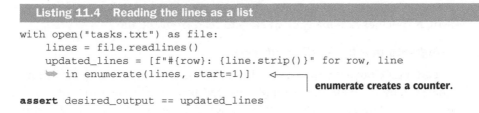

enumerate creates a counter.

```
assert desired_output == updated_lines
```

We use the enumerate function (section 5.3.1) to create a counter for the iteration besides the item. Using list comprehension (section 5.2.1), we create the list object updated_lines, which matches the expected list object, desired_output.

READING A SINGLE LINE

In a rarer case, we may want to read a single line. We may want to read only the header of a file to find the columns of a CSV file, for example. (For more on processing CSV files, see section 11.2.) Although we can read all the lines and retrieve the first item, it can be time-consuming to read that much data. Instead, we can use the readline method to read the text in a single line, which costs less time than reading all the lines.

Notably, we can use readline multiple times. The file object tracks where the reading ends every time (like a generator, a file object knows where the item is in the order), and the next time we call readline, it continues reading from where it left off, as shown in the following listing.

Listing 11.5   Reading a single line

```
with open("tasks.txt") as file:
    print(file.readline())
    print(file.readline())
    print(file.readline(5))
    print(file.readline(8))
    print(file.readline())

# output the following lines:
1001,Homework,5

1002,Laundry,3

1003,
Grocery,
4
```

Prints the following empty line due to the line break

Notice three things in listing 11.5:

- readline optionally takes a size argument, which reads up to the number of characters in that line. file.readline(5) reads 1003, for example, and file .readline(8) reads Grocery,.
- We obtain individual lines by calling readline multiple times.
- The line ends with a line break. When we call readline, it reads the entire line, including the line break; therefore, there are empty lines in the printout message.

NOTE Like readline, both read and readlines can take the size argument, which specifies how many characters to read from the file.

11.1.3 *Writing data to a file in different ways*

We read data from a file to process the stored data. When we're done editing or have prepared data from another source, we need to write the data to a file for long-term preservation. This section describes common use scenarios in terms of writing data.

WRITING STRING DATA TO A NEW FILE

In many cases, we have our data ready and want to save it to a new file. Suppose that we have the following data:

```
data = """1001,Homework,5
1002,Laundry,3
1003,Grocery,4"""
```

To write this data to a new file, we can create a file object by using the with statement. Instead of creating an empty file ahead of time, we call the open function with the path for the new file, which creates the new file at the specified path, as the next listing shows.

Listing 11.6 Writing to a new file

```
with open("tasks_new.txt", "w") as file:   ◁──── Specifies the write mode
    print("File:", file)
    result = file.write(data)
    print("Writing result:", result)

# output the following lines:
File: <_io.TextIOWrapper name='tasks_new.txt' mode='w' encoding='UTF-8'>
Writing result: 45
```

In the open function, besides the file path, we specify that the mode for this file object is "w", meaning that it's write mode as opposed to read mode, which is the default. From the printout message, we see that the file object does have 'w' mode. To write the string data to the new file, we call the write method. Calling this method returns the number of characters that have been written—in our case, 45.

Specifying "w" mode for the file object is required for writing operations. If you open the file using the default read mode, you can't write any data, as in the following example:

```
with open("tasks_new.txt") as file:   ◁──── The default is read mode.
    print("File:", file)
    result = file.write(data)
    print("Writing result:", result)

# ERROR: io.UnsupportedOperation: not writable
```

WRITING A LIST OF LINES TO A NEW FILE

We've seen that we can read data from a file in the form of the lines as a list object. Not surprisingly, we can also write a list of lines to a file. The method involved is writelines. As you do when you write string data, you need to open a file with write mode enabled, as shown in the next listing.

Listing 11.7   Writing a list to a file

```
list_data = [
    '1001,Homework,5',
    '1002,Laundry,3',
    '1003,Grocery,4'
]

with open("tasks_list_write.txt", "w") as file:
    file.writelines(list_data)
```
writelines returns None.

If you open the tasks_list_write.txt file, you'll notice that the data may not appear to be correct:

```
with open("tasks_list_write.txt") as file:
    print(file.read())

# output: 1001,Homework,51002,Laundry,31003,Grocery,4
```

This behavior is expected. writelines writes the data sequentially, there are no line breaks in any item of the data, and you shouldn't expect the file to have multiple lines. Thus, you need to add line breaks to your data if you want to create a file with multiple lines, and I'll leave that task as a challenge (section 11.1.5).

So far, we've seen how to read and write data in different ways by using a variety of methods, including read, write, readline, readlines, and writelines. To help differentiate them, figure 11.2 illustrates these operations.

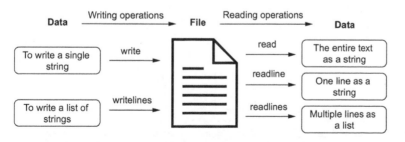

Figure 11.2   Key reading and writing functions with files. When you have data, you can write it to the file by using write and writelines. When you read the file, you can obtain the text data by calling read, readline, and readlines. These functions have different usages.

As you may notice (or be curious about), the operations between reading and writing are almost symmetrical; the only exception is that there's no writeline on the left side. There's no need for one, however. When you want to write a line, use the `write` method.

APPENDING STRING DATA TO AN EXISTING FILE

When you have new data, you want to append the data to an existing file. Suppose that you create a new task, which has the following data:

```
new_task = "1004,Museum,3"
```

You want to write this data to the end of the `tasks.txt` file. Instead of enabling `write` mode, you should use `append` mode, as shown in the next listing.

Listing 11.8   Appending data to an existing file

```
with open("tasks.txt", "a") as file:
    file.write(f"\n{new_task}")        ◁─── Adds a line break
```

In the `open` function, specify `"a"` to open the file in `append` mode; the `write` method adds data to the end of the file. One thing to note is that the `new_task` is prefixed by a line break (`\n`) so that you can add the data as a new line instead of adding it to the last row of the file.

The underlying mechanism for the `append` mode is that when we read or write, we're using the cursor to determine the position of the operation. I've mentioned that a file object represents a stream of data and the cursor sets the position in the stream. Table 11.1 provides more information about the modes and their cursor positions.

Table 11.1   File modes

Mode[a]	read	write	create	truncate	Cursor position
r	*				Start
w		*	*	*	Start
a		*	*		End
r+	*	*			Start
w+	*	*	*	*	Start
a+	*	*	*		End
x			*		Start

[a]`read`: reads the data; `write`: writes new data; `create`: creates a new file; `truncate`: resizes the file; cursor position: when the operation starts.

When we have mode `"a"` for the file, we have the cursor at the end, so the newly added text is appended to the end. For the most-used `"r"` and `"w"` modes, we have the cursor at the beginning, so the corresponding read and write operations start from the beginning.

11.1.4 Discussion

Using the `with` statement when you read and write files is the Pythonic way. The `with` statement is designed more for context management than for processing files. More broadly, we use a context manager when we deal with shared resources, such as a connection to a database. As section 14.3 discusses, when you work with a SQLite database, you can carry out database operations by using the connection under context management, as follows:

```
import sqlite3

with con = sqlite3.connect("database.sqlite"):
    # do your operations here
    pass
```

11.1.5 Challenge

In Leo's daily job as an electrical engineer, he often needs to use Python to write data to files. One day, he tried to write a `list` object to a new file, as we did in listing 11.7. But he found that the file only had one line instead of multiple lines, with each line representing an item of the `list` object. How can he change the `list` object so that the file has multiple lines?

HINT   You can append the line break to each item.

11.2 How do I deal with tabulated data files?

Many people use Microsoft Excel to handle data files, and this data is referred to as *spreadsheets*. More generally, spreadsheets are known as *tabulated data,* which includes rows and columns. A company's sales data can be saved as tabulated data. A school can record exam results as tabulated data. The collected data from a research project can be stored as tabulated data. As you can see, tabulated data has universal usage, so processing tabulated data is an essential data-handling skill. From a general perspective, you can convert tabulated data to CSV (comma-separated values) files to facilitate data exchange between different systems. This section focuses on processing CSV files—a representative format for tabulated data files.

11.2.1 Reading a CSV file using csv reader

As always, we start our data processing jobs by reading the data. For frontend applications, we need to read the data before we can display it. Suppose that our task management application uses a CSV file to store task-related data: the file `tasks.txt` (section 11.1). To show these tasks in our application, we need to know how to read a CSV file, as we'll discuss in this section.

Although I didn't specify it in section 11.1, the `tasks.txt` file is a CSV file. Thus, we've learned how to read a CSV file. But we had to split the string ourselves to obtain the stored data, which is a common operation in dealing with CSV files. Not surprisingly, the standard Python library provides a built-in solution for this purpose: the `csv` module, which allows us to read the data directly with a `csv_reader`, as the next listing shows.

> **Listing 11.9   Reading a CSV file using the `csv` module**

```
import csv         ⟵—— Imports the module

with open("tasks.txt", newline="") as file:
    csv_reader = csv.reader(file)
    for row in csv_reader:
        print(row)
                                        You might see another line if you
# output the following lines:    ⟵—— append data in section 11.1.
['1001', 'Homework', '5']
['1002', 'Laundry', '3']
['1003', 'Grocery', '4']
```

> **TRIVIA**   The official Python documentation recommends specifying the newline character as "" to ensure cross-platform consistency in the way the system treats it. For more information, see https://docs.python.org/3/library/csv.html.

As shown in listing 11.9, we create the `csv_reader` by calling the `reader` function with the file object. The created `csv_reader` is an iterator, so we can iterate over the reader by using a `for` loop. Each item is a `list` object that consists of the values separated by commas—the same output that we obtained in listing 11.5. But we didn't reinvent the wheel; we used the built-in `csv` module!

> **REMINDER**   Don't reinvent the wheel. Always use available solutions, particularly those provided by the standard library.

Notably, we know that `list` constructor can take an iterable to create a `list` object. Thus, we can call the `list` constructor to retrieve all the rows as a `list` object:

```
with open("tasks.txt", newline="") as file:
    csv_reader = csv.reader(file)
    tasks_rows = list(csv_reader)
    print(tasks_rows)

# output the following line:
[['1001', 'Homework', '5'], ['1002', 'Laundry', '3'],
➥ ['1003', 'Grocery', '4']]
```

11.2.2 *Reading a CSV file that has a header*

In the `tasks.txt` file, we only have three fields of data: the ID number, the title, and the urgency level. When your file has many fields, it's hard to know which field keeps what data. Thus, to prevent any ambiguity, many CSV files use a header to mark each field. In this section, you'll learn about reading a CSV file with a header. Suppose that we add the field names to the `tasks.txt` file, which has the following data:

```
task_id,title,urgency
1001,Homework,5
1002,Laundry,3
1003,Grocery,4
```

As you can see, the first row defines the three fields that map to each value in subsequent rows. When you have a CSV file with a header, the best approach is to read each row as a dict object, with the header's field names becoming the keys, as the next listing shows.

Listing 11.10 Reading a CSV file with a header using the `csv_reader`

```
with open("tasks.txt", newline="") as file:
    csv_reader = csv.reader(file)
    fields = next(csv_reader)        ◁——— Obtains the next item
    print("Field:", fields)
    for row in csv_reader:
        task_dict = dict(zip(fields, row))    ◁——— Creates a dict object
        print(task_dict)

# output the following lines:
Field: ['task_id', 'title', 'urgency']
{'task_id': '1001', 'title': 'Homework', 'urgency': '5'}
{'task_id': '1002', 'title': 'Laundry', 'urgency': '3'}
{'task_id': '1003', 'title': 'Grocery', 'urgency': '4'}
```

As a refresher on several techniques that I've covered previously, here are the highlights of listing 11.10:

- Because the csv_reader is an iterator (section 5.1), we can call the next function on it to obtain the first row's data.
- When we consume the first item of the iterator, the iteration continues with the second item. In the for loop, the csv_reader yields items starting from the second row.
- The dict constructor takes an iterable, with each element having two items. We use the zip function to create a zip object by joining fields and row. The output reveals that we obtain three dict objects that correspond to the data in the CSV file.

As you may notice, it's not intuitive to read the first row separately and construct the needed data. But CSV files with a header are so common that an easier solution must exist. Indeed, the csv module provides an additional reader—DictReader—that specifically addresses this need, as shown in the next listing.

Listing 11.11 Reading a CSV file with a header using `DictReader`

```
with open("tasks.txt", newline="") as file:
    csv_reader = csv.DictReader(file)
    for row in csv_reader:
        print(row)
```

```
# output the following lines:
{'task_id': '1001', 'title': 'Homework', 'urgency': '5'}
{'task_id': '1002', 'title': 'Laundry', 'urgency': '3'}
{'task_id': '1003', 'title': 'Grocery', 'urgency': '4'}
```

Instead of calling the reader function, we call the DictReader constructor to create a DictReader object that takes the first row as the keys. As you can see, the solution in listing 11.11 is much cleaner than the one in listing 11.10, which highlights the conciseness of Python code if you use the right technique. As a side note to facilitate your learning process, if you find common problems on your daily job, chances are that Python already has solutions for them, and you only need to locate them! In my experience, you can start your search on Google with the phrase "Python + your job at hand." If you want to read PDF files with Python, for example, you can search "Python read pdf files." Usually, the first few pages of search results should be sufficient for you to find the potential solution.

> **QUESTION**   As csv_reader is an iterator, how can you retrieve all the data as a list object that consists of these dict objects?

11.2.3   *Writing data to a CSV file*

After we have processed our data, it's time to save that data back to a CSV file. reader and DictReader have counterpart writers: writer and DictWriter. As you can imagine, writer writes a list object, and DictWriter writes a dict object. This section shows how. Because the writers are straightforward, this section is short.

Suppose that we want to add the row 1004,Museum,3 to the CSV file. With a writer, we need to convert this string to a list object:

```
new_task = "1004,Museum,3"

with open("tasks.txt", "a", newline="") as file:
    file.write("\n")
    csv_writer = csv.writer(file)             Creates a list to
    csv_writer.writerow(new_task.split(","))  write using split
```

As with writing data to a regular text file, if we know that the last line of data doesn't end with a line break, we should add a line break: file.write("\n").

> **REMINDER**   The file mode should be "a"—append mode. If you use "w", all the existing data will be erased.

Sometimes, data is processed in the form of dict objects. Suppose that we want to save the following data to a new CSV file:

```
tasks = [
    {'task_id': '1001', 'title': 'Homework', 'urgency': '5'},
    {'task_id': '1002', 'title': 'Laundry', 'urgency': '3'},
    {'task_id': '1003', 'title': 'Grocery', 'urgency': '4'}
]
```

The data is a `list` object that consists of multiple `dict` objects. In this case, we should use `DictWriter`, as shown in the following listing.

Listing 11.12   Writing data to a CSV using `DictWriter`

```
fields = ['task_id', 'title', 'urgency']

with open("tasks_dict.txt", "w", newline="") as file:
    csv_writer = csv.DictWriter(file, fieldnames=fields)
    csv_writer.writeheader()
    csv_writer.writerows(tasks)
```

Writes the header points to `csv_writer.writeheader()`

`csv_writer.writerows(tasks)` ◄——— **Writes multiple rows**

Three things are worth noting in listing 11.12:

- When we create an instance of `DictWriter`, we need to specify the field names by setting the `fieldnames` argument.
- We call the `writeheader` method to write the header.
- Because we have the `dict` objects as a `list` object, we can write the entire dataset by calling the `writerows` method instead of the `writerow` method, which writes only one row.

So far, I've covered how to read and write data with a CSV file. As you may realize, reading and writing data involves symmetrical operations: `reader` versus `writer` and `DictReader` versus `DictWriter`. Figure 11.3 provides a visual summary of these operations. If you work with lists, you should choose `reader` and `writer`. If you work with dictionaries, you should choose `DictReader` and `DictWriter`. Another factor to consider is whether the CSV file uses a header; if it does, operations are easier with `DictReader` and `DictWriter`.

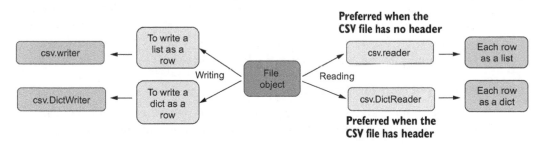

Figure 11.3   Reading and writing operations using the `csv` module. Reading operations involve `reader` and `DictReader`, with the former reading each row as a `list` and the latter reading it as a `dict`. Writing operations involve `writer` and `DictWriter`, with the former writing a `list` to a row and the latter writing a `dict`.

11.2.4   Discussion

Tabulated data can be converted to CSV format. Using the built-in `csv` module, we have the capability to process CSV data conveniently, including reading and writing data. We need to be familiar with these two-way operations. Notably, if we need to perform numeric operations with the CSV data, we need to explore third-party libraries, such as pandas, for advanced processing functions. These packages can read CSV files with a simple function call. We can call `pandas.read_csv("filepath.csv")`, for example, to create a `DataFrame` (a tabulated data model) from a CSV file so that we can use this `DataFrame` for a variety of operations.

11.2.5 Challenge

Leo uses CSV files to store some experimental results for his electrical engineering work. For one project, he called the `writerows` method with a `DictWriter` to write a `list` object that consists of multiple `dict` objects, as in listing 11.12. How can he use this method with a regular CSV `writer` to write multiple `list` objects?

> **HINT**   You need to organize your data in a `list` object, with each item representing the data for a row:

```
tasks = [
    ['1001', 'Homework', '5'],
    ['1002', 'Laundry', '3'],
    ['1003', 'Grocery', '4']
]
```

11.3 *How do I preserve data as files using pickling?*

During the execution of our programs, our code generates hundreds of objects. When data scientists prepare data, they perform multiple processing steps and create a considerable amount of data. Some data is large—hundreds of megabytes or even gigabytes—and it can take a long time to rerun the code to generate the data. It would be nice to store the data permanently in the form of files on a computer.

In section 11.2, we studied how to write tabulated data to files. But our data can be in other forms, such as `dict`, `list`, and `tuple`, as well as classes and functions. Thus, we should have a more general mechanism to preserve data. In this section, you'll learn about pickling, which allows us to preserve various forms of Python data.

11.3.1 Pickling objects for data preservation

The terms *pickle* and *pickling* come from the preservation of food by using vinegar, brine, or similar solutions. In Python, *pickling* refers to the process of converting objects to a binary format for data preservation. When a normal program stops, the data may be lost, which can be undesirable. Some data requires excessive time to process, and we want to preserve data so that we can retrieve it conveniently later. In this section, we'll see how to preserve data with the built-in `pickle` module.

> **CONCEPT**   *Pickling* is the process of creating a binary format from existing objects for data preservation.

We can pickle almost any object in Python. Suppose that we use different forms of data to store a task's information in our task management application. Let's see how we can pickle these objects:

```python
import pickle     ⟵—— Imports the module

task_tuple = (1001, "Homework", 5)
task_dict = {'task_id': '1002', 'title': 'Laundry', 'urgency': 3}

with open("task_tuple_saved.pickle", "wb") as file:
    pickle.dump(task_tuple, file)

with open("task_dict_saved.pickle", "wb") as file:
    pickle.dump(task_dict, file)
```

In this code snippet, we create one tuple and one dict object for pickling. I want to emphasize two key points.

- *The* dump *function saves the data to a file.* When we work with a file, we use the open function to create a file object so that we establish a connection to the pertinent file.
- *When we open the file, we should use* "wb" *mode.* This mode means that we're performing writing operations and that the file should be in binary format. By contrast, when we deal with text files, we don't need to worry about specifying the mode, as we use the default mode: "t" for "text".

After running the code, your current directory has two new files: task_tuple_saved .pickle and task_dict_saved.pickle. If you want to open them with a text editor, you won't see anything meaningful. Likewise, when you try to open an image with a text editor, you'll see some readable content mixed with meaningless text because of the binary format. How can you use the data saved in the pickle files? The next section explains.

11.3.2 Restoring data by unpickling

We pickle objects to preserve them as a file via a process known as pickling. Later, when we need the data again, we retrieve data from a pickle file—the opposite process to pickling, called *unpickling*. In this section, you'll learn about restoring data by unpickling.

When we discussed JavaScript Object Notation (JSON) data serialization (section 9.3), we used dump to create a JSON file, which has the same calling signature as dump for pickling. When we read JSON files, we used the load function. As you may expect, unpickling also uses load:

```python
with open("task_tuple_saved.pickle", "rb") as file:
    task_tuple_loaded = pickle.load(file)

with open("task_dict_saved.pickle", "rb") as file:
    task_dict_loaded = pickle.load(file)
```

Unpickling requires that we open the file in read mode. Remember that pickle files are binary, so we need to use "rb" as the open mode. Unlike the dump function, which returns None, we expect to obtain the data by calling the load function on the file object. Thus, we assign the return value to a variable.

To check the fidelity of data preservation, we can compare the unpickled data with the original objects. The restored objects are equal to the original ones. This fidelity is important, as we're assured that we can recreate the original data after pickling:

```
assert task_tuple == task_tuple_loaded
assert task_dict == task_dict_loaded
```

Can we pickle the instance objects of custom classes too? The answer is yes. Consider the following example:

```
class Task:
    def __init__(self, title, urgency):
        self.title = title
        self.urgency = urgency

task = Task("Laundry", 3)

with open("task_class_saved.pickle", "wb") as file:
    pickle.dump(task, file)

with open("task_class_saved.pickle", "rb") as file:
    task_class_loaded = pickle.load(file)

assert task.__dict__ == task_class_loaded.__dict__
assert task is not task_class_loaded
```

In this code snippet, we pickle and unpickle an instance object of the Task class, and the original object and the pickled/unpickled object have the same attributes, as revealed by the comparison of their dictionary representations. Notably, they're not the same object, as revealed by the identity comparison (is not).

Although we can pickle instances of custom classes, we should pay extra attention to them. The reason is that for built-in classes, when you unpickle these objects, Python knows how to unpickle them because their types are known. By contrast, Python may not know your custom classes if you haven't defined them when you unpickle. That is, if you unpickle an instance object (in our case, an instance of the Task class), you'll encounter an error when the namespace doesn't have the Task class. Consider the following example:

```
del Task      ◁———  Removes Task from the global namespace

with open("task_class_saved.pickle", "rb") as file:
    task_class_loaded = pickle.load(file)

# ERROR: AttributeError: Can't get attribute 'Task' on <module '__main__'
➥ (built-in)>
```

To mimic a situation in which you unpickle an instance when its class is not defined, we remove the Task class from the global namespace by running del Task. After that, we can't obtain the custom instance, as it can't find the Task class for instantiation.

> **MAINTAINABILITY**   When you unpickle instances of a custom class, make sure that you've defined the class in the corresponding namespace.

When you learned about JSON data conversion, you learned that dump and load are for manipulating JSON files, and dumps and loads are for dealing with JSON strings. Pickling has counterpart functions with the same names: dump and load for pickle files, and dumps and loads for pickle strings in binary form (known as bytes; see listing 11.13), as depicted in figure 11.4.

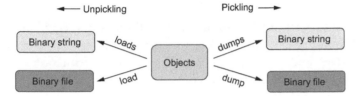

Figure 11.4   Pickling and unpickling in the forms of strings and files. In pickling, you call dumps to create a binary string and dump to create a binary file. In unpickling, you call loads to create an object from a binary string and load to create an object from a binary file.

The preceding examples focus on pickle files, and you'll see some examples of pickle-related binary strings in the next section.

11.3.3 *Weighing the pros and cons of pickling*

We've seen how pickling and unpickling work for data preservation. It's important to know the pros and cons of pickling. This section reviews the most important aspects of pickling, which will help us determine whether pickling is the right choice for data preservation in our project.

COMPATIBILITY WITH MOST OBJECTS

As another common storage and data exchange mechanism, JSON is compatible with the built-in data types, but it doesn't work with custom classes unless we provide specific JSON serialization instructions, such as by setting the default argument in calling dump or dumps (section 9.3). Moreover, JSON can't natively handle all objects, such as functions. By contrast, pickling is compatible with many more kinds of objects out of the box. To see pickling's flexibility, observe an example of preserving a simple function in the next listing.

Listing 11.13   Pickling a function to bytes

```
def doubler(x):
    return x * 2
```

```
doubler_pickle = pickle.dumps(doubler)
print(doubler_pickle)

# output: b'\x80\x04\x95\x18\x00\x00\x00\x00\x00\x00\x00\x8c\x08
⮡ __main__\x94\x8c\x07doubler\x94\x93\x94.'
```

As shown in this code, we pickle the function `doubler` as bytes data, which resumes the look of a string but starts with b to denote that it's a bytes object. We can unpickle this bytes object to reconstruct the function, which should do the same job as `doubler`:

```
doubler_loaded = pickle.loads(doubler_pickle)

assert doubler_loaded(5) == doubler(5)
```

We've seen that pickling works with custom classes without any specific instructions (see listing 11.14), unlike JSON serialization, which requires special instruction for encoding instances (section 9.3). But pickling doesn't work with every object in Python. We can't pickle a module, for example:

```
import os

os_dumped = pickle.dumps(os)

# ERROR: TypeError: cannot pickle 'module' object
```

Also, we can't also pickle file objects and connections to databases, as they use resources in a dynamic manner, which pickling can't handle. Except for these limitations, pickling works with most kinds of objects, serving as a versatile mechanism for data preservation.

DATA SECURITY

When we deal with any data, the first factor we may fail to consider is data security. When we obtain files, we should wonder whether they are safe. The same principle applies to pickle files; we should be cautious about pickled data's security.

Because pickling allows us to preserve almost any object, hackers have the opportunity to embed malicious code inside an object. In sections 11.3.1 and 11.3.2, we've seen how pickling works with built-in data types, such as `tuple` and `dict`. You can't do much with these built-in data types. If someone creates a custom class, however, they can define customized behaviors that can hack the pickling system. Consider the following example:

```
import os

class MaliciousTask:
    def __init__(self, title, urgency):
        self.title = title
        self.urgency = urgency
```

```
def __reduce__(self):                                    Creates one-
    print("__reduce__ is called")                        item tuple
    return os.system, ('touch hacking.txt',)   ◄─┘
```

In this code snippet, someone defines the class `MaliciousTask`. This class has implemented the special method `__reduce__`, which is involved in the pickling process. The return value, if run, results in creating the `hacking.txt` file on your computer. The file is empty, but it can be programmed to contain malicious code that will damage your computer system!

If you're not paying attention to this malicious source code and trying to unpickle an instance of this class, your computer can become vulnerable because of the added file from calling `__reduce__`. The next listing shows this effect.

Listing 11.14 Pickling an instance of a custom class

```
malicious_task = MaliciousTask("Set fire", 5)

with open("test_malicious.pickle", "wb") as file:
    pickle.dump(malicious_task, file)

# output: __reduce__ is called
```

Note that I included the output `"__reduce__ is called"` to show you that `__reduce__` is involved in pickling. The command for creating a potentially malicious file is part of the pickle file. When you unpickle this kind of file, the following problem arises:

```
with open("test_malicious.pickle", "rb") as file:
    pickle.load(file)
```

After unpickling the file, if you check your directory, you'll see that the file `hacking.txt` sneakily shows up! Real malicious code won't leave such apparent traces, however. Thus, you should be cautious when you try to pickle and unpickle objects. The rule of thumb is to pickle only objects that come from trusted sources, such as the built-in ones, classes that you created yourself, or reputable third-party packages.

STORAGE SIZE AND SPEED

Another advantage of pickling is its smaller storage size and faster reading/writing speed compared with text-based storage, such as CSV format. I've mentioned several times that pandas is one of the most prevalent Python packages for data science. Its core data model is known as DataFrame, which is a tabulated data structure. You can save DataFrame objects as CSV files or pickle files. In general, using pickle files to read and write data is much faster than using CSV files, and pickle files tend to be smaller than CSV files for storing the same amount of data.

11.3.4 *Discussion*

Pickling is a convenient storage mechanism that is compatible with most kinds of Python objects, including custom classes. There are pros and cons to using pickles, of course. The rule of thumb is that if you work on data-related projects, pickles can be a great choice, providing faster reading/writing speed than CSV files. As a reminder, be cautious about the security vulnerability of pickling data from untrusted sources.

11.3.5 *Challenge*

As a cybersecurity analyst in a hospital, Roger evaluates security associated with the pickling technique in Python. He tried to pickle an instance of the `MaliciousTask` class that adds a file (`hacking.txt`) to the current working directory, as we did in listing 11.14. How can he modify the class to make it remove the `hacking.txt` file during pickling?

> **HINT** We used the command `touch hacking.txt` to create this file. We can use the command `rm hacking.txt` to remove this file. Don't forget where you should place this command.

11.4 *How do I manage files on my computer?*

No matter what projects you're working on, it's inevitable that you'll deal with files. After all, files are the most versatile containers for storing organized information. In the preceding sections, you learned about reading data from files and writing data to files. But you haven't learned anything about manipulating files in their entirety (not concerned with the content, but the files themselves), as well as manipulating directories, such as by moving and copying files.

Consider the following use scenario. Suppose that you're conducting a scientific experiment in which each participant completes a reaction time test. This test consists of multiple trials, and after the test is run, the software generates several files. Because we run the experiment with multiple subjects, the `data` directory has the following files:

```
subject_123.config
subject_123.dat
subject_123.txt
subject_124.config
subject_124.dat
subject_124.txt
subject_125.config
subject_125.dat
subject_125.txt
```

We are concerned about the files of a specific type. Specifically, when we're done with the data collection, how can we extract only those data files (`.dat`) and move them to a new directory? We also want to delete the text files (`.txt`) because we don't need them.

In this section, we'll address these needs and common file-handling techniques. Please note that Python is a general-purpose language, and when it comes to file handling, there can be multiple solutions involving different libraries, such as os and pathlib. I'll focus on the generalizable ones.

11.4.1   Creating a directory and files

To follow along with the entire section, you'll start by learning how to create a new directory and a bunch of mock files. When you deal with file paths or directory paths, if you've been using the os module, I recommend that you use the pathlib module instead; it's a more compact module that specializes in handling paths. Using pathlib, you can easily make a new directory:

```
from pathlib import Path

data_folder = Path("data")
data_folder.mkdir()          ⟵—— Makes a directory
```

The central data model in the pathlib is Path, a class designated for path-related operations. To make a directory using the Path object, for example, call the mkdir method, which creates the data folder in your current directory. You can check its existence programmatically by calling exists:

```
assert data_folder.exists()
```

When you have the folder ready, you can create a bunch of mock files, and you'll use these files for manipulation later in this section:

```
subject_ids = [123, 124, 125]
extensions = ["config", "dat", "txt"]

for subject_id in subject_ids:
    for extension in extensions:
        filename = f"subject_{subject_id}.{extension}"
        filepath = data_folder / filename          ⟵—— Creates a file path
        with open(filepath, "w") as file:
            file.write(f"It's the file {filename}.")
```

For now, you should know how to create a file with some data by using the open function in a with statement (section 11.1). One thing to note is that you construct a file path by using the operation directory_path / filename. You may know that Windows and macOS use different symbols (backslash versus forward slash) to separate the levels in a directory: data\subject_123.dat vs. data/subject_123.dat. When you create a filepath using directory_path / filename, this operation is operating system agnostic, meaning that the same code can run on either of these platforms. If you arbitrarily create the path—say, data\subject_123.dat—your code may not run on a different system. This cross-platform compatibility is another advantage of using pathlib instead of the os module (in which you may have to use the raw strings as paths), which is platform dependent.

11.4.2 *Retrieving the list of files of a specific kind*

The next step is retrieving all the .dat files in the directory so that we can process these files for scoring data purposes. To retrieve all files of a specific kind, we call the glob method on a directory path in which we specify a pattern for filenames. All files that match this pattern can be found, as the next listing shows.

Listing 11.15   Retrieving files of the same kind

```
data_folder = Path("data")

data_files = data_folder.glob("*.dat")
print("Data files:", data_files)        ⟵——— Creates a generator object

for data_file in data_files:
    print(f"Processing file: {data_file}")
    # applicable data processing steps here

# output the following lines:                          Expect a different
Data files: <generator object Path.glob at 0x100b5c040>  ⟵——┘ memory address on
                                                         your computer.

Processing file: data/subject_124.dat
Processing file: data/subject_125.dat
Processing file: data/subject_123.dat
```

We specify that the pattern is *.dat, locating the files with an extension of .dat. Notably, the file list matching this pattern forms a generator, and we can use it in a for loop. From the printout message, we see that we indeed obtain all the .dat files. One potential drawback is that the list isn't sorted, which may make it hard to eyeball what files have been processed. As an improvement, we can sort the generator to organize the files better:

```
data_files = data_folder.glob("*.dat")    ⟵——— Recreates the generator

for data_file in sorted(data_files):    ⟵——┐ Sorts the generator
    print(f"Processing file: {data_file}")  │ to create a list
    # applicable data processing steps here │

# output the following lines:
Processing file: data/subject_123.dat
Processing file: data/subject_124.dat
Processing file: data/subject_125.dat
```

> **REMINDER**   Generators are consumable. When you exhaust the items in a generator, you must recreate the generator, allowing it to yield its items.

11.4.3 *Moving files to a different folder*

To organize our project's data in a scientific experiment, we can place a participant's data in their own folders. For the participant with ID number 123, for example, we want all their data to reside in the subject_123 folder. In this section, you'll learn about moving files to address this need.

When we move files, the idea is to "rename" the file's path. That is, if you rename the file data/subject_123.dat to subjects/subject_123/subject_123.dat, it moves from the data folder to the subject_123 folder. Using this knowledge, we can come up with the solution in listing 11.16. Please note that we use the mkdir method, which allows us to create a multilevel directory even when some intermediate levels don't exist. We set the parents argument as True in the mkdir call in the next listing; it creates any missing intermediate levels of the path as needed.

Listing 11.16 Moving files to a target folder

```
subject_ids = [123, 124, 125]
data_folder = Path("data")

for subject_id in subject_ids:
    subject_folder = Path(f"subjects/subject_{subject_id}")      Creates the
    subject_folder.mkdir(parents=True, exist_ok=True)   ◄──┘    subject folder

    for subject_file in data_folder.glob(f"*{subject_id}*"):
        filename = subject_file.name
        target_path = subject_folder / filename     ◄───────   Constructs the
        _ = subject_file.rename(target_path)                   target path
        print(f"Moving {filename} to {target_path}")
```

Gets the filename ──►

```
# output the following lines:
Moving subject_123.config to subjects/subject_123/subject_123.config
Moving subject_123.dat to subjects/subject_123/subject_123.dat
Moving subject_123.txt to subjects/subject_123/subject_123.txt
Moving subject_124.config to subjects/subject_124/subject_124.config
Moving subject_124.dat to subjects/subject_124/subject_124.dat
Moving subject_124.txt to subjects/subject_124/subject_124.txt
Moving subject_125.dat to subjects/subject_125/subject_125.dat
Moving subject_125.config to subjects/subject_125/subject_125.config
Moving subject_125.txt to subjects/subject_125/subject_125.txt
```

After running this code, we should see that the current directory has a new folder, subjects, which contains three folders for each subject. Moving a file generally requires four steps (figure 11.5): identify the file you're moving, retrieve the filename, construct the new filename, and rename the file with the new filename.

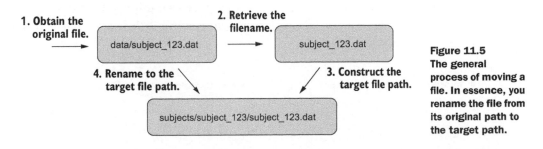

1. Obtain the original file. → data/subject_123.dat → **2. Retrieve the filename.** → subject_123.dat

4. Rename to the target file path. ↘ subjects/subject_123/subject_123.dat ↖ **3. Construct the target file path.**

Figure 11.5 The general process of moving a file. In essence, you rename the file from its original path to the target path.

11.4.4 *Copying files to a different folder*

Copying files allows us to keep the original files and have a second copy. Suppose that instead of moving the files from data to the subjects folder, we copy the data instead. (You need to recreate the initial data files to follow along.) Here, I introduce the shutil module, which provides a high-level application programming interface (API) for manipulating files.

This module has the copy method and the calling signature copy(src, dst), in which src stands for the source file and dst stands for the destination path. Using this method, we can copy the files to each subject's folder, as shown in the next listing.

Listing 11.17   Copying files to a target folder

```
import shutil

shutil.rmtree("subjects")            ◁─┐ Removes a folder
                                         and its contents
subject_ids = [123, 124, 125]
data_folder = Path("data")

for subject_id in subject_ids:
    subject_folder = Path(f"subjects/subject_{subject_id}")
    subject_folder.mkdir(parents=True, exist_ok=True)

    for subject_file in data_folder.glob(f"*{subject_id}*"):    Use an underscore
        filename = subject_file.name                            when you don't use
        target_path = subject_folder / filename                 a function's return
        _ = shutil.copy(subject_file, target_path)   ◁─┘        value.
        print(f"Copying {filename} to {target_path}")

# output the following lines:
Copying subject_123.config to subjects/subject_123/subject_123.config
Copying subject_123.dat to subjects/subject_123/subject_123.dat
Copying subject_123.txt to subjects/subject_123/subject_123.txt
Copying subject_124.config to subjects/subject_124/subject_124.config
Copying subject_124.dat to subjects/subject_124/subject_124.dat
Copying subject_124.txt to subjects/subject_124/subject_124.txt
Copying subject_125.dat to subjects/subject_125/subject_125.dat
Copying subject_125.config to subjects/subject_125/subject_125.config
Copying subject_125.txt to subjects/subject_125/subject_125.txt
```

As shown in listing 11.17, we use the rmtree function to remove a folder and its contents, as rmtree doesn't care about the directory's emptiness. By contrast, we could run into a problem if we use Path.rmdir to remove a directory that is not empty. Observe this feature:

```
Path("subjects").rmdir()
# ERROR: OSError: [Errno 66] Directory not empty: 'subjects'
```

In listing 11.16, we moved files. Copying files involves the same procedure: identify the files, obtain the filename, construct the target path, and use the copy function of the shutil module.

11.4.5   Deleting a specific kind of files

At section 11.4's beginning, I mentioned that one business need is to remove the .txt files in the data folder—specifically, the individual data files that may contain a subject's privacy data—and we must remove the original files for security concerns. From a general perspective, we need to delete a specific kind of files, as we'll discuss in this section.

The Path class provides the unlink method to delete a file. To use this feature, we need to obtain instances of the Path objects and call unlink on them:

```python
data_folder = Path("data")

for file in data_folder.glob("*.txt"):
    before = file.exists()
    file.unlink()
    after = file.exists()
    print(f"Deleting {file}, existing? {before} -> {after}")

# output the following lines:
Deleting data/subject_123.txt, existing? True -> False
Deleting data/subject_124.txt, existing? True -> False
Deleting data/subject_125.txt, existing? True -> False
```

To show that the deletion works, we check the existence of a file before and after the deletion. As you can see, each file exists before the deletion, and it's gone after the deletion.

11.4.6   Discussion

When we manipulate files, we can do the operations manually, but we may lose track of what we've done with the files. Although we can write down each operation, it's tedious and inconvenient to record all the operations. Thus, to make the file operations more reproducible and trackable, we should write code to manipulate the files.

11.4.7   Challenge

Cassi uses Python to manage files on her computer. One lesson she learned is that when she copies files to a different folder, she shouldn't overwrite any files. That is, it's possible that the target folder may have the same files that she moved earlier. Moreover, these files may have been processed and contain new data. How can she update the code in listing 11.17 so that she copies files only if those files don't exist in the target folder?

HINT You can call exists on the Path instance object to determine whether a file exists.

11.5   How do I retrieve file metadata?

In section 11.4, you learned how to manipulate files on a computer. For the moving and copying operations, we retrieved the filename by accessing the name attribute of the Path object. Besides the filename, a file has metadata that can be important in specific use cases. We need to retrieve a file's directory to construct another path to access another file in the same directory, for example.

Suppose that we continue to handle the experimental data in section 11.4. In the data folder, we need to process those data (.dat) files. But we must obtain additional configuration (.config) files for each subject. We can call glob to obtain the list of .dat files. But how can we easily locate the corresponding .config file for each subject? This section addresses this question and other operations related to accessing a file's metadata.

11.5.1   Retrieving the filename-related information

When I say *the filename-related information,* I'm referring to the directory, filename, and file extension. These pieces of information are attributes of the Path class. Let's use some code examples to learn about them.

For the problem, we start with the data file: subjects/subject_123/subject_123.dat. How can we retrieve subjects/subject_123/subject_123.config? These two files have the same directory and filename but have distinct file extensions. Observing these characteristics, we can come up with the solution shown in the next listing.

Listing 11.18   Retrieving filename information

```
from pathlib import Path

subjects_folder = Path("subjects")

for dat_path in subjects_folder.glob("**/*.dat"):    ◁─── Retrieves all data files

    subject_dir = dat_path.parent    ◁─── Retrieves the file directory

    filename = dat_path.stem    ◁─── Retrieves the filename

    config_path = subject_dir / f"{filename}.config"

    print(f"{subject_dir} & {filename} -> {config_path}")

    dat_exists = dat_path.exists()
    config_exists = config_path.exists()
    with open(dat_path) as dat_file, open(config_path) as config_file:
        print(f"Process {filename}: dat? {dat_exists}, config?
        {config_exists}\n")
        # process the subject's data

# output the following lines:
subjects/subject_125 & subject_125 -> subjects/subject_125/subject_125.config
```

Opens both files ⟶ (annotation pointing to the `with open(...)` line)

```
Process subject_125: dat? True, config? True

subjects/subject_124 & subject_124 -> subjects/subject_124/subject_124.config
Process subject_124: dat? True, config? True

subjects/subject_123 & subject_123 -> subjects/subject_123/subject_123.config
Process subject_123: dat? True, config? True
```

In listing 11.18, from the printout message, we see that we process each subject's data by accessing both `.dat` and `.config` files. Four things are worth noting:

- Because there are folders within `subjects_folder`, when you try to access files within these subdirectories, the pattern involves `**/`, meaning that the files reside in subdirectories.
- For each `Path` instance, we can access its `parent` attribute, which returns the directory of the path.
- For each `Path` instance, we can access its `stem` attribute, which returns the filename without the extension of the path.
- In the `with` statement, we can open two files at the same time, creating two file objects that we can work on simultaneously.

You can retrieve the entire filename, including the extension, by accessing `name` (listing 11.17), and you can retrieve only the extension by accessing `suffix`, as follows (please note that the extension includes the dot symbol):

```
dat_path = Path("subjects/subject/subject_123.dat")

assert dat_path.suffix == ".dat"
```

Figure 11.6 shows which attributes correspond to filename data.

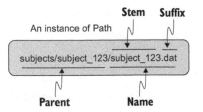

Figure 11.6 Retrieving a file's filename-related data with an instance of the `Path` class. You can access its `parent` (the directory), `name` (filename, including extension), `stem` (filename only, with no extension), and `suffix` (file extension).

11.5.2 Retrieving the file's size and time information

When you use a file-explorer app on your computer, you can see a few columns other than name, such as file size and the time when the file was last updated. This metadata can be useful in specific scenarios. This section discusses a few of those scenarios.

For experimental data, it's typical for each subject's data file to have a stable size if the data recording was done correctly. Thus, without opening the file to check the content, we can check a file's size to quickly determine data integrity before applying any processing procedure. The function shown in the next listing addresses this need.

Listing 11.19   Creating a function to screen file sizes

```
def process_data_using_size_cutoff(min_size, max_size):
    data_folder = Path("data")
    for dat_path in data_folder.glob("*.dat"):
        filename = dat_path.name
        size = dat_path.stat().st_size     ◁—— Retrieves the file size
        if min_size < size < max_size:
            print(f"{filename}, Good; {size},  within
            ⇒ [{min_size}, {max_size}]")
        else:
            print(f"{filename}, Bad; {size}, outside
            ⇒ [{min_size}, {max_size}]")
```

Chained comparisons (annotation pointing to `if min_size < size < max_size:`)

In this code snippet, we call the stat() to retrieve the file's status-related data, among which st_size is the size information in bytes. Using this function, we can test a few variations of the cutoffs to determine data integrity:

```
process_data_using_size_cutoff(20, 40)
# output the following lines:
subject_124.dat, Good; 30,  within [20, 40]
subject_125.dat, Good; 30,  within [20, 40]
subject_123.dat, Good; 30,  within [20, 40]

process_data_using_size_cutoff(40, 60)
# output the following lines:
subject_124.dat, Bad; 30, outside [40, 60]
subject_125.dat, Bad; 30, outside [40, 60]
subject_123.dat, Bad; 30, outside [40, 60]
```

As you can see, when we require the range to be 20–40, all the files are good, as all their sizes are 30. If we define the size window as 40–60, all the files are bad.

Sometimes, we screen files based on their content modification time. To retrieve time-related metadata, we can call the stat method on the Path instance:

```
import time

subject_dat_path = Path("data/subject_123.dat")

modified_time = subject_dat_path.stat().st_mtime     ◁—— The content modification time

readable_time = time.ctime(modified_time)     ◁—— Converts to human-readable time

print(f"Modification time: {modified_time} -> {readable_time}")
```

```
# output: Modification time: 1652123144.9999998 -> Mon May  9 14:05:44 2022
```
Expect a different value.

In this code, we're accessing the attribute st_mtime, which is the time when the file was modified in terms of content (not filename changes or other metadata). This value represents the seconds since the epoch: January 1, 1970, 00:00:00 (UTC). We can use the `ctime` function in the `time` module to convert this value to a human-readable timestamp.

11.5.3 Discussion

This section focused on the file's directory, filename, extension, size, and time-related metadata. Note, however, that a file's metadata contains many other pieces of information, such as the file's permission modes, although your projects may need only the metadata covered in this section. When you're thinking about accessing a file's metadata, you should know that you can call the `stat` method on an instance of the `Path` class.

11.5.4 Challenge

Albert is a graduate student with a major in chemistry. He loves to use Python to manage his computer programmatically. How can he write a function to select a directory's files that were modified in the past 24 hours?

> **HINT** With the `time` module, you can call `time` to retrieve the number of seconds since the epoch. You can compare a file's content modification time with this value for the 24-hour adjustment. Remember that you need to calculate the number of seconds in 24 hours.

Summary

- When you perform reading/writing operations with a file, use the `with` statement, which closes the file automatically, using a context manager.
- The default `open` mode is `"r"` (read). Performing any writing operations requires you to use `"w"` (write) or `"a"` (append), with the latter appending data to the file's end.
- The built-in `csv` module is specialized to read and write CSV data. Although this topic isn't the focus of this book, if you need to perform numeric computations and data processing, consider using a third-party library such as pandas.
- When CSV files have headers, prefer using `csv.DictReader`, which handles the headers, over the other common data reader, `csv.reader`.
- As the counterparts to `csv.reader` and `csv.DictReader`, `csv.writer` and `csv.DictWriter` are used to create CSV files. The latter is better at handling headers.
- Pickling is a built-in mechanism for storing Python objects as binary data. Compared with JSON, pickling is more flexible because it supports more data types, including functions.
- Be cautious about pickling's data security. Don't pickle or unpickle any data from potentially untrusted sources.
- Instead of using CSV files as a storage mechanism for tabulated data, you can use pickling to save data size and increase reading/writing speed.

- The built-in module `pathlib` provides various methods and attributes for its `Path` class. You should be familiar with using `pathlib` to perform file management, such as creating a directory and moving files.
- A file doesn't contain only its content, but also its name, directory, modification time, and other metadata that can contain the information you need. You should know how to retrieve this data through the `Path` class.

Part 5

Safeguarding the codebase

As programmers, we should take responsibility for our code. Taking responsibility means ensuring the quality of our code by making it functional, with the fewest possible bugs (and preferably none). We can improve code quality in four distinct ways:

- We can log important events during the execution of our program, making it possible to know what has happened and to provide a solution quickly should any problem arise.
- We can integrate exception handling into our program, because handling possible exceptions properly prevents our program from crashing.
- We should debug our program during the development phase—the best time to remove bugs, because we have the freshest memory of the code.
- We should test our program thoroughly, making sure that every part works before product delivery.

In this part, you'll learn these four ways to write robust and reliable programs.

Logging and
exception handling

When we move our application into production, we temporarily "lose" control of our product; we must rely on the product itself to behave. If we've been extremely careful during the development phase, we may be lucky enough to have a perfect product that has no bugs. This almost never happens, however. Thus, we should know that a variety of problems, such as an unusual amount of traffic to our web app, can occur. Should any problem arise, we don't panic; we start the problem-solving process.

Sometimes, we don't have the chance to talk to the users who report the problem, and even if we do, the information they provide can be rather limited, which can't help us identify the underlying problems. Fortunately, because we expected that problems could arise with our product, our application logs the user's activities and the related application events, which makes it possible for us to study where things might have gone wrong. These logging records play an essential role in making our product run smoothly by monitoring its performance continuously. Because logging is so useful, we should integrate it into our application during development. In the meantime, because of user input, we should expect specific exceptions to occur. It's not uncommon, for example, for someone to try to get the result of one divided by zero, which causes the `ZeroDivisionError` exception; we should handle this exception properly so that the application will continue to run. In this chapter, we study logging and exception handling.

12.1   *How do I monitor my program with logging?*

The most frustrating thing in software development could well be debugging a problem that you can't reproduce. If you're lucky enough, you may have various anecdotal descriptions from some less tech-savvy end users. These descriptions may be meaningless, however, as the same problem on the surface can have multiple root causes. Thus, it's common sense that you should set up logging properly to monitor the performance of your application before turning it over to end users. When a user encounters any problem in a specific module of your application, you can pull out the pertinent logging information, and it should take much less time to solve the problem. This section introduces the essential features of logging in Python.

12.1.1   *Creating the Logger object to log application events*

Everything is an object in Python, so it's not surprising that we use an object to log application events. Specifically, the `Logger` object does the logging for us. In this section, you'll learn about best practices for creating a `Logger` object.

   In the standard Python library, the `logging` module provides the logging functionalities. This module has the `Logger` class, and that class's constructor takes a name to create an instance object:

```
import logging

logger_not_good = logging.Logger("task_app")
```

This code snippet creates a `Logger` object. But are you wondering why I call this logger `logger_not_good`? Before I explain, take a look at the proper way to create a `Logger` object:

```
logger_good = logging.getLogger("task_app")
```

Here, we call the `getLogger` function by supplying the name of the logger. The reason we should use `getLogger` instead of calling the constructor is that we want a shared instance of the `Logger` class to handle logging. More specifically, in an application or in a module, we may want to retrieve the logger in multiple places. If we use the constructor, we end up with multiple distinct loggers, as in this example:

```
logger0 = logging.Logger("task_app")
logger1 = logging.Logger("task_app")
logger2 = logging.Logger("task_app")
```

```
assert logger0 is not logger1
assert logger1 is not logger2
assert logger0 is not logger2
```
You can combine these comparisons in a single comparison by using AND operations.

You must configure these loggers separately (I discuss configurations in section 12.2), making sure that they have the same configurations so they'll work properly. There is no reason why you should use multiple loggers for the same module, however; only one logger should do the job. As this example shows, using `getLogger` ensures that we always retrieve the same logger:

```
logger0_good = logging.getLogger("task_app")
logger1_good = logging.getLogger("task_app")
logger2_good = logging.getLogger("task_app")
```

```
assert logger0_good is logger1_good is logger2_good
```

Using the `is` comparisons, you can tell that the logger is the same no matter how many times you called `getLogger`. When it's the same logger, you can configure it once, and it'll behave the same way throughout its lifecycle during your application's execution.

As a best practice, if you're creating a module-level logger for each module in your application, I recommend that you create the logger by running `logging.getLogger` (`__name__`). `__name__` is a special attribute for a module name. When you name the module `taskier.py`, for example, the module's `__name__` attribute is `taskier`.

> **MAINTAINABILITY**   Always use `getLogger` to retrieve the same logger for your module or application. For module-level loggers, it's best to use `getLogger` (`__name__`) to get the logger.

12.1.2   *Using files to store application events*

In all the previous chapters, I almost always used the `print` function to show the important messages during the execution of specific code snippets. Suppose that we want to make a log when a user creates a task in our task management application. The following listing shows a simplified version of the code.

Listing 12.1   Creating a log using `print`

```
class Task:
    def __init__(self, title):
        self.title = title

    def remove_from_db(self):
        # operations to remove the task from the database
        task_removed = True
```

```
        return task_removed

task = Task("Laundry")
if task.remove_from_db():
    print(f"removed the task {task.title} from the database")
```

We can print a message after the task is removed successfully. But this approach can work only during the active coding phase because the printout message is showing up in the Python console. When you submit your application for production, it's almost impossible for you to monitor the printout messages in a continuous manner. Thus, a sustainable approach is to store the application events using a permanent medium: files. In this section, I'll show you how to send events to files.

> **NOTE**   When you store events in a file, you can examine these events as many times as you want; thus, your approach is sustainable. By contrast, if you use the print function, the events are sent to the console, and when the console is closed, you lose the recorded information.

We can think of the logger that oversees everything in terms of logging. Thus, to log events in a file, we must provide specific configuration to the logger, which we do by setting *handlers*. The logging module includes a class called FileHandler; we can use this class to specify a file to which the logger should save events, as the next listing shows.

Listing 12.2   Adding a file handler to the logger

```
logger = logging.getLogger(__name__)

file_handler = logging.FileHandler("taskier.log")   ◁——— Specifies the file handler

logger.addHandler(file_handler)     ◁——— Adds the handler to the logger
```

As shown in listing 12.2, we specify that we want all the records to go to the taskier.log file and associate the file with the logger by calling the addHandler method. Notably, after you run this code, you should see that your current directory has the taskier.log file. Now that the logger knows where to save the records, we're ready to check out how logging works in the next listing.

Listing 12.3   Writing a record to the log file

```
task = Task("Laundry")
if task.remove_from_db():
    logger.warning(f"removed the task {task.title} from the database")
```

In this code snippet, we're writing a warning record by calling logger.warning. If we open the taskier.log file, we should be able to see the record.

> **PEEK**   Each logging message is a log record, which is an instance of the LogRecord class. Section 12.2.3 discusses formatting log records.

If you prefer a programmatic way to see the record, run the following code. You know how to read a text file (section 11.1), right? Please note that I wrote a function to check the file content, because we'll check the log file multiple times later, and it's helpful to have a function for this purpose:

```
def check_log_content(filename):
    with open(filename) as file:
        return file.read()

log_records = check_log_content("taskier.log")
print(log_records)

# output: removed the task Laundry from the database
```

> **REMINDER**   Use the with statement to open a file so that it can close the file automatically.

As you can see, we read the entire file, and the content matches what we expected: a single record about removing the task from the database.

12.1.3   Adding multiple handlers to the logger

In section 12.1.2, we saw how to add a file handler to a logger to send log records to a file. A logger can have multiple handlers, as we'll discuss in this section.

Besides file handlers, the logging module provides stream handlers, which can log the records in an interactive console. During the development of the software, we can use files to preserve the log records for later reference, but in the meantime, we can add a stream handler to the logger so that we can view the records in a console for real-time feedback, as in the following listing. This way, we don't need to open or read the log to retrieve the records.

> **Listing 12.4   Using a stream handler with the logger**

```
stream_handler = logging.StreamHandler()

logger.addHandler(stream_handler)

logger.warning("Just a random warning event.")
# output the following: Just a random warning event.
```

We call the StreamHandler constructor to create a stream handler and add it to the logger. When we send a warning log record to the logger, this message gets printed in the console. In the meantime, we can check that the same logger also records the message in the file handler that we added earlier:

```
log_records = check_log_content("taskier.log")

print(log_records)
# output the following lines:
removed the task Laundry from the database
Just a random warning event.
```

As you can see, the log file records the same event as the stream handler. Please note that the log file has the record that we entered earlier.

For a logger, you can set more than a file handler and a stream handler. In fact, you can set multiple file handlers to the logger. Suppose that you want to have two duplicate log files for backup purposes. You can have two file handlers for each of the log files. Moreover, you can set different levels for the handlers (as discussed in section 12.2.2) and achieve finer control of the handlers in terms of what kinds of log records they capture.

In most cases, we'll need to use only stream and file handlers. But several other kinds of handlers can be handy in specific use cases. Although I'm not going to discuss them in detail because they're not often used, it's good to know about their existence (see http://mng.bz/E0pD).

As shown in figure 12.1, we can attach different kinds of handlers to a logger. I've covered stream and file handlers. Some notable handlers include SMTP handlers, which can send log records as an email; HTTP handlers, which can send log records to a web server via an HTTP GET or POST request; and Queue handlers, which can send log records to a queue, such as one in a different thread.

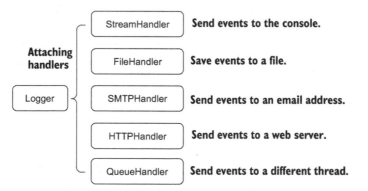

Figure 12.1   Common handlers can be attached to a logger. When we create a logger, we can instantiate a variety of handlers and attach them to the logger. These handlers have their respective intended uses.

12.1.4 Discussion

We should use files to log important application events so that we can locate the necessary information to fix any problems that arise. During the development phase, it would be helpful to set a stream handler to the logger so that you can view the log records on the console in real time.

12.1.5 Challenge

John recently started to integrate logging into his project. He knows that he can call `logging.getLogger(__name__)` to retrieve the logger used by the module. He runs the code in listing 12.2, which adds a file handler to the logger. If he runs the code multiple times, the logger has multiple file handlers, even though these file handlers are referring to the same file. When he logs any events, the file has duplicate records. How can he update the code in listing 12.2 so that it adds the file handler only once? If he does have multiple handlers set to the logger, how can he remove them?

> **HINT 1** A logger has a method called hasHandlers, which you can use to check whether a logger has handlers. You can add a handler if the logger doesn't have any.

> **HINT 2** You can save a logger's handlers as a list object, and you can empty the list so that the handlers will be removed from the logger.

12.2 How do I save log records properly?

Depending on the size of your application, over an extended period of time, the log file can accumulate many records, on the magnitude of thousands or millions. Checking the records to find needed information can be a real pain. For demonstration purposes, I used simple messages for the log records in section 12.1. For a task management application, however, you can expect to see some records like this:

```
-- app is starting
-- created a new task Laundry
-- removed the task from the database
-- successfully changed the tags for the task
-- updated the task's status to completed
-- FAILED to change the task's status!!!
```

As you can see, with minimum formatting (two leading dashes) for the records, it's hard to spot the potential records for a reported problem. Fortunately, we can categorize and format the log records to include more information, making our debugging experience less painful. In this section, I'll show you how to save log records properly by focusing on using different levels for logging, and I'll show you how to apply formatting to the log records for improved readability.

12.2.1 Categorizing application events with levels

Not all problems in software have the same level of priority. Some problems need to be fixed now, while others can wait. We can apply the same logic to our logging system. By using different logging levels, we can highlight the urgency/importance of the problems. In listing 12.3, we call logger.warning to write a record, which is at the warning level. As this section discusses, there are multiple levels higher than a warning, and you'll learn how file handlers and logging work with levels.

In Python's logging module, we have access to five levels (DEBUG, INFO, WARNING, ERROR, and CRITICAL) plus a base level (NOTSET), which has a numeric value of 0 and isn't typically used. Each level has a numeric value, and the higher the value, the more serious the problem. Figure 12.2 shows these levels and the general guidelines regarding what records should be captured at each level.

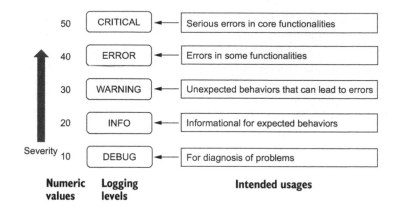

Figure 12.2 The five levels of logging for different usages. There are five logging levels—DEBUG, INFO, WARNING, ERROR, and CRITICAL—with increasing severity.

These five levels are defined as integer constants in the logging module; they have numeric values from 10 to 50, in increments of 10. As shown in figure 12.1, these levels are intended for different purposes, and you should respect the guidelines when you use these levels. But I haven't talked about how to use these levels.

The first use of the levels is to set the level of a logger. Besides the file handlers attribute, a logger has an important attribute called level. When we set a specific level, such as INFO, of a logger, all logging records at the level of INFO or more serious (meaning WARNING, ERROR, and CRITICAL) will be captured by the logger. Let's see it in action:

```
logger = logging.getLogger(__name__)
logger.setLevel(logging.WARNING)

print(logger.level, logging._levelToName[logger.level])    ← Gets the name
# output: 30 WARNING                                          for the level
```

In this code snippet, we set the logger with the level of WARNING, and when we check the logger's level, it's indeed WARNING. With the logger set at a level of WARNING, we expect that only warnings, errors, and critical messages will be captured by the logger. We can observe this effect in the following listing.

Listing 12.5 Logging records at different levels

```
def logging_messages_all_levels():
    logger.critical("--Critical message")
    logger.error("--Error message")
    logger.warning("--Warning message")
    logger.info("--Info message")
    logger.debug("--Debug message")

logging_messages_all_levels()
```

```
log_records = check_log_content("taskier.log")
print(log_records)

# output the following lines:
removed the task Laundry from the database
Just a random warning event.
--Critical message
--Error message
--Warning message
```

As shown in listing 12.5, we send five messages, each corresponding to the five levels. From the printout, you can see that the INFO and DEBUG messages aren't recorded in the log file because the logger is set at the WARNING level.

As you may have noticed, we use logger.critical to send a critical message, logger .error to send an error message, and so on. It's important to know these methods, as we can create log records at different levels. The level settings directly determine how the logger will capture records. File handlers can also accept level settings, as discussed in the next section.

12.2.2 Setting a handler's level

The other use of levels is setting the level of a handler. When we set the level of the logger, the level applies at the logger level, which isn't always desirable. A logger can have multiple handlers, and we might apply different levels to these handlers so that they can save logging records at their designated levels. This section discusses such usage.

Let's use file handlers as an example. Suppose that our task management application has two log files, with one recording WARNING-level records and above, and the other recording only CRITICAL records. The next listing shows a possible implementation.

Listing 12.6   Setting levels to individual file handlers

```
logger.setLevel(logging.DEBUG)      ◁──── Sets the logger's level to DEBUG

handler_warning = logging.FileHandler("taskier_warning.log")
handler_warning.setLevel(logging.WARNING)   ◁─┐
logger.addHandler(handler_warning)            │ Adds a handler at the WARNING level

handler_critical = logging.FileHandler("taskier_critical.log")
handler_critical.setLevel(logging.CRITICAL)   ◁─┐
logger.addHandler(handler_critical)            │ Adds a handler at the CRITICAL level

logging_messages_all_levels()

warning_log_records = check_log_content("taskier_warning.log")
print(warning_log_records)
# output the following lines:
--Critical message
--Error message
--Warning message
```

```
critical_log_records = check_log_content("taskier_critical.log")
print(critical_log_records)
# output the following line:
--Critical message
```

As shown in listing 12.6, we first set the logger's level to DEBUG, which allows the logger to catch any message at the DEBUG level or above. To show how we can customize the levels at the handler level, I'm adding two file handlers to the logger, one at the WARNING level and the other at the CRITICAL level.

After we log multiple messages at all levels, we see that each file captures the records at their designated levels. The taskier_critical.log file has only one CRITICAL record, and the taskier_warning.log file has WARNING, ERROR, and CRITICAL messages.

12.2.3 *Setting formats to the handler*

In the preceding section, you learned about initializing a logger and configuring the logger with a file handler and the desired logging level. Another important configuration is formatting the log records. Without proper formatting, it's hard to locate the problems. The goal of formatting log records is to highlight the key information in each log record, such as the time of the event and the level of the message.

Although we could have continued to configure a file handler for formatting, we must read the log file to retrieve the log records, which is somewhat inconvenient for tutorial purposes. Thus, we'll use a stream handler instead. The stream handler outputs the log records in an interactive console, making it easier to see the results (see the following listing).

> **Listing 12.7 Formatting log records for a stream handler**

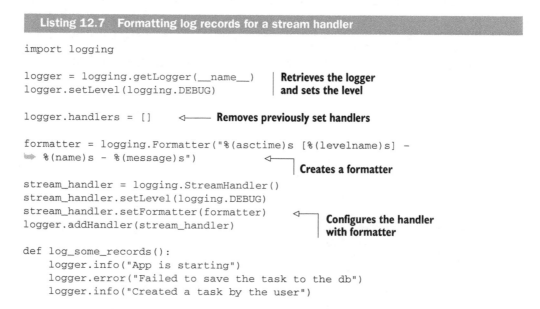

```
import logging

logger = logging.getLogger(__name__)        Retrieves the logger
logger.setLevel(logging.DEBUG)              and sets the level

logger.handlers = []        ←——— Removes previously set handlers

formatter = logging.Formatter("%(asctime)s [%(levelname)s] –
   %(name)s - %(message)s")                 ←┐
                                              │ Creates a formatter
stream_handler = logging.StreamHandler()
stream_handler.setLevel(logging.DEBUG)
stream_handler.setFormatter(formatter)       ←┐ Configures the handler
logger.addHandler(stream_handler)            │ with formatter

def log_some_records():
    logger.info("App is starting")
    logger.error("Failed to save the task to the db")
    logger.info("Created a task by the user")
```

```
        logger.critical("Can't update the status of the task")

log_some_records()

# output the following lines:
2022-05-18 10:45:00,900 [INFO] - __main__ - App is starting
2022-05-18 10:45:00,907 [ERROR] - __main__ - Failed to save the
⇒ task to the db
2022-05-18 10:45:00,912 [INFO] - __main__ - Created a task by the user
2022-05-18 10:45:00,917 [CRITICAL] - __main__ - Can't update the
⇒ status of the task
```

As shown in listing 12.7, the `logging` module has the `Formatter` class, which we can use to create an instance for formatting. Please note that the formatter uses % style instead of f-strings (section 2.1), per the requirement of the class. In essence, the formatter should include the time when the event is recorded, the level of the record, and the message. It's also useful to include the name of the module—in our case, the __main__ module, because we run it in an interactive console.

From the printout records, as you can tell, the readability of the log is much improved. It's much easier for us to focus on records, such as `ERROR` and `CRITICAL`, because the records include the level. In the meantime, we have the timestamps of the events, which we can use to correlate the events with applicable events outside our application. If we see many errors at midnight, for example, is that because the server is under maintenance at that time?

> **READABILITY** Always format the log records to make it easier to locate pertinent problems.

12.2.4 Discussion

By now, you should have a good understanding of how logging works in Python. Figure 12.3 illustrates the general workflow of logging.

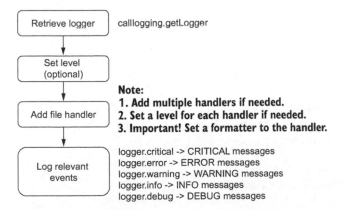

Figure 12.3 The general process of logging. The first step is retrieving the logger by calling `getLogger`. Then (optionally) we can set a level of the logger. To log records in a file, we should add a file handler to the logger. We can call the corresponding method to record a message at a specific level.

We should be clear about what the five levels are and use them in an expected manner. If some functionalities are essential to the normal execution of the software, for example, you should log them as CRITICAL when they go wrong. Because a logger can log only messages at levels equal to or above the set level, if we want to have more-inclusive log records, it's important to set the logger's level to INFO or DEBUG so that more records can be captured.

12.2.5 *Challenge*

John is new to event logging in a project. He has realized that he can set levels to both the logger and the handler. Suppose that the logger has the level of WARNING, and the handler has the level of DEBUG. What happens if he calls logger.info("It's an info message.")? Will the handler capture this record?

> **HINT**   The message is checked against the logger's level before the logger sends it to a handler.

12.3   *How do I handle exceptions?*

When we discussed how to convert strings to obtain their underlying data in section 2.2, you learned that some strings represent numbers (such as "1" and "2") and that we can call the int constructor with these strings to obtain these integer values. Suppose that our task management app has a function that processes string data, which represents a row of data in a text file that stores tasks. For simplicity, suppose that a task has only title and urgency levels as its attributes:

```
from collections import namedtuple          Creates a named
Task = namedtuple("Task", ["title", "urgency"])  ⟵  tuple class
task_text0 = "Laundry,3"

def process_task_string0(text):             Unpacks the
    title, urgency_str = text.split(",")  ⟵  created list object
    urgency = int(urgency_str)
    task = Task(title, urgency)
    return task

processed_task0 = process_task_string0(task_text0)

assert processed_task0 == Task(title='Laundry', urgency=3)
```

In this code snippet, we define the process_task_string0 to process the text data and create an instance of the Task class. Everything seems to be fine. But what can happen if the text is corrupted as Laundry,3#? Let's try it:

```
task_text1 = "Laudry,3#"
processed_task1 = process_task_string0(task_text1)
# ERROR: ValueError: invalid literal for int() with base 10: '3#'
```

We can't convert 3# to a valid integer by calling int("3#"), which leads to the Value-Error exception.

On many occasions, we can't assume things will go as we expect, particularly when dealing with blocks of code that require specific input to work. The `int` constructor, for example, requires an integer or a string representing an integer value. In such a case, we should handle the potential `ValueError` exception during the development phase, preventing the error from stopping our application during its run time. This section discusses the key aspects of exception handling in Python.

12.3.1 Handling exceptions with try...except...

When exceptions such as `ValueError` happen, your application stops running (unless the exception handled as discussed in this section). This phenomenon—when software stops execution abruptly—is commonly known as a *crash*. Software can crash in different ways, some of which are outside the control of the software itself, such as when the computer runs out of memory. When we expect that running a block of code could result in specific exceptions, for example, we should account for this possibility by handling the exceptions properly to prevent the application from crashing. In this section, we'll see the basic code blocks for exception handling.

Exceptions, or *errors,* are a general concept in all programming languages. The standard way to handle exceptions in Python is to use the `try...except...` block. Many other languages use `try...catch...` blocks. Figure 12.4 shows the general workflow of the `try...except...` statement.

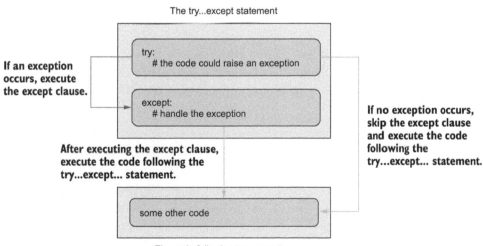

Figure 12.4 The workflow of a `try...except` statement. We include the code that potentially raises an exception in the `try` clause. When such an exception is raised, the `except` clause gets executed, and execution moves to the code outside the statement. If no exception is raised when the code in the `try` clause is executed, Python skips the `except` clause.

As shown in figure 12.4, Python tries to execute the code in the `try` clause. If everything works well, it skips the except clause and continues to run the code outside the try...except statement. If an exception does occur, the except clause gets executed, and any code in the try clause following the code that raises the exception is skipped too. The next listing shows an example of how try...except... works.

Listing 12.8   Using try...except in a function

```
def process_task_string1(text):
    title, urgency_str = text.split(",")
    try:
        urgency = int(urgency_str)
    except:
        print("Couldn't cast the number")
        return None
    task = Task(title, urgency)
    return task
```

> **PEEK**   Don't use a bare except statement. See section 12.3.2.

In listing 12.8, the process_task_string1 function includes the try...except... statement. Specifically, in the try clause, we include code that potentially raises an exception—in this case, the casting of the urgency_str to an integer. As an important note, we don't want to fill the try clause with lots of code because it makes it hard to know which code can lead to an exception.

> **READABILITY**   The try clause should include only the code that can raise an exception.

For simplicity and demonstration purposes, the except clause includes calling the print function. It's important to know that the except clause gets executed only if an exception is caught. We can observe this effect in the following code snippet:

```
processed_task1 = process_task_string1(task_text1)
# output: Couldn't cast the number

assert processed_task1 is None
```

We return None in the except clause, and we can verify it by comparing processed_task1 with None. If the execution of the try clause doesn't raise any exception, the except clause is skipped, and the code outside the try...except... statement continues to execute:

```
processed_task0 = process_task_string1(task_text0)

assert processed_task0 == Task(title='Laundry', urgency=3)
```

> **QUESTION**   Do you think the comparison works with custom class objects instead of a named tuple class like Task in this example?

As you can see, when task_text0 contains the proper data to construct an instance of the Task class, everything works as it does in the process_task_string0 function, as though the try...except... statement doesn't exist in process_task_string1!

12.3.2 *Specifying the exception in the except clause*

In listing 12.8, the except clause uses a bare except by the keyword itself. I don't recommend this usage, however. Instead, the except clause allows us to specify what exception we're handling in the clause. As covered in this section, we should be explicit about the exception to catch.

Specifying the exception is necessary; otherwise, the bare except clause will catch all the exceptions, even those that you don't expect. Suppose that we have a pending task that is to be updated after casting the level of urgency:

```
def process_task_string2(text):
    title, urgency_str = text.split(",")
    try:
        urgency = int(urgency_str)
        pending_task.urgency = urgency
    except:
        print("Couldn't cast the number")
        return None
    task = Task(title, urgency)
    return task
```

> **NOTE** We typically minimize the code in the try clause. I included an extra line of code that results in an exception for teaching purposes only to illustrate the fact that we may have to handle multiple exceptions.

The preceding try clause has an extra line of code: pending_task.urgency = urgency. You may have realized that this code would result in a NameError exception because we never define a variable with this name, and it's not available in any namespace. Observe this effect in the following code snippet:

```
pending_task.urgency = 3
# ERROR: NameError: name 'pending_task' is not defined
```

Thus, when we call process_task_string2, we could have both ValueError and NameError exceptions, and the bare except will handle both exceptions without any differentiation:

```
process_task_string2("Laundry,3")
# output: Couldn't cast the number
```

We should expect task_text0 to get processed without any problems, and we should get a casted urgency level of 3. But the printout message suggests that the number couldn't be casted, suggesting that something is wrong with the casting.

To avoid ambiguity, never use a bare except; instead, be explicit about the exception. In this case, we already know that ValueError is possible; thus, we specify this exception following the except keyword. This clause gets executed if the ValueError exception is raised because the try clause ran, as the next listing shows.

Listing 12.9   Specifying the exception

```
def process_task_string3(text):
    title, urgency_str = text.split(",")
    try:
        urgency = int(urgency_str)
        pending_task.urgency = urgency
    except ValueError:
        print("Couldn't cast the number")
        return None
    task = Task(title, urgency)
    return task
```

With the updated function, the code shows the printout message only if a ValueError exception is caught:

```
process_task_string3("Laundry,3#")
# output: Couldn't cast the number
```

Because the int constructor can't cast "3#" to an integer, the ValueError exception is handled as expected. Note that when we call this function with a string that is expected to produce a correct instance of Task, we should still see a NameError because we don't have code to handle it:

```
process_task_string3("Laudry,3")
# ERROR: NameError: name 'pending_task' is not defined
```

12.3.3   *Handling multiple exceptions*

We know that code executes linearly, and after the casting operation int(urgency_str), the execution continues to pending_task.urgency = urgency, which should raise a NameError exception. As of now, that exception is not handled. We can handle multiple exceptions in the try...except... statement.

We have two ways to handle multiple exceptions. When the exceptions are unrelated, we should use multiple except clauses, with each except handling a distinct kind of exception, as shown in the following listing.

Listing 12.10   Using multiple except clauses

```
def process_task_string4(text):
    title, urgency_str = text.split(",")
    try:
        urgency = int(urgency_str)
```

```
            pending_task.urgency = urgency
    except ValueError:
        print("Couldn't cast the number")
        return None
    except NameError:
        print("You're referencing an undefined name")
        return None
    task = Task(title, urgency)
    return task
```

As shown in listing 12.10, we update the function by adding an extra except clause that handles the potential NameError exception.

> **NOTE**   Our code includes these seemingly "silly" mistakes for demonstration purposes. Some of the mistakes pertain to the quality of the code itself, and these mistakes should be fixed by changing the code instead of handling the exception.

With this update, we can verify that this exception is handled, as shown by the print-out message:

```
process_task_string4("Laundry,3")
# output: You're referencing an undefined name
```

> **MAINTAINABILITY**   Use separate except clauses for exceptions that are unrelated. If the exceptions are semantically related, you can group them by using a single except clause. If you prefer, however, you can still handle these exceptions separately.

Besides using multiple except clauses, you can specify multiple exceptions in a single except clause to handle multiple exceptions. The next listing shows an example.

Listing 12.11   Multiple exceptions in an except clause

```
def process_task_string5(text):
    title, urgency_str = text.split(",")
    try:
        urgency = int(urgency_str)
        pending_task.urgency = urgency
    except (ValueError, NameError):
        print("Couldn't process the task string")
        return None
    task = Task(title, urgency)
    return task
```

In this example, we list both exceptions as a tuple object in a single except clause. This way, if either exception is caught, the same except clause gets executed:

```
process_task_string5("Laundry,3")          ◁——— Expect the NameError.
# output: Couldn't process the task string
```

```
process_task_string5("Laundry,3#")                    ⟵——— Expect the ValueError.
# output: Couldn't process the task string
```

We tried two different strings, with `"Laundry,3"` raising the `NameError` exception and `"Laundry,3#"` raising the `ValueError` exception. Please note that when an exception is caught, the execution jumps to the except clause. In the latter case, when running `int(urgency_str)` raises the `ValueError`, we wouldn't expect the `NameError` too.

12.3.4 *Showing more information about an exception*

The except clause handles the specified exception when such an exception is caught. In the code examples that I've used so far, I've printed out messages as feedback on the exception. But these messages lack details about the exceptions, and I could show users more specific information.

To obtain more information about an exception that is caught, we can assign the exception to a variable, using the `except SpecificException as var_name` syntax. We can update our function to take advantage of this feature as shown in the next listing.

> **Listing 12.12   Creating a variable from the exception**

```
def process_task_string6(text):
    title, urgency_str = text.split(",")
    try:
        urgency = int(urgency_str)
    except ValueError as ex:
        print(f"Couldn't cast the number. Description: {ex}")
        return None
    task = Task(title, urgency)
    return task
```

As highlighted in listing 12.12, we assign the caught `ValueError` exception as ex so that we can use this variable in the clause. For simplicity, we'll print out only the `ValueError` exception:

```
process_task_string6("Laundry,3#")
# output the following line:
Couldn't cast the number. Description: invalid literal
⟿ for int() with base 10: '3#'
```

From the message, we know that the casting fails because `"3#"` can't be converted to an integer number. Please note that I call the `print` function to show a detailed description of the exception for teaching purposes. For a frontend application, such as the task management app, we can display a `WARNING` message to notify users of this mistake, and they can correct it accordingly.

12.3.5 Discussion

Handling exceptions properly is key to improving the user's experience with your applications. We can't overlook the consequences of exceptions; they'll crash your applications when they're not handled properly. Thus, during the development phase of our applications, we should be cautious about code that can easily go wrong. Don't be concerned about using `try...except...` statements in code. Although they may appear to lengthen the code, they make applications more robust; they can still run even when exceptions occur because they're handled properly.

12.3.6 Challenge

Bob is an experienced programmer who uses best practices in his code. He understands that when he writes a `try...except...` statement, he should be explicit about the exact exceptions that he's handling. Many kinds of exceptions exist. How can he find out which exception is appropriate for a specific use case during the development phase? In listing 12.9, for example, how can he know that he needs to handle a possible `ValueError` exception?

> **HINT** Besides looking up information about exceptions in the official Python documentation, you can run the potentially problematic code to see what exceptions you're getting; then you can handle them accordingly.

12.4 How do I use else and finally clauses in exception handling?

The most basic form of handling exceptions in Python is using the `try...except...` statement. This statement consists of one `try` clause and at least one `except` clause. The following example is part of listing 12.12:

```
try:
    urgency = int(urgency_str)
except ValueError as ex:
    print(f"Couldn't cast the number. Description: {ex}")
    return None
task = Task(title, urgency)
```

We know that the code `task = Task(title, urgency)` runs after the `try...except...` statement. Notably, the except clause includes a `return` statement (`return None`). If I didn't include it, we would encounter the `UnboundLocalError` exception due to running `task = Task(title, urgency)` without defining `urgency` in the except clause. But we know that the code `task = Task(title, urgency)` is relevant only if the code in the `try` clause runs without raising exceptions. Is there a better way to make clear that we want some code to run only if there are no exceptions? This question leads to the topic of the next section: adding an `else` clause to the `try...except...` statement. Section 12.4.2 discusses the `finally` clause, another optional component in the full `try...except...` statement.

12.4.1 *Using else to continue the logic of the code in the try clause*

In section 12.3, I mentioned that it's critical to minimize the length of the try clause by including only the code that can raise exceptions. When the try clause completes its execution, Python runs the code after the try...except... statement. The code after the statement, however, makes sense only if executing the code in the try clause doesn't raise any exceptions. To implement this feature, we should use the else clause on top of the try and except clauses.

In the try...except... statement, the try keyword means that we're going to try some code that may raise exceptions, and the except keyword means that we're going to handle the exceptions we're catching. How about the term else? This name may sound confusing. (What *else*?) To understand it, we must acknowledge that the entire try...except...else... statement aims to handle exceptions. More specifically, one objective is to catch such exceptions. Thus, it makes sense to say that if we can catch the exception, we'll handle it; otherwise, we'll continue execution. The else clause does the job for the "otherwise" portion. The next listing shows an example.

> **Listing 12.13   Adding the `else` clause to the `try...except` statement**

```
def process_task_string7(text):
    title, urgency_str = text.split(",")
    try:
        urgency = int(urgency_str)
    except ValueError as ex:
        print(f"Couldn't cast the number. Description: {ex}")
        return None          ⟵
    else:                            You can omit this optional
        task = Task(title, urgency)   return None statement.
        return task
```

As shown in listing 12.13, we include an else clause after the except clause. In the else clause, we create an instance object of the Task class (defined at the beginning of section 12.3) using title and urgency. We should expect to obtain an instance object if we don't have the ValueError exception:

```
processed_task7 = process_task_string7("Laundry,3")

assert processed_task7 == Task("Laundry", 3)
```

As shown in this code snippet, we obtain an instance class of the Task class, which suggests that the code in the else clause executes successfully. What happens when a ValueError exception is raised? Observe the result:

```
processed_task = process_task_string7("Laundry,3#")
# output the following line:
Couldn't cast the number. Description: invalid literal for
➥ int() with base 10: '3#'

print(processed_task)
# output: None
```

The first thing to note is that the except clause executes because of the caught Value-Error exception. The other thing to note is that the return value of calling process_task_string7 is None, which suggests that the code in the else clause doesn't run when the except clause runs and returns None.

12.4.2   *Cleaning up the exception handling with the finally clause*

As you saw in section 12.4.1, only one of the except and else clauses runs. If the try clause raises exceptions, the except clause (handled exceptions) runs; if the try clause raises no exceptions, the else clause runs. Sometimes, however, we have some code that we'd like to run regardless of the exception status. In the function that processes the task string, for example, we may want to notify users that the processing has been done, whether or not it was successful. That task is exactly what the finally clause can do, as we'll see in this section. Figure 12.5 provides a graphic overview of the four possible clauses in exception handling.

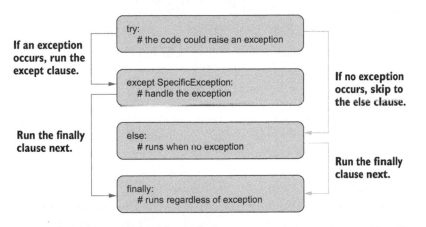

Figure 12.5   The four clauses in a complete try...except...else...finally... statement. The try clause includes the code that could raise an exception. The except clause includes the code that handles the possible exception. The else clause runs only if no exceptions are raised. The finally clause runs after the except clause or the else clause.

As indicated by its name, the finally clause should be placed at the end of the try...except... statement (figure 12.5). If you use an else clause, the finally clause should follow it; otherwise, it follows the except clause. The code in the finally clause runs no matter what the exception-raising status is. The next listing shows how finally works by continuing the example of processing a string that stores a task's data.

Listing 12.14   Using the `finally` clause in the `try...except` statement

```python
def process_task_string8(text):
    title, urgency_str = text.split(",")
    try:
        urgency = int(urgency_str)
    except ValueError as ex:
```

```
            print(f"Couldn't cast the number. Description: {ex}")
            return None
        else:
            task = Task(title, urgency)
            return task
        finally:
            print(f"Done processing text: {text}")
```

In listing 12.14, we add the `finally` clause to the `try...except...` statement. For simplicity, we print out a message showing that the processing is done. This `finally` clause should run whether or not the `ValueError` exception is raised:

```
task_no_exception = process_task_string8("Laundry,3")
# output the following line:
Done processing text: Laundry,3

task_exception = process_task_string8("Laundry,3#")
# output the following lines:
Couldn't cast the number. Description: invalid literal for int()
➥ with base 10: '3#'
Done processing text: Laundry,3#
```

In both invocations of the `process_task_string8` function, we see that the `finally` clause executes by printing out the f-string message. You may wonder what the point of using the `finally` clause is. If it's going to run regardless of exception status, why don't we place it outside the `try...except...` statement? Because we know that code typically executes linearly, by placing it outside the statement, we guarantee that it will follow the except or `else` clause.

As you may notice, I used the word *typically* because an atypical rule applies to the `finally` clause. If the `try` clause reaches a `break`, `continue`, or `return` statement, the `finally` clause runs before executing the `break`, `continue`, or `return` statement. This rule is necessary to ensure that the code in the `finally` clause runs, because in a typical scenario, these statements end the current execution and skip the remaining code. We can observe this effect in the following example:

```
def process_task_string9(text):
    title, urgency_str = text.split(",")
    try:
        urgency = int(urgency_str)
        task = Task(title, urgency)
        return task
    except ValueError as ex:
        print(f"Couldn't cast the number. Description: {ex}")
        return None
    finally:
        print(f"Done processing text: {text}")

task = process_task_string9("Laundry,3")
# output: Done processing text: Laundry,3

assert task == Task("Laundry", 3)
```

As highlighted in the code snippet, we include a return statement in the try clause. Unlike in other scenarios, the return statement ends a function's execution immediately. Here, we see that the print function is called in the finally clause, supporting our earlier notion that the finally clause runs regardless of the exception status and even if the try or except clause contains a return statement. Because a finally clause executes whether or not an exception is raised, we often use a finally clause when we deal with shared resources, such as files and network connections. We want to release those resources (in the finally clause) whether or not the desired operation is done (in the try clause) or an exception is raised (in the except clause).

12.4.3 Discussion

Of the four clauses in the exception handling feature, you should always use try and except because they constitute the fundamentals of handling an exception. The try clause "tries" to run the code, as it may raise exceptions, and the except clause catches and handles the exceptions. Although the else and finally clauses are optional, they have their use cases, which you should know.

12.4.4 Challenge

We know that in the presence of the finally clause, if the try clause includes a return statement, it still runs the code in the finally clause before running the return statement in the try clause. What's the return value of calling the process_task_challenge function in the following example?

```
def process_task_challenge(text):
    title, urgency_str = text.split(",")
    try:
        urgency = int(urgency_str)
        task = Task(title, urgency)
        return task
    except ValueError as ex:
        print(f"Couldn't cast the number. Description: {ex}")
        return None
    finally:
        print(f"Done processing text: {text}")
        return "finally"

processed = process_task_challenge("Laundry,3")
print(processed)
```

HINT   Because the code in the finally clause runs before the return statement in the try clause, it ends the function immediately, as the finally clause includes a return statement itself. The return statement in the try clause is skipped.

12.5 How do I raise informative exceptions with custom exception classes?

When we learn to program in Python, we make various kinds of mistakes. Some errors are due to syntax errors, such as missing the colon in the `if...else...` statement. When we have a basic understanding of all the syntaxes, we may encounter other errors related mostly to the correct use of specific features from a semantic or logical perspective. As extensively used in sections 12.3 and 12.4, `ValueError` is such an error. As another example, when we try to divide a number by zero, we encounter the `ZeroDivisionError`:

```
int("3#")
# ERROR: ValueError: invalid literal for int() with base 10: '3#'

1 / 0
# ERROR: ZeroDivisionError: division by zero
```

In both cases, the error message not only tells us the specific exception name, but also supplies a description of the error, which helps us figure out what we did incorrectly. When we're creating a library or package for other developers to use, it's important to display a proper error message to users so that they know how to debug their code or handle the exception. In this section, you'll learn how to raise informative exceptions with custom exception classes.

12.5.1 Raising exceptions with a custom message

So far, we've seen the exceptions raised when Python evaluates our code. We haven't learned how to raise exceptions ourselves, however. In this section, I'll show how we can raise exceptions and how to provide custom messages for exceptions.

> **CONCEPT**   When we "produce" an exception in the code to indicate some problems, we say that we *raise* an exception. Some other languages use *throw* for this purpose.

I've been using *raise* to state that some code produces an exception. Not surprisingly, raise is a keyword in Python for raising exceptions. When we run the following code in the console, we should also see the traceback:

```
>>> raise ValueError
Traceback (most recent call last):
  File "<stdin>", line 1, in <module>
ValueError

>>> raise ZeroDivisionError
Traceback (most recent call last):
  File "<stdin>", line 1, in <module>
ZeroDivisionError
```

We raise an exception by using the format `raise ExceptionClass`. `ValueError` and `ZeroDivisionError` are two exception classes. Strictly speaking, when we raise an exception, we're raising an instance object of the exception class; thus, the format of this example is syntactic sugar for `raise ExceptionClass()`, in which `Exception-Class()` creates an instance object of the class.

> **CONCEPT**   In programming, *syntactic sugar* refers to usages that are simple but perform the same operations as counterparts that are more complicated.

It's also true that when we handle an exception, we're dealing with an instance of an exception class. Observe the effect in this example:

```
try:
    1 / 0
except ZeroDivisionError as ex:
    print(f"Type: {type(ex)}")
print(f"Is an instance of ZeroDivisionError?
    {isinstance(ex, ZeroDivisionError)}")

# output the following lines:
Type: <class 'ZeroDivisionError'>
Is an instance of ZeroDivisionError? True
```

As shown in this example, we know that `1 / 0` leads to raising the `ZeroDivisionError` exception, and we handle it in the `except` clause. From the printout message, we know that the raised exception is indeed an instance object of the `ZeroDivisionError` class.

Running `raise ValueError` doesn't seem to be useful. If you recall, when we call `int("3#")`, the error message explicitly tells us the cause of this exception: `Value-Error: invalid literal for int() with base 10: ' 3#'`. To supply a custom message to the exception, we use the format `raise ExceptionClass("custom message")`. A few examples follow:

```
raise ValueError("Please use the correct parameter.")
# ERROR: ValueError: Please use the correct parameter.

code_used = "3#"
raise ValueError(f"You used a wrong parameter: {code_used!r}")  ◄──┐
# ERROR: ValueError: You used a wrong parameter: '3#'
```

Uses the repr `!r` conversion to make a string within quotes

When we supply a custom message to the exception class constructor, the raised exception is accompanied by the message, which informs users of the details of the exception. Please note that this message should be concise; we don't want to overwhelm users with a chunky description that may only confuse them.

> **READABILITY**   When you supply custom messages to an exception class, be concise.

12.5.2 *Preferring built-in exception classes*

When we discussed data models in the early chapters, you learned about the built-in data types, such as str (chapter 2), list, and tuple (chapter 3) before you learned about custom classes (chapters 8 and 9). The reason for this order is that built-in data types are the most basic form for representing data, and all Python programmers understand them well. We can apply the same philosophy to exceptions. When we need to raise exceptions, we prefer using built-in exception types.

We know that exceptions are raised by creating instance objects from exception classes. Thus, to use built-in exception classes, we need to know the most common ones. Don't be afraid of not knowing them; everyone who's learning to code makes all kinds of mistakes that raise exceptions. You'll gradually learn which exception is associated with what errors in your code. Figure 12.6 provides an overview of common exceptions.

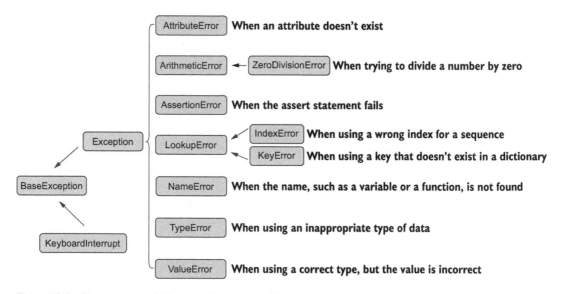

Figure 12.6   The common built-in exception classes. The BaseException class is the superclass for all other exception classes. Most exception classes that we interact with are subclasses of the Exception class.

BaseException is the base class for all built-in exceptions, including system-exiting exceptions such as KeyboardInterrupt and SystemExit. As a rule, we should not inherit this class to define our own custom exception classes; instead, we should use the Exception class (see section 12.5.3) to avoid catching system-exiting exceptions. Common exception classes that we've encountered, such as ValueError and Name-Error, are direct or indirect subclasses of the Exception class.

Although it's not difficult to define custom exception classes, when we think of raising an exception, we should first consider the built-in exception classes because they're better known by ordinary developers. Consider a simple example:

```
class Task:
    def __init__(self, title):
        self.title = title
```

In this code snippet, we define the `Task` class with a `title` attribute, which is a string. As of now, we don't force users to use a `str` object to instantiate the `Task` class. If we do want to enforce this requirement, we can include type checking in our code and raise an exception when the supplied argument isn't a `str` object, as shown in the next listing.

Listing 12.15   Creating a class that raises an exception in its constructor

```
class Task:
    def __init__(self, title):
        if isinstance(title, str):
            self.title = title
        else:
            raise TypeError("Please instantiate the Task
            ➥ using string as its title")

task = Task(100)
# ERROR: TypeError: Please instantiate the Task using string as its title
```

By using the built-in `TypeError` in listing 12.15, we make it easier for users to understand that they used a wrong type for the argument.

> **READABILITY**   Prefer using built-in exception classes when you raise exceptions, as they're more familiar to users.

12.5.3 Defining custom exception classes

When you create your own Python package, it's common to define custom exception classes if the built-in ones can't meet your needs. In this section, I'll show you the best practices for defining custom exception classes.

As mentioned briefly in section 12.5.2, our custom exception classes should inherit from the `Exception` class. For a custom package, the best practice is to create a base exception class for your package and then create additional exception classes by inheriting your base exception class. Creating a base exception for your package allows users to handle all the exceptions of your package, should such a need arise.

Create a base exception class for your package if you need to define your own custom exception classes, which should inherit from the base class. Suppose that for the task management app, we're making the app a package that other developers can use to build their own apps. They can use the `Task` class as the data model to build another app by using a different frontend library, for example. For this package, which might be named `taskier`, we can define a base exception class named `TaskierError`:

```
class TaskierError(Exception):
    pass
```

In this package-specific base exception class, we don't need to have any implementation details. We can simply use a pass statement to fulfill the syntax requirement. (A class's body can't be empty.)

For the taskier package, we can define more specific exception classes. We can allow the users to upload a CSV file from their computers to retrieve the data from multiple tasks, for example. The following listing defines an exception requiring the file to have the .csv extension.

Listing 12.16   Defining a custom exception class

```python
class FileExtensionError(TaskierError):
    def __init__(self, file_path):
        super().__init__()
        self.file_path = file_path

    def __str__(self):
        return f"The file ({self.file_path}) doesn't appear to be a
        ➥ CSV file."


# In another part of our package
from pathlib import Path

def upload_file(file_path):
    path = Path(file_path)
    if path.suffix.lower() != ".csv":
        raise FileExtensionError(file_path)
    else:
        print(f"Processing the file at {file_path}")
```

Notice two significant things in listing 12.16:

- *The custom exception class can take additional arguments for instantiation.* Here, we include the file_path argument (note that the message for creating an exception is optional) because we want to show readers that the file at the specified path isn't in the correct form.
- *We override the __str__ method.* As you may recall from section 8.4, this method is called when we print an instance object.

In another part of our package, we use this exception class. As shown in the preceding code, the upload_file function checks the file's extension (section 11.5) and raises the exception when the extension is incorrect.

When another developer uses our package, they may build a control widget, allowing users to upload a file. They may have the following functionality in their app:

```python
def custom_upload_file(file_path):
    try:
        upload_file(file_path)
    except FileExtensionError as ex:
        print(ex)
```

```
        else:
            print("Custom upload file is done.")


custom_upload_file("tasks.csv")     #A Calling the function with a CSV file
# output the following lines:
Processing the file at tasks.csv
Custom upload file is done.

custom_upload_file("tasks.docx")    #B Calling the function with a docx file
# output: The file at tasks.docx doesn't appear to be a CSV file.
```

In this example, we call the custom function with two different types of files: CSV files and Microsoft Word document files. As you can see, when we don't use the correct file, the except clause catches the FileExtensionError and prints the message that we implement in the __str__ class.

We can define additional custom exception classes in our package if necessary. We can define an exception class called FileFormatError to use when the file doesn't contain the desired data, for example. As another example, we can define an exception class called InputArgumentError to use when developers use wrong arguments for critical functions. Both classes should inherit the TaskierError. Figure 12.7 shows the hierarchy of exception classes in a custom package.

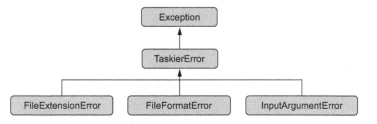

Figure 12.7   The hierarchy of custom exception classes in a custom package. We create a package-specific base exception class by inheriting the Exception class. From this base class, we can define multiple exception classes that raise specific exceptions.

12.5.4 *Discussion*

Although you can define custom exception classes to raise informative exceptions, you should prefer using the built-in exception classes whenever possible. If you're creating a custom package or library, however, you may find that it makes more sense to create your own custom exception classes to produce more specific error messages, thus helping the users of the package (developers) debug the problems. Notably, you should define a package-specific base exception class first. These custom exception classes behave like regular custom classes, and you can override special methods such as __str__ if necessary.

12.5.5 *Challenge*

In listing 12.15, the `Task` class can raise the `TypeError` exception in its constructor. Can you write some code that handles this exception by using the `try...except... else...finally...` statement?

> **HINT**   You should call the constructor in the `try` clause and handle the possible `TypeError` exception.

Summary

- It's best practice to call `getLogger` to retrieve the logger for your module, which guarantees that you obtain the same logger instead of creating multiple ones.
- For long-term storage purposes, it's common to attach a file handler to a logger so that log records can be saved to files.
- During the development phase, it's helpful to show the logs in a console. You can also add a stream handler to the logger.
- To better track the severity of log records, you should categorize those records with different levels: `DEBUG`, `INFO`, `WARNING`, `ERROR`, and `CRITICAL`.
- You can set the logger and the handlers with a proper logging level so that they track records at the desired level.
- For readability, it's always a good idea to format the log records. Key information includes the timestamp, the level of severity, the applicable module, and the message.
- The `try...except...` statement is the basic format for handling exceptions in Python. The `try` clause should include only the code that can raise exceptions. You should be explicit about the exceptions that you're handling in the `except` clause.
- Although you can bundle multiple exceptions as a `tuple` object in a single `except` clause, I recommend that you use multiple `except` clauses instead of one `except` clause—unless the exceptions are indeed closely related.
- The `else` clause runs when the `try` clause doesn't raise exceptions. The `finally` clause can be used to clean up exception handling; it runs no matter whether an exception is raised in the `try` clause.
- You can raise exceptions by using the built-in exception classes and supply custom messages to these exceptions to be more informative.
- When you define custom exception classes, remember that you should inherit the `Exception` class but not the `BaseException` class.
- If your package includes custom exception classes, it's best practice to define a package-specific base exception class from which you define additional custom exception subclasses.

Debugging and testing

13

This chapter covers

- Reading tracebacks
- Debugging your application interactively
- Testing functions
- Testing a class

Completing a programming project from scratch to production is like building a house. After you lay out the foundation, set up the frames and walls, complete the roof, and install the doors and windows, you feel that most of the house is done. But when you proceed to interior decoration, such as flooring, lights, furniture, and closets, you'll realize that it's still far from completion.

You've worked hard on your application for three months, feeling that you've completed 90% of the project. Before you push it into production, however, you must ensure its performance by debugging and testing it rigorously. It wouldn't surprise me if the last estimated 10% costs you another three months—the same amount of time you needed for the first 90%. The debugging and testing phase is analogous to the interior decoration of a house—it's so essential that your application can't live without it—and you don't want to hear your client's complaints after launch day. Thus, let's tackle the debugging and testing jobs while the application

367

is still in our possession. In this chapter, you'll learn the essential techniques that you can apply to conduct a rigorous final touch-up of your application: debugging and testing.

13.1 How do I spot problems with tracebacks?

When our code fails to run due to exceptions, Python not only tells us about the exception, but also provides other information about where the exception is raised. Suppose that when we defined the `Task` class, we misspelled a method call. When we create an instance object of the `Task` class and call the instance method `update_urgency`, we'll encounter an `AttributeError` exception. Try running the code in the next listing in a console.

Listing 13.1 Showing a traceback when running some code

```
class Task:
    def __init__(self, title, urgency):
        self.title = title
        self.urgency = urgency

    def _update_db(self):
        # update the record in the database
        print("update the database")

    def update_urgency(self, urgency):
        self.urgency = urgency
        self.update_db()
```

The line number is 10 without counting empty lines. → `self.update_db()`

```
task = Task("Laundry", 3)
task.update_urgency(4)
# output the following error:
Traceback (most recent call last):
  File "<stdin>", line 1, in <module>
  File "<stdin>", line 10, in update_urgency
AttributeError: 'Task' object has no attribute 'update_db'
```

The line of code that raises the exception → `task.update_urgency(4)`

> **NOTE** When you submit your code to a console, empty lines are removed, so you see a mismatch between the line number in the traceback and the one in the file. Because we often run code in the console and in a file, I'll show you the tracebacks in both modes in this section.

In most previous code snippets involving exceptions, I showed only the last line of the exception. Here, I'm showing the entire output message of the exception. Besides the exception line, the output has information such as the involved method name and line number, all of which can help us locate the buggy problem. These pieces of information in the output are known as *tracebacks*. Using tracebacks to locate a problem is the first step in debugging our code. In this section, you'll learn how to read tracebacks and how to use them to locate problems in our code.

13.1.1 *Understanding how a traceback is generated*

Tracebacks are detailed descriptions of how an exception is raised. In chapter 12, we learned about reading a traceback's last line, which consists of an exception's type and description. Here, let's step back to understand how a traceback is generated, as it's the basis for us to read tracebacks correctly and collect the information about the exception.

During the running of our application, events happen continuously, such as creating instances, accessing their attributes, and calling their methods. When something doesn't work as expected, our application may encounter an exception and stop execution. Although running a specific line of code, such as task.update_urgency(4) in listing 13.1, appears to be the direct cause of our application's termination, the line may not be the one to blame; the exception may be due to an underlying operation somewhere else. Thus, without resorting to tracebacks, we must understand the general execution process to know how an exception is raised.

Let's use the code in listing 13.1 as an example. Figure 13.1 is a simple diagram of the essential execution steps.

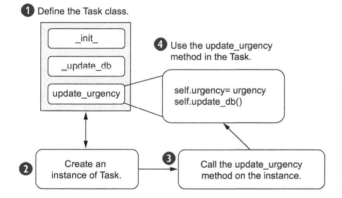

Figure 13.1 **The execution process of the code in listing 13.1. The first step is defining the Task class. The second step is creating an instance of the class. The third step is calling the update_urgency method. The fourth step is using the method's definition in the class.**

The code in listing 13.1 consists of four major steps:

- Defining the Task class
- Creating an instance of Task
- Calling the update_urgency method
- Using the update_urgency method's definition in the class

As annotated in listing 13.1, task.update_urgency(4) leads to the exception, and not because calling the method itself is wrong. Under the hood, something is wrong with the method definition. As you may notice in listing 13.1, update_urgency incorrectly calls update_db instead of _update_db, as it's supposed to do.

These four steps represent a snapshot of execution sequences when running a program, which involves thousands of continuous operations. From a general perspective, we can build an operation tree (figure 13.2). Each box represents a distinct operation. Such an operation can be referred to as a *call*, which corresponds to the term in a traceback's title: `Traceback (most recent call last)`. These operations form the *call stack*, which tracks the progression of the application's execution.

> **CONCEPT**   A *call stack* tracks the sequence of execution from the current call to the underlying operations that are required to complete the execution. These sequential operations form the call stack.

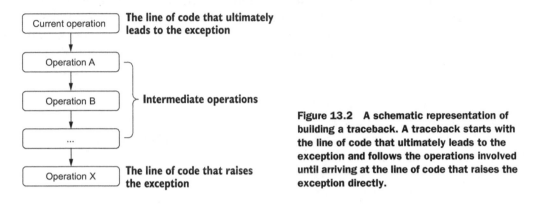

Figure 13.2   **A schematic representation of building a traceback. A traceback starts with the line of code that ultimately leads to the exception and follows the operations involved until arriving at the line of code that raises the exception directly.**

Tracebacks are built on the call stack. They start with the call to the line of code that ultimately leads to the exception and record the operation (or the call) that the line of code invokes. If that operation doesn't raise the exception, tracebacks continue to record the next operation until they locate the code that raises the exception. Figure 13.2 shows a schematic representation of a traceback.

13.1.2 *Analyzing a traceback when running code in a console*

In section 13.1.1, we examined how a traceback is generated under the hood. Now we're ready to find out what elements constitute the traceback generated by running code in a console.

Let's continue with the traceback shown in listing 13.1. Figure 13.3 shows the essential elements of a traceback that is generated by running code in a console.

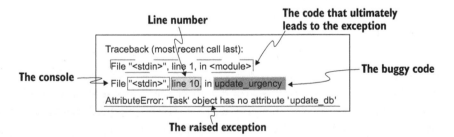

Figure 13.3   **Highlighting the key elements of a traceback generated in a console. Each line represents a distinct operation, as depicted in figure 13.2. For each line, the key elements include the source file of the operation, the line number, and the buggy code. The last line shows the exception.**

Each line in the traceback represents an operation or a call. The first line is the line of code that ultimately leads to the exception: `task.update_urgency(4)`. Let's take a closer look at the second line to examine the key elements. Because we run the code in listing 13.1 in a console, the source of the involved operation is `<stdin>`, which represents the standard input: the console. `Line 10` (annotated in listing 13.1; the line-number counts don't include the empty lines when the code is submitted in the console) is the line where the exception is raised during execution of the `update_urgency` method. Specifically, this line is `self.update_db()`, which can't work because the class doesn't have the `update_db` instance method; therefore, the `AttributeError` exception is raised, as shown in the last line.

13.1.3 *Analyzing a traceback when running a script*

In section 13.1.2, we focused on analyzing a traceback created by running code in a console. From a more general perspective, we often run our code as a script by using a command-line tool. In this section, we'll see more interesting stuff in tracebacks.

To maintain some consistency, save the code in listing 13.1 to a script file named `task_test.py`. Watch for one change toward the end of the code snippet:

```
class Task:
    def __init__(self, title, urgency):
        self.title = title
        self.urgency = urgency

    def _update_db(self):
        # update the record in the database
        print("update the database")

    def update_urgency(self, urgency):
        self.urgency = urgency
        self.update_db()


if __name__ == "__main__":
    task = Task("Laundry", 3)
    task.update_urgency(4)
```

As you can see, instead of creating an instance and calling the method directly, as in listing 13.1, we now include the pertinent code in a conditional statement, which runs only if the special attribute __name__ is equal to "__main__". It's a best practice to include this statement, which allows you to run the file as a script and as a module. When you run the file as a script, the special attribute __name__ has a value of "__main__", so the statement evaluates as `True` and runs the included operations. In the meantime, when you import the file as a module, the module's name is the file's name, which isn't "__main__", so you can't run the included code unexpectedly. In the remaining sections, we'll include the `if` statement in our script files.

> **MAINTAINABILITY**   In most cases, when your Python file is intended to be executed both as a script and a module, you should include the operations in an if statement (if __name__ == "__main__": # operations) if you want these operations to run only as a script. If you don't, when the file is imported as a module, these operations will be executed.

You can run the following command in your command-line tool (listing 13.2), such as the Terminal app if you use a Mac computer or the cmd tool if you use a Windows computer. Please note that you need to navigate to the current directory if you don't use the full path of the script file.

Listing 13.2   Running a Python script that generates a traceback

```
$ python3 task_test.py          ←———————  I use python3, as macOS
                                           defaults to Python version 2.
Traceback (most recent call last):
  File "/full_path/task_test.py", line 17, in <module>
    task.update_urgency(4)
  File "/full_path/task_test.py", line 12, in update_urgency
    self.update_db()
AttributeError: 'Task' object has no attribute 'update_db'. Did you mean:
'_update_db'?
```

$ means the command line's prompt.

Compared with the traceback generated by executing code in a console, the traceback generated by running the script has additional information. As highlighted in listing 13.2, the traceback also shows the exact operation for that call. In the update_urgency method, for example, the code self.update_db() raises the AttributeError exception. The differences between the tracebacks from running the code in the console and running it as a script file arise because Python creates the call stack differently in these two running modes. When the code is running in the console, the call stack tracks only the lines, and while a script is executing, it tracks the specific operations.

13.1.4 *Focusing on the last call in a traceback*

We've seen a couple of tracebacks that are generated by running code in a Python console or executing a script from a command line. You may have noticed where to spot the problem in a traceback, and this section addresses this topic formally.

By design, the traceback shows the call stack in a linear fashion from top to bottom. That is, the last call is shown at the bottom, which directly contributes to the exception that is raised. Thus, to solve the problem, we should focus on the last call. In the examples that we've used, the AttributeError exception informs us of the problem: AttributeError: 'Task' object has no attribute 'update_db'. For the traceback that is generated when we run the file as a script (listing 13.2), the error message even suggests Did you mean: '_update_db'? Please note that this additional information may be not available in earlier Python versions.

TRIVIA   Showing the `Did you mean` exception message is a recent addition to Python. Depending on your Python version and the Python editor you use, you may not see it.

This suggestion is exactly what we should be taking. We go to the definition of the `update_urgency` method, shown in the last call of the traceback (use the line number to locate the code quickly), and replace `update_db` with `_update_db`. Note the difference in using an underscore prefix. After making this change, we can run the script again:

```
$ python3 task_test.py
# output: update the database
```

As expected, we don't see the `AttributeError` exception. Now the script is working properly.

13.1.5 Discussion

In this section, I use a simple example to show the structure of a traceback and how to read it to fix a trivial problem in our code. In general, the last call pertains to the problem that we might fix. When your project uses multiple dependencies, however, it's very likely that you'll see more complicated tracebacks. I bet you'll find that the last call in the traceback isn't your code! When this happens, you must read the traceback upward by tracing to earlier calls, where you'll find the code you wrote. This call is more likely to be the cause of the problem that you want to tackle.

13.1.6 Challenge

Joe is a junior software developer. As part of his job, he's been assigned to debug problems for the work-productivity software that the company develops. As part of his learning experience, he's playing with tracebacks. In listing 13.1, the traceback includes two calls. To have some fun, how can he update the `Task` class by adding and using a few more methods to produce a traceback with more than two calls?

HINT   You can add one or two methods, one of which contains buggy code that raises an exception. Use these methods in other methods to create multiple sequential calls.

13.2 How do I debug my program interactively?

It's always a good idea to identify bugs during the development phase so that you don't have to deal with your clients' complaints after product delivery. You may like to debug the program after every part is (almost) done. But I recommend that you debug your application bit by bit along the road, which minimizes the chances of bugs. Although you can check a traceback from an exception to solve a bug, it's not always enough to let you check each involved operation closely, because an exception crashes your application instantly.

Another essential debugging technique is the *interactive debugger*, which allows you to inspect your application in real time while it's running. In this section, you'll learn about the key features of the built-in debugger. Figure 13.4 shows the general aspects of debugging a program interactively. I cover those aspects in this section.

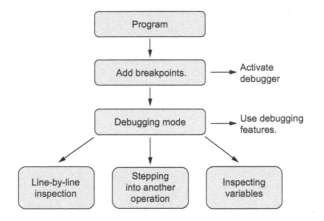

Figure 13.4   **The general aspects of debugging programs in Python. For a program, we add breakpoints to the places where we debug. When the execution encounters the breakpoint, it activates the interactive debugger. Then we can perform a variety of debugging tasks, such as running code line by line.**

As covered in chapters 6 and 7, we know that functions are integral to applications. They also constitute most of the body of a custom class (chapter 8). Writing bug-free functions is the major objective for any programmer, so this section uses functions as examples to show the interactive debugging process.

13.2.1 Activating the debugger with a breakpoint

In most cases, it doesn't take us long to locate a buggy spot, because when our application crashes due to an exception, the generated traceback can inform us about the location of the exception. When we know the problem's location, we can start our intervention by adding a *breakpoint* to activate the debugger.

> **CONCEPT**   A *breakpoint* is a point where you request that your application stop executing for debugging purposes.

As part of the standard Python library, the module pdb provides the essential functionalities for debugging through an interactive debugger. To activate this debugger, you can call its set_trace function:

```
def create_task():
    import pdb; pdb.set_trace()   ◁——— Adding a breakpoint

create_task()
# output the following lines:
--Return--
> <stdin>(2)create_task()->None
(Pdb)
```

In the `create_task` function, you import the `pdb` module and call `set_trace` to insert a breakpoint. (Please note that you could've moved the `import` statement outside the function; it's only a convention to place it before `set_trace`.) When you call this function, you'll notice that the debugger is activated; your Python console has changed its prompt from the default `>>>` to `(Pdb)`, suggesting that Python has entered debug mode.

Although you can activate the debugger by calling `import pdb; pdb.set_trace()`, I'm showing it here so that you'll understand what this line of code means. You may have seen this usage in some legacy projects. A cleaner way, however, is to use a feature that was added in Python 3.7. You call the built-in `breakpoint` function directly, as follows (if you have your debugger on, you can terminate it by pressing q):

```
def create_task():
    breakpoint()

create_task()
```

From the output, you should see that the `breakpoint` function achieves the same effect by activating the debugger; it's a convenience function that calls `set_trace` under the hood. Notably, debug mode is interactive, and many options are available to help you debug your function, as discussed in the next section.

13.2.2 *Running code line by line*

When we carry out an operation, such as a function call, the operations happen instantaneously by executing its entire body. If it succeeds, we get the return value (or `None` implicitly). If it fails, we may get an exception or a value that we don't expect. In either case, the operation is too fast for us to know exactly what's going on with the function. If we can run code line by line, we can gain a better understanding of each step in the operation, giving us a higher chance of solving a possible bug. In this section, I'll show you how to run code line by line. Equally important, you'll see some key options of the debugger.

Suppose that in our task management application, we obtain text data that contains a task's information, and we want to convert this data to an instance object of the `Task` class. For tutorial purposes, let's add a breakpoint in one of the functions and save the code in a script file named `task_debug.py`, as shown in the next listing. Although debugging works when you submit your code in a console, a real project is more like running a script, so we'll use debugging with a script here.

Listing 13.3   Creating a function containing a breakpoint (`task_bebug.py`)

```
from collections import namedtuple
Task = namedtuple("Task", "title urgency")          ◁——— Creating a named tuple class

def obtain_text_data(want_bad):
    text = "Laundry,3#" if want_bad else "Laundry,3"
```

```
        return text

    def create_task(inject_bug: bool):
┌──▷    breakpoint()
        task_text = obtain_text_data(inject_bug)    ◁──── This is line number 10.
        title, urgency_text = task_text.split(",")
        urgency = int(urgency_text)
        task = Task(title, urgency)
        return task


    if __name__ == "__main__":
        create_task(inject_bug=False)
```

Adding a breakpoint

The create_task function creates the task by processing text data from calling obtain_text_data. To allow us to mimic situations when the function call fails, we have a Boolean argument to introduce a bug when needed. With this setup, we can move on to debugging the script without expecting a bug (inject_bug=False). Launch a command-line tool and navigate to the current directory, and then run the following command to execute the script:

```
$ python3 task_debug.py
> /full_path/task_debug.py(10)create_task()
-> task_text = obtain_text_data(inject_bug)
(Pdb)
```

You should see that we're in debug mode with (Pdb) as the prompt. The number (10) informs us of the line number, and current execution stops in the create_task function. It also shows the next line that is going to be executed, which is the calling of the obtain_text_data function.

To execute this line, we can press n, which stands for *next*. You'll see that we complete running the present line, showing the next line of code:

```
> /full_path/task_debug.py(11)create_task()
-> title, urgency_text = task_text.split(",")
(Pdb)
```

If we want to execute the next line, we can press Return (on a Mac) or Enter (on a Windows computer), which should repeat the previous command: n. Execution moves to the next line:

```
> /full_path/task_debug.py(12)create_task()
-> urgency = int(urgency_text)
(Pdb)
```

As you can expect, if we keep pressing Enter or Return, the entire script will complete without any problems. But that's not fun, right? Let's see some other options for debugging.

Sometimes, you may want to see other lines to get a bigger picture of the function. To do that, you can press the l key (lowercase L), because l stands for the `list` command:

```
(Pdb) l
  7
  8      def create_task(inject_bug: bool):
  9          breakpoint()
 10          task_text = obtain_text_data(inject_bug)
 11          title, urgency_text = task_text.split(",")
 12  ->      urgency = int(urgency_text)
 13          task = Task(title, urgency)
 14          return task
 15
 16      if __name__ == "__main__":
 17          create_task(inject_bug=False)
(Pdb)
```

This information is helpful in two ways: it shows all the lines that surround the current line, with the line numbers clearly labeled; and it uses an arrow to indicate the current line.

13.2.3 *Stepping into another function*

In the debugging in section 13.2.2, the first line of code calls another function: `task_text = obtain_text_data(inject_bug)`. You may notice that we get the return value instantaneously. Although it's not the case here, the called function can go wrong, and we may want to zoom into the called function to see its operation. We can quit the current debug session by pressing q and then run the script again in the command-line tool:

```
$ python3 task_debug.py
> /full_path/task_debug.py(10)create_task()
-> task_text = obtain_text_data(inject_bug)
(Pdb)
```

Instead of pressing n, which executes the next line, we want to press s, which stands for *step;* we're asking to execute the next step. In this case, the next step is the calling of the `obtain_text_data` function:

```
(Pdb) s
--Call--
> /full_path/task_debug.py(4)obtain_text_data()
-> def obtain_text_data(want_bad):
```

As you can see, we've zoomed into the function call instead of obtaining its return value directly. If we continue to press s or Return, we'll view the entire function:

```
Pdb) s
> /full_path/task_debug.py(5)obtain_text_data()
-> text = "Laundry,3#" if want_bad else "Laundry,3"
(Pdb) s
> /full_path/task_debug.py(6)obtain_text_data()
-> return text
(Pdb) s
--Return--
> /full_path/task_debug.py(6)obtain_text_data()->'Laundry,3'
-> return text
```

The last operation shows the return value for calling the function: `'Laundry,3'`. If we continue to press s, we'll go back to our original function, `create_task`:

```
(Pdb) s
> /full_path/task_debug.py(11)create_task()
-> title, urgency_text = task_text.split(",")
```

You may notice that the commands n (next) and s (step) are similar, as both commands can execute the next line in most cases. The difference is that step allows you to step into another function call, as you've seen. Figure 13.5 shows the difference between n and s.

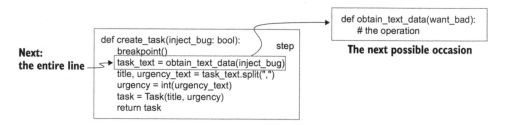

Figure 13.5 The difference between the `next` and `step` commands in debugging. The `next` command executes the entire line; the `step` command attempts to execute the next line but stops at the next possible occasion. In the example, `step` is calling another function.

In figure 13.5, although the step command attempts to execute the next line, it stops at the next possible occasion. In this case, that occasion is the calling of the `obtain_text_data` function.

13.2.4 *Inspecting pertinent variables*

We can see what's being executed, but we haven't done anything proactively. Sometimes, a function call can't work because it doesn't have correct arguments. Even though the arguments may be the correct type, chances are that the values are incompatible, so we want to check the variables' values inside the function. In this section, we'll learn about inspecting variables in a function. We can change the last line of the script (task_debug.py) to `create_task(inject_bug=True)`, and we can run the script from the command line:

```
> /full_path/task_debug.py(10)create_task()
-> task_text = obtain_text_data(inject_bug)
(Pdb) n
> /full_path/task_debug.py(11)create_task()
-> title, urgency_text = task_text.split(",")
(Pdb) n
> /full_path/task_debug.py(12)create_task()
-> urgency = int(urgency_text)
```

Suppose we know that the next line will raise the `AttributeError` exception. We can inspect the pertinent variables to see the potential cause of this exception:

```
(Pdb) p urgency_text
'3#'
```

As shown in the preceding code snippet, we can use the command `p` to retrieve the variable's value. If we want to display multiple variables, we can list them sequentially, with commas as separators:

```
(Pdb) p urgency_text, task_text
('3#', 'Laundry,3#')
```

It can be tedious to list all the variables that we want to check. We can take advantage of the feature that allows us to call a function directly in the debugger. Here, we can call the `locals` function, which shows the local namespace (section 10.4):

```
(Pdb) locals()
{'inject_bug': True, 'task_text': 'Laundry,3#', 'title':
➥ 'Laundry', 'urgency_text': '3#'}
```

We can observe all the variables in the function's local scope, giving us the full picture of the function's status.

13.2.5 Discussion

The tracebacks (section 13.1) provide a snapshot after your application has stopped executing, and everything that leads to the exception happens instantaneously. This static information doesn't give you an opportunity to check each operation in a slow-motion manner; everything happens way too fast. By contrast, the debugger covered in this section is on-demand. You decide when the application can proceed to the next line, which gives you time to study each line closely to identify the possible cause of a bug. More importantly, the debugger is interactive, and you can explore options other than n, l, s, and p. You can find out more about the interactive debugger on the official Python website at https://docs.python.org/3/library/pdb.html.

13.2.6 Challenge

Dylan is an eager learner of Python who wants to know the details of almost every technique. When he learns about debugging, he wants to know what's happening during a function call in terms of the local namespace. For the example discussed in 13.2.4, instead of calling `locals` to retrieve the variables in a local scope after running a few lines, he wants to call `locals` after he starts the debugger. How do you expect the variable lists to change over the course of the function call?

> **HINT**   A namespace is dynamic. After the execution creates a new variable, it's registered in the namespace.

13.3 *How do I test my functions automatically?*

After completing your program's functionalities and removing the obvious bugs through either the tracebacks or interactive debugging, you feel that your application is almost ready for delivery. But you want to do one more thing: test your program thoroughly. Testing is a broad concept that can be manifested in a variety of ways. When you're removing any bugs from your application, you're testing. When you're calling some functions to ensure that they work as expected in your application, you're testing. These examples are manual testing, however.

Although manual testing is acceptable when you work on smaller projects, it can be exhausting if your project's scope is significant; every time you make changes to your code, you may have to go through each involved feature to ensure that it doesn't break due to the changes. As you can imagine, manual testing can be a time-consuming factor that delays your progress. Fortunately, you can develop automatic testing for your application. Specifically, you can write code that tests the codebase of the application. Whenever you make changes to your codebase, you can run the test code, which can save considerable time. In this section, I'll show you some important techniques for implementing automatic testing, with a special focus on functions.

> **MAINTAINABILITY**   Testing is an important tool for ensuring the maintainability of your codebase. Sections 13.3 and 13.4 provide only introductory information. If your job assignment is mainly about testing, you should look at educational materials on testing, such as *The Art of Unit Testing: With Examples in C#*, by Roy Osherove (Manning, 2019).

13.3.1 *Understanding the basis for testing functions*

We know that functions are integral to our application. If we can ensure that every function works as expected, our application will stand strong. This section shows the key elements of testing a function.

Let's start with a simple function, which we can build on when we have more complicated functions to test. Suppose that our task management app has the following function to create a task, as an instance object of the `Task` class, from a string. We're saving the function in the `task_func.py` file so that we can use it in our test, as the next listing shows.

Listing 13.4   Defining a function to be tested (`task_func.py`)

```
class Task:                                    ◄─── Creates a custom class
    def __init__(self, title, urgency):
        self.title = title
        self.urgency = urgency


def create_task(text):
    title, urgency_text = text.split(",")
    urgency = int(urgency_text)
    task = Task(title, urgency)
    return task
```

For a specific functionality in our project (although we can use different implementation details), we generally expect that for given input, a function should return definite output. No matter how we're going to change the implementation details of create_task, for example, we should expect the following to be true:

assert create_task("Laundry,3").__dict__ == Task("Laundry", 3).__dict__

Here, we're using an assert statement to verify the certainty of our function. In this case, we expect the dictionary representation of these two instances to be the same. Please note that instances of a custom class aren't equal out of the box, but their dictionary representations can be compared for equality as a proxy. From a general perspective, this certainty of specific input producing specific output is the basis of testing functions. Figure 13.6 illustrates how testing functions works.

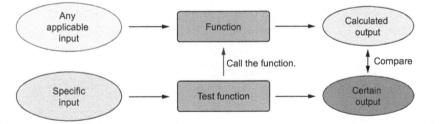

Figure 13.6   The general process of testing functions. In the test function, we use specific input to call the function, and the produced output is compared with the expected output.

13.3.2   Creating a TestCase subclass for testing functions

Now that we know the basis of testing functions, we're ready to implement automatic testing by taking advantage of the unittest module (part of the standard Python library). This module provides important functionalities for testing our program automatically. Specifically, the module's TestCase class allows us to test our function, as shown in the following listing.

Listing 13.5   Testing a function using `TestCase` (`test_task_func.py`)

```
from task_func import Task, create_task
import unittest

class TestTaskCreation(unittest.TestCase):
    def test_create_task(self):
        task_text = "Laundry,3"
        created_task = create_task(task_text)
        self.assertEqual(created_task.__dict__,
        Task("Laundry", 3).__dict__)


if __name__ == "__main__":
    unittest.main()
```

Imports the class and function from the script file

Inherits the TestCase class

Imports the module

Calls the function to be tested

NOTE   If you have problems importing the class and the function, you may want to open the chapter's folder in your Python integrated development environment (IDE).

In listing 13.5, we create the `TestTaskCreation` class by inheriting the `TestCase` class. It's a convention to name our own test classes starting with `Test`. In the body of the class, we define an instance method that is designated to test the `create_task` function. It's important to name this method with the `test_` prefix so that when we run a test, Python knows that this method should be called. Figure 13.7 shows the composition of the test class in relation to the functions we're testing.

READABILITY   Name your test class starting with `Test`, and follow it with the specific functionality your class is testing. Its methods should be named with the `test_` prefix so that Python will run these methods during testing.

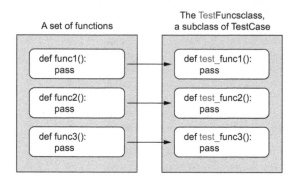

Figure 13.7   **Creating a test class that tests a set of functions. A test function should use `test_` as its prefix, followed by the name of the function that it tests. The class should be named with a prefix of `Test` and is a subclass of the `TestCase`.**

The `test_create_task` method calls the to-be-tested function (`create_task`) with the specific input and compares the return value with the expected output. The comparison is done by calling `assertEqual`, which asserts that the two instances of the `Task` class are equal in their values. If that assertion is true, we're confident that our function works as expected. In the last line, we call `unittest.main()`, which will run all the defined tests in the TestTaskCreation class. With this setup, we're ready to test our function in a command-line tool:

```
$ python3 test_task_func.py
# output the following lines:
.
-------------------------------------------------------------------
Ran 1 test in 0.000s

OK
```

For now, we have one unit of a test case: test_create_task. But we can define multiple test cases.

> **CONCEPT**   A *test case* is an individual unit of testing that checks for a specific response when a particular set of input is provided.

Suppose that we have another function that creates an instance of the Task class from a dict object. We add this function to the task_func.py file as follows:

```
def create_task_from_dict(task_data):
    title = task_data["title"]
    urgency = task_data["urgency"]
    task = Task(title, urgency)
    return task
```

This function should be straightforward: it retrieves the needed values from the dict object and creates the instance object. We can update our test class to test this function too, as shown in the following listing.

Listing 13.6   Testing multiple functions (`test_task_func.py`)

```
from task_func import Task, create_task, create_task_from_dict
import unittest

class TestTaskCreation(unittest.TestCase):
    def test_create_task(self):
        task_text = "Laundry,3"
        created_task = create_task(task_text)
        self.assertEqual(created_task.__dict__,
        ➥ Task("Laundry", 3).__dict__)

    def test_create_task_from_dict(self):
        task_data = {"title": "Laundry", "urgency": 3}
        created_task = create_task_from_dict(task_data)
        self.assertEqual(created_task.__dict__,
        ➥ Task("Laundry", 3).__dict__)


if __name__ == "__main__":
    unittest.main()
```

As with `test_create_task`, we define a method that starts with `test_`. In this added method, we're ensuring that the function works with the special case we've been using. We can run the test again:

```
$ python3 test_task_func.py
# output the following lines:
..
----------------------------------------------------------------------
Ran 2 tests in 0.000s

OK
```

As you can see, we defined two methods in the test class, so Python ran two tests for us, and both were OK. By the way, you may notice the two dots in the first line; the number of dots represents the number of tests that were run.

13.3.3 *Setting up the test*

We've seen how our test class can test two functions together. Notably, these two functions have something in common: both create an instance of the `Task` class. When we test them, we also create an instance of the `Task` class so that we can do the comparison. If you recall (section 2.1.4), repetition is a signal that there may be a need for refactoring. In this section, we set up the test, which can extract things in common in testing functions.

> **MAINTAINABILITY**   Always pay attention to possible opportunities for refactoring, such as code repetition. Refactoring improves your codebase's maintainability.

The `TestClass` has a `setUp` method that we can override. This method is called before running any test, so we can take advantage of this opportunity to carry out the operations that our test method shares. (Please note that these operations depend on what data we set up for our testing.) See the next listing for an example.

Listing 13.7   Overriding the `setUp` method (`test_task_func.py`)

```python
from task_func import Task, create_task, create_task_from_dict
import unittest

class TestTaskCreation(unittest.TestCase):
    def setUp(self):
        task_to_compare = Task("Laundry", 3)
        self.task_dict = task_to_compare.__dict__

    def test_create_task(self):
        task_text = "Laundry,3"
        created_task = create_task(task_text)
        self.assertEqual(created_task.__dict__, self.task_dict)

    def test_create_task_from_dict(self):
        task_data = {"title": "Laundry", "urgency": 3}
```

```
        created_task = create_task_from_dict(task_data)
        self.assertEqual(created_task.__dict__, self.task_dict)


if __name__ == "__main__":
    unittest.main()
```

As highlighted in listing 13.7, we update the class by adding an attribute. Specifically, we're defining the `task_dict`, which holds the `dict` object that our test methods will use for equality comparisons. In the test methods, we can refer to the instance attribute `task_dict` directly; we don't need to create duplicate instance objects for comparison. If we run the test script file again, we'll see the same result.

> **TRIVIA**   As you may have noticed, the methods in the `unittest` module use the lowercase camel naming convention (such as `setUp` and `assertEqual`) instead of snake case (such as `set_up` and `assert_equal`). The methods are named as they are for legacy reasons; they were adapted from Java-based tools, which use camel case.

13.3.4 *Discussion*

In the test class's methods, we only use `assertEqual` to test equality between the desired output and the generated output. But there are other convenient methods to assert that the generated output meets the requirement of the desired output. `assertIn(a, b)`, for example, checks whether a is in b, and `assertTrue(a)` checks whether a is `True`. These methods are straightforward to use, and you should get familiar with them. You can find these methods in the official documentation of the `unittest` module (https://docs.python.org/3/library/unittest.html).

13.3.5 *Challenge*

Aaron is building software for weather forecasting, and he's learning to run some unit tests in his project. While he's following along with this section, in which we defined two functions and tested them with the `TestTaskCreation` class, he's tasked with writing another function and its corresponding test method. Suppose that the function creates an instance of the `Task` class from a `tuple` object `("Laundry", 3)`. Can you provide a solution?

> **HINT**   You can probably name this function `create_task_from_tuple`, in which you can use tuple unpacking (section 4.4) to get the title and urgency level for instantiation.

13.4   *How do I test a class automatically?*

Although functions are integral to our application, the custom classes are the cornerstone of our application, as they're the data models that bundle the necessary data and functionalities as a coherent entity. Typically, we don't need to worry about testing the attributes of a custom class, as those attributes should be defined in a straightforward fashion. Thus, testing a class is mainly about testing its methods, as discussed in this section.

13.4.1 Creating a TestCase subclass for testing a class

Methods are functions, and they're called *methods* because they're defined within a class. Thus, testing a class's methods boils down to testing these functions, which is covered extensively in section 13.3. As you'll see in this section, we'll still create a TestCase subclass for testing a class. The examples use class methods, but the same testing principle applies to instance and static methods too.

In section 13.3, we worked on two functions: create_task and create_task_ from_dict. As you may have realized, we can convert them to custom methods. Because these two methods use the constructor to create an instance of the Task class, they're perfect use cases for class methods, as the next listing shows.

Listing 13.8   Creating a class for testing (`task_class.py`)

```python
class Task:
    def __init__(self, title, urgency):
        self.title = title
        self.urgency = urgency

    @classmethod
    def task_from_text(cls, text_data):
        title, urgency_text = text_data.split(",")
        urgency = int(urgency_text)
        task = cls(title, urgency)
        return task

    @classmethod
    def task_from_dict(cls, task_data):
        title = task_data["title"]
        urgency = task_data["urgency"]
        task = cls(title, urgency)
        return task
```

In listing 13.8, the Task class has the task_from_text and task_from_dict class methods, which are converted from the create_task and create_task_from_dict functions, respectively.

> **REMINDER**   The class method uses cls as its first argument, which refers to the class. See section 8.2.

To test this class, we'll create the TestTask class as a subclass of the TestCase class, in which we define two methods that correspond to the two class methods. Save the code in the next listing in a file called test_task_class.py.

Listing 13.9   Creating a class for testing a class (`test_task_class.py`)

```
from task_class import Task
import unittest

class TestTask(unittest.TestCase):        | Sets up the test
    def setUp(self):                   ◄──┘
        task_to_compare = Task("Laundry", 3)
        self.task_dict = task_to_compare.__dict__

    def test_create_task_from_text(self):
        task_text = "Laundry,3"
        created_task = Task.task_from_text(task_text)
        self.assertEqual(created_task.__dict__, self.task_dict)

    def test_create_task_from_dict(self):
        task_data = {"title": "Laundry", "urgency": 3}
        created_task = Task.task_from_dict(task_data)
        self.assertEqual(created_task.__dict__, self.task_dict)

if __name__ == "__main__":
    unittest.main()
```

As we did with the `TestCreationTask` class, we define the test methods with names starting with `test_` in the `TestTask` class so that when we run the script, all these test methods will run automatically. Observe the effect in the following code snippet:

```
$ python3 test_task_class.py
..
----------------------------------------------------------------------
Ran 2 tests in 0.000s

OK
```

As expected, two tests were run, and neither had problems.

13.4.2 *Responding to test failures*

The purpose of testing is to ensure that the units we're testing work as expected. As you can imagine, the success of all tests is never guaranteed. When some tests fail, we need to know how to respond to those failures. Consider adding the following function to the `Task` class from listing 13.8:

```
def formatted_display(self):
    displayed_text = f"{self.title} ({self.urgency})"
    return displayed_text
```

This instance method creates a formatted display for the task. To test this instance method, we can add the following test method to the `TestTask` class (listing 13.9):

```
def test_formatted_display(self):
    task = Task("Laundry", 3)
    displayed_text = task.formatted_display()
    self.assertEqual(displayed_text, "Laundry(3)")
```

As you may have noticed, to simulate a test failure, I intentionally omitted the space between the task's title and its urgency level in the assertEqual call. If we're running the test, we should expect a failure:

```
$ python3 test_task_class.py
..F
======================================================================
FAIL: test_formatted_display (__main__.TestTask)
----------------------------------------------------------------------
Traceback (most recent call last):
  File "/full_path/test_task_class.py", line 22, in test_formatted_display
    self.assertEqual(displayed_text, "Laundry(3)")
AssertionError: 'Laundry (3)' != 'Laundry(3)'
- Laundry (3)
?        -
+ Laundry(3)


----------------------------------------------------------------------
Ran 3 tests in 0.001s

FAILED (failures=1)
```

Instead of seeing three dots, which correspond to three successful tests, we're seeing ..F. The F indicates a test failure, and the detailed description of the failure informs us why the test fails: because of the AssertionError between these two strings. This error message should give us enough information to solve the problem. We can add a space in the string 'Laundry(3)' to make the comparison equal.

13.4.3 *Discussion*

Testing should be an integral step in software development to ensure the quality of the product. During development, you should focus on removing bugs at the smallest possible scale. That is, you should do some manual testing whenever you complete a feature, even it's a tiny one. You shouldn't think "I'll do the development now without doing any manual testing." It's much easier to solve any problem while you're working on it. Although automatic testing can be powerful, you may have to refresh your memory before you can solve any problems that arise.

13.4.4 *Challenge*

A test that fails doesn't have to be an AssertionError in our test class. It's also possible that something is wrong with our code itself. Can you update the formatted_display method to make it raise an exception and see what happens during the test?

> **HINT** The simplest way to raise an exception is to do so manually, such as raise TypeError.

Summary

- Tracebacks are detailed information that shows you how an exception is raised. The detailed information represents a series of operations or calls.
- When you try to solve the problem from a traceback, you should focus on the last call in a traceback where the exception is raised.
- To examine some code's execution closely, you can set a breakpoint, which activates the debugger. The pdb module is specifically designed for interactive debugging.
- With the interactive debugger, you can move execution line by line (the n command) so that we can know which line is the source of a problem.
- When you want to step into another operation, such as calling a function, you should use the s command instead of the n command, which executes the entire line instantly.
- The unittest module provides functionalities for automatic testing. It has the TestCase class, from which you can define your own test cases by creating a subclass.
- You should respect the naming rules in terms of creating a testing method. It should start with test_, and the class should start with Test.
- The basis of testing a function is the certainty of a function's intended operation. When you provide some defined input, the function should generate the output without any ambiguity.
- In most cases, you can use assertEqual to evaluate the test results. You can use other methods in the TestCase class.
- Testing a class is effectively testing its methods, and you can apply the same techniques that you use to test functions to test methods.

Part 6

Building a web app

The best way to evaluate a chess player's skill level is to let them play a real game against another player instead of asking them how many openings they can play. To play a real game, a player must know the opening game, the middle game, and the end game.

For a programmer, completing a project is like playing chess: you must have comprehensive knowledge, including (but not limited to) choosing the right data models, writing good functions, and defining well-structured classes. In this part, we complete the task management app that we talked about in the first five parts. We not only review the techniques we've learned but also use these techniques in the context of a realistic project. Completing a project is always fun and creates a sense of accomplishment. Don't you agree?

Completing a real project

Chapters 2–12 focused on individual techniques, with considerable cross-referencing of pertinent techniques. When I introduced built-in data types (chapters 2–5), for example, we created functions to perform some repeated work. When I discussed functions (chapters 6 and 7) and classes (chapters 8 and 9), we used built-in data types. From examples in the context of the task management app, you've seen that these techniques depend on one another to solve realistic problems. Solving these isolated problems is fun in the sense of learning pertinent techniques. The ultimate purpose of learning these individual techniques, however, is to use them collectively to complete a real project from beginning to end.

In this chapter, we're going to complete the task management app project (section 1.4.3) from the beginning, creating a virtual environment (section 14.1), defining the proper data models (section 14.2), using the backend database (section 14.3), implementing the frontend app (section 14.4), and publishing our package for distribution (appendix E online). As an important note, although we're going to learn a few new techniques, such as using a local database, we'll focus on synthesizing the techniques that we learned in chapters 2–12.

14.1 How do I use a virtual environment for my project?

As mentioned in chapter 1 (section 1.2), we have many choices of open source Python packages to use in our project. We can install third-party packages with Python's package installer `pip` (see appendix B online), which is a command-line tool that allows you to install and uninstall Python packages with one line of command.

By default, these packages are installed at the system level, which means that all your projects must share these packages. Different projects, however, may require distinct versions of the packages, and you can't reconcile these conflicts easily if the systemwide packages that your projects share are in different versions than the ones required by your project. In this section, I'll show you how to reconcile this dilemma by using virtual environments.

14.1.1 Understanding the rationale for virtual environments

Virtual environments reconcile the problem of different projects requiring packages in multiple versions. What is a virtual environment, and what can it do? This section answers these questions.

First, I'll elaborate on the package conflict problem. When you have only one project, you're fine in terms of using packages. Often, you're probably working on multiple projects simultaneously—a situation that can introduce a package management problem. In one project, you use package A, version 1.0; in another project, you need package A, version 1.5, so you upgrade the package to version 1.5. You've likely created a dilemma. When you go back to your first project, your code may break, because chances are that some of the features in package A are removed in version 1.5.

You can certainly downgrade to version 1.0 to work on the first project, but when you want to work on your second project, you must run the upgrade again. I don't think you want to do a lot of back-and-forth downgrading and upgrading.

The best solution is to use virtual environments. *Virtual environments* are isolated work directories in which you install the packages you need for a project. Because each project has its own virtual environment, you can install different packages (or packages of different versions) in their respective work directories. Moreover, in advanced virtual environment management tools such as `conda`, you can have a distinct Python version for each virtual environment, together with different packages, giving you greater flexibility to manage environments for separate projects, as shown in figure 14.1.

> **CONCEPT** A *virtual environment* is a directory tree that contains Python and third-party dependencies that are isolated from the installations—including Python and third-party dependencies—on the computer.

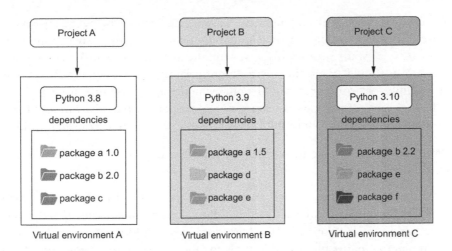

Figure 14.1 **Creating multiple virtual environments for each project. In each virtual environment, you can have a distinct version of Python and a different set of third-party dependencies.**

Figure 14.1 shows three projects with virtual environments. In the virtual environment, you use the needed Python version and the third-party dependencies with their applicable versions. By using a distinct virtual environment, you don't need to worry about different projects requiring conflicting versions of a package, because each project uses its own dependencies.

> **MAINTAINABILITY** Create a distinct virtual environment for each project to prevent your projects from having conflicting dependencies.

14.1.2 *Creating a virtual environment for each project*

The root cause of the dilemma described in section 14.1.1 is that you share packages on your computer because you installed them at the system level. What if you could install packages separately for each project? This is exactly how a virtual environment works.

As part of the standard Python library, the venv module provides the core functionalities for virtual environment management. Several third-party tools, such as conda and virtualenv, can manage virtual environments in Python. Although they have slightly different features, the fundamentals are about the same as what the built-in venv module offers. For this reason, I'll use the venv module to show the core techniques.

To create a virtual environment, you need to open a command-line tool, such as Terminal for Mac or the cmd tool for Windows. For your app project, you create the taskier_app directory, which I refer to throughout this chapter. Navigate to the taskier_app directory (use the cd command to change the directory), and run the following command:

```
$ python3 -m venv taskier-env
```

If you use Windows, you may need to use `python` instead of `python3`, which I use because I'm using a Mac. The command creates a virtual environment named `taskier-env`, as you're using this environment to build your task management app `taskier`. You should name the environment related to the project so that when you have multiple environments, you'll know which environment is for which project. That is, each project will have its own properly named virtual environment for dependency management, and there will be no dependency conflicts between projects.

> **MAINTAINABILITY**   Name the virtual environment related to the project that it serves.

You'll notice that a folder named `taskier-env` appears in the directory. This folder holds all the folders and files needed for the virtual environment. If you're curious, the `bin` folder (macOS only; in Windows, you'll see a folder called `Scripts` or something similar) contains the essential tools for the environment, including the link to the Python interpreter, `pip` (section 14.1.3), and activation scripts (section 14.1.3).

14.1.3 *Installing packages in the virtual environment*

You understand that virtual environments are isolated work directories for your projects and that it's safe to install any packages needed for this project without affecting other projects. In this section, I'll show you how to install packages in a virtual environment.

First, create the virtual environment `taskier-env` for the project. To use this environment, run the following command:

```
# for Mac:
$ source taskier-env/bin/activate

# for Windows:
> taskier-env\Scripts\activate.bat
```

> **NOTE**   If the command doesn't work in your command-line tool, see this page of the official Python website for further instructions: https://docs.python .org/3/library/venv.html.

The command activates the virtual environment, allowing you to install packages in the virtual environment. You'll see that the command line has the virtual environment's name as a prefix (`taskier-env`), which signifies that the environment is activated and ready for package installation.

The most common Python package installation tool is `pip`; you can find detailed instructions on how to use `pip` in appendix B online. In brief, you'll install the `streamlit` library for the task management app, and this library will provide the tools to build the frontend for the project as a web app. I chose this library because it's easy to build a web app with it, which allows you to focus on the content instead of the layout of the web elements. This command installs `streamlit` (version 1.10.0 at the time this book was written):

```
$ pip install streamlit==1.10.0
```

For best reproducibility, I recommend that you install the same version. It's entirely possible, however, that your web app will still run with the latest streamlit version.

14.1.4 Using virtual environments in Visual Studio Code

For this project, you'll use Visual Studio Code (VSC) as your coding tool because it's an open source integrated development environment (IDE) with powerful extension capability. (See appendix A online for installation instructions.) In this section, I'll show you how to use virtual environments in VSC.

Open the project directory (taskier_app) in VSC; press Cmd+Shift+P (Mac) or Ctrl+Shift+P (Windows) to display the command menu; and enter Python: Select Interpreter, which brings up the list of available virtual environments. You should be able to see the virtual environment taskier-env in the list. Select the 'taskier-env': venv option (figure 14.2).

> **NOTE** You need to open the project directory (taskier_app) by choosing File > Open Folder in VSC. Otherwise, you may not see the environment in the list.

Figure 14.2 Selecting the proper interpreter in the correct virtual environment. Note that you may not see other options on your computer; this figure shows the full list of virtual environments available on my computer.

To verify that you're indeed using this environment, create a file (say, test_env.py) in the parent directory (taskier_app). When you open this file, you should see the status bar at the bottom of the VSC window, as shown in figure 14.3.

Please note that although your project is going to be completed with Python 3.10.4, it should be compatible with earlier versions (Python 3.8 and later), as the techniques I've been covering are stable core features of Python.

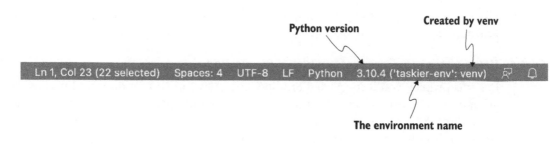

Figure 14.3   The status bar showing key information on running Python in VSC, including the Python version, the virtual environment, and the environment's creation tool (venv).

14.1.5 Discussion

The venv module provides essential features for creating a virtual environment and is convenient to use because it comes with the standard Python library. The module has a drawback, however: by default, it uses the systemwide Python. If you want to use a specific version of Python for your project, you should use other virtual environment management tools, such as conda. With conda, you can enjoy all the benefits of installing environment-specific packages that you have with venv. Moreover, you can have an isolated Python installation in the virtual environment, giving you greater flexibility in project configuration in terms of Python version and third-party packages.

> **Using conda for virtual environment management**
>
> To have a distinct Python interpreter for your project, you can use conda to manage the virtual environments. You can find installation instructions on its official website: https://conda.io. After you install conda, you can use it to create virtual environments in your preferred command-line tool.
>
> For your project, you have Python 3.10.4 and the dependency of streamlit 1.10.0. You can use the following command to create the desired virtual environment:
>
> ```
> conda create -n taskier-env python=3.10.4 streamlit=1.10.0
> ```
>
> (Please note that if you run the following code after creating the virtual environment with venv, you may see two virtual environments with the same name and distinct file paths.) After running this command, you can activate this environment by running conda activate taskier-env and then work on this virtual environment. To set up the environment in VSC, bring up the Python interpreter list, and choose the one in the taskier-env environment.

14.1.6 Challenge

Jerry works as a data scientist at a real estate company. He knows that it's a good idea to have separate virtual environments for his project. As a practice, how can he create a virtual environment named python-env? In the environment, he needs to install the pandas library. After the installation, he also wants to configure VSC to use this environment.

HINT Follow the instructions covered in this section.

14.2 *How do I build the data models for my project?*

The core of any application is data, although data takes a variety of forms, such as text and image. Regardless of the form of the data, when we build an application, we typically define custom classes to represent the data as attributes. We prepare and process data through functions or methods within the custom classes. This data and related operations are collectively referred to as *data models* for an application. In this section, we'll review the data models used in our task management app.

14.2.1 *Identifying the business needs*

The data models should serve the business needs of our project. To build the data models properly, we must first identify the features of our task management app. The app is a demonstration project, so I'll include sufficient features to serve as a backbone to show you the essential techniques of Python. Please note that I don't want to overcomplicate the app, which would make it hard to focus on learning these essentials.

In our app, users can create a new task, view the list of tasks, edit a task, and delete a task. It would also be helpful if users could sort and filter the tasks by specific criteria. Figure 14.4 summarizes these features.

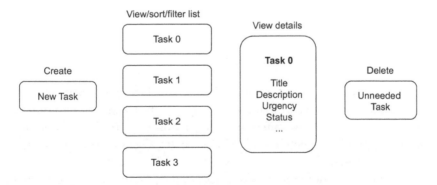

Figure 14.4 The key features of the task management app. In the app, users can create a new task; view, sort, and filter tasks; view a task's details; and delete a task.

As shown in figure 14.4, each task has a few attributes: `title` (title), `desc` (description), `urgency` (level of urgency), and `status` (status). When you build a real application with many more features, you'll need to design the app's user interface (the frontend) in such a way that you can determine whether you have all the features you need and how the features interact. For our task management app, I'll keep the interface simple, focusing on the coding portion instead of on the app's interface design.

PEEK We'll build a web app as our app's frontend. Because the streamlit framework helps us lay out the elements of a web app (such as text display and input boxes), we'll use it as our tool.

14.2.2 *Creating helper classes and functions*

Before analyzing the code for the Task class (section 14.2.3), I want to introduce the needed helper classes and functions in this section. We're going to create a file named taskier.py to store the Task class. At the head of this file, we're importing the necessary dependencies as follows (and please note that I'll cover the use of these modules when I discuss the pertinent code):

```
import csv
import re
import sqlite3
from enum import IntEnum, Enum
from pathlib import Path
from random import choice
from string import ascii_lowercase
```

A task has three possible statuses: created, ongoing, and completed. We'll use enumeration to represent these statuses:

```
class TaskStatus(IntEnum):
    CREATED = 0
    ONGOING = 1
    COMPLETED = 2

    @classmethod
    def formatted_options(cls):
        return [x.name.title() for x in cls]
```

In section 9.1, we learned about enumeration by subclassing the Enum class. Here, we subclass IntEnum class, which is like the Enum class but has an added benefit: we can sort statuses because their raw values are integer numbers. In this enumeration class, we define a class method (section 8.2), which creates a list of strings to be used in our web app (section 14.4).

In section 11.2, we studied how to process tabulated data by using the csv module. To show you the pertinent techniques, I'll use a CSV file as the data source, even though a CSV file typically isn't preferred as the database; as a formal database choice, I'll show you how to use SQLite in section 14.3. To include both options in the web app, we can use an enumeration class:

```
class TaskierDBOption(Enum):
    DB_CSV = "tasks.csv"
    DB_SQLITE = "tasks.sqlite"

app_db = TaskierDBOption.DB_CSV.value
```

We created a global variable app_db to track the database option. Now we default it to the CSV file option. In the web app, for demonstration purposes, we let users choose the database option, and we use the function in the next listing to update the database choice.

> **Listing 14.1   Setting the database option for the app**

```
def set_db_option(option):
    global app_db
    app_db = option
    db_path = Path(option)
    if not db_path.exists():      ◄─── Checks a path's existence
        Task.load_seed_data()
    elif app_db == TaskierDBOption.DB_SQLITE.value:
        Task.con = sqlite3.connect(app_db)
```

Because we're changing the variable in the global scope, we need to use the global keyword before we can change it (section 10.4). If the file doesn't exist at the path, we're going to create the data file and load some seeding data for demonstration purposes, using the Task's load_seed_data method (section 14.2.3). Although I'll talk more about the SQLite database in section 14.3, listing 14.1 includes a line of code (Task.con = sqlite3.connect(app_db)) that creates a connection to the database when the database option is SQLite.

From the exception-handling perspective, we'll create our own exception class, allowing us to raise custom exceptions. As discussed in section 12.5, our exception class is a subclass of the Exception class:

```
class TaskierError(Exception):
    pass
```

Because we can provide custom error messages when we use this class, we don't need to implement any methods; we'll use the pass statement to fulfill the syntax requirement. Please note that if we want to provide more specific exceptions, we can create subclasses from the TaskierError class.

14.2.3   Creating the Task class to address these needs

We've identified the core features of our app, and we're ready to implement the Task class to address our business needs. In this section, we'll build the Task class. To facilitate teaching, I'll analyze the code directly with an emphasis on individual methods.

CREATING AND SAVING TASKS

In our app, each task is modeled as an instance of the Task class. We create instance objects to model the tasks. In this section, I'll show you the code that creates and saves instance objects to a file.

The initialization method allows us to define custom attributes for the instance objects (section 8.1). We override the __init__ method to configure the instantiation.

In the definition, we use the type hints (section 6.3) for each of the arguments. We also provide docstrings for the method by using Google style (section 6.5.1):

```
class Task:
    def __init__(self, task_id: str, title: str, desc: str, urgency:
    ➥ int, status=TaskStatus.CREATED, completion_note=""):
        """Initialize the instance object of the Task class

        Args:
            task_id (str): The randomly generated string as the identifier
            title (str): The title
            desc (str): The description
            urgency (int): The urgency level, 1 - 5
            status (_type_, optional): The status. Defaults to
            ➥ TaskStatus.CREATED.
            completion_note (str, optional): The note when a task is
            ➥ completed. Defaults to "".
        """
        self.task_id = task_id
        self.title = title
        self.desc = desc
        self.urgency = urgency
        self.status = TaskStatus(status)
        self.completion_note = completion_note
```

We use a form to collect the title, description, and urgency level, and then use this information to create an instance of the Task class. As you can see in the following code snippet, task_from_form_entry is a class method because we don't need to access or manipulate per-instance data. Instead, this method accesses the class's constructor:

```
@classmethod
def task_from_form_entry(cls, title: str, desc: str, urgency: int):
    """Create a task from the form's entry

    Args:
        title (str): The task's title
        desc (str): The task's description
        urgency (int): The task's urgency level (1 - 5)

    Returns:
        Task: an instance of the Task class
    """
    task_id = cls.random_string()
    task = cls(task_id, title, desc, urgency)
    return task
```

NOTE I could have specified that the class method's return type is `Self`, which refers to the class, but it's not available until Python 3.11. For compatibility with earlier Python versions, I omitted the type hints for the return type.

In this class method, we call the `random_string` method to get a random string as the new task's ID number. Because the generation of the random string can be a utility function for other purposes, we implement it as a static method, as it doesn't use the class or instance-related attributes:

```python
@staticmethod
def random_string(length=8):
    """Create a random ASCII string using the specified length

    Args:
        length (int, optional): The desired length for the random
        ➥ string. Defaults to 8.

    Returns:
        str: The random string
    """
    return "".join(choice(ascii_lowercase) for _ in range(length))
```

In this method, we use the lowercase ASCII character set (imported from the `string` module) as our source, randomly pick eight characters using the `choice` function in the `random` module, and concatenate these characters using the `join` method (section 2.3). When we've created the instance, we need to save it to the database, and we can use the `save_to_db` method, as shown in the following listing.

Listing 14.2   Saving a record to the database

```python
def save_to_db(self):
    """Save the record to the database
    """
    if app_db == TaskierDBOption.DB_CSV.value:
        with open(app_db, "a", newline="") as file:
            csv_writer = csv.writer(file)
            db_record = self._formatted_db_record()
            csv_writer.writerow(db_record)
    else:
        # operations when the database is the SQLite3
        pass

def _formatted_db_record(self):
    db_record = (self.task_id, self.title, self.desc, self.urgency,
    ➥ self.status.value, self.completion_note)
    return db_record
```

We open the CSV file in append mode using the `with` statement (section 11.1). Using the CSV writer, we can write a row of data into the CSV file. As you may notice, we call the protected method `_formatted_db_record` to obtain the record we're going to write to the file. The underscore prefix indicates that the method is nonpublic (section 8.3.1).

READING TASKS FROM THE DATA SOURCE

When we have multiple tasks in the database, it's time to read and display the tasks. To load tasks from the database, we create the load_tasks method, as the next listing shows.

Listing 14.3 Loading tasks from the database

```
@classmethod
def load_tasks(cls, statuses: list[TaskStatus]=None, urgencies:
➥ list[int]=None, content: str=""):
    """Load tasks matching specific criteria

    Args:
        statuses (list[TaskStatus], optional): Filter tasks with
        ➥ the specified statuses.
            Defaults to None, meaning no requirements on statuses
        urgencies (list[int], optional): Filter tasks with the
        ➥ specified urgencies.
            Defaults to None, meaning no requirements on urgencies
        content (str, optional): Filter tasks with the specified
        ➥ content (title, desc, or note).
            Defaults to "".

    Returns:
        list[Task]: The list of tasks that match the criteria
    """
    tasks = list()
    if app_db == TaskierDBOption.DB_CSV.value:
        with open(app_db, newline="") as file:
            reader = csv.reader(file)
            for row in reader:
                task_id, title, desc, urgency_str, status_str, note = row
                urgency = int(urgency_str)
                status = TaskStatus(int(status_str))
                if statuses and (status not in statuses):
                    continue                                      Uses find
                if urgencies and (urgency not in urgencies):    to search a
                    continue                                     substring
                if content and all([note.find(content) < 0,
                ➥ desc.find(content) < 0, title.find(content) < 0]):  ◄──┘
                    continue
                task = cls(task_id, title, desc, urgency, status, note)
                tasks.append(task)
    else:
        # using the SQLite as the data source
        pass
    return tasks
```

NOTE The type hint usage list[TaskStatus] is available in Python 3.9 and later. If you experience an exception related to this usage, it's likely that you're using an older version of Python.

In listing 14.3, I want to highlight the following techniques:

- The created CSV reader from the file can be used as a generator (section 11.2), with each item representing a row of data.
- We use tuple unpacking (section 4.4) to obtain the six data elements sequentially. Each of these elements is in the form of a string.
- We obtain the desired urgency and status attributes by using the int and Task-Status constructors, respectively. Please note that we could have used a try...except... statement to obtain the data, but we're sure about the data integrity here, so the conversion should work. When we're processing outside data, we should use the exception-handling techniques.
- When we search a substring, we prefer using find, as it doesn't raise an exception, unlike the index method (section 4.3.2).
- Related to the substring searching, the built-in all function returns True if all the items in the list are evaluated to be True. The entire line means that if the function call specifies the content argument, and we can't find any match in the note, desc, or title, we'll skip the current row by triggering the continue statement.
- Because our app allows users to select tasks that meet specific criteria—including statuses, urgencies, and content (for title, description, and completion note)—we want to define the load_tasks method that can load not only all the tasks, but also a subset of tasks. If the argument statuses is not None, and the current row's status is not in the statuses, we can skip the current row by calling the continue statement. The same logic applies to the urgencies and content arguments.

UPDATING A TASK IN THE DATA SOURCE

When the user makes changes to a task, we need to update the record in the database. For this purpose, we use the update_in_db method, as the next listing shows.

Listing 14.4 Updating a record in the database

```
def update_in_db(self):
    """Update the record in the database
    """
    if app_db == TaskierDBOption.DB_CSV.value:
        updated_record = f"{','.join(map(str,
        ➥ self._formatted_db_record()))}\n"
        with open(app_db, "r+") as file:
            saved_records = file.read()
            pattern = re.compile(rf"{self.task_id}.+?\n")      ⟵ Compiles the regular
            if re.search(pattern, saved_records):                  expression pattern
                updated_records = re.sub(pattern,
                ➥ updated_record, saved_records)
                file.seek(0)
                file.truncate()
                file.write(updated_records)
```

```
        else:
            raise TaskierError("The task appears to be
        ⇨ removed already!")
    else:
        # using the SQLite as the data source
        pass
```

In this method, I want to show you the usefulness of regular expressions. In essence, we read all the text data from the CSV file. The pattern is to search the string that starts with the task ID number and ends with a newline break. The replacement is the updated record that we obtain by calling the _formatted_db_record method. Note that because we're writing text data to the file, we need to convert the formatted record's data to strings using the map function (section 7.2.2).

From a performance perspective, we can replace the updated record directly without searching for its existence. But because of the design of our app (section 14.4.3), it's possible that the user may be trying to update a task that has been removed. To accommodate this need, we're raising an exception when the record doesn't exist.

Although we didn't have a chance to discuss the seek and truncate methods in section 11.1, they're easy to understand. In essence, we call seek(0) to move the cursor of the file stream to the beginning and call truncate to remove all the text data. When the file is empty, we can write the updated_records to the file.

DELETING A TASK FROM THE DATA SOURCE

If the user wants to delete a task, it's possible for them to do so. We can define the delete_from_db method to address this need, as shown in the next listing.

Listing 14.5   Deleting a record from the database

```
def delete_from_db(self):
    """Delete the record from the database
    """
    if app_db == TaskierDBOption.DB_CSV.value:
        with open(app_db, "r+") as file:
            lines = file.readlines()
            for line in lines:
                if line.startswith(self.task_id):
                    lines.remove(line)
                    break
            file.seek(0)
            file.truncate()
            file.writelines(lines)
    else:
        # using the SQLite as the data source
        pass
```

In this method, we call readlines (section 11.1) to obtain the text data as a list object. We use this method because list objects are mutable (section 3.1), allowing us to remove a task. For each line, we examine whether it starts with the task ID number, and when we find it, we call the break statement to exit the for loop immediately.

After the `lines` object is updated, we can write it back to the file by calling the `write-lines` method.

We define a method, `load_seed_data`, to load some tasks so that the app can display some data. In this method, we create three tasks and save them to the database by calling the `save_to_db` method:

```python
@classmethod
def load_seed_data(cls):
    """Load seeding data for the web app
    """
    task0 = cls.task_from_form_entry("Laundry", "Wash clothes", 3)
    task1 = cls.task_from_form_entry("Homework", "Math and physics", 5)
    task2 = cls.task_from_form_entry("Museum", "Egypt things", 4)
    for task in [task0, task1, task2]:
        task.save_to_db()
```

Last but not least, we define the string representation methods, `__str__` and `__repr__` (section 8.4):

```python
def __str__(self) -> str:
    stars = "\u2605" * self.urgency
    return f"{self.title} ({self.desc}) {stars}"

def __repr__(self) -> str:
    return f"{self.__class__.__name__}({self.task_id!r},
    {self.title!r}, {self.desc!r}, {self.urgency},
    {self.status}, {self.completion_note!r})"
```

> **NOTE** _str_ is for informational purposes and _repr_ is for coding development purposes, if you're wondering about the difference between these two methods.

14.2.4 Discussion

Our data models should serve our business needs. It's important to identify the app's features before we implement our data models. Although I'm showing the final version of the code, it has taken me considerable time with multiple iterations of the code to arrive at this version. Be patient with yourself when you work on any project.

> **PEEK** The Task class serves the web app that we're going to build in section 14.4.

14.2.5 Challenge

While Kathy is studying this book, she writes all the code to learn all the topics covered in this book. When she works on the `Task` class, she thinks it's possible that users may try to delete a task that has already been removed from the database. How can she update the `delete_from_db` method to make it raise an exception when the record doesn't exist?

HINT   You can examine whether the record has been located before carrying out the desired operation.

14.3   *How do I use SQLite as my application's database?*

A database hosts the data for your application. Depending on the nature of your application, such as data volume and processing requirements, you have a variety of options for the database—Microsoft SQL, Oracle, MySQL, and PostgreSQL, to name a few. These options are generally for enterprise-level applications, and it takes time and resources to set up the infrastructure and maintain its performance. Unlike these enterprise database solutions, SQLite is a kind of lightweight database that requires virtually no setup on your computer, as it uses your computer's disk directly as the storage mechanism. In this section, I'll show you how to use SQLite as our application's database.

14.3.1   *Creating the database*

The creation of an SQLite database is almost instant, requiring only a few function calls. Specifically, we'll use the built-in `sqlite3` module, which is in the standard Python library. This module provides all the application programming interfaces (APIs) needed to create and manipulate the SQLite database. We'll start with creating a database.

Because the database is shared by all the instances of the `Task` class, we'll define the connection to the database as a class attribute. Through this connection, we'll perform all database-related operations, such as data query and updating. We don't work on the database directly at the physical level because we want other processes to use the database if necessary. Therefore, we establish a connection and work on it as we create a file object on a file instead of manipulating the file directly:

```
class Task:
    con: sqlite3.Connection
```

To create a database, we define the `create_sqlite_database` method:

```
@classmethod
def create_sqlite_database(cls):
    """Create the SQLite database
    """
    with sqlite3.connect(TaskierDBOption.DB_SQLITE.value) as con:
        cls.con = con
        cursor = con.cursor()
        cursor.execute("CREATE TABLE task (task_id text, title text,
          desc text, urgency integer, status integer, completion_note text);")
```

Saves it as a class variable ⇨ [pointing to `cls.con = con`]

We perform two operations in this method:

- *By calling* connect *function, we're establishing a connection to the database at the specified path.* Notably, if the database doesn't exist at the path, this function call also creates the database. We use the `with` statement, which creates a context manager to commit the execution automatically.

- *We're adding a new table,* task, *to the database.* Please note that this code runs only when there is no database. The command is CREATE TABLE table_name (field0_name field0_type, field1_name field1_type, ...). Another thing you may notice is that we create a cursor to run the statement—a standard operation in SQLite and SQL databases in general.

We intend to call this create_sqlite_database method when users set the database option, so we need to update the set_db_option function in listing 14.1 as follows:

```
def set_db_option(option):
    global app_db
    app_db = option
    db_path = Path(option)
    if not db_path.exists():
        if app_db == TaskierDBOption.DB_SQLITE.value:
            Task.create_sqlite_database()
        Task.load_seed_data()
    elif app_db == TaskierDBOption.DB_SQLITE.value:
        Task.con = sqlite3.connect(app_db)
```

I boldfaced the added code, which is a simple call of the create_sqlite_database method when the database doesn't exist. As a side note on the elif portion, when the SQLite database exists and the database choice is SQLite, we establish a connection to the database. Before we jump into the code to perform data operations using the SQLite database, take a quick look at figure 14.5, which depicts the most common operations.

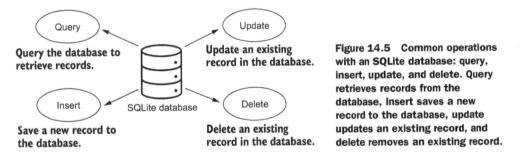

Figure 14.5 Common operations with an SQLite database: query, insert, update, and delete. Query retrieves records from the database, insert saves a new record to the database, update updates an existing record, and delete removes an existing record.

Query the database to retrieve records.

Update an existing record in the database.

Save a new record to the database.

Delete an existing record in the database.

As shown in figure 14.5, we perform four common operations when we use an SQLite database (or any database in general): query (retrieving records from the database), insert (saving a new record to the database), update (updating an existing record), and delete (removing a record from the database). The following sections address these four operations individually.

14.3.2 Retrieving records from the database

To display data in our app, we need to retrieve records from the database. We've seen how we can use the csv module to read data from a CSV file (section 14.2.3). Here, I show you how to retrieve data by using the SQLite database.

We've defined the `load_tasks` method (listing 14.3) to obtain the tasks data. Now we'll update this method to let it work with the SQLite database (listing 14.6). Please note that I'm showing you only the code that is pertinent for reading data from the SQLite database and omitting the code for using the CSV file.

Listing 14.6   Loading data from the SQLite database

```
@classmethod
def load_tasks(cls, statuses: list[TaskStatus]=None,
➥ urgencies: list[int]=None, content: str=""):
    """The docstring as before
    """
    tasks = list()
    if app_db == TaskierDBOption.DB_CSV.value:
        # csv-related code from listing 14.3
        pass
    else:
        with cls.con as con:
            if statuses is None:
                statuses = tuple(map(int, TaskStatus))
            else:
                statuses = tuple(statuses) * 2
            if urgencies is None:
                urgencies = tuple(range(1, 6))
            else:
                urgencies = tuple(urgencies) * 2
            sql_stmt = f"SELECT * FROM task WHERE status in {statuses}
            ➥ and urgency in {urgencies}"
            if content:
                sql_stmt += f" and ((completion_note LIKE '%{content}%')
                ➥ or (desc LIKE '%{content}%') or (title LIKE
                ➥ '%{content}%'))"
            cursor = con.cursor()
            cursor.execute(sql_stmt)
            tasks_tuple = cursor.fetchall()
            tasks = [Task(*x) for x in tasks_tuple]
    return tasks
```

Note the following points about this code:

- Because I want to create a single SQL statement to handle two scenarios—all the tasks (using no filtering conditions for the arguments) and a subset of tasks (using filtering conditions for the arguments)—I list all the statuses when the `statuses` argument is `None` by running `statuses = tuple(map(int, TaskStatus))`.
- Similar logic applies to the `urgencies` argument. When the user wants to retrieve all the tasks, we require the records' urgency field to fall in the range 1–5, which is the possible range of urgency levels.
- One tricky part to understand is that when `statuses` and `urgencies` are not `None`, I use `tuple(statuses) * 2` and `tuple(urgencies) * 2`. I do this to fulfil the SQL statement syntax requirement when users pick only one item for `status` or `urgency`. Specifically, if users specify one urgency level, such as 2, from this input,

we're going to have a one-item `tuple` object `(2,)`. Using this `tuple` object directly in the `sql_stmt` is invalid, so we duplicate the items in the `tuple` object, changing `(2,)` to `(2,2)`, which is a valid SQL statement.

- The `LIKE` operation is SQL syntax for obtaining records that match the specified substring. We update the `sql_stmt` only when the `content` argument is set. The portion `content` is evaluated as `True` if the string contains any characters.
- The `fetchall` function retrieves all the records as a `list` object based on the executed SQL statement. Each record is returned as a `tuple` object in the form of `(task_id, title, desc, urgency, status, completion_note)`. Using `list` comprehension, we convert these `tuple` objects to `Task` instance objects.
- During the conversion from a `tuple` object to an instance, we use the asterisk operation, which unpacks the `tuple` object and sends the items to the constructor.

14.3.3 Saving records to the database

When we have created records, we need to save them to the database. We can save the records one by one or save them all together. In this section, I'll show both techniques.

Listing 14.2 defines the `save_to_db` method for the CSV file as the data source. We're going to update this method to make it compatible with the SQLite database (listing 14.7).

Listing 14.7 Saving a record to the SQLite database

```python
def save_to_db(self):
    """Save the record to the database
    """
    if app_db == TaskierDBOption.DB_CSV.value:
        # operations when the database is the CSV file
        pass
    else:
        with self.con as con:
            cursor = con.cursor()
            sql_stmt = f"INSERT INTO task VALUES (?, ?, ?, ?, ?, ?);"
            cursor.execute(sql_stmt, self._formatted_db_record())
```

The syntax for saving a record to an SQLite database is `INSERT INTO table VALUES (?, ?, ...)`. The question mark represents a placeholder, and the number of placeholders (six, in our case) should match the number of items in the record, as obtained by calling `_formatted_db_record`. Please note that you can execute a statement without using placeholders, as we did in listing 14.6. If you use the placeholders, you specify these values as the second argument in the `execute` function call.

Another thing to note is that we call `self.con` to retrieve the connection to the database. Although we define `con` as the class attribute, when we access the `con` attribute of an instance, it uses the class attribute as the fallback.

What should we do if we want to save multiple records in a single SQL statement? That feature is supported. Instead of calling `execute`, we call the `executemany` function. In the function call, the second argument is a list of records. Although we're not going to implement it in the Task class (the instance method save_to_db is sufficient for demonstration purposes), the next listing shows how to save multiple records to an SQLite database.

Listing 14.8   Saving multiple records to the SQLite database

```python
task0 = Task.task_from_form_entry("Laundry", "Wash clothes", 3)
task1 = Task.task_from_form_entry("Homework", "Math and physics", 5)
task2 = Task.task_from_form_entry("Museum", "Egypt things", 4)

with Task.con as con:
    cursor = con.cursor()
    tasks = [task0, task1, task2]
    formatted_records = [task._formatted_db_record() for task in tasks]
    sql_stmt = f"INSERT INTO task VALUES (?, ?, ?, ?, ?, ?);"
    cursor.executemany(sql_stmt, formatted_records)
```

14.3.4 *Updating a record in a database*

Our task management app allows users to edit a task. After editing the task, we need to update the record in the database. This section shows how to update a record in the SQLite database.

The update_in_db method is responsible for updating a record. The following code updates the method to include the code for the SQLite database portion:

```python
def update_in_db(self):
    """Update the record in the database
    """
    if app_db == TaskierDBOption.DB_CSV.value:
        # operations when the database is the CSV file
        pass
    else:
        with self.con as con:
            cursor = con.cursor()
            count_sql = f"SELECT COUNT(*) FROM task WHERE          Counts the
            ➥ task_id = {self.task_id!r}"                          existing
            row_count = cursor.execute(count_sql).fetchone()[0]  ◄─┘ records
            if row_count > 0:
                sql_stmt = f"UPDATE task SET task_id = ?, title = ?,
                ➥ desc = ?, urgency = ?, status = ?, completion_note = ?
                ➥ WHERE task_id = {self.task_id!r}"
                cursor.execute(sql_stmt, self._formatted_db_record())
            else:
                raise TaskierError("The task appears to be
                ➥ removed already!")
```

Note that we first examine the number of records that match the task ID number, which should be 1—thus, greater than 0. If the record has been removed, we raise an exception indicating that fact, as we did in listing 14.4 when we implemented this method using a CSV file as our data source.

The syntax for updating a record in an SQLite database is `UPDATE table SET field0_name = ?, field1_name = ?, ... WHERE condition`. In this syntax, we shouldn't omit the `WHERE` clause, which filters the record; if we do, we'll update all the records accidentally. Again, we're using placeholders for the `execute` function call. In the clause, we specify the `task_id` using `!r` as the conversion, which produces the task ID in single quotes (`'example_id'`) as opposed to `example_id`.

14.3.5   Deleting a record from the database

Our task management app allows users to remove a task. When a task is removed, we need to delete the record from the database. In this section, I'll show how to address this need.

The `delete_from_db` method is responsible for deleting a record. The following code updates the method to include the code for the SQLite database portion:

```
def delete_from_db(self):
    """Delete the record from the database
    """
    if app_db == TaskierDBOption.DB_CSV.value:
        # operations when the database is the CSV file
        pass
    else:
        with self.con as con:
            cursor = con.cursor()
            cursor.execute(f"DELETE FROM task WHERE task_id =
            ➥ {self.task_id!r}")
```

The syntax for deleting a record in an SQLite database is `DELETE FROM table WHERE condition`. The only thing to note is that we still use `!r` for the task's ID number to create a string within single quotes.

14.3.6   Discussion

Because SQLite is a lightweight database with little configuration, we can use it when we prototype our application. When we're moving the application to production, we can upgrade it by using a larger database, such as Oracle and MySQL. Although I've focused on text and integers as the data types, which satisfies our business needs, SQLite has limitations. For one, it doesn't support all data types, such as date and Boolean values. As a workaround, we can use strings in the format MMDDYY-HHMMSS, the number of seconds since a reference date for the date, and integers 0 and 1 for `false` and `true`.

14.3.7   Challenge

We've seen that we can use a CSV file and SQLite as our database option. Can you write a decorator to log the time needed to call a method? You can compare which is faster by using a CSV file or an SQLite database for data-related manipulations.

HINT   Section 7.3 discusses creating a decorator.

14.4   How do I build a web app as the frontend?

Web apps are a popular choice for many programming projects. Their most significant benefit is their cross-platform compatibility. They can run on any web browser, which means that you can acccss the app on any computer, any smartphone, and even any television set that supports web browsers. In addition, web apps require zero installation and configuration on the client's side because they run on a web browser, and all the features of a web app are loaded as web elements.

As you can tell, web apps provide the most attractive outlet for any business. In this section, I'll show you how to build a web app by using `streamlit`, a third-party Python framework for web developments. Please note that this framework provides a wide range of features, and I won't provide a comprehensive tutorial on using this framework. Instead, I'll focus on implementing the features of our task management application in the form of a web app.

14.4.1   Understanding the essential features of streamlit

To use `streamlit` to create the web app, you should have a good understanding of this framework. In this section, I'll introduce essential knowledge of this framework.

After we install `streamlit` in our virtual environment (`taskier-env`; section 14.1), in addition to using the framework in our Python files, the installation of `streamlit` includes using command line-based functionalities—that is, we can use a command-line tool as the interface to invoke actions relevant to manipulating web apps built with `streamlit`. The most important command is `streamlit run taskier_app.py`. As indicated by its name, this command launches a web app running in your default web browser, using `taskier_app.py` as the source file.

The first essential feature of `streamlit` is converting a Python script file to a web app. That's the major reason why `streamlit` is a popular web framework choice for Python developers. If you know Python, you can use `streamlit` to build a web app.

The other essential feature of `streamlit` is automatic layout of web elements, such as buttons and text-input boxes. This framework provides common web elements (widgets) out of the box. Figure 14.6 shows the available widgets implemented in the framework. Please note that these widgets may change in the latest release of the `streamlit` framework.

I won't discuss how to use the widgets because they're straightforward to use; also, you can find instructions at https://streamlit.io/. I'll show some screenshots in section 14.4.2. You'll see that when you use these widgets in your script, you specify the widget type with the necessary configurations, such as the text shown on the button, leaving the heavy work of laying out the elements to the framework.

Another notable feature of the `streamlit` framework is the reloading of the entire script linearly (from top to bottom) when there is any change in the input, such as users having selected an option of the radio widget. This feature is the core of this framework's execution model. Some beginning users of this framework may be frustrated because their experience of using a web app has taught them that a page doesn't reload

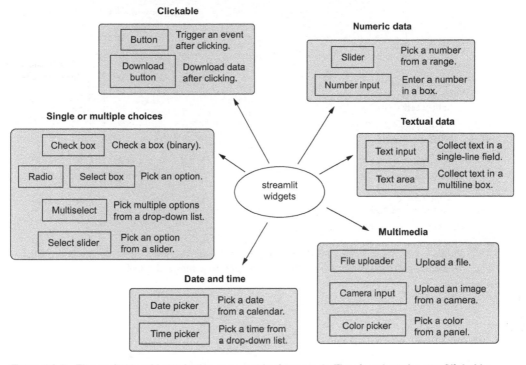

Figure 14.6   The available widgets in the `streamlit` framework. The six categories are Clickable (buttons), Single or Multiple Choice, Numeric Data, Textual Data, Multimedia, and Date and Time.

automatically when they click an option of the radio widget. Although it can be a drawback in some use cases, we have a workaround to address this problem: session state (section 14.4.3).

14.4.2   Understanding the app's interface

Before I show you the code for creating the web app, you need to see what the app looks like. This section shows the app's interface.

The first page shows the list of tasks (figure 14.7). On the left side is a sidebar, which includes the menu options, such as showing tasks and choosing the database option. On the right side is the main content area. In this case, the content is the list of tasks. You can choose how to sort and filter the list of tasks by using the sidebar. For clarity, we show the sort/filter menu only when we show the list of tasks.

For each task in the list, you can click the View Detail button to display the details of the task (figure 14.8). On the left side, we're adding some widgets, which allow users to delete the task. On the right side, we're showing the task's details in the main content area, which includes an Update Task button for saving the updated task to the database.

If users click the New Task button on the sidebar, they'll be directed to a form where they can create a task (figure 14.9). In the main content area, we're displaying a form, which collects the data needed for a new task. Users click Save Task to save the record to the database.

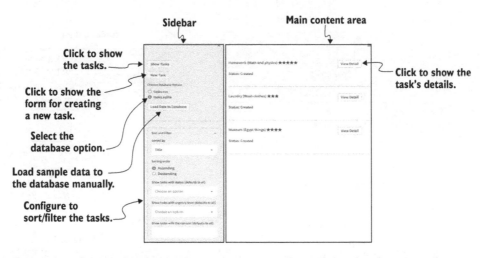

Figure 14.7   The interface for showing the list of tasks. The main interface includes a sidebar, which shows menu information. The main content area shows the tasks.

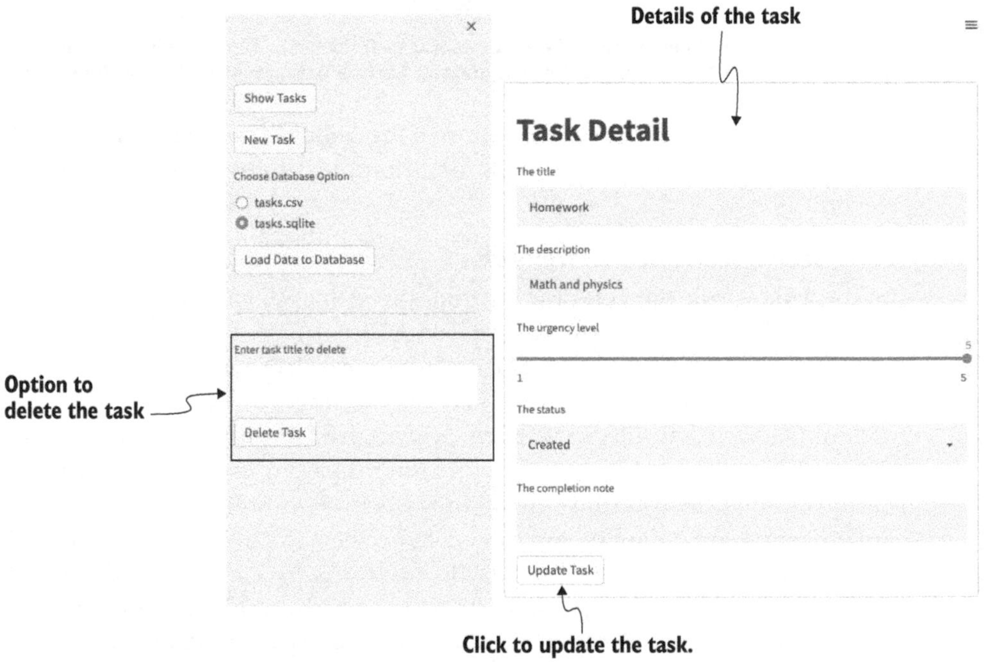

Figure 14.8   The interface for showing a task's details. In the sidebar, we display some widgets that allow users to delete the task. In the main content area, we display the task's details.

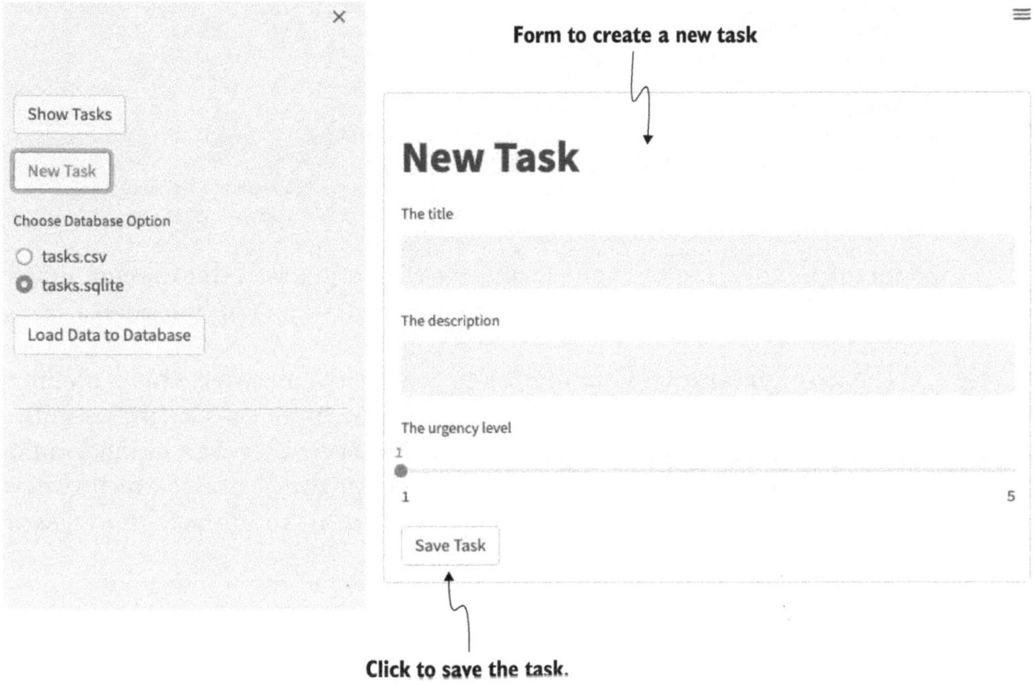

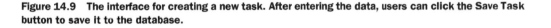

Form to create a new task

Show Tasks

New Task

Choose Database Option

○ tasks.csv
● tasks.sqlite

Load Data to Database

New Task

The title

The description

The urgency level

1

1   5

Save Task

Click to save the task.

Figure 14.9   The interface for creating a new task. After entering the data, users can click the Save Task button to save it to the database.

14.4.3 *Tracking user activities using session state*

As a loose definition to facilitate the discussion of streamlit, I refer to a *session* as users accessing a web app in a web browser, typically in the form of a tab in modern browsers. While the tab is active without being refreshed, we can use session state to track users' activity, stored as key-value pairs. This section shows what data we need to track for our app.

We'll create the taskier_app.py file as the script for our web app, and all the code discussed in this section will go into this file unless noted otherwise. At the top of this file, we import the dependencies. We'll talk about these dependencies when they become relevant in the context of the code; for now, we'll focus on streamlit. As a convention, we typically use st as an alias for streamlit, making it easier to refer to the framework. We call st.session_state to retrieve session data, for example:

```
import copy
import streamlit as st
from taskier import Task, TaskierDBOption, set_db_option,
    TaskStatus, TaskierError
from taskier_app_helper import TaskierMenuOption, TaskierFilterKey

session = st.session_state
```

```
sidebar = st.sidebar
status_options = TaskStatus.formatted_options()
menu_key = "selected_menu_option"
working_task_key = "working_task"
sorting_params_key = "sorting_params"
sorting_orders = ["Ascending", "Descending"]
sorting_keys = {"Title": "title", "Description": "desc", "Urgency":
➥ "urgency", "Status": "status", "Note": "completion_note"}
```

Besides dependencies, this code includes variables that we refer to often in the app, and all of these variables are concerned either with setting up the sidebar or the session state.

The first item that we want to track in a session is the selected menu option. We want to show three main pages (section 14.4.2): the list of tasks, a task's details, and a form for creating a new task. Because a session state stores data in the form of key-value pairs, for this item, we'll call the key selected_menu_option, which saves one of these three menu options that are implemented as an enumeration class in the taskier_app_helper.py file:

```
from enum import Enum

class TaskierMenuOption(Enum):
    SHOW_TASKS = "Show Tasks"
    NEW_TASK = "New Task"
    SHOW_TASK_DETAIL = "Show Task Detail"


class TaskierFilterKey(Enum):
    SORTING_KEY = "sorting_key"
    SORTING_ORDER = "sorting_order"
    SELECTED_STATUSES = "selected_statuses"
    SELECTED_URGENCIES = "selected_urgencies"
    SELECTED_CONTENT = "selected_content"
```

You may notice that we define the TaskierFilterKey class in the helper file. This class pertains to the second item we're tracking in session state: how users choose to sort and filter the list of tasks. Users can view only tasks with an urgency level of 3, for example. These sorting and filtering parameters are saved as a dict object by means of the key sorting_params in session state.

> **NOTE** We could have used two dict objects to track sorting and filtering parameters separately. But many web apps, including ours, have the same user interface for filtering and sorting. It's cleaner for us to use one dict object to track these parameters generated from a single user interface. Unless I specify otherwise, I refer to sorting and filtering parameters interchangeably.

When the user wants to view a task's details, we need to track which task the user is viewing. In session state, we use the `working_task` key to store this task, which is an instance of the `Task` class. As we need to update several key-value pairs in a variety of functions in the session, it's a good idea to define a function for this job in the `taskier_app.py` file:

```python
def update_session_tracking(key, value):
    session[key] = value
```

We can use the `update_session_tracking` function to update the values for the corresponding keys. Notably, `streamlit` runs the entire script from top to bottom whenever any change in user input occurs. Thus, we want to set the keys to their initial values only when the session doesn't have these keys. If these keys have been set, we don't want to override their existing values, which we use to track users' activity. The following code snippet shows how we set the initial session state:

```python
def init_session():
    if menu_key not in session:
        update_session_tracking(menu_key,
            ➥ TaskierMenuOption.SHOW_TASKS.value)
        update_session_tracking(working_task_key, None)
        update_session_tracking(sorting_params_key, {x.value: None for x
            ➥ in TaskierFilterKey})
```

Because we use `streamlit` to run the file as a script, it's good practice to use `if __name__ == "__main__"` at the end of the file in case we want to use this file as a module, as shown in the following listing.

Listing 14.9   Calling the functions to create the web app

```python
if __name__ == "__main__":
    init_session()          ⟵——— Initiates the session
    setup_sidebar()
    if session[menu_key] == TaskierMenuOption.SHOW_TASKS.value:
        show_tasks()
    elif session[menu_key] == TaskierMenuOption.NEW_TASK.value:
        show_new_task_entry()
    elif session[menu_key] == TaskierMenuOption.SHOW_TASK_DETAIL.value:
        show_task_detail()
    else:
        st.write("No matching menu")
```

As annotated in listing 14.9, we call the `init_session` function, which sets up the session state that can track users' activity. The next function we call is `setup_sidebar`, discussed in section 14.4.4.

14.4.4 Setting up the sidebar

We typically use a sidebar to show menu or optional configuration settings. In this section, I'll show how to set up the sidebar for our app. We configure the sidebar by calling the setup_sidebar function, as shown in the next listing.

Listing 14.10   Setting up the sidebar

```
def setup_sidebar():
    sidebar.button("Show Tasks", on_click=update_session_tracking,
      args=(menu_key, TaskierMenuOption.SHOW_TASKS.value))     ◁——— Adds a button

    sidebar.button("New Task", on_click=update_session_tracking,
      args=(menu_key, TaskierMenuOption.NEW_TASK.value))

    selected_db = sidebar.radio("Choose Database Option", [x.value for x
      in TaskierDBOption])     ◁
    set_db_option(selected_db)            Adds a radio

    sidebar.button("Load Data to Database", on_click=Task.load_seed_data)

    sidebar.markdown("___")   ◁——— Adds a divider

    if session[menu_key] == TaskierMenuOption.SHOW_TASKS.value:
        setup_filters()
    elif session[menu_key] == TaskierMenuOption.SHOW_TASK_DETAIL.value:
        setup_deletion()
```

> **CONCEPT**   Markdown is a lightweight markup language for creating formatted text. In these examples, we use three underlines ___, which translate to a divider widget that forms a visual separator between sections.

Listing 14.10 is the first time that we add widgets to our web app. In general, we add a widget in the following syntax: st.widget_name(widget_label, value_or_options, key=widget_id, on_click=on_click_if_applicable, args=args_if_any). For a sidebar, we can use sidebar.widget_name. Using the button and radio widgets as examples, figure 14.10 illustrates the anatomy of the pertinent code.

When we add a widget, such as a radio (figure 14.10), we can optionally use the return value of the function call. st.radio adds the radio, for example, and when users pick an option, we can obtain the index from this function call. In our case, we use this index to know which database option is chosen by calling the set_db_option function (listing 14.1). When the database option is selected, we'll configure the database behind the scenes, such as by creating the SQLite database and adding the task table. Related to this widget, to help you interact with this app from the learning perspective, I'm adding a Load Data to Database button to add more data to the database.

When users elect to show the tasks, we display the options for sorting and filtering by calling the setup_filters function. In case you wonder whether it's necessary to make this function private (we're writing a script for developers, not for other users),

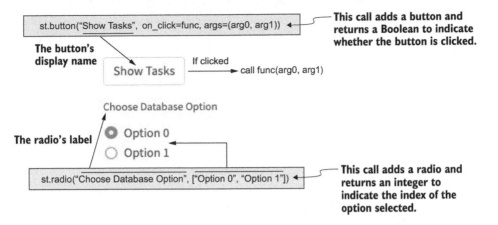

Figure 14.10   Dissecting the code for adding a button and a radio in streamlit. **Calling** st.button **adds a button to the web page and returns a Boolean that indicates the button's click status. Calling** st.radio **adds a radio to the web page and returns an integer that indicates the selected option's index. Each function includes additional arguments that configure the widgets.**

it's fine to name functions without using an underscore prefix, which would otherwise reduce readability:

```
def setup_filters():
    filter_params = session[sorting_params_key]
    with sidebar.expander("Sort and Filter", expanded=True):
        filter_params[TaskierFilterKey.SORTING_KEY.value] =
        ➡ st.selectbox("Sorted by", sorting_keys)
        filter_params[TaskierFilterKey.SORTING_ORDER.value] =
        ➡ st.radio("Sorting order", sorting_orders)
        filter_params[TaskierFilterKey.SELECTED_STATUSES.value] =
        ➡ st.multiselect("Show tasks with status (defaults to all)",
        ➡ options=status_options)
        filter_params[TaskierFilterKey.SELECTED_URGENCIES.value] =
        ➡ st.multiselect("Show tasks with urgency level (defaults to all)",
        ➡ options=range(1, 6))
        filter_params[TaskierFilterKey.SELECTED_CONTENT.value] =
        ➡ st.text_input("Show tasks with the content (defaults to all)")
```

Because the sorting and filtering parameters belong to the same conceptual category, I use an expander widget named Sort and Filter. In the expander, we define five widgets: a selectbox to pick one of the tasks' attributes (title, description, urgency, status, or completion note) for sorting; a radio to determine the sort order (descending or ascending); a multiselect to specify the selected statuses; another multiselect to specify the selected urgency levels; and a text_input to filter tasks with the specified content. Figure 14.11 shows how to select a subset of tasks by specifying these parameters.

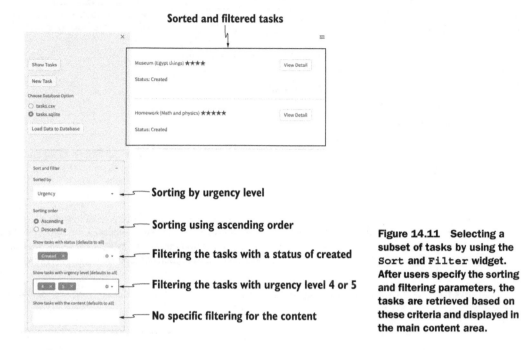

Figure 14.11 Selecting a subset of tasks by using the `Sort` and `Filter` widget. After users specify the sorting and filtering parameters, the tasks are retrieved based on these criteria and displayed in the main content area.

When the user views a task's detail in the main content area, we show the deletion option in the sidebar by calling the `setup_deletion` function:

```python
def setup_deletion():
    task = session[working_task_key]
    text_title = sidebar.text_input("Enter task title to delete",
    ➥ key="existing_delete")
    submitted = sidebar.button("Delete Task")
    if submitted:
        if text_title == task.title:
            task.delete_from_db()
            sidebar.success("Your task has been deleted.")
        else:
            sidebar.error("You must enter the exact text for the
            ➥ title to delete.")
```

In this function, we retrieve the task by accessing the session's `working_task` key. To prevent users from deleting a task accidentally, we require them to type the task's title before removing it from the database. The new feature calls the `success` and `error` functions, which are useful for providing real-time positive and negative feedback on the actions the users performed (figure 14.12).

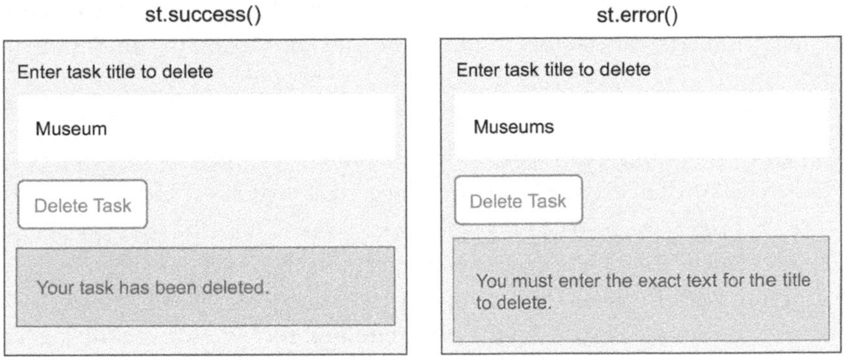

st.success()   st.error()

Enter task title to delete   Enter task title to delete

Museum   Museums

Delete Task   Delete Task

Your task has been deleted.   You must enter the exact text for the title
                                              to delete.

**Figure 14.12   Success and error feedback in the web app. We call `st.success` to
provide positive feedback and `st.error` to provide negative feedback.**

14.4.5 Showing the tasks

In a task management app, it's useful to show the list of available tasks that users can
work on. Thus, the page that shows the tasks is important. This section shows how to
implement this feature by using streamlit. In listing 14.9, we called the show_tasks
function to configure the web elements for showing the tasks. The next listing shows
how the show_tasks function is implemented.

Listing 14.11   Showing the tasks in the web app

```
def show_tasks():
    filter_params = session[sorting_params_key]
    if filter_params[TaskierFilterKey.SORTING_KEY.value] is not None:
        reading_params = get_reading_params(filter_params)
        tasks = Task.load_tasks(**reading_params)
        sorting_key = sorting_keys[filter_params[
            TaskierFilterKey.SORTING_KEY.value]]
        should_reverse = filter_params[
            TaskierFilterKey.SORTING_ORDER.value] == sorting_orders[1]
        tasks.sort(key=lambda x: getattr(x, sorting_key),
            reverse=should_reverse)
    else:
        tasks = Task.load_tasks()

    for task in tasks:
        col1, col2 = st.columns([3, 1])
        col1.write(str(task))
        col2.button("View Detail", key=task.task_id,
            on_click=wants_task_detail, args=(task,))
        st.write(f"Status: {task.status.name.title()}")
        st.markdown("___")
```

Retrieves the data → `else: tasks = Task.load_tasks()`

Creates two columns as a grid for clearer display → `col1, col2 = st.columns([3, 1])`

Displays the data → `st.write(f"Status: {task.status.name.title()}")` `st.markdown("___")`

This code has two parts. The first part retrieves the data, with and without using the sorting and filtering parameters, and the second part displays the data by using the widgets.

The first part of listing 14.11 involves two steps:

1 *Obtain the filtering parameters from user input by calling the* get_reading_params *function.* We'll discuss this function later in this section.

2 *Sort the tasks based on the sorting parameters provided.* Because we use list, a mutable object (section 3.1), to store tasks, we can sort the tasks by using the sort method (section 3.2). Because the sorting key can change, such as from title to desc, it can be tedious if we're creating different lambda functions as the key argument, such as lambda x: x.title to sort by the title and lambda x: x.urgency to sort by the urgency level. Thus, we're using a generic approach to retrieve the corresponding attribute dynamically: lambda x: getattr(x, sorting_key).

The second part of listing 14.11 uses applicable widgets to display the tasks. Here, I'm using a new widget called columns, which is an invisible widget used for organizational purposes. Specifically, the call st.columns([3, 1]) creates two columns with a width ratio of 3:1, and the return value of this call is a tuple that represents these two columns. Using tuple unpacking, we're getting the references to them, named col1 and col2, and we can add widgets to the columns. One of these widgets is the View Detail button, and when it's clicked, we show the details for the task in the main content area, as discussed next in section 14.4.6. Here's how the get_reading_params function works:

```
def get_reading_params(filter_params):
    reading_params = dict.fromkeys(["statuses", "urgencies", "content"])
    if selected_statuses := filter_params[
      TaskierFilterKey.SELECTED_STATUSES.value]:
        reading_params["statuses"] = [status_options.index(x) for x
          in selected_statuses]
    if selected_urgencies := filter_params[
      TaskierFilterKey.SELECTED_URGENCIES.value]:
        reading_params["urgencies"] = selected_urgencies
    if selected_content := filter_params[
      TaskierFilterKey.SELECTED_CONTENT.value]:
        reading_params["content"] = selected_content
    return reading_params
```

As shown in figure 14.11, users can configure three filtering parameters: status, urgency, and content. Everything should be straightforward in this code snippet except for one new technique that we haven't seen before: *assignment expression.* This technique uses the := symbol (nicknamed the *walrus operator*), which was introduced in Python 3.8. The code selected_statuses := filter_params[TaskierFilter-Key.SELECTED_STATUSES.value], for example, means that we're trying to retrieve the value of the selected_statuses key in the filter_params dictionary and assign it to a variable called selected_statuses. If this value isn't None, we're going to run the code within the if statement. Typically, an assignment is a statement, so we can't use it in an `if` statement, which requires the clause to be an expression. As you can see, assignment expression does two things: assigns a value and evaluates it.

> **REMINDER** An expression evaluates to an object, whereas a statement performs an action without returning a value. See section 2.1.3 for a detailed discussion of the differences between expressions and statements.

14.4.6 *Showing a task's details*

The list of tasks provides overall information for each task. We can display more detailed information about the task. This section shows how to address this need.

For the View Detail button, we set the `on_click` argument using the `wants_task_detail` function and the `args` argument using `(task,)`. If a user clicks this button, we'll call `wants_task_detail(task)`:

```
def wants_task_detail(task: Task):
    update_session_tracking(working_task_key, task)
    update_session_tracking(menu_key,
    ➥ TaskierMenuOption.SHOW_TASK_DETAIL.value)
```

This function call does two things:

- It sets the task associated with the View Detail button as the current working task.
- It changes the selected menu to show a task's details. By changing the menu, when the web app reloads, we show the task detail page by calling the `show_task_detail` function, as shown in the next listing.

Listing 14.12 Showing a task's detail

```
def show_task_detail():
    task = session[working_task_key]
    form = st.form("existing_task_form", clear_on_submit=False)

    form.title("Task Detail")

    task.title = form.text_input("The title", value=task.title,
    ➥ key="existing_task_title")

    task.desc = form.text_input("The description", value=task.desc,
    ➥ key="existing_task_desc")

    task.urgency = form.slider("The urgency level", min_value=1,
    ➥ max_value=5, value=task.urgency)

    status = form.selectbox("The status", index=task.status,
    ➥ options=status_options, key="existing_task_status")
    task.status = TaskStatus(status_options.index(status))

    task.completion_note = form.text_input("The completion note",
    ➥ value=task.completion_note, key="existing_task_note")
```

```
submitted = form.form_submit_button("Update Task")
if submitted:
    try:
        task.update_in_db()
    except TaskierError:
        form.error("Couldn't update the task as it's maybe
    ➥ deleted already.")
    else:
        session[working_task_key] = task
        form.success("Your Task Was Updated!")
```

Note three things in listing 14.12:

- We're using the `form` widget to group individual widgets, such as `slider` and `text_input`. The `form` widget can remember the user's input for its contained widgets so that when the web page is reloaded, it shows the user's input.
- When we're done with the updating, we call the `form_submit_button`, which adds the Submit button to the form and uses the return value, which is `True` when the button is clicked.
- When we're submitting this form to update the record in our database, we're using the `try...except...else...` statement (sections 12.3 and 12.4). We use exception handling here because it's possible that the user may have deleted the task by using the deletion option on the sidebar or may have used another tab to delete the task.

Please note that in an actual web app, you may not want to design your interface this way. If the user has deleted an item, you should direct them to a page that doesn't show the deleted item. I provide this example purely for demonstration purposes to show how to use exception handling in a project.

14.4.7 Creating a new task

In the task management app, we allow users to create a new task. This section shows how to implement this feature in our web app. For this feature, we're defining the `show_new_task_entry` function, as the following listing shows.

Listing 14.13   Creating a new task in the web app

```
def show_new_task_entry():
    with st.form("new_task_form", clear_on_submit=True):
        st.title("New Task")

        title = st.text_input("The title", key="new_task_title")

        desc = st.text_input("The description", key="new_task_desc")

        urgency = st.slider("The urgency level", min_value=1, max_value=5)

        submitted = st.form_submit_button("Save Task")
```

```
    if submitted:
        task = Task.task_from_form_entry(title, desc, urgency)
        task.save_to_db()
        st.success("Your Task Was Saved!")
```

As we did in the task detail page, we're using the form widget for new task entry. What's different from listing 14.12 is that we're using the with statement for the form, creating a context manager (section 11.1). In the with statement, when we call st.text_input to create a text-input box, streamlit knows that the box should be placed within the form because of the context manager. By contrast, when we didn't use a context manager in listing 14.12, we explicitly called form.text_input to add a text-input box to the form. Both approaches—using and not using a context manager—are acceptable.

14.4.8 *Organizing your project*

We've seen how we implement our features individually. From the maintainability perspective, it's essential to organize your project so that it's easier for team members to read and locate the pertinent functionalities. In this section, I'll show the best practice to organize your project by using streamlit to develop the web app. Because the final product is a web app, I'll focus first on the script file taskier_app.py, which is responsible for creating the web app.

In general, this script consists of three components: dependencies, global variables, and functions for configuring the interface. For our web app, the script uses the Task class as its core data model. Although the script file is the only place to use the Task class in our app, we don't want to put the class in the script file for two reasons:

- We're making it hard to read the script file to understand how the web app is built because the Task class occupies considerable space in the code, and it doesn't contribute to the web app's interface.
- It would be inconvenient to use this class for other purposes, such as building a desktop app. Thus, it's critical to use a separate file to implement our data model.

When we use the data model in our app, we import it as a dependency. For the script file, we place the dependencies at the top of the file, as shown in the following code snippet. The dependencies not only serve the code in the script, but also provide important information that readers of the code (such as teammates) want to know, such as what libraries and packages the script uses:

```
import streamlit as st
from taskier import Task, TaskierDBOption, set_db_option,
➥ TaskStatus, TaskierError
from taskier_app_helper import TaskierMenuOption, TaskierFilterKey
```

As you may notice, we're saving the TaskierMenuOption and TaskierFilterKey classes in a different file (taskier_app_helper.py) so that the taskier_app.py file includes only the code for building the web's interface.

After clarifying the organization of the dependencies, we can analyze the organization of the script file's components. Figure 14.13 provides a graphic analysis.

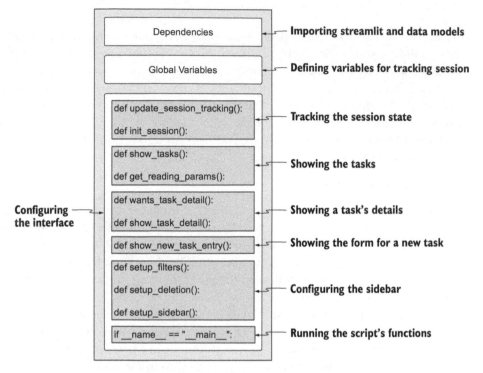

Figure 14.13   The organization of the `taskier_app.py` file. The file has three components: dependencies, global variables, and configuration of the interface.

For the code that configures the interface, I've organized the functions based on their intended purposes. Related functions are grouped together. The code for session tracking is at the top because it's the driving force for tracking user activity. In the middle are the functions for configuring the main content area. At the end are the functions that set up the sidebar.

14.4.9 *Running the app*

We've completed the code and organized it nicely. It's time to run the app and give it a try. (Please note that when you work on app development, you should run the app in a browser so that you can see the code's performance in real time.) To run the app, enter the `streamlit` command in the command-line tool:

```
$ streamlit run taskier_app.py
```

Make sure that you run the command after you navigate to the directory where the `taskier_app.py` file is saved; otherwise, you need to specify the full path to the script file. You should see a new tab in your default browser, with our app running in the tab.

14.4.10 Discussion

It takes some time to get familiar with a framework such as streamlit. This section isn't about the technicalities of using this framework. Instead, by building this web app, including its interface and its supporting data models, you saw how the techniques covered in the book contribute to a real project. Toward the end of this section, I showed you how to organize the project. Although this app is a toy project, it's still important to organize your code in a readable, maintainable way.

> **NOTE** The company behind the streamlit framework allows you to publish your web app for free if you host your app's code publicly on GitHub. You can find information about sharing your apps at https://share.streamlit.io/.

14.4.11 Challenge

One of the global variables that we define is sorting_keys, which is a dict object: {"Title": "title", "Description": "desc", "Urgency": "urgency", "Status": "status", "Note": "completion_note"}. We use this object when we create a selectbox widget: st.selectbox("Sorted by", sorting_keys). In this call, we use the dict object as options for the widget. Why can we use a dict object instead of a list object, such as list(sorting_keys.keys())?

> **HINT** We can send any iterable to the selectbox as the options. A dict object is iterable, using its keys as the iterator's elements by default.

Summary

- You should create a virtual environment for each project, forming an isolated environment to manage the dependencies for the project and avoiding dependency requirements between projects.
- The venv module is the built-in solution for managing virtual environments.
- Some third-party tools, such as conda, allow you to have a distinct Python interpreter for each virtual environment, which can give you more flexibility if your projects use different versions of Python.
- Data models should serve the business needs of your project. Thus, before writing code for implementing your data models, you should identify your needs.
- Your code files should be readable. For a class, you should write docstrings for each method you're defining.
- SQLite is a lightweight database that requires no preconfiguration. You can create an SQLite database in all major operating systems, including those for portable devices such as smartphones.
- Compared with CSV files, an SQLite database is a more formal database choice. I used a CSV file as a data source for tutorial purposes, but for a real project, you should always consider using a formal database.

- Web apps are great options for showcasing your projects, as they're platform-agnostic. Python supports several web frameworks, including `streamlit`, which all Python developers can use to build a web app easily.
- Although the project you created for this book is a tiny one, you should organize your files and their internal code. This is critical for improving readability and maintainability.

solutions to the challenges

Chapter 1

No challenges to get started with Python. You *win!*

Chapter 2

Section 2.1

We start with the following `dict` object:

```
product = {"name": "Vacuum", "price": 130.675}
```

Following is the solution for producing the desired output:

```
product_tag = f"{product['name']}: {{{product['price']:.2f}}}"

assert product_tag == "Vacuum: {130.68}"
```

Normally, we use curly braces to interpolate variables, so to make them mean the brace symbols themselves instead of interpolations, you need to use {{ to mean the brace symbol itself. Thus, {{{var_name} is interpreted as one left curly brace plus an interpolated string from var_name.

Section 2.2

When we use the input function to collect users' input, we're getting strings. When we expect numeric values, we need to convert them to a corresponding numeric value. We can have the following code:

```
x = input("What's today's temperature in your area?")
x_num = float(x)    ◀──┐ Converts a string to a floating-point number
if x_num < 10:
    x_output = f"You entered {x_num:.1f} degrees. It's cold!" ◀──┘
```

.1f is the floating-point format specifier.

431

```
elif 10 <= x_num < 25:
    x_output = f"You entered {x_num:.1f} degrees. It's cool!"
else:
    x_output = f"You entered {x_num:.1f} degrees. It's hot!"

print(x_output)
```

If you look at how x_output is created multiple times, you may notice a pattern of repetition: the only difference is the adjective that describes weather. Thus, a better solution is

```
x = input("What's today's temperature in your area?")
x_num = float(x)
if x_num < 10:
    x_whether = "cold"
elif 10 <= x_num < 25:
    x_whether = "cool"
else:
    x_whether = "hot"

x_output = f"You entered {x_num:.1f} degrees. It's {x_whether}!"
print(x_output)
```

Section 2.3

The argument maxsplit specifies the maximal number of splits when you use split or rsplit. When you ignore this argument, both methods will use all occurrences of the separator. Alternatively, if you set this argument that is greater than the number of occurrences, you expect the same result for both methods as follows:

```
fruits = "apple,orange,pineapple,cherry,watermelon"
assert fruits.split(",") == fruits.split(",", 10) ==
➥ fruits.rsplit(",") == fruits.rsplit(",", 10) ==
➥ ['apple', 'orange', 'pineapple', 'cherry', 'watermelon']
```

If you use a number that is smaller than the maximally available splits, however, you expect split and rsplit to produce different results:

```
assert fruits.split(",", 3) == ['apple', 'orange', 'pineapple',
➥ 'cherry,watermelon']

assert fruits.rsplit(",", 3) == ['apple,orange', 'pineapple',
➥ 'cherry', 'watermelon']
```

Section 2.4

Suppose that you want to split the following string:

```
data_to_split = "abc_,abc__,abc,,__abc_,_abc"
```

As you can see, the separators are a variable mixture of _ and , . To split such string data, we can use the following pattern: [,_]+, which means that there can be multiple matching occurrences of _ or , in the string. Applying this pattern, we can create the desired split:

```
import re                          Uses the raw string
pattern = r"[,_]+"         ◀────   for pattern creation
splitted = re.split(pattern, data_to_split)
print(splitted)
# output: ['abc', 'abc', 'abc', 'abc', 'abc']
```

Section 2.5

When we process multiline text, we can use \n to identify the end of a line. Thus, to extract the needed records without splitting the lines, we can try the following pattern by specifying that the record ends with a newline character:

```
text_data = """101, Homework; Complete physics and math
some random nonsense
102, Laundry; Wash all the clothes today
54, random; record
103, Museum; All about Egypt
1234, random; record
Another random record"""

import re
pattern = r"(\d{3}), (\w+); (.+)\n"
splitted = re.findall(pattern, text_data)
print(splitted)

# output: [('101', 'Homework', 'Complete physics and math'), ('102',
➡ 'Laundry', 'Wash all the clothes today'), ('103', 'Museum',
➡ 'All about Egypt'), ('234', 'random', 'record')]
```

Everything appears to work, but there is one exception: we also include the incorrect record ('234', 'random', 'record'). If we compare this record with our pattern, matching it isn't a surprise because we don't have any restriction in terms of what precedes the three-digit identifier. Following is a more accurate way to build the pattern:

```
pattern = r"(?<!\d)(\d{3}), (\w+); (.+)\n"
splitted = re.findall(pattern, text_data)
print(splitted)

# output: [('101', 'Homework', 'Complete physics and math'), ('102',
➡ 'Laundry', 'Wash all the clothes today'), ('103', 'Museum',
➡ 'All about Egypt')]
```

The part (?<!\d) is known as the *negative look-behind assertion*, which means that it matches text that has a three-digit number only if it's not preceded by any number. Please note that this example shows advanced use of regular expressions. You can find

more information on the official Python website at https://docs.python.org/3/library/re.html.

Chapter 3

Section 3.1

When you need to hold a series of places, such as a person's trip history, you want to use list as the data model because you expect that users may change the places they've visited (to add new ones, for example).

A place has a specific coordinate, and you don't expect it to change. Thus, you want to use tuple to hold the coordinate data:

```
(latitude, longitude)
```

Section 3.2

Following is the list that we want to sort based on the length of the descriptions:

```
tasks = [
    {'title': 'Laundry', 'desc': 'Wash clothes', 'urgency': 3},
    {'title': 'Homework', 'desc': 'Physics + Math', 'urgency': 5},
    {'title': 'Museum', 'desc': 'Egyptian things', 'urgency': 2}
]
```

We know that we need to set a function to the key argument, and the function should calculate the length of a task's description as follows:

```
def using_by_desc_len(task):
    return len(task["desc"])

tasks.sort(key=using_by_desc_len, reverse=True)
print(tasks)

# output: [{'title': 'Museum', 'desc': 'Egyptian things', 'urgency':
➡ 2}, {'title': 'Homework', 'desc': 'Physics + Math', 'urgency':
➡ 5}, {'title': 'Laundry', 'desc': 'Wash clothes', 'urgency': 3}]
```

We define the function using_by_desc_len, which returns the task's description length. As a reminder, this function will serve as the key argument, which must take exactly one argument. It's necessary to set the reverse argument to True, as the challenge requires the task to have a higher rank if its description is longer. If you already know lambda functions (section 7.1), you can use the following code to sort:

```
tasks.sort(key=lambda x:len(x["desc"]), reverse=True)
```

Section 3.3

Because a named tuple is a tuple object, we can't change it due to its immutability. If we insist, we'll encounter an AttributeError:

```
from collections import namedtuple

Task = namedtuple("Task", "title desc urgency")
task = Task(title='Laundry', desc='Wash clothes', urgency=3)

task.urgency = 4
# ERROR: AttributeError: can't set attribute
```

But named tuples provide a workaround in the form of the _replace method:

```
task._replace(urgency=4)
# output: Task(title='Laundry', desc='Wash clothes', urgency=4)
```

Please note that this method creates a new tuple object that has the changed value instead of making an in-place change of the original object.

Section 3.4

Suppose that we have the dict object numbers:

```
numbers = {"one": 1, "two": 2, "three": 3}
numbers_key = numbers.keys()
id_key = id(numbers_key)
print(id_key)

# output 140660045849520   ⟵⎯  Expect a different value
                              on your computer.
```

In this code snippet, we also obtain the keys by using the keys method, which is a dictionary view object. The built-in id function can get the memory address of this view object. We'll change the dict object by adding a new key-value pair:

```
numbers["four"] = 4
```

After this change, we see that the keys are updated automatically in the numbers_key object and that the memory address stays the same because the update manipulates the same object:

```
print(numbers_key)
# output: dict_keys(['one', 'two', 'three', 'four'])

print(id_key)
# output: 140660045849520
```

Section 3.5

The keys in a dict object must be hashable because the hash values will be used by the underlying hash table as the storage mechanism. When you have keys that have the same hash values, the *last-seen rule applies:* the value associated with the key that is set later becomes the value for the key. In our case, an integer of 1 and a floating-point number of 1.0 have the same hash value:

```
assert hash(1) == hash(1.0) == 1
```

Thus, under the last-seen rule, we should expect the value associated with 1.0 to become the key's value:

```
numbers = {1: "one", 1.0: "one point one"}

print(numbers)
# output: {1: 'one point one'}
```

Section 3.6

As indicated in the hint, these evaluations are known as *short-circuit evaluations*. When Python tries to evaluate expr_a or expr_b, if it finds the first expression to be True, it uses the first object; otherwise, it uses the second expression. Some examples support this rule:

```
assert ({1, 2, 3} or {4, 5, 6}) == {1, 2, 3}
assert (False or []) == []
assert ("Hello" or "World") == "Hello"
```

When Python tries to evaluate expr_a and expr_b, if it finds the first expression to be False, it uses the first object; otherwise, it uses the second expression. Some examples support this rule:

```
assert ({1, 2, 3} and {4, 5, 6}) == {4, 5, 6}
assert (False and []) == False
assert ("Hello" and "World") == "World"
```

This rule may be trickier to remember than the or operations. Here's a hint: because they're short-circuit evaluations for and operations, they're evaluated to be True only if both are True. Thus, if Python finds the first expression to be False, the evaluation is done; the result must be False. For this reason, Python uses the first expression.

Chapter 4

Section 4.1

When you create a subsequence from a slice, it should be exactly like the original sequence. A few examples follow:

```
num_list = [1, 2, 3, 4]
num_tuple = (1, 2, 3, 4)
num_str = "1234"

print(num_list[:2])
# output: [1, 2]

print(num_tuple[:2])
# output: (1, 2)

print(num_str[:2])
# output: 12
```

You can do the same slicing with a range object. As you might expect, the subsequence is also a range object:

```
num_range = range(1, 5)

print(num_range[:2])
# output: range(1, 3)
```

Section 4.2

We need to obtain sales for November. Following is the entire year's data:

```
revenue_by_month = [95, 100, 80, 93, 92, 110, 102, 88, 96, 98, 115, 120]
```

As discussed in the section, we can obtain this data point with `revenue_by_month[-2]` using the negative index. If we want to use a positive index, we can obtain it by calculating the length:

```
assert revenue_by_month[-2] ==
➥ revenue_by_month[len(revenue_by_month) - 2]
```

Section 4.3

If you run the following code snippet, you'll encounter a `ValueError`:

```
class Task:
    def __init__(self, title, urgency):
        self.title = title
        self.urgency = urgency


tasks = [
    Task("Laundry", 3),
    Task("Museum", 4),
    Task("Homework", 5),
    Task("Ticket", 2)
]

task_to_search = Task("Homework", 5)
tasks.index(task_to_search)
# ERROR: ValueError: <__main__.Task object at 0x7fee281be3e0>
➥ is not in list
```

The reason for this error is that although `task_to_search` appears to have the same attributes for the third item in the `tasks` list, the instance objects of a custom class aren't comparable out of the box. Built-in data, such as strings, is comparable, so you can use the `index` method to locate the item. To make the comparison work, you must override the `__eq__` special method:

```
class Task:
    def __init__(self, title, urgency):
        self.title = title
```

```
        self.urgency = urgency

    def __eq__(self, __o: object):
        return self.__dict__ == __o.__dict__


tasks = [
    Task("Laundry", 3),
    Task("Museum", 4),
    Task("Homework", 5),
    Task("Ticket", 2)
]

task_to_search = Task("Homework", 5)
print(tasks.index(task_to_search))
# output: 2
```

Please note that you'll learn about defining custom classes in chapter 8.

Section 4.4

When you unpack a list object with embedded structures, you can unpack the inner ones as though they stand alone. The following code shows how:

```
data_to_unpack = [1, (2, 3), 4]

a, (b, c), d = data_to_unpack
print(a, b, c, d)
# output: 1, 2, 3, 4
```

Section 4.5

If you multiply the nested list object by 3 directly, you're repeating the elements three times:

```
numbers = [[1, 2, 3], [4, 5, 6], [7, 8, 9], [10, 11, 12]]
print(numbers * 3)

# output: [[1, 2, 3], [4, 5, 6], [7, 8, 9], [10, 11, 12], [1, 2, 3],
➥ [4, 5, 6], [7, 8, 9], [10, 11, 12], [1, 2, 3], [4, 5, 6], [7, 8, 9],
➥ [10, 11, 12]]
```

The desired output, however, multiplies each element by 3. With this kind of data, you must use for loops:

```
numbers_multiplied = []
for number_list in numbers:
    embedded_list = []
    for number in number_list:
        number_multiplied = number * 3
        embedded_list.append(number_multiplied)
    numbers_multiplied.append(embedded_list)

print(numbers_multiplied)
# output: [[3, 6, 9], [12, 15, 18], [21, 24, 27], [30, 33, 36]]
```

The embedded for loops are not easy to read. A better solution is to use list comprehension, as discussed in section 5.2:

```
numbers_multiplied2 = [x*3 for number_list in numbers for x in number_list]
assert numbers_multiplied == numbers_multiplied2
```

Notably, if your application involves lots of numeric computation, data structures such as array in the NumPy library (see the package-installation instructions in appendix B online) are better options. You can find a cleaner solution by using the NumPy library as follows:

```
import numpy as np

numbers_array = np.array(numbers)

print(numbers_array * 3)

# output the following lines:
[[ 3  6  9]
 [12 15 18]
 [21 24 27]
 [30 33 36]]
```

As shown in this code snippet, multiplication with a NumPy array is like other algebraic operations that you normally do with numbers. Isn't this approach much more convenient?

Chapter 5

Section 5.1

To join three or even more iterables, we list them sequentially. Each item of the zip iterator consists of one member from each iterable, forming a tuple object, as in this example:

```
numbers_int = [1, 2, 3]
numbers_word = ("one", "two", "three")
letters = "abc"
for item in zip(numbers_int, numbers_word, letters):
    print(item)

# output the following lines:
(1, 'one', 'a')
(2, 'two', 'b')
(3, 'three', 'c')
```

The number of items forming from the zip depends on the iterable with the fewest items. The following example provides an illustration:

```
numbers_fewer = [1, 2]
numbers_more = [3, 4, 5, 6]
```

```
for item in zip(numbers_fewer, numbers_more):
    print(item)

# output the following lines:
(1, 3)
(2, 4)
```

One iterable, `numbers_fewer`, has two items, whereas the other, `numbers_more`, has four items. When we zip them, we have two pairs, matching the number of `numbers_fewer`.

Section 5.2

Try running the code using `(expression for item in iterable)`. Consider the following example:

```
numbers = [1, 2, 3]

numbers_gen = (x*x for x in numbers)

print(type(numbers_gen))
# output: <class 'generator'>
```

As shown in this code snippet, the expression `(x*x for x in numbers)` creates a generator, which is a kind of memory-efficient iterator (section 7.4). Apparently, it's not a `tuple` object, and there's no such thing as tuple comprehension in Python.

Section 5.3

Suppose that we have the following `dict` object:

```
numbers = {"one": 1, "two": 2}
```

We can iterate through the keys of this `dict` object:

```
for key in numbers.keys():
    print(key)

# output the following lines:
one
two
```

We can iterate through the values of this `dict` object:

```
for value in numbers.values():
    print(value)

# output the following lines:
1
2
```

We can iterate through the key-value pairs:

```
for key, value in numbers.items():
    print(f"{key}: {value}")

# output the following lines:
one: 1
two: 2
```

In the preceding code, the items form the key and value as tuple objects, and we can unpack the tuple. Notably, there is syntactic sugar. When we iterate over the keys, we can use the dict object itself directly, as follows:

```
for key in numbers:
    print(key)

# output the following lines:
one
two
```

Section 5.4

For your reference, the list of tasks that you need to search through is

```
from collections import namedtuple

Task = namedtuple("Task", "title, description, urgency")

tasks = [
    Task("Toaster", "Clean the toaster", 2),
    Task("Camera", "Export photos", 4),
    Task("Homework", "Physics and math", 5),
    Task("Floor", "Mop the floor", 3),
    Task("Internet", "Upgrade plan", 5),
    Task("Laundry", "Wash clothes", 3),
    Task("Museum", "Egypt exhibit", 4),
    Task("Utility", "Pay bills", 5)
]
```

When you try to find the urgent task by using a break statement, you can do the following (as shown in listing 5.7):

```
first_urgent_task1 = None

for task in tasks:
    if task.urgency == 5:
        first_urgent_task1 = task
        break

print(first_urgent_task1)
# output: Task(title='Homework', description='Physics and math', urgency=5)
```

The challenge is asking about what happens if we don't set an initial value for `first_urgent_task1`. Because it's possible that we may not encounter any urgent task, the `first_urgent_task1` is never set, making it unusable. Consider the following modification to see the potential problem:

```
for task in tasks:
    if task.urgency > 5:
        first_urgent_task2 = task
        break

print(first_urgent_task2)
# ERROR: NameError: name 'first_urgent_task2' is not defined.
```

As shown in this code snippet, we require a task to be urgent if its urgency level is greater than 5. With this condition, it appears that no tasks meet this criterion, so `first_urgen_task2` is never set. When we try to print it out, we encounter a `Name-Error` (see section 10.4).

Chapter 6

Section 6.1

We can embed a timestamp as a default argument. This timestamp reflects the time when it's defined instead of the time when it's called:

```
from datetime import datetime
from time import sleep

def set_start_time(time=datetime.today()):
    print(f"Time: {time}")

for _ in range(3):
    set_start_time()
    sleep(1.0)

# output the following lines:
Time: 2022-04-25 20:22:06.337848
Time: 2022-04-25 20:22:06.337848
Time: 2022-04-25 20:22:06.337848
```

As you can see, we call the function multiple times, thinking that we could get different timestamps. But every timestamp is the same, showing the time when the function was created.

Section 6.2

The return value has the same structure, `latitude` and `longitude`, and we can create a named tuple to capture these two values. Following is a possible refactored version:

```
from collections import namedtuple

Coordinate = namedtuple("Coordinate", ["latitude", "longitude"])
```

```
def locate_me():
    # look up the user's current location
    return coordinate0

def locate_home():
    # look up the user's home location
    return coordinate1

def locate_work():
    # look up the user's work location
    return coordinate2
```

Instead of returning two values, now we can return only a `tuple` object for each of these functions.

Section 6.3

The following function can take an argument as a `list` of `int` or `str`, with the type hints provided:

```
def run_computation(numbers: list[int | str]):
    pass
```

In the example, we use the type hint: `list[int | str]`, meaning that the `list` object can consist of integers or strings.

Section 6.4

The call `example(a=1, b=2)` is valid, as we're using two keyword arguments. The call `example(1, 2)` is invalid, as we're using positional arguments, but the function accepts keyword arguments. The call `example(2a=1, 2b=2)` is invalid, as these identifiers are invalid (they can't start with a number). The call `example()` is valid, as it's using zero keyword arguments. `**kwargs` means a variable number of keyword arguments, including zero keyword arguments.

Section 6.5

We can have the following docstring using Google style:

```
def quotient(dividend, divisor, taking_int=False):
    """
    Calculate the product of two numbers with a base factor.

    Args:
        dividend: int | float, the dividend in the division
        divisor: int | float, the divisor in the division
        taking_int: bool, whether only taking the integer part of
        ⮡ the quotient;
            default: False, which calculates the precise quotient of the
            ⮡ two numbers

    Returns:
```

```
      float | int, the quotient of the dividend and divisor

  Raises:
    ZeroDivisionError, when the divisor is 0
  """

  if divisor == 0:
      raise ZeroDivisionError("division by zero")
  result = dividend / divisor
  if taking_int:
      result = int(result)
  return result
```

Chapter 7

Section 7.1

All lambda functions have the name <lambda>, a nominal name for them, which is also why lambda functions are known as anonymous. By contrast, a regularly defined function has a name that matches the identifier defined in the function head:

```
add_five = lambda x: x + 5

print(add_five.__name__)
# output: <lambda>

def add_ten(x):
    return x + 10

print(add_ten.__name__)
# output: add_ten
```

Section 7.2

As stated in the hint, it's possible that the user might use an argument that doesn't match any of the specified conditions. We should be prepared for this kind of undesired calling. By using get, we can use the fallback_action when the specified action isn't in the actions dict object.

Section 7.3

As shown in the hints, we need to add another layer of function that deals with the argument. Here's the solution:

```
import functools
import time

def logging_time_app(app_name):
    def decorator(func):
        @functools.wraps(func)
        def logger(*args, **kwargs):
            """Log the time"""
            print(f"{app_name} --- {func.__name__} starts")
```

```
        start_t = time.time()
        value_returned = func(*args, **kwargs)
        end_t = time.time()
        print(f"{app_name} *** {func.__name__} ends; used time:
        ➥ {end_t - start_t:.2f} s")
        return value_returned

    return logger

    return decorator

@logging_time_app("Task Tracker")
def example_app():
    pass

example_app()
# output the following lines:
Task Tracker --- example_app starts
Task Tracker *** example_app ends; used time: 0.00 s
```

The outmost function `logging_time_app` is the decorator, which takes the app name as its argument. Within this function, we define our typical decorator as we normally do, and this decorator takes the actual function that we're going to decorate.

Section 7.4

Based on the hint, we can write the following generator function, which yields numbers in the Fibonacci sequence:

```
def fibonacci(n):
    a, b = 0, 1
while a < n:
        yield a
        a, b = b, a + b
```

As the Fibonacci sequence is built up by summing two consecutive numbers to create the next one, we initialize the sequence with its first two numbers and create the subsequent ones accordingly. We can try this function by creating a `list` object:

```
below_fiften = fibonacci(15)

numbers = list(below_fiften)

print(numbers)
# output: [0, 1, 1, 2, 3, 5, 8, 13]
```

The list represents a Fibonacci sequence up to 13.

Section 7.5

Suppose that we have the function `run_stats_model` and the partial function `run_stats_model_u`.

```
from functools import partial

def run_stats_model(dataset, model, output_path):
    calculated_stats = 123
    return calculated_stats

run_stats_model_a = partial(run_stats_model, model="model_a",
    output_path="project_a/stats/")
```

The partial function is created from run_stats_model. Using the hint, we can see this partial function's attributes:

```
print(dir(run_stats_model_a))
# output: ['__call__', '__class__', '__class_getitem__', '__delattr__',
    '__dict__', '__dir__', '__doc__', '__eq__', '__format__', '__ge__',
    '__getattribute__', '__gt__', '__hash__', '__init__',
    '__init_subclass__', '__le__', '__lt__', '__module__', '__ne__',
    '__new__', '__reduce__', '__reduce_ex__', '__repr__', '__setattr__',
    '__setstate__', '__sizeof__', '__str__', '__subclasshook__',
    '__vectorcalloffset__', 'args', 'func', 'keywords']
```

As you may see, the function has an attribute called func, which may be the one telling us which function is the source function:

```
print(run_stats_model_a.func)
# output: <function run_stats_model at 0x7fedf82c30a0>
```

Indeed, it's the function run_stats_model. You can also try finding out what the attributes args and keywords are.

Chapter 8

Section 8.1

In section 6.1, I said that we should use None as the default value for a mutable argument. We should do the same thing with the __init__ method:

```
class Task:
    def __init__(self, title, desc, urgency, tags=None):
        self.title = title
        self.desc = desc
        self.urgency = urgency
        if tags is None:
            self.tags = []
        else:
            self.tags = tags
```

We can also try the ternary expression var = value_true if condition else value_false. Thus, we can update the preceding code this way:

```
class Task:
    def __init__(self, title, desc, urgency, tags=None):
```

```
        self.title = title
        self.desc = desc
        self.urgency = urgency
        self.tags = [] if tags is None else tags
```

Section 8.2

As we create an instance object from the `tuple` object, we need access to the class's constructor. Thus, we need to define a class method to access a class's data:

```
class Task:
    def __init__(self, title, desc, urgency):
        self.title = title
        self.desc = desc
        self.urgency = urgency

    @classmethod
    def task_from_tuple(cls, data):
        title, desc, urgency = data
        return cls(title, desc, urgency)
```

Section 8.3

Following the example shown in listing 8.9, we can apply the same thing to urgency:

```
class Task:
    def __init__(self, title, desc, urgency):
        self.title = title
        self.desc = desc
        self._urgency = urgency

    @property
    def urgency(self):
        return self._urgency

    @urgency.setter
    def urgency(self, value):
        if value in range(1, 6):
            self._urgency = value
        else:
            raise ValueError("Can't set a value outside of 1 - 5")
```

For detailed explanations, see listing 8.9.

Section 8.4

Instead of hardcoding the class name, we can use its special attributes to retrieve this information programmatically:

```
class Task:
    def __init__(self, title, desc, urgency):
        self.title = title
        self.desc = desc
        self.urgency = urgency
```

```
        def __repr__(self):
            return f"{self.__class__.__name__}({self.title!r}, {self.desc!r},
            ➡ {self.urgency})"
```

The __class__ special attribute gets the instance object's class, which has the __name__ special attribute to get its class name.

Section 8.5

The following code shows how to override the initialization method in a subclass:

```
class Employee:
    def __init__(self, name, employee_id):
        self.name = name
        self.employee_id = employee_id

class Supervisor:
    def __init__(self, name, employee_id, subordinates):
        super().__init__(name, employee_id)
        self.subordinates = subordinates
```

In the Supervisor class's __init__ method, we use super() to create a proxy object to its superclass Employee, so we can use its __init__ method by sending name and employee_id.

Chapter 9

Section 9.1

Because move_to is related to a specific instance, we can convert it to an instance method of the Direction class:

```
from enum import Enum

class Direction(Enum):
    NORTH = 0
    SOUTH = 1
    EAST = 2
    WEST = 3

    def __str__(self):
        return self.name.lower()

    def move_to(self, distance: float):
        if self in self.__class__:
            message = f"Go to the {self} for {distance} miles"
        else:
            message = "Wrong input for direction"
        print(message)
```

As shown in this code snippet, we rename the move_to method's first argument as self, which refers to the instance object. Within the body, we can use self.__class__ to get a reference to the class Direction.

Section 9.2

When we create a data class, if we're setting a default value for a field, we can use the dataclasses module's field function, which handles setting the default value for mutable fields. The following code shows how to implement this feature:

```
from dataclasses import dataclass, field

@dataclass
class Bill:
    table_number: int
    meal_amount: float
    served_by: str
    tip_amount: float
    dishes: field(default_factory=list)
```

In this code, the dishes field is mutable, and we can specify the default_factory argument as list so that it creates an empty list object.

Section 9.3

As stated in the hint, tuple objects are serializable, and we can convert them directly to JavaScript Object Notation (JSON) strings as follows:

```
import json
from collections import namedtuple

User = namedtuple("User", "first_name last_name age")
user = User("John", "Smith", "39")

print(json.dumps(user))
# output: ["John", "Smith", "39"]
```

Section 9.4

Suppose that you build a client management app, using the following Client data model:

```
class ClientV0:
    def __init__(self, first_name, last_name, middle_initial='-'):
        self.first_name = first_name
        self.last_name = last_name
        self.middle_initial = middle_initial
        self.initials = first_name[0] + middle_initial + last_name[0]
```

Everything should be straightforward. When you get an instance object's initials, it's using the value that you set initially. But the app has a function that allows users to change their names, so their initials may be updating too. To make the initials calculate on the go, we can convert the attribute `initials` to a function as follows:

```python
class ClientV1:
    def __init__(self, first_name, last_name, middle_initial='-'):
        self.first_name = first_name
        self.last_name = last_name
        self.middle_initial = middle_initial

    def initials(self):
        return self.first_name[0] + self.middle_initial + self.last_name[0]
```

This approach works—but it may break your code. Previously, you used `client.initials` to access a client's initials; now you must use `client.initials()`. To avoid using the call operator, you can apply the `property` decorator:

```python
class ClientV2:
    def __init__(self, first_name, last_name, middle_initial='-'):
        self.first_name = first_name
        self.last_name = last_name
        self.middle_initial = middle_initial

@property
    def initials(self):
        return self.first_name[0] + self.middle_initial + self.last_name[0]
```

This way, you can keep your application programming interface (API) consistent by using just `client.initials`, but you provide the calculation on the go by calling a function for this property. Thus, using a decorator can help you avoid API break changes. You can keep your API consistent even though the implementation has become a property instead of an attribute.

Section 9.5

Because all these methods can be nonpublic, I'm converting them to protected methods by using an underscore prefix:

```python
class Account:
    def __init__(self, student_id):
        self.student_id = student_id
        # query the database to get additional information using student_id
        self.account_number = self._get_account_number_from_db()
        self.balance = self._get_balance_from_db()

    def _get_account_number_from_db(self):
        # query database to locate the account number using student_id
        account_number = 123456
        return account_number

    def _get_balance_from_db(self):
        # query database to get the balance for the account number
        balance = 100.00
        return balance
```

```
class Demographics:
    def __init__(self, student_id):
        self.student_id = student_id
        # query the database to get additional information
        age, gender, race = self._get_demographics_from_db()
        self.age = age
        self.gender = gender
        self.race = race

    def _get_demographics_from_db(self):
        # query database to get the demographics using student_id
        birthday = "08/14/2010"
        age = self._calculated_age(birthday)
        gender = "Female"
        race = "Black"
        return age, gender, race

    @staticmethod
    def _calculated_age(birthday):
        # get today's date and calculate the difference from birthday
        age = 12
        return age
```

Chapter 10

Section 10.1

As mentioned in the hint, the collections.abc module has the Iterable class, and iterables should generally have implemented the required method __iter__. Thus, we can use the isinstance function on this class to examine whether an object is an iterable:

```
from collections.abc import Iterable

def is_iterable(obj):
    if isinstance(obj, Iterable):
        outcome = "is an iterable"
    else:
        outcome = "is not an iterable"
    print(type(obj), outcome)
```

Using this updated function, we can check some common data types:

```
is_iterable([1, 2, 3])
# output: <class 'list'> is an iterable

is_iterable((404, "Data"))
# output: <class 'tuple'> is an iterable

is_iterable("abc")
# output: <class 'str'> is an iterable

is_iterable(456)
# output: <class 'int'> is not an iterable
```

Section 10.2

To test how using a variable in a function changes the reference count, we can write a trivial function:

```python
import sys

class Task:
    def __init__(self, title):
        self.title = title

task = Task("Homework")

def get_detail(obj):
    print(sys.getrefcount(obj))
```

If we call `get_detail` with the `task` variable, the reference count becomes

```python
get_detail(task)
# output: 4
```

Why 4? The first count is the `task` variable itself. When you call `get_detail`, you send `task`, making the count 2. The function `get_detail` takes `task`, making the count 2. Within the function's body, calling `sys.getrefcount` adds another count, making the count 4.

Section 10.3

According to the requirements specified in the challenge, we can update our `Task` class to the following edition:

```python
class Task:
    def __init__(self, title, desc, tags = None):
        self.title = title
        self.desc = desc
        self.tags = [] if tags is None else tags

    def __copy__(self):
        new_title = f"Copied: {self.title}"
        new_desc = self.desc
        new_tags = self.tags.copy()
        new_task = self.__class__(new_title, new_desc, new_tags)
        return new_task
```

In the `__copy__` method, we create a new `title` and a new `tags` list for the copied object. We can check whether the `__copy__` method works as intended by using this code:

```python
from copy import copy

task = Task("Homework", "Math and physics", ["school", "urgent"])

new_task = copy(task)
```

```
print(new_task.__dict__)
# output: {'title': 'Copied: Homework', 'desc': 'Math and physics',
➥ 'tags': ['school', 'urgent']}
```

To double-check whether the tags attributes of these two objects are indeed different, we can try changing one list:

```
task.tags.append("red")
print(task.tags)
# output: ['school', 'urgent', 'red']

print(new_task.tags)
# output: ['school', 'urgent']
```

Everything works as expected: task.tags and new_task.tags are two distinct list objects.

Section 10.4

In Python, the if...else... statement doesn't form its own scope, unlike classes and functions. As there is no scope, you can change a global variable without using the global keyword, as shown in this example:

```
import random

weather = "sunny"

if random.randint(1, 100) % 2:
weather = "cloudy"
else:
    weather = "rainy"

print(weather)              You may get a different result
# output: cloudy    ◁────┘  because of the randomness.
```

As shown in this code snippet, we change the weather variable without the global keyword, indicating that the if...else... statement doesn't form a scope, making weather fall outside it.

Section 10.5

When you define a decorator as a class, to keep the metadata for a decorated function, you know that you need to wrap the function. But unlike a decorator function, in which you use the wraps decorator, a class-based decorator uses the method update_wrapper, which helps keep the metadata:

```
import time
import functools

class TimeLogger:
    def __init__(self, func):
```

```
        functools.update_wrapper(self, func)
        def logger(*args, **kwargs):
            start = time.time()
            result = func(*args, **kwargs)
            print(f"Calling {func.__name__}: {time.time() - start:.5f}")
            return result
        self._logger = logger

    def __call__(self, *args, **kwargs):
        return self._logger(*args, **kwargs)

@TimeLogger
def calculate_sum(n):
    return sum(range(n))


print(calculate_sum.__name__)
# output: calculate_sum
```

Using update_wrapper is like using the wraps decorator. You update the wrapper in the __init__ method of the TimeLogger class. Notably, the wraps decorator is syntactic sugar, as it's invoking the update_wrapper under the hood.

Chapter 11

Section 11.1

We need to add a line break to each item. Using the list comprehension, we can create a new list object by using the list_data:

```
list_data = [
'1001,Homework,5',
'1002,Laundry,3',
'1003,Grocery,4'
]

updated_list_data = [f"{x}\n" for x in list_data]
```

With the updated list, we can use the writelines function to produce the desired file. We can double-check whether the writing is successful by reading the data:

```
with open("tasks_list_write.txt", "w") as file:
    file.writelines(updated_list_data)

with open("tasks_list_write.txt") as file:
    print(file.read())

# output the following lines:
1001,Homework,5
1002,Laundry,3
1003,Grocery,4
```

Section 11.2

The writerows works with a list object, so we can embed each row's data (list object) within an outer list object, as suggested by the hint:

```
tasks = [
    ['1001', 'Homework', '5'],
    ['1002', 'Laundry', '3'],
    ['1003', 'Grocery', '4']
]
```

Then we can run the following code to write this list:

```
import csv

with open("tasks_writer.txt", "w", newline="") as file:
    csv_writer = csv.writer(file)
    csv_writer.writerows(tasks)
```

If we open the file tasks_writer.txt, we should see that the data is entered correctly.

Section 11.3

We override the __reduce__ method within the MaliciousTask class as follows:

```
import os

class MaliciousTask:
    def __init__(self, title, urgency):
        self.title = title
        self.urgency = urgency

    def __reduce__(self):
        print("__reduce__ is called")
        return os.system, ('rm hacking.txt',)
```

Specifically, we use ('rm hacking.txt',) instead of ('touch hacking.txt'). The command rm means that we'll delete the specified file. After updating the class, we can run the code in listing 11.14 to see the effect.

Section 11.4

We can call the exists method on an instance of the Path class to check a file's existence. Thus, we can update listing 11.17 to the following version:

```
from pathlib import Path
import shutil

shutil.rmtree("subjects")    ◁——— Removes the existing folder

subject_ids = [123, 124, 125]
data_folder = Path("data")

for subject_id in subject_ids:
```

```
subject_folder = Path(f"subjects/subject_{subject_id}")
subject_folder.mkdir(parents=True, exist_ok=True)

for subject_file in data_folder.glob(f"*{subject_id}*"):
    filename = subject_file.name
    target_path = subject_folder / filename
    if not target_path.exists():
        _ = shutil.copy(subject_file, target_path)
        print(f"Copying {filename} to {target_path}")
    else:
        print(f"{filename} already exists at {target_path}")
```

As highlighted in this code, we copy the files only if the file at the target path doesn't exist, preventing us from overwriting already-processed files.

Section 11.5

We know that we can find a file's modification time by accessing st_mtime of a file's status. Thus, we can create the following function to return the files whose modification times are within the past 24 hours:

```
from pathlib import Path
import time

def select_recent_files_24h(directory):
    dir_path = Path(directory)
    current_time = time.time()
    time_cutoff = current_time - 24 * 3600
    good_files = []
    for file_path in dir_path.glob("*"):
        file_time = file_path.stat().st_mtime
        if time_cutoff <= file_time <= current_time:
            good_files.append(file_path)

    return good_files
```

The pattern "*" allows us to go over all the files in the directory. We specify that the file's modification time must reside in the range of the previous 24 hours. If a file meets this requirement, we add it to the good_files list as this function's final output.

Chapter 12

Section 12.1

We can call the logger's hasHandlers method to check whether the logger has any handlers before we add the handler:

```
import logging

logger = logging.getLogger(__name__)

if not logger.hasHandlers():
    file_handler = logging.FileHandler("taskier.log")
    logger.addHandler(file_handler)
```

To clear the handlers, we can manipulate the logger's `handlers` attribute, which is a `list` object:

```
print(logger.handlers)
# output: [<FileHandler /directory/taskier.log (NOTSET)>]

logger.handlers.clear()   ⟵—— Removes all the handlers

print(logger.handlers)
# output: []
```

Section 12.2

To demonstrate what happens, I use a stream handler so that the messages can be printed in the console:

```
import logging

logger = logging.getLogger(__name__)
logger.handlers = []
logger.setLevel(logging.WARNING)

stream_handler = logging.StreamHandler()
stream_handler.setLevel(logging.DEBUG)
logger.addHandler(stream_handler)

logger.info("It's an info message.")
# output: None (hide automatically in the console)
logger.warning("It's a warning message.")
# output: It's a warning message.
```

If you run this code in the console, you'll see that only the warning message is shown; the logging message at the `INFO` level is lower than the logger's level, so it won't be sent to the handler. By contrast, the message at the `WARNING` level meets the logger's level requirement and is forwarded to the handler.

Section 12.3

As suggested by the hint, you can run the potentially problematic code in the console and see what happens. Here's an example:

```
>>> urgency = int("3#")
Traceback (most recent call last):
  File "<stdin>", line 1, in <module>
ValueError: invalid literal for int() with base 10: '3#'
```

You'll see that you encounter the `ValueError` exception. Step backward and add this exception in the `try...except...` statement:

```
try:
    urgency = int(urgency_str)
except ValueError:
    # the operation when ValueError happens
```

Section 12.4

If you run the code in the challenge, you'll see that your console has the following output:

```
Done processing text: Laundry,3
finally
```

You don't see the `task` get returned, as the `return` statement in the `finally` gets executed before the `try` clause's `return` statement.

Section 12.5

To allow you to try the code multiple times, I'm defining a function that can create a task based on different kinds of input:

```python
def create_task(task_title):
    try:
        print(f"Trying to process {task_title}")
        task = Task(task_title)
    except TypeError as e:
        print(f"Couldn't create the task, error: {e}")
    else:
        print(f"Created task: {task}")
    finally:
        print(f"Done processing {task_title}")
```

This function uses all four clauses in exception handling. Try calling this function:

```
>>> create_task(100)
Trying to process 100
Couldn't create the task, error: Please instantiate the Task using
➥ string as its title
Done processing 100
>>> create_task("Laundry")
Trying to process Laundry
Created task: <__main__.Task object at 0x1043e7b80>
Done processing Laundry
```

When you use a non-`str` object, you see that the try, except, and `finally` clauses get executed. When you use a `str` object, you see that the try, else, and `finally` clauses get executed.

Chapter 13

Section 13.1

There are different ways to make the tracebacks more complicated. Following is a possible solution:

```python
class Task:
    def __init__(self, title, urgency):
        self.title = title
```

```
            self.urgency = urgency

        def _report(self):
            print("report")
            report = "Urgency: " + self.urgency

        def _send_report(self):
            print("send report")
            self._report()

        def _update_db(self):
            # update the record in the database
            print("update the database")
            self._send_report()


        def update_urgency(self, urgency):
            self.urgency = urgency
            self._update_db()

task = Task("Laundry", 3)
task.update_urgency(4)

# output the following lines:
update the database
send report
report
Traceback (most recent call last):
  File "<stdin>", line 1, in <module>
  File "<stdin>", line 17, in update_urgency
  File "<stdin>", line 14, in _update_db
  File "<stdin>", line 10, in _send_report
  File "<stdin>", line 7, in _report
TypeError: can only concatenate str (not "int") to str
```

In the class, we use multiple methods to call one another, resulting in a traceback that has multiple calls.

Section 13.2

Namespaces track variables dynamically. Calling the built-in `locals` function reveals what's available in the local namespace at the specific moment. The following code snippet is a snapshot of the changes:

```
$ python3 task_debug.py
> /fullpath/task_debug.py(10)create_task()
-> task_text = obtain_text_data(inject_bug)
(Pdb) locals()
{'inject_bug': False}
(Pdb) n
> /fullpath/task_debug.py(11)create_task()
-> title, urgency_text = task_text.split(",")
(Pdb) locals()
{'inject_bug': False, 'task_text': 'Laundry,3'}
(Pdb)
```

Section 13.3

We can have the following function create an instance of the `Task` class from a `tuple` object:

```
def create_task_from_tuple(task_tuple):
    title, urgency = task_tuple
    task = Task(title, urgency)
    return task
```

We can define the following test function in the test class for the `create_task_from_tuple` function:

```
import unittest

class TestTaskCreation(unittest.TestCase):
    def setUp(self):
        task_to_compare = Task("Laundry", 3)
        self.task_dict = task_to_compare.__dict__

    def test_create_task_from_tuple(self):
        task_tuple = ("Laundry", 3)
        created_task = create_task_from_tuple(task_tuple)
        self.assertEqual(created_task.__dict__, self.task_dict)
```

Section 13.4

You can update the method to make it raise an exception explicitly. You need to change the `Task` class in the `test_class.py` file as follows:

```
class Task:
    def __init__(self, title, urgency):
        self.title = title
        self.urgency = urgency

    def formatted_display(self):
        displayed_text = f"{self.title} ({self.urgency})"
        raise TypeError("This is a TypeError")
        # the next return statement will be skipped due to raising
        ➡ an exception
        return displayed_text
```

When you run the `test_task_class.py` again, you'll see the following output in the command-line tool, showing that we encounter an error due to the `TypeError` in our code. Note that the output shows `..E` instead of `..F` because it's an error instead of a test failure:

```
$ python3 test_task_class.py
..E
======================================================================
ERROR: test_formatted_display (__main__.TestTask)
----------------------------------------------------------------------
```

```
Traceback (most recent call last):
  File "/fullpath/test_task_class.py", line 21, in test_formatted_display
    displayed_text = task.formatted_display()
  File "/fullpath/task_class.py", line 22, in formatted_display
    raise TypeError("This is a TypeError")
TypeError: This is a TypeError


----------------------------------------------------------------
Ran 3 tests in 0.001s

FAILED (errors=1)
```

Chapter 14

Section 14.1

Use a tool such as Terminal if your computer is a Mac or a command-line tool if your computer operates under Windows. Navigate to the desired directory, and then run the following command to create a virtual environment:

```
$ python3 -m venv python-env
```

After creating the virtual environment, you need to activate it by running the following command:

```
# for Mac:
$ source taskier-env/bin/activate

# for Windows:
> taskier-env\Scripts\activate.bat
```

To install the pandas library, run the following command:

```
$ pip install pandas
```

To use this virtual environment in Visual Studio Code, see section 14.1.4 for detailed instructions.

Section 14.2

We can use a Boolean flag to indicate whether the record is found:

```
def delete_from_db(self):
    """Delete the record from the database
    """
    if app_db == TaskierDBOption.DB_CSV.value:
        with open(app_db, "r+") as file:
            lines = file.readlines()
            found_record = False
            for line in lines:
                if line.startswith(self.task_id):
                    found_record = True
```

```
        lines.remove(line)
        break
    if not found_record:
        raise Exception("Record not found error.")
    else:
        file.seek(0)
        file.truncate()
        file.writelines(lines)
```

As shown in this code snippet, we set an initial `False` value for the flag. If we find the record, we make it `True`. We can raise an exception when the Boolean value is `False`.

Section 14.3

Chapter 7 covered how to create a time-logging decorator. Here's a possible implementation taken from listing 7.9:

```
import functools
import time

def logging_time_wraps(func):
    @functools.wraps(func)
    def logger(*args, **kwargs):
        """Log the time"""
        print(f"--- {func.__name__} starts")
        start_t = time.time()
        value_returned = func(*args, **kwargs)
        end_t = time.time()
        print(f"*** {func.__name__} ends; used time: {end_t -
        ⇢ start_t:.10f} s")
        return value_returned

    return logger
```

You can use this decorator to decorate the methods in the class. To show a proof of concept, I decorate the `load_tasks` method:

```
@classmethod
@logging_time_wraps
def load_tasks(cls, statuses: list[TaskStatus]=None,
⇢ urgencies: list[int]=None, content: str=""):
```

Although I don't intend to perform a formal comparison, it appears that the SQLite 3 database outperforms the CSV file in terms of data-reading speed. Please note that we're dealing with a small amount of data, so the difference between these two sources appears to be trivial:

```
# Using the CSV file as the data source
*** load_tasks ends; used time: 0.0008411407 s
--- load_tasks starts
*** load_tasks ends; used time: 0.0005502701 s
--- load_tasks starts
```

```
*** load_tasks ends; used time: 0.0004429817 s
--- load_tasks starts
*** load_tasks ends; used time: 0.0002791882 s
--- load_tasks starts
*** load_tasks ends; used time: 0.0003058910 s
--- load_tasks starts
*** load_tasks ends; used time: 0.0005359650 s
--- load_tasks starts
*** load_tasks ends; used time: 0.0002870560 s
--- load_tasks starts
*** load_tasks ends; used time: 0.0004091263 s
--- load_tasks starts
*** load_tasks ends; used time: 0.0004007816 s
--- load_tasks starts
*** load_tasks ends; used time: 0.0002658367 s

# Using the SQLite as the data source
--- load_tasks starts
*** load_tasks ends; used time: 0.0003259182 s
--- load_tasks starts
*** load_tasks ends; used time: 0.0002837181 s
--- load_tasks starts
*** load_tasks ends; used time: 0.0004198551 s
--- load_tasks starts
*** load_tasks ends; used time: 0.0002789497 s
--- load_tasks starts
*** load_tasks ends; used time: 0.0003492832 s
--- load_tasks starts
*** load_tasks ends; used time: 0.0003030300 s
--- load_tasks starts
*** load_tasks ends; used time: 0.0004410744 s
--- load_tasks starts
*** load_tasks ends; used time: 0.0003309250 s
--- load_tasks starts
*** load_tasks ends; used time: 0.0003337860 s
--- load_tasks starts
*** load_tasks ends; used time: 0.0002810955 s
```

Section 14.4

We can use any iterable as the option in the `selectbox` widget in `streamlit`. When we use a `dict` object as an iterable, using the `dict` and `dict.keys()` is the same, as in this example:

```
numbers = {0: "zero", 1: "one", 2: "two"}

assert list(numbers) == list(numbers.keys())
```

index